MENLO SCHOOL

founded 1915

MENLO COLLEGE

Gift of

College Student Council

Library Fund

Established Fall of 1972

A Study of
SHELLEY'S
POETRY

A STUDY OF
Shelley's Poetry

by

SEYMOUR REITER

THE UNIVERSITY

OF NEW MEXICO PRESS

1967

*The publication of this book was assisted by a grant
from the Ford Foundation*

MANUFACTURED IN THE UNITED STATES OF AMERICA
BY THE UNIVERSITY OF NEW MEXICO PRINTING PLANT

Library of Congress Catalog Card No. 67-22735
First Edition

TO JODY, MY WIFE

CONTENTS

1819

1820

1821

1822

PREFACE

THIS critical study has as its main theme the many kinds of great poetry Shelley wrote. The wide range of his artistry has not been much recognized, although Shelley scholars are aware of it, and has never been critically demonstrated. He wrote significantly in the three characteristic structures of poetry, the lyric, the reflective, and the narrative; in numerous and complex tones; and in various styles. If his dominant vision as an artist is as everybody knows romantic, there are also the realistic and classic in his work.

Since my purpose is to demonstrate the wide-ranging accomplishment of Shelley's career as a poet, my approach is primarily critical, using much close analysis. There are in the book, of course, also other critical techniques and scholarly matters. The biographical content is intended not only to have an intrinsic interest for the reader and to give unity to the book, but also, as is sometimes necessary, to serve criticism. My views on the complex connections between biography and criticism are given where aspects of that critical issue come up. (I spend time on Harriet Shelley; it is necessary to do so to clear the way to Shelley's poetry.)

The quotations from Shelley will, I think, be a revelation to those who have been encouraged to disapprove of him, as has been the fashion, without having read him or who have read too little of him and that with preformed antipathy. My commentary is designed to help them see what is there. It should also give pleasure and justification to readers who like Shelley, and, I intend, deepen their appreciation.

I am not interested in Shelley's trivia, I am interested only in the large body of his work which is great. The measure of a poet is not taken by striking an average in his work any more than one would weigh the chaff in setting a price on the grain. In like manner, I do not deal with the eccentricities in Shelley's life, which too often have characterized the man in lieu of his essential self. In anything less than a full-length study the eccentricities could not be portrayed in the right perspective. I give nothing that is not true of the essential man and I have tried to give everything needed to form an image of that man. For the complete person I warmly and admiringly commend Newman Ivey White's *Portrait of Shelley*.

In setting forth what is in Shelley's poetry I divide my book into two parts, *Early Career* and *Exile in Italy*. The book's chief emphasis is the explication of *Prometheus Unbound*. This is Shelley's greatest work, in the opinion of C. S. Lewis the greatest in his age, but it is the least read. It is the least read because it is the most difficult. My explication interprets every difficulty in the poem, including many never before coped with, and reveals things never seen before, e.g., Shelley in both language and structure anticipated techniques of Cubism (others have already seen that he anticipated Impressionism). The explication, of course, should be read with the poem at hand. Sometimes simple declarative statements are less straightforward paraphrase than a clarification of complex, much-debated matter.

Bennett Weaver concluded his bibliography on Shelley in *The English Romantic Poets* by saying, "It is in the field of criticism that advances are to be made—criticism . . . fixing its interest faithfully upon the page which Shelley wrote."

Because this book is not primarily for specialists, I have dispensed with a formal apparatus for footnotes. My bibliography, however, lists every book and article that I have used in this study. Rather than drop explanatory notes to the foot of the page, I have bracketed such material and run it into the text for the sake of ease of reading. With the exceptions that are identified, all direct quotations are from Shelley's writings or from the writings of contemporaries who knew him.

I include little of Shelley's prose in the body of the work, but print in an appendix the Socrates-Diotima discourse from Shelley's translation of the *Symposium*. That translation, connected to important thought in his poetry, has not been printed in any book that a private person is likely to own.

At the last I am glad to express my debt to my friends and colleagues Richard H. Barker, Bernard Grebanier, and Julian B. Kaye, who gave my manuscript the advantage of their valuable criticism.

Early Career

PART ONE

Early Career

IT IS STRANGE that even those parents who are decent human beings, perhaps admirable outside their families, can make a botch of things with their own children. Squire Timothy Shelley, a member of Parliament by favor of the liberal Duke of Norfolk, was a good farmer, and a good man until young Bysshe inevitably acted as though he had a right to a mind and spirit of his own. Domestic history plays itself out in the larger march or scramble of the history of nations. While refugees were being disgorged in English ports and crossing Sussex farmlands on the way to London, and in Europe the allied powers were readying themselves to invade France, Percy Bysshe was born on his father's estate in Sussex in 1792. The boy Bysshe learned crops, livestock, hunting, riding, and marksmanship. Riding through Sussex with his father's steward, Bysshe discovered people out of work; the steward, moved by the boy's generosity, recorded, "he would give lavishly, and if he had no money with him would borrow of me." Again and again in Shelley's lifetime the man gave what he could of money and himself to lessen the harsh distress of the poor.

The character of his mind also began to show itself early. At six he recited Gray's charming, mock-heroic *On the Death of a Favorite Cat* after hearing it once—a measure of his appreciative sense of fun as well as of his precocity. In later years, in face of illness, contumely, and deep emotional distress, at times he could be "merry, cheerful, overflowing with animal spirits" and "full of life and fun," and "his wit flowed in a continuous stream"—so his friends recorded. Only when the risible offended his moral sense would he take no pleasure in the comic. That he was a passionately serious man, religiously dedicated, is profoundly true, but even without the testimony to his comic sense we should know that was part of him by the humor and wit, whether quiet or hilarious, in his mature poetry.

A slip of a boy at ten, easily enraged, girlish-looking, who fought like a girl—a natural enough consequence of his hav-

3

ing played only with his sisters—young Bysshe was baited and bullied at Syon House Academy and two years later at Eton. But he won a place for himself at Eton, and there was nothing effeminate about the mature man. His face and features were firm and hard; fairly tall and thin (in an age of sensibility the thinness was sometimes translated to "delicate-looking"), he had unusual physical stamina; and was absolutely fearless. Of his sensitiveness, or sensibility, as though his nerve ends were nakedly exposed, I shall speak later.

During those brutal school years the child dedicated himself to quell moral and physical outrage in the world. But I doubt that we can explain his intense consciousness of the world's evil and his lifelong radical opposition to that evil by his schoolboy or other experiences, such as those due to his father's alienation and oppression. Much wiser to think of those experiences as the occasion, not the cause, of his remarkable dedication. Nor need we look to his grandfather, old Bysshe Shelley, imaginative and enterprising, his mind distinctly his own, for the youngster's endowments. Old Bysshe wanted grandeur; he had married two heiresses, amassed wealth, and was building a never-completed castle. The old patriarch, who swore at the uselessness of his son Timothy for his ambitions, thought that Timothy's heir could grow up to people the castle with a splendid family and a name to reckon with. Old Bysshe, while Shelley was at Eton, became a baronet. But young Bysshe was heir not only to a baronetcy; old Bysshe settled matters so that the boy would inherit his wealth. However, after Percy Bysshe eloped with Harriet Westbrook, daughter of a retired tavern keeper and no wife for the old man's ambitions, Sir Bysshe looked beyond his grandson and changed his will so that the inheritance would go on to his great grandsons; but luckily for Percy Bysshe the old man overlooked resettling a portion of his estate. Consequently, on his grandfather's death in 1815, Shelley could arrange matters with Sir Timothy so that he, Bysshe, had an annuity of £1,000 a year, later £2,000. But for four years, from the summer of that elopement in 1811, money worries plagued Shelley; he never had enough for the generous impulses he acted on. Himself in debt, in 1813 he assumed a burden of £3,000 for William Godwin out of admiration for the philosopher. Often Shelley had to dodge arrest, and matters worsened, harrowing his life first with Harriet Westbrook and then with Mary Godwin. To the self-centered old Bysshe, or rather to the old man's oversight, Shelley owed his escape and independence of means but not his independence of mind. What Shelley was he was. His essence was neither inherited nor shaped by circumstance and cannot finally be explained, at least not with our present knowledge of the universe.

The elopement with Harriet (Shelley nineteen and the girl sixteen) finally brought misery to him and suicide to her. For over two years they lived happily together—in Scotland, England, Ireland, Wales—Harriet's love, loyalty, and bloom sustaining that happiness. But the marriage was doomed in the beginning, for whatever the beguilements that made the union, they were not love on his part nor an equal mind or a like purpose for a lifetime on hers. Shelley thought to rescue her from persecution suffered because of her friendship for him. "Gratitude and admiration," he wrote, "all demand that I should love her *for ever*." But love is indifferent to moral suasion and chivalry cannot joust to make a marriage victorious. The day that Harriet, looking miserable, confessed her violent attachment and her fear that he should not return her love—a cause for her drooping that Shelley had been ignorant of—the young man hurried into sentiment. A few days earlier he had been able to say, "If I know anything about love, I am *not* in love." But now, "It was impossible to avoid being much affected, I promised to unite my fate with hers." [Thomas Jefferson Hogg, to whom Shelley wrote these remarks, was Shelley's closest friend at the time. When the authorities at Oxford expelled Shelley because of *The Necessity of Atheism*, which the two young men had collaborated on, Hogg loyally got himself expelled also. It was a severe shock to Shelley, after his marriage to Harriet, to learn of Hogg's having tried to seduce Harriet. Hogg tried again with Mary Shelley, and perhaps succeeded; if he did, Shelley never learned of his betrayal. They remained friends for the rest of Shelley's life. Hogg followed a career as a lawyer; was an amateur man of letters; still apparently pursuing women close to Shelley united himself with Jane Williams, the wife of the man who died with Shelley in a Mediterranean storm; and began a biography of Shelley but

Shelley's family, justifiably dissatisfied, withdrew the materials which Hogg needed for continuing the biography.]

From the happiness that followed Shelley's marriage to Harriet emerged poems that seem to make a strong case that he learned to love her genuinely. But Shelley in those years was capable of believing what he needed to believe although the emotional reality was otherwise—that self-deception ironically a consequence of his own moral values. Out of chivalry and pity he had given himself to her; and, as he could not in his own mind live in a union without love, he sealed the first error with another. Harriet was an amiable physical beauty and they were happy together—so he let himself believe—in their perfect sympathy and love. Or was it worse? In the midst of their apparent happiness and love, in an essay on a line in *Queen Mab*, Shelley wrote, "Persons of delicacy and virtue, unhappily united to one whom they find it impossible to love, spend the loveliest season of their life in unproductive efforts to appear otherwise than they are, for the sake of the feelings of their partner or the welfare of their mutual offspring." Although Harriet was intelligent, she had none of her husband's intellectuality; and, after the novelty wore off, none of his passion to change the world. (When Shelley went to Ireland to urge on the Irish the best means of freeing themselves, Harriet traveled along full of excitement. Experiences like the failure in Ireland and the difficulty of joining philanthropy to science to build a community in Wales that would be a social glory, together with his recognition of what limited people, shifted Shelley from action to poetry, from changing immediate circumstance to changing the mind and moral life of mankind.) With the birth of their daughter Harriet gave up trying to mold herself to a mind and temperament foreign to her own; however, she loved him until she died.

Had there been a mutual love, like minds and like temperaments, Shelley would not have broken away. Years later the emotional distance from Harriet was so great that on the occasion of a pirated edition of *Queen Mab* Shelley could remark that the publisher showed "delicacy" in not having printed the "foolish dedication to my late wife." He never broke away from Mary, was never adulterous, never ceased loving her even during the lacerating time of her spiritual desertion. To say that he was not always spiritually monogamous to Mary, as though that were an arraignment, assumes that infinity can be circumscribed, a belief that Shelley cut loose from his own mind.

By the spring of 1814 the marriage of Shelley and Harriet, nearly three years old, drifted into unhappiness but survived his brief passion for a young married woman in the circle of their acquaintance, a passion that he unwittingly grasped at to medicine the emotional illness in his life. Later on Shelley had to leave Harriet to make a trip to London on money matters. For three weeks he ate in Godwin's house. In those weeks Shelley and Mary Godwin, who seemed perfectly formed for each other, linked their lives. Shelley tried to hide his feelings from himself, but Mary, frankly confessing her love, shone light on his in a "sublime & rapturous moment." They disclosed their love to Godwin, who promptly forbade Shelley entrance to his house, accusing his disciple of impiety, betrayal, and seduction.

Deeply in love with Mary, Shelley wanted Harriet to release him—"friendship and not passion," he wrote, had held them together. His moral argument on the grounds for divorce Shelley had written earlier, in the *Queen Mab* essay that speaks of persons "unhappily united." Here are fragments of that essay: "How long then ought the sexual connection to last? what law ought to specify the grievances which should limit its duration? A husband and wife ought to continue so long united as they love each other: any law which should bind them to cohabitation for one moment after the decay of their affection would be a most intolerable tyranny, and the most unworthy of toleration." And again: the connection is "naturally dissolved when its evils are greater than its benefits. There is nothing immoral in the separation." Carrying his second child and believing that they could still have a life together, Harriet refused. In the turmoil of his mind "the balance between two opposing importances of morality" hung quivering, making him wretched beyond restraint. He attempted suicide. After his recovery he was of a single mind, although his judgment was not perfectly clear: again perhaps believing what he needed to believe, he accused Harriet of adultery to justify to Mary their union and escape to France. It was a moral lapse, but let no man carelessly throw stones. Not many souls in the world's history are freer of stain than Shelley's. Byron's testimony is a tribute owed to a hero, and no tribute could be worth more, coming as it does from Byron's vitality and honesty of mind, his knowledge of men and experience, his unsparing realism: Shelley was "without exception the *best* and least selfish man I ever knew," a man "about whom the world was ill-naturedly, and ignorantly, and brutally mistaken."

In a letter to Harriet, about two months after leaving her, Shelley allowed himself open to only one charge. "Perhaps I have done you injury, but surely most innocently & unintentionally, in having commenced any connection with you." That connection could not have been sustained without wrecking Shelley's moral life by thwarting its purpose. Before he left England with Mary he provided for Harriet's maintenance and a year later, when he came into his inheritance, made the provision comfortable. Two and a half years after Shelley ended the marriage, Harriet drowned herself in Hyde Park's Serpentine, possibly pregnant. Her death shook him badly, and gave emotional reality to a remarkable lyric that issued from his "agony of mind," an agony he concealed. The lyric, headed *November, 1815* in its posthumous publication, antedates Harriet's death by a year, but the general scholarly judgment takes her death as the occasion of the poem.

LINES: "The cold earth slept below"

I

THE cold earth slept below,
Above the cold sky shone;
And all around, with a chilling sound,
From caves of ice and fields of snow,
The breath of night like death did flow
Beneath the sinking moon.

II

The wintry hedge was black,
The green grass was not seen,
The birds did rest on the bare thorn's breast,
Whose roots, beside the pathway track,
Had bound their folds o'er many a crack
Which the frost had made between.

8

Thine eyes *glowed* in the *gl*are
Of the moon's *d*ying *l*ight;
As a *fen-fire*'s beam on a *s*luggish *s*tream
Glea*ms* di*ml*y, *s*o the *m*oon sh*o*ne there,
And it yellowed the strings of th*y* raven hair,
That shook *i*n the w*i*nd of n*i*ght.

The *m*oon *m*ade thy *l*ips pale, be*l*oved—
The w*i*nd made thy bosom ch*i*ll—
The night *d*id shed on thy *d*ear head
*I*ts frozen *d*ew, and thou *d*i*d*st lie
Where the *b*itter *b*reath of the naked sky
Might v*i*sit thee at w*i*ll.

He speaks of Harriet as his beloved, and the deep emotional
reality of the poem would persuade us that it is so. But emotion being shaped out of chaos into form, which is ever the
work of art, may suffer a change in its elements. That is why
we cannot surely argue from a poem to the actuality of a
man's experience. The intensity of the emotion, I think, corresponds to Shelley's agony, and that is the only sincerity we
need look for. It takes no profound insight to understand the
change suffered in the lyric. In any case personal sincerity may
measure a man but not a poem. Artistic sincerity—a man's
encroaching on flux and chaos to give enduring life in the
best form he can to that worth giving life to—is quite another
matter.

These lines, among the earliest of Shelley's great lyrics,
curiously suggest two poets who, although they both admired
Shelley greatly, are no way alike, Swinburne and Hardy. The
mood of the waste imagery is Hardy's; the music of the assonance and alliteration, which I have italicized, Swinburne's
(as in *Atalanta in Calydon* or *Ave Atque Vale* the music here
never usurps the emotional meaning in which it is an element).
The tone of passionate personal intensity is Shelley's own,
inimitably, all the more powerful for its economy of means
and for the shock of surprise which illuminates the poem. We
know nothing of the woman in relation to the speaker in the
lyric until the evocative, *beloved,* in the final stanza; and only

one other word, *dear,* connects his emotional life to her dead person. We take that much in only to have the waste terror become a spiritual terror in the sexual image at the lyric's end, the impersonal ravishment of the dead girl by the naked sky, bitter to her, impossible to check.

Before leaving this lyric, that would do honor to any poet, we may as well explicitly make short work of the cliché that Shelley was emotionally unrestrained, was incapable of emotional restraint, as a poet. Observe that although we feel the personal intensity of the speaker in the lyric, he says nothing of himself at all. If that is not restraint admirably put to artistic purposes, what is? The instances of his capacity for restraint are many. If elsewhere he sometimes speaks with less restraint than suits the taste of certain modern critics (including mine), we must yet consider that restraint is a classical virtue and that Shelley was a romantic poet. The speaker in Shakespeare's sonnets often cares little for restraint. A critic who categorically judges against an artistic vision—whether classical, romantic, metaphysical, or realistic—we may pity as incapable of profiting from the function of literature to give a larger life to our sympathies.

I confess that I am unable to read *The New Life* of Dante with any emotional understanding or sympathy. Am I therefore to dismiss that document, judging the work as valueless? Or am I to think that if the meaning of his experience is inaccessible to me, the limitation is mine? More than inaccessible, it seems invalid to me. Yet Dante embraced the nature of that experience, which issued from values of his age, as true. Those values, governing the connection between men and women, are not ours. But I must think myself the poorer for not being able to look with his eyes, love with his love.

Shelley, whose sensitiveness was "quick and deep," was born into an age that valued feeling. In 1790 sensibility was "a word which in modern times we hear in the mouth of every one" (*Hibernian Magazine,* 1790, ii: 132). "Sensibility!—what is it?— Is it not that delicate perception of natural and moral beauty, which the Creator has implanted in the soul to exalt its happiness, and awaken its noblest passions?" (*Universal Magazine,* 86: 60-61). Not perception only. "Our author distinguishes the true sensibility from that which is false and . . . leads us to the most brilliant example of true sensibility in our Saviour.

10

He wept, but he healed; he felt, but his feelings did not delay his compassionate assistance" (*Critical Review*, 69: 33).

So much for the voices of men whose names we do not know. Let us listen to a greater: "the human mind is capable of being excited without the application of gross and violent stimulants; and he must have a very faint perception of its beauty and dignity who does not know this, and who does not further know, that one being is elevated above another in proportion as he has this capability. It has therefore appeared to me, that to endeavour to produce or to enlarge this capability is one of the best services in which, at any period, a Writer can be engaged." Thus Wordsworth (in his Preface to the second edition of *Lyrical Ballads*, 1800) justified the place of sensibility in his poetic credo. In our own time the gross and violent stimulants needed to excite our minds are alike causes of violence in New York City streets, of Nazi atrocity and a people's bearing with, if not rejoicing in, that atrocity, and of what may destroy most of us.

Coleridge also believed that "Sensibility indeed, both quick and deep, is not only a characteristic feature, but may be deemed a component part of genius" (*Biographia Literaria*, 1817, chapter II). But we must not think that because these men valued feeling more than we do, they valued the intellect less. In a footnote Coleridge added, "a more than usual rapidity of association, a more than usual power of passing from thought to thought, and image to image, is a component equally essential" to genius; without this power "profound sensibility . . . might be fairly described as exposing the individual to a greater degree of mental derangement." As Coleridge balanced profound and acute feeling with the working of thought and imagination, so Wordsworth wrote in his Preface, "Poems to which any value can be attached were never produced on any variety of subjects but by a man who, being possessed of more than usual sensibility, had also thought long and deeply."

Some of us may dislike the intense sensitivity and outpouring of feeling in the Romantic poets. To those poets our expression of emotional experience would perhaps seem barren and uninviting. The only absolute measure of the validity of an emotional response is the determination of whether or not (to borrow the language of physical science) the strain be

11

proportional to the stress, but not always can we make that determination in the emotional world. When the response is too much for the stress, we are confronted with a sentimentality rather than with a genuine emotion, and sentimentalities are present as typical flaws in the great Romantic poets, mainly in their earlier poetry. Sentimentalities are infrequent in modern poetry because modern poets, valuing intellect preeminently and thinking irony always a virtue (excepting the few modern poets who are romantic), have typically no personal emotion not cut down, a neat way of escaping the sentimentality they are deathly afraid of being caught with. The typical flaw of modern poetry in which the emotional response is too little for the stress is barrenness. One word more: we should be presumptuous to think that there is more or better intellect in modern than in Romantic poetry.

ALASTOR

When Shelley and Mary, out of money, had to return to England in September of 1814, they found themselves almost friendless—a hard thing for Shelley to bear. "Social enjoyment," he later wrote to Peacock, "is the alpha and omega of existence." [Shelley's extraordinary descriptive letters from Italy were written to Thomas Love Peacock. They were close in 1814, when Shelley in the profound agitation of his mind as he separated himself from Harriet turned to Peacock; and after Shelley and Mary came back from the Continent, Peacock visited almost every day. They were close again in the winter of 1815, when Shelley and Mary lived at Bishopsgate, near Windsor, and Peacock at Great Marlow; and their intimacy continued when Shelley settled in Great Marlow after his second return from the Continent in the autumn of 1816. Peacock had made himself into a fine classical scholar; his love of Greek poetry excited Shelley's, and that seems an ample exchange for the pension Shelley gave him for a time. Shelley reviewed with high praise Peacock's elaborate poem *Rhododaphne, or the Thessalian Spell,* published in 1818. His best literary gifts were for satirical fiction. *Nightmare Abbey,* also published in 1818, caricatured Shelley, who responded good-naturedly; the glazed terrace atop the house where he composed *The Cenci* Shelley

called Scythrop's tower, Scythrop being the Shelley in Peacock's extravaganza. Letters were Peacock's avocation. He
found his vocation in 1819 in the India House, where he rose
to succeed James Mill as chief examiner for twenty years and
retired in favor of John Stuart Mill.] Shelley and Mary constantly changed lodgings to escape arrest for debt, and Shelley
at last had to go into hiding alone. Mary's father, the philosopher Godwin, was behaving like most fathers in like
circumstances, badly. Matters could not be settled with Harriet. An eminent doctor thought Shelley's life nearly over because of a lung disease. Suffering nervously and physically, in
nine months he composed almost nothing. When Sir Bysshe
died in 1815 and their affairs were reasonably in order, Shelley
and Mary retreated to a cottage on the edge of Windsor Forest,
near the winding Thames. During a thoroughly delightful
expedition on the Thames to the source of the river, which they
made with two friends, Shelley's dejection and irritability
vanished. On their return to the cottage he began to study
six hours a day without difficulty; and here, at twenty-three,
composed *Alastor,* the first promise of his genius.

Shelley wrote a preface of two paragraphs. The second is a
reflection on the moral implication of the poem. The first
gives an epitome:

THE poem entitled *Alastor* may be considered as allegorical of one
of the most interesting situations of the human mind. It represents
a youth of uncorrupted feelings and adventurous genius led forth
by an imagination inflamed and purified through familiarity with
all that is excellent and majestic, to the contemplation of the universe. He drinks deep of the fountains of knowledge, and is still
insatiate. The magnificence and beauty of the external world sinks
profoundly into the frame of his conceptions, and affords to their
modifications a variety not to be exhausted. So long as it is possible
for his desires to point towards objects thus infinite and unmeasured,
he is joyous, and tranquil, and self-possessed. But the period arrives
when these objects cease to suffice. His mind is at length suddenly
awakened and thirsts for intercourse with an intelligence similar
to itself. He images to himself the Being whom he loves. Conversant
with speculations of the sublimest and most perfect natures, the
vision in which he embodies his own imaginations unites all of
wonderful, or wise, or beautiful, which the poet, the philosopher, or

13

the lover could depicture. The intellectual faculties, the imagination, the functions of sense, have their respective requisitions on the sympathy of corresponding powers in other human beings. The Poet is represented as uniting these requisitions, and attaching them to a single image. He seeks in vain for a prototype of his conception. Blasted by his disappointment, he descends to an untimely grave.

Five years later in a letter Shelley reflected, "I think one is always in love with something or other. The . . . error consists in seeking in a mortal image the likeness of what is perhaps eternal." The pressure to incorporate the ideal in a living woman was constant in Shelley's life, a deep cause of his spiritual tension. The Romantic poets (to quote part of a statement by Hoxie Fairchild) endeavored "an imaginative fusion of . . . the real and the ideal, the finite and the infinite, the material and the spiritual." Hoxie Fairchild made that statement disparagingly. To me that endeavor seems high wisdom. When Romantic poets make that fusion successfully, one must resist doggedly not to respond with excitement. Shelley often succeeds, astonishing us by his assurance and ease of execution even in the familiar style. But Shelley made that endeavor in the actual world too, and therein never succeeded. The undertaking itself is a tribute to him. Not only Shelley had this Romantic vision. Wordsworth chants in *The Recluse, or Views on Man, Nature, and Society:*

> Paradise, and groves
> Elysian, Fortunate Fields—like those of old
> Sought in the Atlantic Main—why should they be
> A history only of departed things,
> Or a mere fiction of what never was?
> For the discerning intellect of Man,
> When wedded to this goodly universe
> In love and holy passion, shall find these
> A simple produce of the common day.
> —I, long before the blissful hour arrives,
> Would chant, in lonely peace, the spousal verse
> Of this great consummation.
> (800-810)

> How exquisitely the individual Mind
> (And the progressive powers perhaps no less

14

Of the whole species) to the external World
Is fitted:—and how exquisitely, too—
Theme this but little heard of among men—
The external World is fitted to the Mind;
And the creation (by no lower name
Can it be called) which they with blended might
Accomplish:—this is our high argument.
(816-824)

In *Alastor* the imaginative fusion succeeded only in parts.
A vision comes to a Poet in a dream.

Her voice was like the voice of his own soul
Heard in the calm of thought . . .
Knowledge and truth and virtue were her theme,
And lofty hopes of divine liberty,
Thoughts the most dear to him, and poesy. (153-154, 158-160)

The solemn mood kindles a fire in her, and her hands sweep
from a "strange harp Strange symphony," tumultuous like her
breathing; and her body glows in the warm light of its own
life "beneath the sinuous veil Of woven wind" (the veil a
symbol of illusoriness, which hides truth).

she drew back a while,
Then, yielding to the irresistible joy,
With frantic gesture and short breathless cry
Folded his frame in her dissolving arms. (184-187)

It is not her arms that are dissolving. Her passion and beauty
make the poet dissolve, as "limbs, and breath, and being
intertwined," into infinity. In this dream-experience the "intellectual faculties, the imagination, the functions of sense" of
the poet are in perfect sympathy—as one tuning fork will
vibrate when another of the same frequency sounds—with
those of the vision. Pursuing her into wakefulness in vain, the
poet laments:

Lost, lost, for ever lost,
In the wide pathless desert of dim sleep,
That beautiful shape! Does the dark gate of death
Conduct to thy mysterious paradise,
O Sleep? Does the bright arch of rainbow clouds,

15

And pendent mountains seen in the calm lake,
Lead only to a black and watery depth? (209-215)

The poet's search for an embodiment of his vision begins ten lines later and that search brings the extinction of his life by Alastor, the spirit of solitude, for none can live alone. (Harriet had not the intellect and imagination for sympathy with her husband; Mary had such corresponding powers. Shelley escaped death by solitude.) The journey the poet makes in his search is the radical fault of the poem, but neither for its length nor for the sentimental and Gothic details that mar passages. The elegiac beauty haunting the poet's journey overcomes the awkward details. The descriptiveness seems less and less lengthy with successive readings, as we perceive that such passages do not exist for their own sake. Sometimes the descriptive purpose is openly interpreted: A stream,

Wanton and wild, through many a green ravine
Beneath the forest flowed. Sometimes it fell
Among the moss with hollow harmony
Dark and profound. Now on the polished stones
It danced; like childhood laughing as it went:
Then, through the plain in tranquil wanderings crept,
Reflecting every herb and drooping bud
That overhung its quietness.—"O stream!
Whose source is inaccessibly profound,
Whither do thy mysterious waters tend?
Thou imagest my life. Thy darksome stillness,
Thy dazzling waves, thy loud and hollow gulfs,
Thy searchless fountain, and invisible course
Have each their type in me: and the wide sky,
And measureless ocean may declare as soon
What oozy cavern or what wandering cloud
Contains thy waters, as the universe
Tell where these living thoughts reside, when stretched
Upon thy flowers my bloodless limbs shall waste
I' the passing wind!" (495-514)

Sometimes we feel the meaning as a living presence, as in this passage (the concrete imagery shows how closely Shelley observed the actual): The oak,

16

Expanding its immense and knotty arms,
Embraces the light beech. The pyramids
Of the tall cedar overarching, frame
Most solemn domes within, and far below,
Like clouds suspended in an emerald sky,
The ash and the acacia floating hang
Tremulous and pale. Like restless serpents, clothed
In rainbow and in fire, the parasites,
Starred with ten thousand blossoms, flow around
The grey trunks, and, as gamesome infants' eyes,
With gentle meanings, and most innocent wiles,
Fold their beams round the hearts of those that love,
These twine their tendrils with the wedded boughs
Uniting their close union; the woven leaves
Make net-work of the dark blue light of day,
And the night's noontide clearness, mutable
As shapes in the weird clouds. Soft mossy lawns
Beneath these canopies extend their swells,
Fragrant with perfumed herbs, and eyed with blooms
Minute yet beautiful. One darkest glen
Sends from its woods of musk-rose, twined with jasmine,
A soul-dissolving odour, to invite
To some more lovely mystery. Through the dell,
Silence and Twilight here, twin-sisters, keep
Their noonday watch, and sail among the shades,
Like vaporous shapes half seen; beyond, a well,
Dark, gleaming, and of most translucent wave,
Images all the woven boughs above,
And each depending leaf, and every speck
Of azure sky, darting between their chasms;
Nor aught else in the liquid mirror laves
Its portraiture, but some inconstant star
Between one foliaged lattice twinkling fair,
Or, painted bird, sleeping beneath the moon,
Or gorgeous insect floating motionless,
Unconscious of the day, ere yet his wings
Have spread their glories to the gaze of noon. (432-468)

In a work of such meditative tone as *Alastor* descriptiveness
may sustain itself and claim our regard so long as it reveals
meaning.—The radical fault is this: we do not believe in the

17

reality of the journey; Shelley endeavored an "imaginative fusion of . . . the natural and the supernatural" and failed.

But the promise of genius is there, as in the forest passage just given, where there is a subtle and sure mastery of music changing in accord with imagery and meaning. The meanings of the passage intervolve with the imminence of death: as in the imagery of pyramids and cathedrals in the opening lines; in the light and color glowing at a middle height as in a cathedral; in the beauty and love gleaming around the boles (the blossoms like "gamesome infants' eyes" and the tendrils "with the wedded boughs Uniting their close union"), and the scents inviting to more lovely mystery; in the Silence and Twilight taking on existence in the visible world; and in the image of the reflections creating for us a glimpse of the continuity between the finite and the infinite.

The promise is in the invocation:

> Earth, ocean, air, belovèd brotherhood!
> If our great Mother has imbued my soul
> With aught of natural piety to feel
> Your love, and recompense the boon with mine;
> If dewy morn, and odorous noon, and even,
> With sunset and its gorgeous ministers,
> And solemn midnight's tingling silentness;
> If autumn's hollow sighs in the sere wood,
> And winter robing with pure snow and crowns
> Of starry ice the grey grass and bare boughs;
> If spring's voluptuous pantings when she breathes
> Her first sweet kisses, have been dear to me;
> If no bright bird, insect, or gentle beast
> I consciously have injured, but still loved
> And cherished these my kindred; then forgive
> This boast, belovèd brethren, and withdraw
> No portion of your wonted favour now!
>
> Mother of this unfathomable world!
> Favour my solemn song, for I have loved
> Thee ever, and thee only; I have watched
> Thy shadow, and the darkness of thy steps,
> And my heart ever gazes on the depth
> Of thy deep mysteries. I have made my bed
> In charnels and on coffins, where black death

Keeps record of the trophies won from thee,
Hoping to still these obstinate questionings
Of thee and thine, by forcing some lone ghost
Thy messenger, to render up the tale
Of what we are. In lone and silent hours,
When night makes a weird sound of its own stillness,
Like an inspired and desperate alchymist
Staking his very life on some dark hope,
Have I mixed awful talk and asking looks
With my most innocent love, until strange tears
Uniting with those breathless kisses, made
Such magic as compels the charmèd night
To render up thy charge: . . . and, though ne'er yet
Thou hast unveiled thy inmost sanctuary,
Enough from incommunicable dream,
And twilight phantasms, and deep noon-day thought,
Has shone within me, that serenely now
And moveless, as a long-forgotten lyre
Suspended in the solitary dome
Of some mysterious and deserted fane,
I wait thy breath, Great Parent, that my strain
May modulate with murmurs of the air,
And motions of the forests and the sea,
And voice of living beings, and woven hymns
Of night and day, and the deep heart of man. (1-49)

Wordsworthian as this passage is, we yet hear Shelley's genuine
voice, as we hear Beethoven's in his early Haydnesque works.

   In Wordsworth the presences in nature, spiritual powers,
shape his soul with the instruments of fear and beauty. On his
part there are love and worship. In Shelley's invocation there
are love and kinship. The mythopoeic impulse, therefore, di-
verges in the two poets. Unlike Wordsworth, Shelley makes us
feel earth, ocean, and air—with whom he claims brotherhood—
as living beings. His invocation to these beings and their great
Mother must not be mistaken as a poetic convention. Rather
the invocation is a genuine prayer to spiritual powers to whose
race the poet, although a lesser being, belongs. This noble
conception of God and Man sprung from one Mother, although
unequally, was also Pindar's: "One is the race of Gods and of
men; from one mother [the Earth-Mother] we both draw our

breath. Yet are our powers poles apart; for we are nothing, but for them the brazen Heaven endures for ever, their secure abode" (as translated by H. D. F. Kitto). This religious conception of Shelley's was to change, but that it changed makes the experience no less a religious one in this invocation.

In the single periodic structure of the first seventeen lines, the rhythm of the clauses is incantatory, obliquely summoning the days and seasons into life as persons even as the poet invokes spiritual powers. As the period moves to its culmination, assonance and alliteration in twelve lines running (6-17), sometimes more sometimes less insistent, intensify the emotion in the appeal. The vocalic designs in the last line of the opening verse paragraph and in the first line of the second paragraph are masterly, as is the contrapuntal effect of long syllables playing against stress and the patterns of caesuras in the first nearly six-line sentence of the second paragraph. [I can best illustrate what I mean by contrapuntal effect with these lines from Milton's sonnet on his blindness:

> When I consider how my light is spent,
>   E're half my days, in this dark world and wide . . .

The form demands five stresses to the line. Were we to give either line four or six, we should destroy the music. The lines scan with classical evenness:

$$- / - / - / - / - /$$
$$- / - / - / - / - /$$

Only *this dark world* may raise a question. *World* clearly takes a stress. The choice is perhaps less clear in *this dark*. As the meaning is *this* world, in which it is that Milton must serve his God, *this* must take the stress, that is, must be pronounced with more force than *dark*. Were we to stress *dark* also, we should create six stresses in the line and the pattern would offend our ear. However, *dark* is a long syllable (long syllables are those with a long vowel or a cluster of consonants). We hear its length although the sound is unstressed (i.e., it is pronounced with less force than *this* and *world*), and the length of the sound has musical importance. Counterpoint in music consists of two or more melodies heard at the same time. In Milton's line the metrical pattern of the syllables and the length or shortness of the syllables are heard at the same time; and *dark*, playing against the meter, gives a contrapuntal dimension to the line.] There follows another six-line sentence and then one of nearly twenty-one lines managed with remarkable clarity. As he nears the end of his invocation, he again uses the musical resources of assonance and alliteration, this time in nine lines running (41-49). The invocation comes to a close with a line that musically accentuates his serene waiting for the breath of the Great Parent, long syllables coinciding with the stresses. The suppleness of the rhythms is less a function of suppleness of mind, which it is in Wordsworth, than it is of suppleness of temperament, and in Shelley depends less on polysyllabic words.

The religious conception, the music, the sense of architectural design in the syntax, are Shelley's own; so are the obstinate questionings, although that phrase is Wordsworth's. Shelley thought to compel knowledge from the far side of the grave. Gothic and young though they may seem, Shelley in his mature work transforms such questionings to dignity and power. We may take the beautiful closing lines of the invocation as summoning a sustained response not to be found elsewhere in *Alastor* but in later work.

> I wait thy breath, Great Parent . . .

HYMN TO INTELLECTUAL BEAUTY

The quiet days on the Thames and in Windsor Forest came to an end. Like Coleridge writing in *Biographia Literaria*, Shelley "regarded the obligations of intellect among the most sacred of the claims of gratitude"; but although he acknowledged Godwin as the "philosopher who first awakened" his "understanding," the man's intruding letters—strident in their egoism and moral hypocrisy, and clamoring for money—were too much to bear. Mary and Shelley, too, began to live uneasily in the face of the prejudice and contempt they were enduring. Ripe to leave, they let Mary's stepsister, Claire Clairmont, who had her own private reasons, persuade them to go to Geneva. There, although on a blue gem of a lake, Mont Blanc beyond ridges facing their window, spring bursting up all around, Shelley realized his intense love of England.

21

Ten days later Byron (Claire's private reason) reached their hotel. The two men were soon at ease with each other and enjoyed a fine season of friendship. Only a vineyard divided their houses; they spent days and nights together, sailing and talking their chief pleasures. In their sailboat they made a journey of a week or so around Lake Leman, visiting places made memorable by Rousseau and Voltaire and also visiting the castle of Chillon, which Shelley thought a monument of "cold and inhuman tyranny," none "more terrible." Byron wrote stanzas for the third canto of *Childe Harold's Pilgrimage* and his two poems on Chillon; Shelley, the *Hymn to Intellectual Beauty*, an amazing new version of Platonism. There were impulses for the hymn—Shelley's first articulation of the power in the universe that could shape a man as "immortal, and omnipotent," the power to which he had consecrated himself as a boy—in Rousseau's worship of love (which "coincided with Shelley's own disposition"), in the dreadful symbol of Chillon, in the beauty of the voyage on every turn.

The shadow of that Power floats inconstantly among us, unseen.

> Spirit of Beauty, that dost consecrate
> With thine own hues all thou dost shine upon
> Of human thought or form,—where art thou gone?
> Why dost thou pass away and leave our state,
> This dim vast vale of tears, vacant and desolate?
> Ask why the sunlight not for ever
> Weaves rainbows o'er yon mountain-river,
> Why aught should fail and fade that once is shown,
> Why fear and dream and death and birth
> Cast on the daylight of this earth
> Such gloom,—why man has such a scope
> For love and hate, despondency and hope? (13-24)

We do not know; therefore, we cannot sever doubt, chance and mutability from our experience of the world. Only the light of the Spirit of Beauty can give "grace and truth to life's unquiet dream." Were that Spirit and its ministers Love, Hope, and Self-esteem constant in man, he would be godlike. But our lives are dark and against the everlastingness of that reality Shelley appeals,

22

Thou—that to human thought art nourishment,
   Like darkness to a dying flame!
   Depart not as thy shadow came,
   Depart not—lest the grave should be,
Like life and fear, a dark reality. (44-48)

Even as a boy Shelley pursued the knowledge that he thought lay beyond the grave, in vain.

   When musing deeply on the lot
Of life, at that sweet time when winds are wooing
   All vital things that wake to bring
   News of birds and blossoming,—
   Sudden, thy shadow fell on me;
I shrieked, and clasped my hands in ecstasy. (55-60)

The mystical revelation the boy experienced had an authority that shaped his life.

I vowed that I would dedicate my powers
   To thee and thine—have I not kept the vow? (61-62)

The hours of his study and love bear witness.

They know that never joy illumed my brow
   Unlinked with hope that thou wouldst free
   This world from its dark slavery,
   That thou—O awful Loveliness,
Wouldst give whate'er these words cannot express. (68-72)

The man has lived as a prophet of that Power, singing of freedom, and he closes the hymn with expectant calm and genuine religious emotion.

The day becomes more solemn and serene
   When noon is past—there is a harmony
   In autumn, and a lustre in its sky,
Which through the summer is not heard or seen,
As if it could not be, as if it had not been!
   Thus let thy power, which like the truth
   Of nature on my passive youth
Descended, to my onward life supply
   Its calm—to one who worships thee,
   And every form containing thee,

23

Whom, Spirit fair, thy spells did bind
To fear himself, and love all human kind. (73-84)

The genuineness of the religious experience, in which context freedom is a spiritual necessity, gives the poem its passion and dignity. Were the poem not an expression of the religious life, its meaning would be rooted in no reality, it would be mere fancy. What, then, is the religious life? William James in *The Varieties of Religious Experience* concludes that these are its governing beliefs:

1. That the visible world is part of a more spiritual universe from which it draws its chief significance;
2. That union or harmonious relation with that higher universe is our true end;
3. That prayer or inner communion with the spirit thereof—be that spirit "God" or "law"—is a process wherein work is really done, and spiritual energy flows in and produces effects, psychological or material, within the phenomenal world.

The *Hymn to Intellectual Beauty* tallies with these common elements in the world's diversity of religious experience, formal and private, past and present, Eastern and Western. Religious experience, as James empirically studied it, testifies only that the power in the unseen world is larger and other than ourselves—not necessarily one, infinite, or personal—and that in union with that power we find our greatest peace. That power "might conceivably even be only a larger and more godlike self, of which the present self would then be the mutilated expression, and the universe might conceivably be a collection of such selves," a conception we shall return to in *Prometheus Unbound*.

Shelley looks to that power—he calls it now Intellectual Beauty, and later Love—for the deliverance of "This world from its dark slavery," a spiritual necessity because no spiritual values can exist without freedom. Life and hope, truth and love have never been utterly quenched, the semichoruses of *Hellas* sing,

Semichorus
Yet were life a charnel where
Hope lay coffined with Despair;

24

Yet were truth a sacred lie,
Love were lust—

Semichorus
                    If Liberty
Lent not life its soul of light,
Hope its iris of delight,
Truth its prophet's robe to wear,
Love its power to give and bear. (37-45)

[Let me make perfectly clear what is not obvious to everyone,
that Hope, Truth, and Love are not lending to Life; rather,
Liberty lends its soul to Life, its iris of delight to Hope, its
prophet's robes to Truth, its power to give and bear to Love.
"Yet were life" translates in prose to "Nevertheless life would
be."]

MONT BLANC

Shelley's religious experience expressed itself again some
weeks later in *Mont Blanc,* this time in another vision and so in
another form and tone. In this vision the power in the unseen
world is not Beauty but Strength. We hear a voice expressive
of largeness and grandeur, with a depth and resonance of
ringing movement. The poem "was composed," Shelley wrote,
"under the immediate impression of the deep and powerful
feeling excited by the objects which it attempts to describe;
and, as an undisciplined overflowing of the soul, rests its claim
to approbation on an attempt to imitate the untameable
wildness and inaccessible solemnity from which those feelings
sprang." Unlike the controlled congruency of the stanzaic
form in *Hymn to Intellectual Beauty,* the five-stress lines of
the overflowing *Mont Blanc* rhyme irregularly, sometimes not
at all; Strength has not the symmetry of Beauty. Less formally
disciplined than the *Hymn*—rightly so because of what it imi-
tates—*Mont Blanc* is nonetheless a firm intellectual structure.
Shelley witnessed the things that excited his deep and powerful feeling in the Alpine valley of Chamouni, to which he,
Mary, and Claire climbed on muleback. We have in the poem
a vivid awareness of the natural world: of the dark, deep
ravine; the caves out of which torrents welled and the loud

25

waters of the Arve River; the pine trees and savage crags; the rainbow in the high waterfall; the destructive glaciers blue as the sky, with their towering cones and pyramids; and the snow-covered pinnacles of mountains dominated by Mont Blanc. The vividness bears witness to the reality of the universe of things.

[Shelley's prose fragment *On Life* apparently committed him to a different ontology from the theory of reality that *Mont Blanc* affirmed in 1816. Although James Notopoulos in a careful article on the dating of Shelley's prose fixed on 1819 for the writing of *On Life,* David Clark in his edition of Shelley's prose decided that 1812 to 1814 were likely. As the earlier years put a harder case to me, I shall assume those. In *On Life* Shelley repudiated a dualism of mind and matter. "The shocking absurdities of the popular philosophy of mind and matter . . . had early conducted me to a materialism . . . a seducing system to young and superficial minds." But the spirit within man is characteristically "at enmity with nothingness and dissolution," and such characteristic contemplation is "only consistent with the intellectual system," that is, with a monism that is intellectual: "The view of life presented by the most refined deductions of the intellectual philosophy is that of unity. Nothing exists but as it is perceived. The difference is merely nominal between those two classes of thought which are vulgarly distinguished by the names of ideas and of external objects. . . . By the word *things* is to be understood any object of thought—that is, any thought upon which any other thought is employed with an apprehension of distinction." By "Life" Shelley meant "that which includes all"; it constitutes the universe, which is of the nature of thought. Human minds do not generate the content of the universe, for "mind cannot create, it can only perceive." Like things, human minds are "different modifications of the one mind." The one mind, therefore, its thought constituting the universe, is life; the one mind is being or existence; it is reality.

But I submit that a man's mind works differently in composing poetry than in writing prose, and we therefore cannot be certain that a prose passage puts us on the way to meaning in his poetry. For example, in his *Speculations on Metaphysics* (Notopoulos dates these fragments from 1816 to 1821, and Clark from 1812 to 1815) Shelley wrote, "Words . . . are not mind, nor are they portions of mind." In *Prometheus Unbound* (1819) Asia, or Love, demands of Demogorgon, or Eternity, "Who made the living world?" and "Who made all That it contains? thought, passion, reason, will, Imagination?" The living world, then, is mind, of which thought is a portion. Some speeches later Asia reflects that Prometheus "gave man speech, and speech created thought" (II. iv. 9-11, 72). Words here are a portion of mind. In his prose metaphysical speculations Shelley's mind worked systematically, although he never constructed a philosophic system, but in his poetry, as he wrote to Keats, "I have tried to avoid system"; and so his prose and poetry were liable to contradiction. In reaching the meaning of his poetry, which after all has its own objective existence, we may profit from his prose, but we must finally depend on our esthetic sense rather than on our logical sense.

Although in his systematic prose the "most refined abstractions of logic conduct to a view of life," that is, a view of being, which is intellectual, we are conducted by his poetry to another view. A poet, sings a Spirit in *Prometheus Unbound,*

> will watch from dawn to gloom
> The lake-reflected sun illume
> The yellow bees in the ivy-bloom,
> Nor heed nor see, what things they be;
> But from these create he can
> Forms more real than living man. (I. 743-749)

If a poet neither heeds nor sees "The lake-reflected sun illume The yellow bees in the ivy-bloom," the Spirit vividly responds to these concrete things, which (the main stress in the line falling on *things*) are physical reality; that is to say, Shelley saw that reality. But the poet, like Shelley, penetrates to the forms, or essences, to make poetry from. "I always seek *in what I see* [italics mine] the manifestation of something beyond the present and tangible object." That his poetry is more perfect than living man, "is the very image of life expressed in its eternal truth" as Shelley wrote in *A Defence of Poetry* (1821), makes it more real than *things,* which carries its ordinary meaning. *Things,* if less real (they are perishable), are not therefore unreal. Here again, as in *Mont Blanc,* Shelley expresses a dualism of thought and things. And a song of celebration near the close of *Prometheus Unbound* affirms

27

physical reality in "This true fair world of things" (IV. 384). I give one more passage, from *Adonais* (1821), in which the images seem to me to affirm a universe in which both the spirit and matter are real:

> the one Spirit's plastic stress
> Sweeps through the dull dense world, compelling there,
> All new successions to the forms they wear;
> Torturing th' unwilling dross that checks its flight
> To its own likeness, as each mass may bear. (381-385)

"Forms" here—in "the dull dense world," of "unwilling dross" —must mean physical shapes, physical beings, not essences.

In *Hellas* (later in 1821) Shelley presented thought as the only reality:

> this Whole
> Of suns, and worlds, and men, and beasts, and flowers,
> With all the silent or tempestuous workings
> By which they have been, are, or cease to be,
> Are motes of a sick eye, bubbles and dreams;
> Thought is its cradle and its grave, nor less
> The Future and the Past are idle shadows
> Of thought's eternal flight—they have no being:
> Nought is but that which feels itself to be. (776-785)

That Shelley, when his mind was working in poetry, now believed in thought as the only reality is open to question. *Hellas* is a play, and these lines are spoken by the character Ahasuerus in a passage, as Shelley explains in a note, "tempting Mahmud to that state of mind in which ideas may be supposed to assume the force of sensations through the confusion of thought with the objects of thought." By now the reader is perhaps tempted to think, in an ironic sense that Shelley did not intend in his metaphysical speculations, "It imports little to inquire whether thought be distinct from the objects of thought," and so I shall stop.]

Shelley first put his experience of the white mountain into a prose letter; let us juxtapose a passage with the poem.

Mont Blanc was before us but was covered with cloud, & its base furrowed with dreadful gaps was seen alone. Pinnacles of snow, intolerably bright, part of the chain connected with Mount Blanc shone thro the clouds at intervals on high. I never knew, I never imagined what mountains were before. The immensity of these aerial summits excited, when they suddenly burst upon the sight, a sentiment of extatic wonder, not unallied to madness—And remember this was all one scene. It all pressed home to our regard and to our imagination. Though it embraced a great number of miles the snowy pyramids which shot into the bright blue sky seemed to overhang our path—the ravine, clothed with gigantic pines and black with its depth below—so deep that the very roaring of the untameable Arve which rolled through it could not be heard above—was close to our very footsteps. All was as much our own as if we had been the creators of such impressions in the minds of others, as now occupied our own.—Nature was the poet whose harmony held our spirits more breathless than that of the divinest.

A day later he composed *Mont Blanc,* whose imaginative power and harmony create in the minds of others the impressions Shelley experienced; more than that, the poem reflects on the meaning of the experience.

I

The everlasting universe of things
Flows through the mind, and rolls its rapid waves,
Now dark—now glittering—now reflecting gloom—
Now lending splendour, where from secret springs
The source of human thought its tribute brings
Of waters,—with a sound but half its own,
Such as a feeble brook will oft assume
In the wild woods, among the mountains lone,
Where waterfalls around it leap for ever,
Where woods and winds contend, and a vast river
Over its rocks ceaselessly bursts and raves.

These lines are an expression of philosophy in images; although the images of river, woods, waterfalls, and winds have a physical existence in the next section of the poem, here their life is purely tropal. The physical universe brings its tribute of waters to the source of human thought, which is in the mind. While the source of human thought is known, in Shelley's view, the springs of the universe are secret; we also know that the universe is everlasting. The river flowing through our mind, or our experience, brings gloom and splendor. The connotation of *tribute* suggests that our mind is a greater power than the universe. Our mind gives the river of the universe, as it flows through, half its sound, as waterfalls, contending winds, and river give sound to a brook. That sound, I take it, is a symbol for meaning. The theme echoes lines in *Tintern Abbey:*

> all the mighty world
> Of eye and ear,—both what they half create,
> And what perceive. (105-107)

II

Thus thou, Ravine of Arve—dark, deep Ravine—
Thou many-coloured, many-voicèd vale,
Over whose pines, and crags, and caverns sail
Fast cloud-shadows and sunbeams: awful scene,
Where Power in likeness of the Arve comes down
From the ice-gulfs that gird his secret throne,
Bursting through these dark mountains like the flame
Of lightning through the tempest;—thou dost lie,
Thy giant brood of pines around thee clinging,   20
Children of elder time, in whose devotion
The chainless winds still come and ever came
To drink their odours, and their mighty swinging
To hear—an old and solemn harmony;
Thine earthly rainbows stretched across the sweep
Of the aethereal waterfall, whose veil
Robes some unsculptured image; the strange sleep
Which when the voices of the desert fail
Wraps all in its own deep eternity;—
Thy caverns echoing to the Arve's commotion,   30
A loud, lone sound no other sound can tame;
Thou art pervaded with that ceaseless motion,
Thou art the path of that unresting sound—
Dizzy Ravine— and when I gaze on thee

I seem as in a trance sublime and strange
To muse on my own separate fantasy,
My own, my human mind, which passively
Now renders and receives fast influencings,
Holding an unremitting interchange
With the clear universe of things around;   40
One legion of wild thoughts, whose wandering wings
Now float above thy darkness, and now rest
Where that or thou art no unbidden guest,
In the still cave of the witch Poesy,
Seeking among the shadows that pass by
Ghosts of all things that are, some shade of thee,
Some phantom, some faint image; till the breast
From which they fled recalls them, thou art there!

This section is a single sentence elaborately constructed in
thirty-seven lines. The architecture of the sentence, although
elaborate, need cause no difficulty. To compass it from lines
19 through 34, we need merely see that parallel to "thou" in
19 are "Thy giant brood" in 20, "Thine earthly rainbows" in
25, and "Thy caverns" in 30—elaborate architecture, but remarkably symmetrical. There are difficulties in the images,
but nothing in the poem is opaque.

"Thus thou, Ravine"—the section begins by establishing a
comparison with the content of the first section. The Ravine
is like the mind, and the Arve River like the flowing universe
of things. The Arve is also a likeness of Power (16), which "is
as a law" both to thought and the physical universe (139-141).
The vivid reality of the scene is full of awe (15) because of its
beauty and power and mystery. Deep in the mystery is the
unsculptured (in the sense of unshaped, immaterial) image
veiled by the ethereal (high) waterfall textured with rainbows;
that image, that "strange sleep" (24-26), is death, to whose
eternity all will come "when the voices of the desert fail" (27-
28). The voices of the desert suggest the prophets, who keep
the world going; they are also the great natural forces in the
world, like the energy of storms in the desert of frozen floods
and mountains (62-67).

The Ravine symbolizes, we come to understand, not a
single mind but the universal mind. When the poet gazes on

the dizzy-making ravine, the path of the Arve's sound, he seems to muse in a sublime and strange trance on his own human mind, a fantasy separated from the poet's *I* and from the universal mind. His own mind now passively (because he is in a trance) is influenced by and influences the universe around (34-40); and now floats—a fantasy, it is a "legion of wild thoughts"—over the ravine (in its duple aspect as the Ravine of Arve and as a symbol of the universal mind): and now rests in the cave of contemplative poetry, where his own human mind and the ravine are rightfully present (41-44). There his mind searches. Among the shadows in that cave his mind makes a double search. It searches for the "ghosts"— the essences—of "things that are." The force of "are" establishes the "things" as reality. They may have, in the dualistic universe that this poem envisions, their ideal essences which are also reality.

In Platonic philosophy the only reality is of the nature of thought and has its existence in the intellectual world. The visible, or material, world is not real. Its things are merely shadows, or imperfect manifestations, of their ideas in the intellectual world. In geometry, for example, our triangles and circles are imperfect manifestations of figures that exist perfectly in idea only. Many beautiful things, each with its idea in the intellectual world, "may be brought under a single idea," absolute beauty, "which is called the essence of each." We see things imperfectly during our life in the visible world because we can perceive only through our senses, which clog the vision of the soul. When death releases the soul from the prison of the body, the soul will look upon the reality of the intellectual world. In this poem Shelley views both the visible and the intellectual worlds as real; Plato, believing in a single reality, is monistic in his philosophy whereas Shelley is dualistic. In Plato's view, as I have said, the things of this world are only shadows—Shelley's "shade" and "faint image" are shadows. The expression *shadows* comes from Plato's allegory of the cave in *The Republic*. There are human beings in a cave facing away from the entrance. They are chained so that they cannot turn their heads. Behind them a fire blazes, and between the prisoners and the fire is a wall. Other men walk along the wall, holding higher than the wall "all sorts of vessels and

32

statues and figures of animals made of wood and stone and various materials." The fire throws on the wall of the cave that the prisoners face the shadows of the prisoners and the shadows of the objects. The prisoners, who cannot move their heads, see nothing but shadows, and as they know of no other existences, they mistake the shadows for the realities. Only a man released from the cave to the world which the sun lights up, although dazzled at first, will see things as they really are and understand that the sun "gives the season and the years, and is the guardian of all that is in the visible world, and in a certain way the cause of all things which he and his fellows have been accustomed to behold." This, Socrates says to a disciple, is the meaning of the allegory: "The prisonhouse is the world of sight, the light of the fire is the sun, and you will not misapprehend me if you interpret the journey upwards to be the ascent of the soul into the intellectual world according to my poor belief, which, at your desire, I have expressed—whether rightly or wrongly God knows. But, whether true or false, my opinion is that in the world of knowledge the idea of good appears last of all, and is seen only with an effort; and, when seen, is also inferred to be the universal author of all things beautiful and right and of the lord of light in this visible world, and the immediate source of reason and truth in the intellectual; and that this is the power upon which he who would act rationally either in public or private life must have his eye fixed" (as translated by B. Jowett).

The speaker's mind in *Mont Blanc* searches not only for the essences of "things that are" but also searches for some "shade" —some manifestation as a thing—of the universal mind. "Some phantom, some faint image" are a repetition of ghost and shade; the lyrical technique of repetition is used, of course, for its emotional effect. Until the shadows are recalled to their ultimate source, the "breast From which they fled" (47-48), the ravine in its duple aspect will endure in the cave of poetry (45-48). The universe is "everlasting" (1). We are not to believe that the "breast From which they [the shadows] fled"—the breast is the "secret Strength" (139)—*will* recall the shadows. If a man says, "I'll wait till hell freezes over," he does not mean that he expects hell to freeze, at which time he will stop waiting.

III

Looking up, the poet at the beginning of the third section wonders whether a veil hides life and death from knowledge, or whether, his spirit driven from him, sleep reveals gleams of the spiritual world (49-59).

> Far, far above, piercing the infinite sky,
> Mont Blanc appears,—still, snowy, and serene—(60-61)

An infinite sky has no limit; yet Mont Blanc pierces that sky. The intellectual paradox in the visually firm image springs imaginatively from the symbolic value of Mont Blanc. The serenity of Mont Blanc, inhabited by Power (127), contrasts with the savagery and destructiveness of the mountains of ice and rock heaped around—among them the spreading and winding glacial floods, the storms, the eagle with the hunter's bone tracked by the wolf. There is tension in the contrast, hard for knowledge to loosen. Did earthquake or fire make the hideous shapes of this desert, this wasteland? "None can reply" (60-75); its beginning, like the secret springs of the universe, is unknowable. This wilderness may teach religious doubt or religious faith: "man may be, But for such faith, with nature reconciled" (76-79). [The phrase "But for such faith" was Shelley's revision, printed in 1817, of a manuscript version which reads "In such a faith." The revision, which makes the line opposite in meaning to the manuscript version, is fitting, powerful and admirable, and is a remarkable instance of how far a poet can go in revising. Shelley often uses the word "faith" in a derogatory sense, as though it were a synonym for superstition; but here faith is mild, solemn, and serene—clearly no derogation is intended.] That is, without such faith he would have to reconcile himself to the existence of a savage naturalistic world only. But the great mountain, unlike the wilderness, speaks with no ambiguity, repealing

> Large codes of fraud and woe; not understood
> By all, but which the wise, and great, and good
> Interpret, or make felt, or deeply feel. (81-83)

The "wise, and great, and good" are the prophets of mankind, without whom we should live savagely, at last to be wrapped in the eternity of death (27-29).

34

IV

In twelve lines Shelley portrays the mutable physical universe (84-95); only the Power is not subject to mutability (96-97). The primeval mountains of the wilderness teach the heedful mind. The glaciers move on, their precipices shaped by Frost and Sun into a city of death (98-106), or rather they are a flood of ruin descending from the highest limits of the world, shattering much of the life and joy of its living things (107-120). Power is a destroyer and preserver. Below, the majestic Arve, which is the "breath and blood"—the life—"of distant lands, for ever Rolls its loud waters to the ocean-waves," which wash the farthest shores of the world, and in the sure cycles of the world, "Breathes its swift vapours to the circling air" (120-126).

V

Mont Blanc gleams in silence and solitude, that silence and solitude vivified by images whose purpose is to make us feel a presence (127-138). The "secret Strength of things," governing thought and the infinite universe, inhabits that mountain (139-141). And what were Mont Blanc—that is, what were the Strength it symbolizes,—

> and earth, and stars, and sea,
> If to the human mind's imaginings
> Silence and solitude were vacancy? (142-144)

The reply wrapped in the question is "Nothing." But not in the sense of nonexistent. Mont Blanc, the earth, the stars, the sea would exist as facts without meaning. In other words, if the imaginative faculty of the human mind recognized no spiritual presence, if to the human mind silence and solitude were empty of spiritual meaning, neither the Power nor the universe would have any value. That conception makes the human mind the only conferrer of meaning and value.

THE REVOLT OF ISLAM

By summer's end Claire had so complicated her life, Godwin his own finances, and Sir Timothy his son's business affairs that Shelley had to set off for England. Shelley, by the way, handled complex business and legal matters with patience and acumen. Harriet's suicide broke upon him in December—he had had no news of her for half a year—and her family proceeded against Shelley in the Court of Chancery for custody of the two children. The Lord Chancellor ruled that Shelley would inculcate immorality were the children in his care, and gave them to a guardian named by Shelley, allowing Shelley to visit the children twelve times a year. But Shelley could make no visit. Before the proceedings were over, he had to leave England, never to return.

The Shelleys early in 1817 leased a house on the outskirts of Marlow (somewhat over thirty miles west of central London by land, nearly twice as long on the river), at an easy walk from the Thames. Here they had fine social pleasures. With friends that came to visit or lived nearby, they hiked in the open country or woods and boated on the river; evenings they enjoyed music. Shelley attended the poor and the sick with broth, clothes, blankets, money; discouraged boys from hurling stones at squirrels; and had crayfish purchased from street mongers and given back to the Thames—the man lived the universal love and sympathy his poetry celebrates. Always, of course, in his solitary hours he wrote or studied. Knowledge was a passion. He learned literature in seven languages, physical and social sciences, history, philosophy. Among the arts (other than poetry) music evoked his deepest response.

There were social pleasures in London, too, happily dissipating Shelley's anxiety and depression during the protracted Chancery business. He turned to Leigh Hunt, whose politics and editorial courage had first attracted Shelley; their lasting, fine friendship made the thwarting circumstances of Shelley's life less difficult to bear. As editor of the *Examiner*, a weekly newspaper, Hunt set a standard that raised the tone of journalism in England. When the *Morning Post* printed a fulsome adulation of the Prince Regent, later George IV, as the "Protector of the Arts," the "Maecenas of the Age," the "glory of the People," an "Adonis of Loveliness, attended by Pleasure, Honour, Virtue, and Truth," Hunt erupted. "This Adonis in loveliness," he wrote, "was a corpulent man of fifty!—in short, this delightful, blissful, wise, honourable, virtuous, true, and immortal prince was a violator of his word, a libertine over head and ears in disgrace, a despiser of domestic ties, the companion of gamblers and demireps, a man who has just closed half a century without one single claim on the gratitude of his country or the respect of posterity." For which Hunt and his brother were thrown into jail. Hunt's prison room, Charles Lamb declared, had its like only in fairy tale. The walls were papered with a trellis of roses, the ceiling with sky and clouds. There were fresh flowers, books, a pianoforte, and no bar to the company of his wife and friends. It was there that he met Byron, whose regard he won. During the two years in Surrey gaol he never stopped editing the *Examiner*. As a poet Hunt wrote little to commend, but he was a fine essayist and critic. His *Autobiography* Carlyle reckoned as a chronicle second only to Boswell's *Life of Johnson*, and praised the author as "a gifted, gentle, patient, and valiant human soul."

About a year after leaving Surrey gaol, Hunt went to Hampstead to live, where Shelley had been his guest at the close of 1816. A remarkable company visited Hunt's cottage in Hampstead, among them Keats, Hazlitt, Lamb. Keats and Shelley each agreed to compose a long poem within half a year; they set to work on *Endymion* and *The Revolt of Islam*.

Shelley had come upon the idea for a work on the meaning of the French Revolution during the journey from Lake Leman to England. For him and Mary, Fontainebleau and Versailles were monuments of tyranny. Byron, to whom Shelley had suggested the idea in his efforts to make Byron take on greater purposes as a poet, let the matter slide. Now Shelley turned to that idea and worked (as he put it in a letter to Godwin) with the " 'agony and bloody sweat' of intellectual travail." His power as a poet, he believed, consisted in "sympathy, and that part of the imagination which relates to sentiment and contemplation." If he had uncommon gifts, they were "to apprehend minute and remote distinctions of feeling, whether relative to external nature or the living beings which surround us, and to communicate the conceptions which result from considering either the moral or material universe as a whole." His immediate impulse for engaging in the task (he told Godwin in that letter) was to leave some record of himself for, ill at the time, he felt the precariousness of his life. For six steady months Shelley executed the design, sometimes working high in Bisham Wood, sometimes in his boat moored on the Thames, and issued in the autumn of 1817 *Laon and Cythna or The Revolution of the Golden City, a Vision of the Nineteenth Century*, named *The Revolt of Islam* after the revisions pressed on him by his publisher to make the protagonists, Laon and Cythna, cousins rather than brother and sister, and to make changes in lines on God and Christ. The religious changes were three or four times as many as the incest changes. None were radical; only surfaces were altered.

Here is an epitome of the story, taken from Leigh Hunt's review in the *Examiner* in 1818:

Laon, the hero, relates it. He was an ardent and speculative youth, born in modern Greece; and grew up with great admiration of the beauties and kindnesses of external nature, and a great horror of the superstitions and other oppressions with which his country and mankind in general were afflicted. A beautiful female orphan under the care of his parents shared these feelings with him; and a mutual love was the consequence. She even speculated upon taking some extraordinary though gentle step to deliver the world from its thraldom; when she was torn away from him by some slaves of the Grand Turk's Seraglio; and he himself, for endeavouring to rescue her, and for taking that opportunity of proclaiming freedom, was shut up in a prison in a rock, where his senses forsook him. The effect of the circumstance however is not lost. He is delivered from his dungeon by an old man, and after a second but milder insanity, is informed by his preserver that the people had been awakened to new ideas, and that there was a maiden who went about exciting them to a bloodless freedom. It was his love *Cythna*, after having been made a victim of the tyrant's lust, and having been likewise imprisoned, and robbed of her senses. A considerable interval elapses while *Laon* recovers his reason, but on so doing, and hearing of the exploits of her whom he justly supposed to be his lovely friend, he takes leave of the old man, and journeys for Constantinople, or the Golden City, where he finds the people risen, the tyrant fallen, and *Cythna* the predominant spirit of the change. He goes with others to the palace, and sees the "sceptred wretch" sitting silent and sullen on the footstool of his throne. She clasps the tyrant's feet, and then stands up when the strangers come nigh. *Laon* saves his life from the fury of the crowd; a festival is held at which *Cythna* presides like a visible angel, and every thing seems happiness and security. The Revolters however are suddenly assailed by the allies of the tyrant; and the fortune of the contest is changed. *Cythna* reaches *Laon* through the lost battle on a huge black Tartarian horse "whose path makes a solitude"; and they fly to a distance through a desolate village, in the dwellings of which the flames and human beings were now dead. The only survivor is a female, who has gone mad, and fancies herself the Plague. The description of her desperate laughter and actions is appalling, though not without a tendency, we think, to something overwrought and artificial. When the travellers arrive at a place of rest, *Cythna* tells *Laon* her adventures. They have been briefly alluded to, and include a finely-fancied and pathetic account of a child she had in her dungeon, and which was taken from her. *Laon* goes out from the retreat occasionally to get food and intelligence, and finds that Revenge, and subsequently Pestilence and Famine, have been making terrible havoc in the city. The tyrant and his slaves, in their terror, make frightened addresses to heaven, and a priest advises them to expiate its "vengeance" by sacrificing *Laon* and *Cythna*. He accordingly dispatches members to hunt them out; upon which *Laon* comes forward disguised and offers to give up the man provided the woman be spared. They take an oath to do so, and he declares himself; but it is then declared impious to have made the oath; and at last, *Cythna* comes voluntarily forward, and shares the funeral pyre with her beloved friend, from which they find themselves suddenly sailing on a beautiful sea to the Paradise in which the Spirit of Good resides, where *Cythna* meets with her child who had died of the plague; and the poem concludes.

After the sustained middle flight of twelve cantos, some passages darting upward to look through the gate of heaven, in a relaxed mood Shelley wrote the dedication to Mary, a conversation poem.

> So now my summer's task is ended, Mary,
> And I return to thee, mine own heart's home;
>
> (Ded. i. 1-2)

Nor let Mary disdain the doubtful promise of his fame which he would unite with her, "Child of love and light." We can almost hear Mary's complaints of his spending too little time with her, complaints many a husband absorbed by work has heard:

The toil which stole from thee so many an hour,
   Is ended,—and the fruit is at thy feet!
No longer where the woods to frame a bower
   With interlacèd branches mix and meet,
   Or where with sound like many voices sweet,
Waterfalls leap among wild islands green,
   Which framed for my lone boat a lone retreat
Of moss-grown trees and weeds, shall I be seen:
But beside thee, where still my heart has ever been. (Ded. ii)

There is a quiet ease in the flow of the rhythm and in the subdued alliteration or vocalic assonance in each line of the stanza and in the assonance sometimes linking lines. And the warmth of the tone is here quiet. The deep love has a more enduring human reality than the rapture in the green ruin, the hall whose shattered portal looked to the eastern stars, during Laon and Cythna's retreat after the ugly battle.

XXIX
We know not where we go, or what sweet dream
   May pilot us through caverns strange and fair
Of far and pathless passion, while the stream
   Of life, our bark doth on its whirlpools bear,
   Spreading swift wings as sails to the dim air;
Nor should we seek to know, so the devotion
   Of love and gentle thoughts be heard still there
Louder and louder from the utmost Ocean
   Of universal life, attuning its commotion.

XXX
To the pure all things are pure! Oblivion wrapped
   Our spirits, and the fearful overthrow
Of public hope was from our being snapped,
   Though linkèd years had bound it there; for now
   A power, a thirst, a knowledge, which below
All thoughts, like light beyond the atmosphere,
   Clothing its clouds with grace, doth ever flow,
Came on us, as we sate in silence there,
Beneath the golden stars of the clear azure air:—

XXXI
In silence which doth follow talk that causes
   The baffled heart to speak with sighs and tears,

When wildering passion swalloweth up the pauses
    Of inexpressive speech:—the youthful years
    Which we together passed, their hopes and fears,
The blood itself which ran within our frames,
    That likeness of the features which endears
The thoughts expressed by them, our very names,
And all the wingèd hours which speechless memory claims,

XXXII

Had found a voice—and ere that voice did pass,
    The night grew damp and dim, and through a rent
Of the ruin where we sate, from the morass,
    A wandering Meteor by some wild wind sent,
    Hung high in the green dome, to which it lent
A faint and pallid lustre; while the song
    Of blasts, in which its blue hair quivering bent,
Strewed strangest sounds the moving leaves among;
A wondrous light, the sound as of a spirit's tongue.

XXXIII

The Meteor showed the leaves on which we sate,
    And Cythna's glowing arms, and the thick ties
Of her soft hair, which bent with gathered weight
    My neck near hers, her dark and deepening eyes,
    Which, as twin phantoms of one star that lies
O'er a dim well, move, though the star reposes,
    Swam in our mute and liquid ecstasies,
Her marble brow, and eager lips, like roses,
With their own fragrance pale, which Spring but half uncloses.

XXXIV

The Meteor to its far morass returned:
    The beating of our veins one interval
Made still; and then I felt the blood that burned
    Within her frame, mingle with mine, and fall
    Around my heart like fire; and over all
A mist was spread, the sickness of a deep
    And speechless swoon of joy, as might befall
Two disunited spirits when they leap
In union from this earth's obscure and fading sleep.

41

XXXV

Was it one moment that confounded thus
　　All thought, all sense, all feeling, into one
Unutterable power, which shielded us
　　Even from our own cold looks, when we had gone
　　Into a wide and wild oblivion
Of tumult and of tenderness? or now
　　Had ages, such as make the moon and sun,
The seasons, and mankind their changes know,
Left fear and time unfelt by us alone below?

XXXVI

I know not. What are kisses whose fire clasps
　　The failing heart in languishment, or limb
Twined within limb? or the quick dying gasps
　　Of the life meeting, when the faint eyes swim
　　Through tears of a wide mist boundless and dim,
In one caress? What is the strong control
　　Which leads the heart that dizzy steep to climb,
Where far over the world those vapours roll,
Which blend two restless frames in one reposing soul?

XXXVII

It is the shadow which doth float unseen,
　　But not unfelt, o'er blind mortality,
Whose divine darkness fled not, from that green
　　And lone recess, where lapped in peace did lie
　　Our linkèd frames till, from the changing sky,
That night and still another day had fled;
　　And then I saw and felt. The moon was high,
And clouds, as of a coming storm, were spread
Under its orb,—loud winds were gathering overhead.

XXXVIII

Cythna's sweet lips seemed lurid in the moon,
　　Her fairest limbs with the night wind were chill,
And her dark tresses were all loosely strewn
　　O'er her pale bosom:—all within was still,
　　And the sweet peace of joy did almost fill
The depth of her unfathomable look;—
　　And we sate calmly, though that rocky hill,

The waves contending in its caverns strook,
For they foreknew the storm, and the gray ruin shook.

XXXIX

There we unheeding sate, in the communion
    Of interchangèd vows, which, with a rite
Of faith most sweet and sacred, stamped our union.—
    Few were the living hearts which could unite
    Like ours, or celebrate a bridal-night
With such close sympathies, for they had sprung
    From linkèd youth, and from the gentle might
Of earliest love, delayed and cherished long,
Which common hopes and fears made, like a tempest, strong.

(Canto VI)

In xxix we come upon images we may remember from earlier poems. In *Alastor* an individual life was likened to a stream. In that poem the young man made a journey in a bark; here the bark is a symbol for the person. Ocean is a metaphor for universal life. [A symbol, unlike a metaphor or simile, does not make a comparison; it purports to be, or rather to participate in the nature of, an unstated something else; often symbols are used as visible manifestations of invisible realities.] Shelley gradually worked toward a symbolic language. Believing that a human being is "pre-eminently an imaginative being," he evolved thought that demanded for expression an original language, which would convey multiplicity rather than singleness of meaning. We may learn that symbolic language through much reading of his poetry if we like the pleasure of the journey or we may take a shortcut through scholarship. Often in Shelley the trope changes from a metaphor or simile in an earlier poem to a symbol in a later poem; for example, in the metaphor "ocean of universal life," "of universal life" disappears and "ocean" becomes a symbol for life. Sometimes an image changes its symbolic meaning; we must be flexible in our response. Other times although the intellectual significance of a symbol in a passage, nowhere used as a metaphor, may seem impermeable, another context may make it clear.

Often when we read the poetry of a man to whom knowledge is important, we discover that he expects us to be coversant

43

with his knowledge. Milton, Shelley, Eliot are such poets. When the knowledge is significant in the world's thought, art or science, we have no reasonable choice but to get the knowledge if we do not already have it. Plato and Plotinus make Shelley easier to understand. Finally, through much reading of his poetry we learn the nature of his thought and imagination, his vision; and we learn his own ways of controlling the formal elements, such as imagery, musical attributes of language, tone, structure; as we begin to understand the whole, the parts naturally take on more and clearer meaning. Although it is critically valid that a poet's whole work illuminate any single poem or passage, we must be cautious lest the light of one work give a wrong color to another. For a poet's thought and language, of course, may change. The value of knowing a poet's whole work is especially demonstrable in modern poetry. A single poem by Gerard Manley Hopkins, say, or by Dylan Thomas, may seem insuperably difficult, but as we get to know their whole work, difficulties unravel.

In the original version of xxx, the quotation from St. Paul, "To the pure all things are pure," rather daringly justified the incestuous union of Laon and Cythna. That quotation loses somewhat of its force in the revised version where Paul protects only a union outside marriage. (In like manner the allusion to the likeness of the lovers' features in xxxi loses intensity when the likeness belongs to cousins rather than to brother and sister.) More important than that in xxx is to realize how much "public hope" (that is, the hope for public good) meant to Laon and Cythna; consciousness of the overthrow of public good, to which they had dedicated themselves for years, had to be snapped from their being before they could take any private happiness. We live in a world today in which most people who ought to know better and who are capable of better are circumscribed by private good; perhaps it has always been so except for moments now and then. But that there have been such moments, as in Periclean Athens or in Chartres, means that there can be a wider span.

The rapture and mystery of the act of love as portrayed in these stanzas was something new in literature, perhaps not possible of expression before the Romantic movement, and no poet has ever come anywhere near Shelley in such portrayals. Nor will it do to say that the emperor is wearing no clothes; his garments are glorious; the vexed beholder would do better to learn to see than to accuse blindly. There are those who would speak presumably as clinicans and say, "No, no, not 'the sickness of a deep And speechless swoon of joy,' not that," but they give away their own emotional lives, for after all they can speak out of no experience at such a moment but their own. Although many have had the experience and recognize it in these stanzas which portray the ideal reality, it does not follow that they can give the experience their own expression. Shelley's accuracy may be more than psychologically factual, it may be true. The experience is spiritual: either "All thought, all sense, all feeling" become "one Unutterable power"—not of course for those who believe that one plus one can never equal one—or the lovers are outside the mutable universe (xxxv). The questions of xxxvi are answered in xxxvii; it is Intellectual Beauty, the Spirit of Beauty—"the shadow which doth float unseen"—that gives spiritual essence to the physical act.

If it is not a human reality that this scene reveals, so much the worse for us. Not everybody, for various reasons easy enough to imagine, is attracted to that reality. In any case, it is hard to imagine anybody's not being attracted to the warmth in the lines quoted from the first two dedicatory stanzas, of a kind with the love in Coleridge's conversation poems. In the third stanza the mood changes to early "thoughts of great deeds." The modulation is not erratic; it serves structural design. The Dedication is not only a tribute to Mary; it gives life to and takes life from the purpose and accomplishment of the poem.

> I do remember well the hour which burst
>   My spirit's sleep: a fresh May-dawn it was,
>   When I walked forth upon the glittering grass,
> And wept, I knew not why; until there rose
>   From the near schoolroom, voices, that, alas!
> Were but one echo from a world of woes—
> The harsh and grating strife of tyrants and of foes. (Ded. iii. 3-9)

That echo and others, as of the desolation caused by war that Shelley had seen in France in 1814, reverberate horrifyingly in the poem. (Not only the eyewitness experience profited him. He could not have created so dark a moral thunderstorm without his experience of literature and philosophy and without his imagination, which in Coleridge's eloquence is the "soul moving everywhere.") After Islam has been "Made free by love" (X. xiv. 4), the dictators of other nations command their armies and navies—steel and flame—to destroy freedom and restore Islam's (France's) tyrant: "they knew his cause their own" (X. vii. 7). The bloody work begun,

> The tyrant passed, surrounded by the steel
> Of hired assassins, through the public way,
>   Choked with his country's dead:—his footsteps reel
>   On the fresh blood—he smiles. "Ay, now I feel
> I am a King in truth!" (X. viii. 2-6)

His is the insanity of a Hitler or Stalin. After the slaughter there was peace,

> Peace in the desert fields and villages,
>   Between the glutted beasts and mangled dead!
> Peace in the silent streets! save when the cries
>   Of victims to their fiery judgement led,
>   Made pale their voiceless lips who seemed to dread
> Even in their dearest kindred, lest some tongue
>   Be faithless to the fear yet unbetrayed;
> Peace in the Tyrant's palace, where the throng
> Waste the triumphal hours in festival and song! (X. xii)

"Over the death-polluted land . . . the sky became Stagnate with heat" (X. xiii. 2-6), and plague visited.

> The fish were poisoned in the streams; the birds
>   In the green woods perished; the insect race
> Was withered up; the scattered flocks and herds
>   Who had survived the wild beasts' hungry chase
>   Died moaning, each upon the other's face
> In helpless agony gazing. (X. xv. 1-6)

Then Famine and Misrule made the world groan.

> There was no food, the corn was trampled down,
>   The flocks and herds had perished; on the shore
> The dead and putrid fish were ever thrown. (X. xviii. 1-3)

46

There was no corn—in the wide market-place
   All loathliest things, even human flesh, was sold;
   They weighed it in small scales— (X. xix. 1-3)

The horrors become more ghastly in the rage of thirst and madness. The plague at last pounces upon the tyrant and his guards and priests, who are pale with terror.

"O God!" they cried, "we know our secret pride
   Has scorned thee, and thy worship, and thy name;
Secure in human power we have defied
   Thy fearful might; we bend in fear and shame
   Before thy presence; with the dust we claim
Kindred; be merciful, O King of Heaven!
   Most justly have we suffered for thy fame
Made dim, but be at length our sins forgiven,
Ere to despair and death thy worshippers be driven.

"O King of Glory! thou alone hast power!
   Who can resist thy will? who can restrain
Thy wrath, when on the guilty thou dost shower
   The shafts of thy revenge, a blistering rain?
   Greatest and best, be merciful again!
Have we not stabbed thine enemies, and made
   The Earth an altar, and the Heavens a fane,
Where thou wert worshipped with their blood, and laid
Those hearts in dust which would thy searchless works have weighed?"
                (X. xxvii-xxviii)

They are dramatic stanzas, powerfully ironic, that prayer of the rulers and priests who

Worshipped their own hearts' image, dim and vast,
   Scared by the shade wherewith they would eclipse
   The light of other minds. (X. xxx. 2-4)

To appease their God's wrath the priests set three hundred furnaces blazing with human sacrifice (like an anticipation of the Nazi horror), for "Fear is never slow To build the thrones of Hate" (X. xliii. 4-5):

The noontide sun was darkened with that smoke,
   The winds of eve dispersed those ashes gray.

The madness which these rites had lulled, awoke
 Again at sunset.—Who shall dare to say
 The deeds which night and fear brought forth, or weigh
In balance just the good and evil there?
 He might man's deep and searchless heart display,
 And cast a light on those dim labyrinths, where
Hope, near imagined chasms, is struggling with despair. (X. xlvi)

In creating a "world of woes" the assassins destroyed a world in which justice was "the light of love, and not revenge" (V. xxxiv. 8-9). Laon had persuaded the multitudes that even those who kill

 "For hire, are men; and to avenge misdeed
On the misdoer, doth but Misery feed
 With her own broken heart!" (V. xi. 4-7)

After the victorious revolution Cythna had sung a hymn containing this vision:

 "Our toil from thought all glorious forms shall cull,
To make this Earth, our home, more beautiful,
 And Science, and her sister Poesy,
Shall clothe in light the fields and cities of the free!"
        (V. li. 5. 12-15)

The world was to be shaped to the ideality of thought, and such a world can be created only by the free; "a happier condition of moral and political society" go together (Preface to *The Revolt of Islam*). Some say that it is not realistic to think that the world can be shaped ideally, that Shelley was incompetent to measure books by experience. They must also deny a moral world governed by love, for such a world is counter to all experience, and in this poem "Love is celebrated as the sole law which should govern the moral world" (Preface). Yet they accept, ostensibly, a Christian civilization, and so they must either be described as schizophrenic or be accused of plain hypocrisy. Much better is it, in any case, to measure experience by books, the "precious life-blood of a master spirit," than the other way around—realists notwithstanding, the Romantic vision is the world's only hope.

In his radical desire for a "happier condition of moral and

political society," a desire surviving the tempests of the age, Shelley never lost sight of the human condition, which always must contend with sorrow. The people of Islam were free, and a great treasure of freedom, as Cythna sang in her hymn, is this:

> man and woman,
> Their common bondage burst, may freely borrow
> From lawless love a solace for their sorrow;
> For oft we still must weep, since we are human. (V. li. 4. 3-6)

In like manner, in the Dedication, Shelley wrote to Mary that at a time when he had searched for sympathy in love and had been deluded, when despair,

> The shadow of a starless night, was thrown
> Over the world in which I moved alone

her presence on his wintry heart

> Fell, like the bright Spring upon some herbless plain;
> How beautiful and calm and free thou wert
> In thy young wisdom.

Mary broke the "chain Of custom . . . And walked as free as light" (Ded. vi. 4-5; vii. 2-4, 5), eloping with him. In a time

> When Poverty can blight the just and good,
> When Infamy dares mock the innocent,
> And cherished friends turn with the multitude (Ded. viii. 6-8)

their lawless, or unmarried, love sustained them.

Darker than sorrow in the human condition is the nature of the human mind. Cythna, urging the sailors whose work is a traffic in slavery to "live, as if to love and live were one" (VIII. xii. 7) tells them not to disguise their evil, for

> " 'we have one human heart—
> All mortal thoughts confess a common home;' " (VIII. xix. 1-2)

and again,

> " 'Look on your mind . . .
> Ah! it is dark with many a blazoned name
> Of misery—all are mirrors of the same.' " (VIII. xx. 3-5)

49

Nonetheless,

> " 'Reproach not thine own soul, but know thyself,
>   Nor hate another's crime, nor loathe thine own.
> It is the dark idolatry of self,
>   Which, when our thoughts and actions once are gone,
>   Demands that man should weep, and bleed, and groan;
> O vacant expiation! Be at rest.—
>   The past is Death's, the future is thine own;
> And love and joy can make the foulest breast
> A paradise of flowers, where peace might build her nest.' "
>
> (VIII. xxii)

"If aught survive," Shelley believed, "It must be love and joy" (XI. xvii. 8-9).

They learned to live in love and joy, as do multitudes, until barbarity destroys them and "moral dignity and freedom" sink once more to "slavery and degradation" (Preface). With pitifully inadequate weapons the people war against the hired soldiers, for passive resistance will not work against moral natures governed by money, fear, and cruelty. They are right "who war but on their native ground For natural rights" (VI. xii. 3-4). And so Shelley, although he hated violence, celebrated armed revolution against contemporary European tyrannies. Yet even battles for natural rights are ghastly, and Shelley knew, as Laon saw,

>   how ugly and how fell
>   O Hate! thou art, even when thy life thou shedd'st
>   For love. (VI. xvi. 2-4)

Millions destroyed by barbarity, themselves defeated, Cythna nonetheless justifies their work to Laon.

> "This is the winter of the world;—and here
>   We die, even as the winds of Autumn fade,
> Expiring in the frore and foggy air.—
>   Behold! Spring comes, though we must pass, who made
>   The promise of its birth,—even as the shade
> Which from our death, as from a mountain, flings
>   The future, a broad sunrise; thus arrayed
> As with the plumes of overshadowing wings,
> From its dark gulf of chains, Earth like an eagle springs.

50

"O dearest love! we shall be dead and cold
　　Before this morn may on the world arise;
　Wouldst thou the glory of its dawn behold?
　　Alas! gaze not on me, but turn thine eyes
　　On thine own heart—it is a paradise
　Which everlasting Spring has made its own,
　　And while drear Winter fills the naked skies,
　Sweet streams of sunny thought, and flowers fresh-blown,
Are there, and weave their sounds and odours into one.

"In their own hearts the earnest of the hope
　　Which made them great, the good will ever find;
　And though some envious shades may interlope
　　Between the effect and it, One comes behind,
　　Who aye the future to the past will bind—
　Necessity, whose sightless strength for ever
　　Evil with evil, good with good must wind
　In bands of union, which no power may sever:
They must bring forth their kind, and be divided never!

"The good and mighty of departed ages
　　Are in their graves, the innocent and free,
　Heroes, and Poets, and prevailing Sages,
　　Who leave the vesture of their majesty
　　To adorn and clothe this naked world;—and we
　Are like to them—such perish, but they leave
　　All hope, or love, or truth, or liberty,
　Whose forms their mighty spirits could conceive
To be a rule and law to ages that survive." (IX. xxv-xxviii)

[On "Necessity" in xxvii: In his earlier career Shelley believed in Necessity as the absolute ruling force of the world.
By Necessity he meant physical, psychological, and moral
determinism. That is to say, every effect has its cause or causes,
themselves the effects of antecedent causes, and so it is throughout eternity. The continuity of cause and effect is unbreakable.
Somewhat inconsistently, Shelley also believed that men could
hasten or retard ("some envious shades may interlope") the
inevitable destiny of the race, although not divert it. That destiny, judging from the intellectual and moral evolution history
revealed, was a more perfect physical, mental, and moral being,
a being capable of becoming infinitely better. Some scholars

of considerable reputation—Kenneth Cameron for one—think that Shelley never stopped believing in Necessity, and they interpret crucial matters in his poetry as an emanation of that belief. But the word Necessity does not appear in any of his poems after *The Revolt of Islam* (1817); and, it seems to me, the concept went to the periphery of his thought. It appears again in his *Essay on the Devil and Devils* (possibly as late as 1820), but here it is used for a satirical thump, not in a reasoned argument. "The art of persuasion," he wrote elsewhere, "differs from that of reasoning. . . . All reformers have been compelled to practice this misrepresentation of their own true feelings and opinions." More important, some of his prose excepted, the best of his thought and art is in his poetry. In *Hellas* (1821) a chorus speaks of "The world's eyeless charioteer, Destiny" but Destiny and Necessity are interpretable as very different concepts. Destiny is what does happen, or what is envisioned as belonging to a person although not necessarily to be his; Necessity is what *must* happen. In *Prometheus Unbound* (1818-1819), the protagonist cries:

> I would fain
> Be what it is my destiny to be,
> The saviour and strength of suffering man,
> Or sink into the original gulf of things. (I. 815-819)

The envisioned destiny may or may not be realized. At least so thinks Prometheus, wisest of beings, who has no belief in the must of Necessity. In *Hellas* the conception of Destiny is simply what does happen:

> The world's eyeless charioteer,
> Destiny, is hurrying by! (711-712)

Because Destiny rushes on eyeless, its path cannot be foretold. Such a Destiny is closer to blind Chance than to Necessity, to which it has been equated. In Necessity's progress consequence can be foretold from cause. Chance, according to Demogorgon in *Prometheus Unbound,* is one of the ruling forces of the world (II. iv. 119-120). Shelley was too deeply religious—too deeply believed that the power or powers in the invisible universe could affect human life and the physical universe—to hold to the idea of Necessity. A spiritual power can make no difference in a deterministic universe, and so can have no meaning in human life. The *Hymn to Intellectual Beauty* (1816), in creating which Shelley discovered language for his religious belief, spelled the end of Necessity's misrule. That does not mean to say that consequences are haphazard. It means only that in the moral world a man may choose his action, whether good or evil (obviously there are innumerable limits to his action in the physical world); the moral act he chooses becomes a cause that will have its necessary consequence. This is free will in a universe of law.

What I have said may seem contradicted by what Shelley wrote in *A Philosophical View of Reform* (late 1819–early 1820), that reform "is inevitable and must be"—but this does not say that everything is inevitable or that the inevitability of reform always existed. Moreover, the essay tries to persuade the people to act in a certain way, as though they had free will, to achieve lasting reform—a meaningless persuasion in a deterministic world. What I have said may seem contradicted again in *A Defence of Poetry* (1821): in Greek tragedy "even crime is disarmed of half its horror and all its contagion by being represented as the fatal consequence of the unfathomable agencies of nature; error is thus divested of its wilfulness; men can no longer cherish it as the creation of their choice." Shelley is here stating (wrongly, I think) the cause for an effect of Greek tragedy. He does not give the statement as his own opinion. If it is his opinion, we must accept contradiction in his thought. In *Essay on Christianity* (probably composed between 1816 and 1819) he wrote, "There is a Power by which we are surrounded, like the atmosphere in which some motionless lyre is suspended, which visits with its breath our silent chords at will"—the "at will" and the effect of that Breath upon us are irreconcilable with the idea of Necessity. Perhaps we must conclude, as Shelley said of a greater person, "It is not here asserted that no contradictions are admitted to have place in the system of Jesus Christ, between doctrines promulgated in different states of feeling or information, or even such as are implied in the enunciation of a scheme of thought various and obscure through its immensity and depth."]

Like those "good and mighty" Shelley left the vesture of his "majesty To adorn and clothe this naked world." To that end the boy on a fresh May dawn, hearing the harsh voices from the near schoolroom, dedicated his manhood.

> "I will be wise,
> And just, and free, and mild, if in me lies
> Such power, for I grow weary to behold
> The selfish and the strong still tyrannise
> Without reproach or check." (Ded. iv. 4-8)

Like Laon, from "deathless minds" Shelley "drew Words which were weapons" and "adamantine armour" for his heart (II. xx. 1, 5, 6). Out of knowledge the man

> Wrought linkèd armour for my soul, before
> It might walk forth to war among mankind. (Ded. v. 5-6)

The Revolt of Islam issued from that dedication, that high intent. So he conceived song: a peopling of the universe with thoughts "strong . . . to disperse The cloud of that unutterable curse Which clings upon mankind" (II. xxx. 3-6). Shelley never blinded himself to that curse, the evil clinging to us. In the twisted circumstances of his own life he had enough experience of despair. Out of knowledge, his "linkèd armour," came power and hope, and, as they strengthened, loneliness beset him (Ded. v.). Love is the only escape from loneliness; but when he searched for "all sympathies in one" (Ded. vi. 2), love was a withering blight. Then on his "wintery heart" Mary "Fell, like bright spring" (Ded. vii. 1-2);

> And what are thou? I know, but dare not speak. (Ded. xi. 1)

The familiar language of that line and the reserve disarm our disbelief. In this conversation poem Shelley makes the real and the ideal one: Mary incarnates intellectual beauty, which for Shelley was the spiritual matrix of the world. (Later in his thought intellectual beauty fused with love or, rather, they were aspects of the power governing the universe.) To find intellectual beauty embodied in a woman was a constant pressure in Shelley's imaginative and daily life because nothing else would answer to his intensest love.

Mary, in whose soul a sacred fire burns, was lovely from her birth, "Of glorious parents" (Ded. xii. 2).

> One then left this earth
> Whose life was like a setting planet mild,

54

Which clothed thee in the radiance undefiled
Of its departed glory; still her fame
    Shines on thee, through the tempests dark and wild
Which shake these latter days. (Ded. xii. 3-8)

Only a niggardly spirit, thinking himself a realist, would care to contract that praise of Mary Wollstonecraft, among the world's most remarkable of women, who died of an infection soon after giving birth to her daughter. We do not like William Godwin, who contrary to his own teaching howled when Mary eloped with Shelley, and who constantly plagued them although they returned generosity for his meanness. But his writings, although too abstract in dealing with human experience, do not deserve contempt. Like Carlyle writing of Boswell, we must believe that a book which has greatness in it is a spiritual accomplishment and must have been created, despite the meanness defacing a man, out of greatness in his soul's resources. Shelley owed much to Godwin and, himself large-souled, he could divide the man's accomplishment from his irksomeness. For Shelley (and many others) *Political Justice* was a great book:

    One voice came forth from many a mighty spirit,
        Which was the echo of three thousand years;
    And the tumultuous world stood still to hear it,
        As some lone man who in a desert hears
        The music of his home. (Ded. xiii. 1-5)

    Tennyson understood well the theme of those first two lines, himself writing,

        Our echoes roll from soul to soul,
        And grow for ever and for ever.

Godwin's echo grew finer and greater in Shelley, whose own voice echoed the Bible, Aeschylus, Plato, Lucretius, Jesus, Dante, Shakespeare, Milton. Shelley's cry, *The Revolt of Islam,* was, like Godwin's, levelled against the oppressors of our race, wrong beliefs and customs and "low-thoughted cares" (Ded. xiii. 7). The stanzas and themes of the Dedication, we note, are organically joined, as is the Dedication to the poem. If there is no response to his cry but blind fury, Mary and Shelley can look, conscious of their own worth,

> Like lamps into the world's tempestuous night,—
> Two tranquil stars, while clouds are passing by
> Which wrap them from the foundering seaman's sight,
> That burn from year to year with unextinguished light.
>
> (Ded. xiv. 6-9)

Well, doubtless there is much dust on the pages of the poem. He played his lyre with "inexperienced fingers." A "loftier strain" (Ded. x. 1, 2) was yet to come. But the reader is perverse who will not stoop to a dusty road to collect the jewels lying there. The loftier strain he promised in a letter to Godwin: "if I live, or if I see any trust in coming years, doubt not but that I shall do something, whatever it may be, which a serious and earnest estimate of my own powers will suggest to me, and which will be in every respect accommodated to their utmost limits." Spelled out for the unimaginative Godwin, that promise nonetheless carries excitement to us, like Milton's wonderful "To morrow to fresh Woods, and Pastures new." Both promises, modest and confident, were fulfilled in the greatest poems of their time.

Now for an esthetic issue. There are modern critics who hold stoutly to the esthetic doctrine that the virtue of a poem is self-contained, that biography is inadmissible in interpretation or appreciation, that the excellence of a poem is made impure by a graft of knowledge of its maker. I make no dispute. That literary principle is defensible, perhaps impregnable, as an abstraction. But it is profound error to rule human experience, whether moral or esthetic, by abstract principles for such reduce goodness and pleasure. Faithful to that abstract doctrine, we should have to lament the form of Milton's sonnet on his blindness, for without knowledge of the man's blindness (which the poem does not tell us) and without knowledge of the cardinal meaning to his life of his work as a poet (which the poem does not tell us) our experience of the sonnet would be incomplete, even puzzled, although we could feel the greatness present. Yet it is hard to imagine a better poem containing what is unstated, for much of the power is in the direct and immediate voice of the man. (By the way, this poem cancels the notion that classic poetry is equivalent to the objective, as Shakespeare's plays cancel the notion that romantic is equivalent to subjective.)

Because it makes for more pleasure, I have conjoined knowledge of Shelley's life with his poetry. But beginning with "So now my summer's task is ended, Mary," I have said nothing of Shelley that is not implicit in *The Revolt of Islam*, its Dedication and its Preface. This work called for the use of the modern critical principle that we understand the *I* not as a self-portrait but as a mask donned, a *persona* created for artistic purposes. When Pope showed certain of his satires to his close friend Dr. Arbuthnot, the good doctor questioned the propriety of Pope's tone and his attack on nonentities. In his *Epistle to Dr. Arbuthnot*—brilliant in design, superb in control of tonal shifts from the witty to the passionate, highly serious in purpose—Pope justified himself. But the image of Pope, the *I* in the poem, we are told (by Maynard Mack), is the public image of a satirist, an image assuming the authority that will sway minds. Thus the technique of the apparent self-portraiture is really fictional and rhetorical. In like manner a story whether in prose or poetry, whether narrated in the first or third person, has an "implied author" (the phrase is Wayne Booth's) whose voice we hear, whose values we understand. The tone of his voice, the values that bear on the story have the rhetorical intention of shaping our response. A novelist or narrative poet may don another mask or create a different implied author with each story he tells.

We may regard the *I* of Shelley's dedication as a *persona.* Wordsworth, who intimately knew the pains of craftsmanship, often laboring to exhaustion when he composed, and who rarely praised a contemporary, said of Shelley that he was "one of the best *artists* of us all." And Shelley's intelligence was subtle and comprehensive. His artistic instincts and intelligence are enough to justify our regarding the *I* as a created *persona.* We do not really need to justify ourselves if the modern critical principle at issue is true, for if it is, donning the right mask must be an elementary instinct for a writer. If we regard the *I* as a *persona,* questioning the accuracy or sincerity of the apparently subjective elements becomes irrelevant. For it is, for purposes of literary experience, a fictional being we are contending with. We must understand that *persona* deeply and well if we are to understand the many connections

—in structural design, theme, metaphor, tone—between the Dedication and the rest of *The Revolt of Islam*. Those connections understood, the poem, I think, takes on a new dimension.

As the narrative came to an end at Marlow, illness and lethargy began to oppress Shelley. When the winter cold and dampness settled into their house, Mary, wretchedly watching his heavy illness, wished for the bright skies and Italian sun that physicians gave as the remedy for her husband's disease. Much of the autumn Shelley had to spend in London, coping with money harassments over the payment of Harriet's debts, the Chancery expenses, and his support of Claire, Leigh Hunt, Godwin, and others. In December he somehow managed to work things out, and with the nervous pressure gone the physical suffering abated. Shelley and Mary left Marlow early in 1818, spent a month of pleasure in London, and travelled south through France and Savoy to Italy, that "Paradise of exiles."

Exile in Italy

PART TWO

Exile in Italy

IN MARCH AND APRIL of 1816 Claire Clairmont persistently (like many other women) offered herself to Byron, and after several bored rebuffs succeeded in climbing into a bed with him. During Byron's last week in England the independent-minded, excited girl put to him this proposal, after saying that she did not expect him to love her, "Have you any objection to the following plan? On Thursday Evening we may go out of town together by some stage or mail about the distance of ten or twelve miles. There we shall be free and unknown; we can return early the following morning." The liaison began. In pursuit of Byron, Claire persuaded Shelley and Mary to go to Geneva when the dejected Shelley resolved, chiefly because of the vexatious Godwin, to escape from the contempt that he and Mary were enduring. From the conjunction of the two poets, as of two planets, issued bright beams in the literary heavens. Shelley dosed Byron with Wordsworth and talk of love; the dosing streamed into passages of the third canto of *Childe Harold's Pilgrimage.* He also urged on Byron larger purposes as a poet, which Shelley later admired as accomplished in *Cain* and *Don Juan.* To Byron, Shelley perhaps owed a leaven of toughening realism, as in the vision of nature's destructiveness in *Mont Blanc,* written that summer. Aside from the direct influences in their poetry, each mind profited, we may believe, from the friendly opposition of the other. Byron's talk helped Shelley know himself (*Julian and Maddalo,* 558-560). But Claire's emotionally erratic adventure ruined her and caused misery in the Shelleys' marriage. Her intimacy with Byron lasted until the end of the summer. Byron never had any love for her. Bearing his child, Claire returned to England with the Shelleys.

In 1818, Shelley embarked from England forever. In the party were Shelley and Mary, their two children, Claire and her daughter Allegra, and two nurses. At Milan, Shelley mediated in a controversy between the unhappy Claire and Byron, who took Allegra into his charge when Claire (letting herself

61

believe that Byron would soften) at the end of April resigned the child absolutely to him. Byron grew fond of "my bastard." By August the unsettled Claire, at the Baths of Lucca with Shelley and Mary, stubbornly insisted on a surreptitious visit to Allegra. Shelley, fearful that Claire would succeed only in provoking Byron into ill conduct, travelled with her to Venice to do what he could.

1818

JULIAN AND MADDALO: A CONVERSATION

Byron was at his best. *Julian and Maddalo: a Conversation* records the fine reunion of the two men. The first part of the poem, before the visit to the madhouse, is incomparable, a triumph of the familiar style; but Shelley paid dearly for the occasion of that triumph.

The preface speaks of Maddalo (Byron), Julian (Shelley), and the Maniac, who if he is not Shelley is "one like" Shelley (line 195). Let me give here only the passage on Julian, "an Englishman of good family, passionately attached to those philosophical notions which assert the power of man over his own mind, and the immense improvements of which, by the extinctions of certain moral superstitions, human society may yet be susceptible. Without concealing the evil in the world, he is forever speculating how good may be made superior. . . . Julian, in spite of his heterodox opinions, is conjectured by his friends to possess some good qualities. How far this is possible the pious reader will determine. Julian is rather serious." Here, I think, Shelley and the *persona* created for the poem are one. Julian is rather serious, but not solemn. There is a fine if quiet sense of humor, in the next to the last two sentences about Julian, which blossoms into glee as the two men ride on the sands of the Lido. Whether or not there is anything deeper in the character of man than laughter, I do not know. Aristotle thought laughter divided the man from the animal; Rousseau, tears. *In Shelley neither laughter nor tears but the consciousness of evil and the vision of good were the flywheels of being.* "Without concealing the evil in the world

. . ."—curiously, there are those who think that Shelley was naive about the nature of the universe. Curiously, I say, because there are few darker and more terrifying visions than those we encounter again and again in his poetry. If ever a man was "twice-born," that man was Shelley.

William James made the classic distinction between the "once-born" and the "twice-born" in *The Varieties of Religious Experience*. The once-born, or the healthy-minded, are people of an unwaveringly cheerful temperament. They look upon the world as everywhere and always a beautiful and harmonious place, and do not feel the need to look into themselves; they think of God as only merciful, and if they recognize the existence of evil at all, they certainly spend no time worrying about it. The temperament of the once-born is incapable of prolonged suffering.

The twice-born are people whose temperament cannot always escape melancholy. They do not avert their minds from the evil facts that pervade the world we live in because, they believe, evil is a "genuine portion of reality." Only shallow natures can easily "throw off the burden of the consciousness of evil." Evil is a mystery that must be wrestled with, the twice-born say, and we must force it to reveal the true significance of our life, no matter what price we pay in suffering, for therein is our deliverance. It is the realization of all this that brings on a second (spiritual) birth, the first birth being the natural one.

But although a dark mood claims the poem after a third of the way through, there is no melancholy in the beginning. The preface, written in the first person, refers to Julian in the third person. The first line of the poem,

> I rode one evening with Count Maddalo,

subtly impinges Julian on Shelley, beginning as it does in the first person—at the line's end we know it is Julian speaking. I should think a craftsman such as Shelley was conscious of the artistic effect, but whether so or not, the artistry is there. Now, if Shelley and the *persona* in the preface are one, as I believe, if the self-portraiture is truthful, what was in the world of fact comes together with what is ideal in art. May we in like manner use the biography of Shelley as a *persona* for his poetry? I shall take up that important critical issue later.

I rode one evening with Count Maddalo
Upon the bank of land which breaks the flow
Of Adria towards Venice: a bare strand
Of hillocks, heaped from ever-shifting sand,
Matted with thistles and amphibious weeds,
Such as from earth's embrace the salt ooze breeds,
Is this; an uninhabited sea-side,
Which the lone fisher, when his nets are dried,
Abandons; and no other object breaks
The waste, but one dwarf tree and some few stakes   10
Broken and unrepaired, and the tide makes
A narrow space of level sand thereon,
Where 'twas our wont to ride while day went down.
This ride was my delight. I love all waste
And solitary places; where we taste
The pleasure of believing what we see
Is boundless, as we wish our souls to be:
And such was this wide ocean, and this shore
More barren than its billows; and yet more
Than all, with a remembered friend I love   20
To ride as then I rode;—for the winds drove
The living spray along the sunny air
Into our faces; the blue heavens were bare,
Stripped to their depths by the awakening north;
And, from the waves, sound like delight broke forth
Harmonising with solitude, and sent
Into our hearts aëreal merriment.
So, as we rode, we talked; and the swift thought,
Winging itself with laughter, lingered not,
But flew from brain to brain,—such glee was ours,   30
Charged with light memories of remembered hours,
None slow enough for sadness: till we came
Homeward, which always makes the spirit tame.
This day had been cheerful but cold, and now
The sun was sinking, and the wind also.
Our talk grew somewhat serious, as may be
Talk interrupted with such raillery
As mocks itself, because it cannot scorn
The thoughts it would extinguish:—'twas forlorn,
Yet pleasing, such as once, so poets tell,   40

64

The devils held within the dales of Hell
Concerning God, freewill and destiny:
Of all that earth has been or yet may be,
All that vain men imagine or believe,
Or hope can paint or suffering may achieve,
We descanted, and I (for ever still
Is it not wise to make the best of ill?)
Argued against despondency, but pride
Made my companion take the darker side.
The sense that he was greater than his kind   50
Had struck, methinks, his eagle spirit blind
By gazing on its own exceeding light.
Meanwhile the sun paused ere it should alight,
Over the horizon of the mountains;—Oh,
How beautiful is sunset, when the glow
Of Heaven descends upon a land like thee,
Thou Paradise of exiles, Italy!
Thy mountains, seas, and vineyards, and the towers
Of cities they encircle!—it was ours
To stand on thee, beholding it: and then,   60
Just where we had dismounted, the Count's men
Were waiting for us with the gondola.—
As those who pause on some delightful way
Though bent on pleasant pilgrimage, we stood
Looking upon the evening, and the flood
Which lay between the city and the shore,
Paved with the image of the sky . . . the hoar
And aëry Alps towards the North appeared
Through mist, an heaven-sustaining bulwark reared
Between the East and West; and half the sky   70
Was roofed with clouds of rich emblazonry
Dark purple at the zenith, which still grew
Down the steep West into a wondrous hue
Brighter than burning gold, even to the rent
Where the swift sun yet paused in his descent
Among the many-folded hills: they were
Those famous Euganean hills, which bear,
As seen from Lido thro' the harbour piles,
The likeness of a clump of peakèd isles—
And then—as if the Earth and Sea had been   80

Dissolved into one lake of fire, were seen
Those mountains towering as from waves of flame
Around the vaporous sun, from which there came
The inmost purple spirit of light, and made
Their very peaks transparent. "Ere it fade,"
Said my companion, "I will show you soon
A better station"—so, o'er the lagune
We glided; and from that funereal bark
I leaned, and saw the city, and could mark
How from their many isles, in evening's gleam,   90
Its temples and its palaces did seem
Like fabrics of enchantment piled to Heaven.
I was about to speak, when—"We are even
Now at the point I meant," said Maddalo,
And bade the gondolieri cease to row.
"Look, Julian, on the west, and listen well
If you hear not a deep and heavy bell."
I looked, and saw between us and the sun
A building on an island; such a one
As age to age might add, for uses vile,   100
A windowless, deformed and dreary pile;
And on the top an open tower, where hung
A bell, which in the radiance swayed and swung;
We could just hear its hoarse and iron tongue:
The broad sun sunk behind it, and it tolled
In strong and black relief.—"What we behold
Shall be the madhouse and its belfry tower,"
Said Maddalo, "and ever at this hour
Those who may cross the water, hear that bell
Which calls the maniacs, each one from his cell,   110
To vespers."—"As much skill as need to pray
In thanks or hope for their dark lot have they
To their stern maker," I replied. "O ho!
You talk as in years past," said Maddalo.
"'Tis strange men change not. You were ever still
Among Christ's flock a perilous infidel,
A wolf for the meek lambs—if you can't swim
Beware of Providence." I looked on him,
But the gay smile had faded in his eye.
"And such,"—he cried, "is our mortality,   120

And this must be the emblem and the sign
Of what should be eternal and divine!—
And like that black and dreary bell, the soul,
Hung in a heaven-illumined tower, must toll
Our thoughts and our desires to meet below
Round the rent heart and pray—as madmen do
For what? they know not,—till the night of death
As sunset that strange vision, severeth
Our memory from itself, and us from all
We sought and yet were baffled." I recall   130
The sense of what he said, although I mar
The force of his expressions. The broad star
Of day meanwhile had sunk behind the hill,
And the black bell became invisible,
And the red tower looked gray, and all between
The churches, ships and palaces were seen
Huddled in gloom;—into the purple sea
The orange hues of heaven sunk silently.
We hardly spoke, and soon the gondola
Conveyed me to my lodging by the way.   140
    The following morn was rainy, cold and dim:
Ere Maddalo arose, I called on him,
And whilst I waited with his child I played;
A lovelier toy sweet Nature never made,
A serious, subtle, wild, yet gentle being,
Graceful without design and unforeseeing,
With eyes—Oh speak not of her eyes!—which seem
Twin mirrors of Italian Heaven, yet gleam
With such deep meaning, as we never see
But in the human countenance: with me   150
She was a special favorite: I had nursed
Her fine and feeble limbs when she came first
To this bleak world; and she yet seemed to know
On second sight her ancient playfellow,
Less changed than she was by six months or so;
For after her first shyness was worn out
We sate there, rolling billiard balls about,
When the Count entered. Salutations past—
"The word you spoke last night might well have cast
A darkness on my spirit—if man be   160

67

The passive thing you say, I should not see
Much harm in the religions and old saws
(Tho' I may never own such leaden laws)
Which break a teachless nature to the yoke:
Mine is another faith"—thus much I spoke
And noting he replied not, added: "See
This lovely child, blithe, innocent and free;
She spends a happy time with little care,
While we to such sick thoughts subjected are
As came on you last night—it is our will   170
That thus enchains us to permitted ill—
We might be otherwise—we might be all
We dream of happy, high, majestical.
Where is the love, beauty, and truth we seek
But in our mind? and if we were not weak
Should we be less in deed than in desire?"
"Ay, if we were not weak—and we aspire
How vainly to be strong!" said Maddalo:
"You talk Utopia." "It remains to know,"
I then rejoined, "and those who try may find   180
How strong the chains are which our spirit bind;
Brittle perchance as straw . . . We are assured
Much may be conquered, much may be endured,
Of what degrades and crushes us. We know
That we have power over ourselves to do
And suffer—what, we know not till we try;
But something nobler than to live and die—"

The first line in its meter $(-/-/--//-/)$ and bare statement could begin a prose passage, say a letter, but the music of
the line (made of the meter, the sounds of the syllables, and the
rhetorical movement) gives it a genuine place in poetry. Cun-
ningly the familiar style takes hold. The rhythms and sentence
constructions resemble those of speech, and the rhymes, while
visible, are submerged. The images of the opening scene (lines
1-13), realistic and vivid, show Shelley mastering realism for his
purposes. Then he impregnates the scene with romantic meaning (14-19). The tact of the modulation is perfect. He asserts of
this ocean and shore as emblems of infinitude only that here
"we taste The pleasure of believing what we see Is boundless,
as we wish our souls to be." The best of the pleasures was rid-

ing with a friend (19-21)—that best pleasure of Julian's, the human interchange, shapes and colors the first part of the poem. The winds, spray, sky, and waves make their hearts merry, and their talk is winged with laughter (21-32). Their spirits tamer in the homeward ride, their mood changes with nature, which seems like a third companion in converse with them. First their seriousness is mixed with raillery, and then becomes too deep for their good-humored ridicule. They descant "Of all the earth has been or yet may be" and of what "suffering may achieve"—the romantic faith, although it sees clearly what has been, believing that suffering may, not will, change the world, lets Julian accept without despondency the meaning of suffering in a contract of existence that makes profit unlikely. For "for ever Is it not wise to make the best of ill?" (32-49). Maddalo takes the darker side. From philosophic reflection the lines modulate with ease to Maddalo's motive and character. Then the metaphor of Maddalo's "own exceeding light" blinding his "eagle spirit" gives place to the literal light of the sun descending on the mountains, and the mood changes to quiet rapture as they behold Italy glowing (50-60). With fine artistic judgment Shelley lets an ordinary detail interrupt, the Count's men waiting with the gondola, not to lose the familiar tone, and then creates the majestic and gorgeous vision Julian and Maddalo look upon from the Lido across the lagoon to Venice, the Euganean hills and the Alps, "half the sky . . . roofed with clouds of rich emblazonry," the colors and shapes in motion as they gaze. This, too, Shelley interrupts, now with the evenly conversational, as Maddalo suggests a better vantage. They glide on the lagoon and Venice seems a city of enchantment (61-92). At the place Maddalo meant, Julian hears a heavy bell; a madhouse stands strong and black against the sun. The enchantment has been shattered by the dreary and somber. The "hoarse and iron tongue" summons the maniacs to vespers. Julian, with irony and yet with earnest compassion, reflects:

> "As much skill as need to pray
> In thanks or hope for their dark lot have they
> To their stern maker." (93-113)

Maddalo retorts with light mockery of Julian. The gay smile fades from Maddalo as a magnificent and dark conception pos-

69

sesses him: his image likens the soul, which summons "Our thoughts and our desires to meet below Round the rent heart and pray," to that "black and dreary bell" tolling the maniacs. After Maddalo's darkness the day's gloom settles in among the churches, ships and palaces (114-140). The mind of man and the world around seem exquisitely fitted to each other in this poem.

But for Shelley, unlike Wordsworth, deeper meaning gleams in the human countenance than in the face of nature. He says as much in speaking of Maddalo's child (147-150). The child is Allegra, whom Shelley loved almost as his own. Prompted by love, he spun out of verse an ideal grace to clothe her in. Notwithstanding, her presence and person are not accidental in the narrative on the next day; she is there not because in fact she was. Rather she is an emblem denying the Count's dark vision of human existence, the night's gloom, and the rainy cold and dim mood of the morning (141-170). The moral and the physical bear on each other.

Julian's faith is different from Maddalo's; their opposition is superbly expressed in lines 170 to 187, a classic opposition between the idealism and realism of two extraordinary good men, *personae* who are remarkable creations. In what remains before they leave the Count's villa, Maddalo proposes that experience—in the example of the madman, who was one like Julian—will show the vanity of theory although Julian might make a "system refutation-tight As far as words go" (194-195). Then unexpectedly come two serious errors, one intellectual and the other artistic. Julian hopes to prove that theory is not vain, that the ideal does work and that a man's life must correspond to ideal truth. He believes that the madman's being has been bowed because his life has not corresponded to "that true theory . . . Which seeks a 'soul of goodness' in things ill" (203-204). The intellectual error is in the implicit assumption that we can always find a soul of goodness in things ill. Jupiter in *Prometheus Unbound,* in composition at the time that Shelley wrote *Julian and Maddalo,* is irreclaimably evil. I doubt that Julian's statement is strictly dramatic characterization, that is, only his view and not Shelley's. Rather, I believe that a pressure in his life forced Shelley into the poem as a *persona* different from the Julian-Shelley, that immediate circumstance shaped what he believed against his better knowledge.

70

We are various persons in connection with other people. Julian is Shelley in connection with Byron. The *persona* making the intellectual error is Bysshe, husband of Mary. What Julian says of the madman, that he is among those who must "love and be beloved with gentleness; And being scorned, what wonder if they die Some living death" (208-210), is artistically inadmissible because Julian as yet knows next to nothing of the man's story. Again not Julian but Bysshe, who has entered the poem emotionally, is speaking. The quality of the second part of the poem, the visit to the madhouse, is erratic. The brief third part, the return of Julian after many years, is a weak ending.

We cannot be certain that circumstances in Shelley's marriage broke into the poem. Carlos Baker and earlier Raymond D. Havens have argued that Shelley had as his model for the Maniac not himself but Tasso. However, if Newman Ivey White's persuasion is true (as I believe it is), that the Maniac's story is a disguised version of crushing experiences of Shelley's, we see the unhappy working out of a principle of artistic creation.

> Grief must run on, and pass
> Into the memory's more quiet plain,
> Before it can compose itself in song.
> He who is agonised, and burns to show
> His agony to those who sit around,
> Seizes the pen in vain: thought, fancy, power,
> Rush back into his bosom: all the strength
> Of genius cannot draw them into light
> From under mastering Grief.

At least so thought Walter Savage Landor in *Remonstrance and Reply*. Shelley had no desire to show his agony to the world; he took pains to disguise himself. But "mastering Grief," breaking in, disrupted *Julian and Maddalo*.

While Shelley made the journey with Claire to Venice, Mary stayed dejectedly at the Baths of Lucca with their two children, Clara and William. In Venice, Byron, unexpectedly tractable, invited Shelley—and Mary and Claire, whom he thought at nearby Padua—to spend their visit at his villa in Este, outside Venice, with Allegra. Not knowing his daughter, Clara, had fallen mildly ill, Shelley wrote to Mary to come at once to

71

Este. "I have been obliged to decide on all these things without you—I have done for the best and, my own beloved Mary, you must soon come and scold me if I have done wrong, and kiss me if I have done right—for, I am sure, I do not know which—and it is only the event that can show." During the difficult several days' travel in the summer heat to Este, dysentery attacked little Clara. Some weeks later the child seemed much recovered. Her parents took her along to Venice on a visit to Byron. On the way she suddenly turned worse, convulsions distorted her face, and she died at an inn in Venice only hours after they crossed the lagoon. Mary, resenting Shelley's affection for Claire, which had taken him on the journey to Venice, in her misery blamed him for the death of Clara and turned away bitterly from her husband. [In the end Byron hardened against Claire and would not let Allegra visit the Shelley household to "perish of Starvation, and green fruit, or be taught to believe that there is no Deity." Four years later Allegra died of typhus fever. In Claire's mind Byron murdered the child; and the Shelleys, because they had not consented to take part in her unbalanced schemes to retrieve Allegra, shared in the crime. Claire's persistence had got her a liaison with Byron, but neither her persistence nor her child (whom she surrendered to Byron against Shelley's advice) gave her any claim on Byron, unless Byron's careless, easygoing continuance of the affair in Geneva, where the child was conceived, be allowed for a claim. Claire was no fool, but she let sentimentality be her motive for a liaison and for her surrendering the child.]

Mary's aversion protected her like a shell even in her despair. Shelley's suffering tightened, intense as frenzy. That internal pressure thrust him as another *persona* into *Julian and Maddalo*. The first part of the poem, the "Conversation" proper, Shelley perhaps composed at Este while Clara seemed to be recovering. Devastated by her death and Mary's bitterness, he let out his agony by changing the tenor of the conversation to an eruption of unmodulated grief, the monologue of the madman—grief not in his own voice because he did not want Mary to hear his cry.

As Julian and Maddalo embark in the gondola through the rain to the madhouse, the lines are still restrained. Maddalo knows little of the Maniac. Like Shelley,

72

He seemed hurt,
Even as a man with his peculiar wrong,
To hear but of the oppression of the strong. (237-239)

When his lady left him, he wandered about until he grew wild.
The police brought him to the madhouse, and he would not
leave. Maddalo fitted up these "rooms beside the sea, to please
his whim" and gave sculpture, books, urns for flowers, and
musical instruments to the "gentle and unfortunate" man.

"Nay, this was kind of you—he had no claim,
As the world says"—"None—but the very same
Which I on all mankind, were I as he
Fallen to such deep reverse." (262-265)

There is a Shakespearian generosity of spirit in those lines, a
grace that goes into the balance against pain. They enter the
apartment of the Maniac, who, unseeing and unhearing, gives
voice to his despair. The monologue (lines 300 to 510) takes
a third of the poem. Passages are deeply moving. The Maniac
speaks to the woman who left him:

"Didst thou not seek me for thine own content?
Did not thy love awaken mine? I thought
That thou wert she who said, 'You kiss me not
Ever, I fear you do not love me now'—
In truth I loved even to my overthrow." (401-405)

That is done with the simplest of means, inimitably.
    For people such as Shelley and Mary the act of love is either
a spiritual experience or a horror. The Maniac cannot forget
that in her terrible curses his lady desired (it is he speaking),

"That you had never seen me—never heard
My voice, and more than all had ne'er endured
The deep pollution of my loathed embrace—
That your eyes ne'er had lied love in my face—
That, like some maniac monk, I had torn out
The nerves of manhood by their bleeding root
With mine own quivering fingers, so that ne'er
Our hearts had for a moment mingled there
To disunite in horror—" (420-428)

73

He goes on, partly unable to escape his searing memory, partly to justify himself.

> "Thou wilt tell,
> With the grimace of hate, how horrible
> It was to meet my love when thine grew less;
> Thou wilt admire how I could e'er address
> Such features to love's work . . . this taunt, though true,
> (For indeed Nature nor in form nor hue
> Bestowed on me her choicest workmanship)
> Shall not be thy defence . . . for since thy lip
> Met mine first, years long past, since thine eye kindled
> With soft fire under mine, I have not dwindled
> Nor changed in mind or body, or in aught
> But as love changes what it loveth not
> After long years and many trials." (460-472)

Still he returns "love for hate"; and that she "have less bitter cause to grieve," he refrains from "that sweet sleep which medicines all pain" (495-499). The man ceases and Julian and Maddalo weep without shame, their argument quite forgot. Later, in a return of the conversational mood, Bysshe's cry ended, Julian thinks that were he an unconnected man he would stay on. There is all, in Venice,

> We seek in towns, with little to recall
> Regrets for the green country. I might sit
> In Maddalo's great palace, and his wit
> And subtle talk would cheer the winter night
> And make me know myself, and the firelight
> Would flash upon our faces, till the day
> Might dawn and make me wonder at my stay. (556-563)

But Julian "had friends in London too: the chief Attraction here, was," he imagined perhaps idly, that he might reclaim the Maniac from "his dark estate" (564-574). If Shelley and the madman were one identity, it would seem incredible that the thought of reclaiming another could enter his mind. By the same token, if they are one identity the passage is a tribute to the imaginative distance Shelley could reach after his utterance, which was like a leech taking agony away.

Many years later Julian returned to Venice. Maddalo's daughter had become a woman,

a wonder of this earth,
        Where there is little of transcendent worth,—
        Like one of Shakespeare's women. (590-592)

That incidentally reminds us that Shakespeare, a romanticist, also created ideally. We remember, too, that Allegra died as a child, and must reflect that Shelley was writing poetry not strict autobiography. From Maddalo's daughter Julian learns that the lady came again and her coming made the Maniac better, but again deserted the man. The girl tells Julian the story, and the poem ends "but the world shall not know." It is a weak ending, as I have said, and indeed it would not be difficult to show the erratic quality of *Julian and Maddalo* once Shelley began to cope with the emotions and events of his marriage. Out of that chaos Shelley could create only a flawed masterpiece. It may be, as Maddalo said,

        "Most wretched men
    Are cradled into poetry by wrong,
    They learn in suffering what they teach in song." (544-546)

We ourselves may think: Not unless they have the skill. Be that as it may, if a man writes while suffering, his powers lose mastery. Nevertheless a flawed masterpiece is yet a masterpiece. The modulations of the first part, like harmonics of the fundamental familiar style, are artful beyond praise. In the poem are elegance and courtesy, a cultivated and strong intelligence, and later, extremest sensibility and depth of passion.

LINES WRITTEN AMONG THE EUGANEAN HILLS

The alchemical failure to convert raw materials utterly into other substance in *Julian and Maddalo* was redeemed in the almost flawless *Lines written among the Euganean Hills*. Shelley said that the poem "was written after a day's excursion among those lovely mountains which surround what was once the retreat, and where is now the sepulchre, of Petrarch" and spoke of "the sudden relief of a state of deep despondency by the radiant visions disclosed by the sudden burst of an Italian sunrise in autumn on the highest peaks of those delightful mountains." (The Shelleys were still living in Byron's villa in

75

Este, inland at the foot of the Euganean Hills. Padua lies northeast of Este, on a plain, and Venice east of Padua.) Beauty and love—impulses perhaps from the mountains and from Petrarch's love poetry—are motifs in the poem. Clara's death and Mary's desolation occasioned the "deep despondency," a fact which we need not know for our response to the poem but which is worth knowing for what it reveals of the poet's art and thereby of a literary principle.

The poem does not exist as a subjective expression of isolated pain; rather *it records a state that is common to humanity in personal experience and connects that state to public experience,* a city's or a nation's. The most important criterion of great art is its universality. In accord with that principle Shelley begins with a mariner who is any one of us voyaging on the sea of misery which is life.

> Many a green isle needs must be
> In the deep wide sea of misery,
> Or the mariner, worn and wan,
> Never thus could voyage on—

the *many* is insisted on by the opening stress in contrast to the two unstressed syllables beginning the second line, and the greenness by the stress lingering on the long *green* after the two quick syllables. That these green isles *are* set in the dark sea is subtly certified by the vocalic sounds of the middle five words of the first line being in the middle five words of the dark image of the second line, and again by the contrapuntal dimension of the assonance in *isle* and *wide* being set in long unstressed syllables, and again by the effect of shimmering light in the long *i* sounds surrounded by the long *e* sounds. This much of the music in the lines must be said to underscore the balance of a "twice-born" mind which sees clearly the darkness of human experience *and* that, as the speaker states again when he turns to his own personal experience,

> Ay, many flowering islands lie
> In the waters of wide Agony, (66-67)

where music is also in conjunction with theme. Were it otherwise, were there not many such flowering islands, the mariner, we, could not voyage on—

76

> Day and night, and night and day,
> Drifting on his dreary way,
> With the solid darkness black
> Closing round his vessel's track;
> Whilst above the sunless sky,
> Big with clouds, hangs heavily. (5-10)

The cyclical repetition in the fifth line is interpenetrated by the alliteration and image in the sixth; and in the next four lines the sounds are thick tones, like the quality of the symbolic atmosphere. The mariner voyages through the darkness, his ship hurried on and riven by the storm of life, almost destroyed by the overbrimming misery; as in a dream the ship of his being seems to welter through eternity while the shore of death, the haven of the grave for which he longs with divided will, ever recedes. With divided will because, although death is a haven of rest, it is life that counts. If he can find no refuge from distress in friendship or love while alive, whether they exist or not on that distant shore will wreak him little woe (27-44).

Other meaning, which we cannot yet grasp, exists in "the sunless sky, Big with clouds, hangs heavily." In any work of art meaning depends on the relationships among the parts and of each part to the whole, on the harmony and unity of its structure. Because a poem, like a play or a piece of music, takes place in time, we may not understand an earlier line fully until we have read a later line or understand either fully until we have considered their place in the whole design. But let us proceed without foreknowledge.

On a tempest-shaken northern beach lie a skull and seven bones,

> Where a few gray rushes stand,
> Boundaries of the sea and land. (45-52)

Those "few gray rushes" (also dividing life and death) are the right detail for the mood.

> Nor is heard one voice of wail
> But the sea-mews, as they sail
> O'er the billows of the gale; (53-55)

the sea-mew, or mew gull, exists all over Europe and the Medi-

77

terranean. It has a harsh, querulous voice, and its wild cries having something of a distorted human quality can be heard through a storm. It is a fit voice for this desolate world in which a wretch died. The only other voice of wail is the whirl-wind's,

> Howling, like a slaughtered town,
> When a king in glory rides
> Through the pomp of fratricides. (57-59)

Nature, like humanity, is out of joint. None laments the wretch whose unburied bones lie there (60-65). Who that wretch is and where the sea, are indeterminable. Scholars variously suggest little Clara on the northern Adriatic, Shelley's dead past in England, Frankenstein's monster (of Mary Shelley's novel) in the Arctic. But it really does not matter, and we do wrong to distract ourselves with the shrouded identity. What does matter is the clarity of the emotional bleakness. In the passage the personal state of the mariner, which will end in cold death (36), is common to the desolate world.

Now the narrator shifts to the first person. This morning soft winds piloted his bark to one of the many flowering islands in the wide Agony of the world. (We learn in line 327 that the soft winds are soft dreams.) He listens to the rooks hailing the "sun's uprise majestical" and watches them soar into the bursting eastern heaven, "their plumes of purple grain, Starred with drops of golden rain." Not his mood alone, even the dark ill-omened birds are transformed. In contrast to the "solid darkness black" around the mariner, the sunless sky, and the storm, here "all is bright, and clear, and still, Round the solitary hill," his flowering isle (66-89).

Shelley wrote that these first eighty-nine lines were "introductory" and that "they were not erased at the request of a dear friend" (Mary). The remark reflects a personal reserve too rarely appreciated. That the lines are "introductory" must not mislead us into thinking that they are not integral to the poem. Shelley had a comprehensive mind, which saw things as wholes, and in his best work has a strong sense of structure. Indeed, his structural power is a distinguishing mark of his greatness. In Oliver Elton's praise, "This poem is perfectly put together, and it is an intellectual pleasure to see its firm development."

"Bright, and clear, and still," the world can now be seen before him. And as what is revealed is intellectual as well as physical, we come to understand that sunlight is also the light of the mind. On the Lombard plain, as on a green sea, are islands of fair cities. There "Venice lies, A peopled labyrinth of walls"—an ominous image—and "Lo! the sun upsprings behind" Venice:

> As within a furnace bright,
> Column, tower, and dome, and spire,
> Shine like obelisks of fire,
> Pointing with inconstant motion
> From the altar of dark ocean
> To the sapphire-tinted skies. (105-110)

The city seems like the flames of a sacrifice to Apollo, the god of light who "spoke of old" (and whose voice is in the intellectual light of this utterance), even as there were bloody sacrifices to the Minotaur in the labyrinth on Crete (90-114).

The once glorious, sun-girt city must be sacrificed, a prey to Ocean, because she exists enslaved (to Austria), if Ocean will so hallow her who was once "his child, and then his queen." The sea-mew will fly over the depopulated isles, and palace gates overgrown with sea-flowers will topple into the sea as the tides change. The fisherman will hurry from these shores, afraid of a dance of the dead. It is a desolation connected by the sea-mew to the desolate world of the northern sea (115-141).

Looking only at the towers "Quivering through aëreal gold," none would imagine that Venice was a mouldering corpse of greatness to which human forms cling like pollution-nourished worms. Yet even the most rotten evil can be transformed by Freedom. But if Venice and a hundred cities like her in chains do not overthrow the Celtic Anarch (the Teutonic, or Austrian, dictator; there is little to choose between the Austrian Emperor Francis I and his chancellor, Metternich), let them perish,

> Clouds which stain truth's rising day
> By her sun consumed away. (161-162)

In the new day of truth the sun of freedom, which lends "life its soul of light" (*Hellas*, 41), will consume these cities, and in the cycle of decay and regeneration better nations will blossom

(142-166). That uprising day is a flowering island like the "sun's uprise majestical" in the Euganean Hills, a radiant vision that lifts Shelley out of despondency. And now we may more fully understand the meaning of "the sunless sky, Big with clouds, hangs heavily" (9-10): a world without freedom is an oppressive atmosphere intensifying the mariner's distress. The analogy between the sun, which was his green isle, and liberty is made again at the end of the passage on Venice:

> Lo, the sun floats up the sky
> Like thought-wingèd Liberty. (206-207)

Personal destiny is inextricable from public destiny. That theme makes the introductory lines inextricable from the rest.

Only that a great English poet, a swan soaring through the tempests of life (a swan has strength and beauty), was driven from Albion by the "might of evil dreams" and found a nest in Venice, only this will redeem remembrance of the dead city of the sea,

> As the garment of the sky
> Clothes the world immortally. (169-170)

When the poet left England, Ocean welcomed him with joy (fittingly he found a refuge in Venice, child and queen of Ocean); the joy grew the poet's and in his song had power to chasten terror (167-183). Although the sins and foul slaveries of Venice stain his sunlike soul, the city will take fame from him as the river Scamander's wasting springs, near Troy, from Homer; as Shakespeare filled "Avon and the world with light Like omniscient power" (the light of mind is spiritual as well as intellectual), so this sunlike soul will illumine Venice and the world; and as love burns from Petrarch's urn in the Euganean Hills, so the effluence of love from this "Mighty spirit" in Venice will reveal "things unearthly" to the human heart (192-205). This great poet is among those who—as Cythna consoled Laon in the winter of their world, after love and freedom were defeated by barbarity—make the promise of the "future, a broad sunrise" (IX. xxv).

Now, this English poet, this "Mighty spirit," can be no fiction, for Shelley speaks of dreadful actualities of the world's history, which are central to the poem. The poet must be an historical person capable of what Shelley claims for him; a

80

persona, an idealized poet, would water the wine. It was otherwise in *Julian and Maddalo*, whose action and characters depended on no necessary connection with historical actuality for their value. Thus, not to weaken the poem by accepting a fictional cause for an historical consequence, we must know who the poet is. As many of Shelley's English audience recognized, and as all Shelley scholars know, the poet is Byron. Although a man stained by his degraded life in Venice (192-193), Byron was "a great poet" as "the address to ocean proves." [So Shelley wrote. This is the passage in *Childe Harold's Pilgrimage* to which the paragraph on Byron gives tribute:

> There is a pleasure in the pathless woods,
> There is a rapture on the lonely shore,
> There is society, where none intrudes,
> By the deep sea, and music in its roar:
> I love not man the less, but nature more,
> From these our interviews, in which I steal
> From all I may be, or have been before,
> To mingle with the universe, and feel
> What I can ne'er express, yet cannot all conceal.

> Roll on, thou deep and dark-blue ocean—roll!
> Ten thousand fleets sweep over thee in vain;
> Man marks the earth with ruin—his control
> Stops with the shore;—upon the watery plain
> The wrecks are all thy deed, nor doth remain
> A shadow of man's ravage, save his own,
> When, for a moment, like a drop of rain,
> He sinks into thy depths with bubbling groan,
> Without a grave, unknell'd, uncoffin'd, and unknown.

> His steps are not upon thy paths,—thy fields
> Are not a spoil for him,—thou dost arise
> And shake him from thee; the vile strength he wields
> For earth's destruction thou dost all despise,
> Spurning him from thy bosom to the skies,
> And send'st him, shivering in thy playful spray
> And howling, to his gods, where haply lies
> His petty hope in some near port or bay,
> And dashest him again to earth:—there let him lay.

The armaments which thunderstrike the walls
Of rock-built cities, bidding nations quake,
And monarchs tremble in their capitals,
The oak leviathans, whose huge ribs make
Their clay creator the vain title take
Of lord of thee, and arbiter of war;
These are thy toys, and, as the snowy flake,
They melt into thy yeast of waves, which mar
Alike the Armada's pride, or spoils of Trafalgar.

Thy shores are empires, changed in all save thee—
Assyria, Greece, Rome, Carthage, what are they?
Thy waters wasted them while they were free,
And many a tyrant since; their shores obey
The stranger, slave, or savage; their decay
Has dried up realms to deserts:—not so thou,
Unchangeable save to thy wild waves' play—
Time writes no wrinkle on thine azure brow—
Such as creation's dawn beheld, thou rollest now.

Thou glorious mirror, where the Almighty's form
Glasses itself in tempests; in all time,
Calm or convulsed—in breeze, or gale, or storm,
Icing the pole, or in the torrid clime
Dark-heaving; boundless, endless, and sublime—
The image of Eternity—the throne
Of the Invisible; even from out thy slime
The monsters of the deep are made; each zone
Obeys thee; thou goest forth, dread, fathomless, alone.

And I have loved thee, ocean! and my joy
Of youthful sports was on thy breast to be
Borne, like thy bubbles, onward: from a boy
I wanton'd with thy breakers—they to me
Were a delight; and if the freshening sea
Made them a terror—'twas a pleasing fear,
For I was as it were a child of thee,
And trusted to thy billows far and near,
And laid my hand upon thy mane—as I do here.

(IV. clxxviii-clxxxiv)

For Shelley *Cain* and *Don Juan* set the seal on Byron's greatness.]

Perhaps Shelley had Byron in mind when he wrote, "The persons in whom this power resides may often, as far as regards many portions of their nature, have little apparent correspondence with that spirit of good of which they are the ministers. But even while they deny and abjure, they are compelled to serve the power which is seated upon the throne of their own soul." Shelley believed that the poets of his age surpassed beyond comparison any English poets since Milton. Of the poets of his age, he thought Byron the greatest; Goethe also admired Byron prodigiously. Given Shelley's belief in the power of poetry to make men and society more perfect (argued in his noble document *A Defence of Poetry*), and given his judgment of Byron as a poet, the paragraph (167-205) is unassailable. But time has done injury: if we no longer think of Byron as so great a poet as Shelley and Goethe did, the paragraph becomes weakened by overstatement. Byron cannot do all that Shelley claims for him. It is the one flaw in the poem. We are thrown back to this position: although not among the greatest poets, Byron was an excellent one, and as such shares in the work of heroes, poets, and philosophers who leave, not to Venice but to the world, "All hope, or love, or truth, or liberty, Whose forms their mighty spirits could conceive, To be a rule and law to ages that survive" (*The Revolt of Islam*, IX. xxviii).

For Venice herself there is little hope, and the poem foretells no regeneration. Her glory died long ago. Nearby stands Padua, "a peopled solitude"—without freedom and love they of the city live each alone. The peasant harvests his grain and the oxen strain with the load of the vineyard wagons for the brutal, drunken Celt (Austrian). The sickles are not yet changed to swords, but sheaves of overlords "are ripe to come To destruction's harvest-home." The shift in the use of the harvest image from political and economic injustice to murderous justice is excellently done.

> Men must reap the things they sow,
> Force from force must ever flow,
> Or worse; but 'tis a bitter woe
> That love or reason cannot change
> The despot's rage, the slave's revenge. (210-235)

Not the justice of revenge, only the justice of love must rule the world; but neither love nor reason can stop violence from begetting violence. The change from trochaic to iambic lines sets off the bitter hopelessness of the prospect.

In Padua, older in slavery than Venice, Death won an earlier tyrant from Sin, and to assuage his mother made her Vice-Emperor (the wit is grim), when the time came, under the Austrian. The incestuous mother and son follow, inevitably,

> Tyrants as the sun the swallow,
> As Repentance follows Crime,
> And as changes follow time.

The three similes work in two ways. They contain not only inevitability in their analogy, but also contrast with tyranny: the simple warmth the swallow enjoys, moral compunction, and mutability (236-255).

Austrian tyranny has, in Shelley's view, trampled out the lamp of learning, which once burned in Padua's university with a sacred flame of knowledge and freedom. But although the tyrant, like a Norwegian woodsman, put out one flame, the fire has already spread, and liberty is a light, fearful as a forest fire howling in the darkened sky, surrounding the tyrant (256-284). Shelley was writing at a time when Metternich's design for repressive rule, which emerged from the Congress of Vienna in 1813, was being imposed on Europe by the Quadruple Alliance (Austria, Russia, Prussia, Great Britain); in 1818 the admission of France under Louis XVIII made it the Quintuple Alliance—power that seemed hopeless to defy. Yet his faith was justified: two years later revolutions flared up in Spain and Greece and within a generation had swept over Europe and through Spain's colonies in the New World.

The morning gives way to a glowing autumnal noon descending around the poet, the morning star of love dissolving as amethyst light and fragrance in the sky. The world around, all living things,

> And my spirit which so long
> Darkened this swift stream of song,—
> Interpenetrated lie
> By the glory of the sky:
> Be it love, light, harmony,

Odour, or the soul of all
Which from Heaven like dew doth fall,
Or the mind which feeds this verse
Peopling the lone universe. (285-318)

He is sure of the value of the experience although not sure of
its cause; the philosophical hesitation, although mystical authority invites dogmatism, makes the reality of the experience
more persuasive. The lambency of that mystical experience in
the first paragraph of the third movement is connected to the
flaming vision of freedom in the last paragraph of the middle
movement (the passages on Venice and Padua) not by direct
statement but by trope and, in the classical Greek manner
elucidated by H. D. F. Kitto, by structure: by trope in the light
imagery; by structure in the implicit cause and consequence in
the paragraphic sequence. Public destiny and private destiny
are no more separable in the third movement, the last eighty-
nine lines, than in the first movement of eighty-nine lines; the
symmetry of design enforces that theme. And as we now know
the speaker is a poet ("this swift stream of song"), we understand the precise nature of his destiny, typified in Byron. Within the three-movement structure change takes place: experience of the flowering islands has given life to knowledge and
hope, which have irradiated the darkness.

Now evening brings the infant moon, to which the evening
star of love (the planet Venus, "that one star," being both
morning and evening star) seems to minister crimson sunlight
for the infant's growth to bright maturity. Although the day
has been glorious, it must go, passing to other sufferers, and in
the night the pilot of the speaker's being, "Pain, Sits beside the
helm again" (321-334).

Love's ministration of intellectual light, which is the beautiful and the true, may bring to maturity a healing paradise,
"Far from passion, pain, and guilt," where the poet may live
with those he loves—the best flowering isle. In those he loves,
then, is his hope for paradise. Were the polluting multitude to
break in, enticed by envy, the multitude would change, chiefly
because of that

love which heals all strife
Circling, like the breath of life,

85

All things in that sweet abode
With its own mild brotherhood. (335-373)

Even in the midst of his imaginative refuge the poet realizes
that private experience cannot be an island unto itself. As
Matthew Arnold claimed in *Culture and Anarchy*: "because
men are all members of one great whole, and the sympathy
which is in human nature will not allow one member to be
indifferent to the rest or to have a perfect welfare independent
of the rest, the expansion of humanity . . . must be a *general*
expansion. Perfection . . . is not possible while the individual
remains isolated."

Our echoes roll from soul to soul.

INVOCATION TO MISERY

Other poems composed during this autumn and winter had
their origin in grief. In *Invocation to Misery* the figure of
Misery is abstracted from Mary's desolation. Meaning thereby
again transcends the circumscription of personal experience
and is perfectly visible in a complete intellectual and emotional
statement.

The speaker and Misery must together "live some Hours or
ages yet to come" (14-15).

IV

'Tis an evil lot, and yet
Let us make the best of it;
If love can live when pleasure dies,
We two will love, till in our eyes
This heart's Hell seem Paradise.   20

V

Come, be happy!—lie thee down
On the fresh grass newly mown,
Where the Grasshopper doth sing
Merrily—one joyous thing
In a world of sorrowing!   25

But their only refuge is a "bridal bed—Underneath the grave
'tis spread" (41-42). Dreaming in "that long sleep" (51),

XII

Let us laugh, and make our mirth,
At the shadows of the earth,
As dogs bay the moonlight clouds,
Which, like spectres wrapped in shrouds,
Pass o'er night in multitudes.   60

XIII

All the wide world, beside us,
Show like multitudinous
Puppets passing from a scene;
What but mockery can they mean,
Where I am—where thou hast been?   65

The shadows are earth's unrealities, a puppet show whose
meaning is a mockery, a falseness, he himself now in Misery's
state. The mirth they make watching the show is joyless, even
tinged with madness. It is a dark imagining, the death-mar-
riage with Misery and the eternal bad dream.

PROMETHEUS UNBOUND: INTRODUCTION

Mary had arrived at Este from the Baths of Lucca early in
September. Byron's villa, in her words, stood "on the very
overhanging brow of a low hill at the foot of a range of higher
ones. The house was cheerful and pleasant; a vine-trellised
walk, a *pergola*, as it is called in Italian, led from the hall-
door to a summer-house at the end of the garden, which
Shelley made his study, and in which he began the *Prometheus;*
and here also, as he mentions in a letter, he wrote *Julian and
Maddalo*. A slight ravine, with a road in its depth, divided the
garden from the hill, on which stood the ruins of the ancient
castle of Este. . . . We looked from the garden over the
wide plain of Lombardy, bounded to the west by the far
Apennines, while to the east the horizon was lost in misty
distance." During that September, Byron in a palace on the
Grand Canal in Venice worked on the fourth canto of *Childe
Harold's Pilgrimage* and the first canto of *Don Juan*. In October Shelley composed *Lines written among the Euganean
Hills*.

In November the Shelleys travelled south to spend the

87

winter in the mildness of Naples. On an excursion to ancient places they visited Baiae in the Bay of Naples. The seaweed in the bed of the still water, perfectly distinct, Shelley later transplanted to *Ode to the West Wind*. In the transparent water, too, lay antique ruins of Baiae, submerged by earthquake,

> palaces and towers,
> Quivering within the wave's intenser day,
> All overgrown with azure moss and flowers. (33-35)

It is perhaps too little realized how much of the actuality of Shelley's experience makes texture in his poetry. He steadily regarded the visible world even while he searched for the "manifestations of something beyond the present and tangible object."

During these winter months Shelley, still inwardly suffering, wrote little. In March they were in Rome, where spring had come. Stirred by the continuity of evil in "every attitude of humiliation and slavery" of the prisoners decorating the Arch of Constantine and of the prisoners working in the Square of St. Peter's preparing the grounds for the visit of the Austrian Emperor, his own spirit revivified by the seasonal rebirth of the world, Shelley set to work again on *Prometheus Unbound,* apparently possessed by a demon. At Este, until Clara died, he had worked on the first act. Now in less than a month the three acts were done, "chiefly written upon the mountainous ruins of the Baths of Caracalla," we learn from the pleasurable remembrance in the Preface, "among the flowery glades, and thickets of odoriferous blossoming trees, which are extended in ever winding labyrinths upon its immense platforms and dizzy arches suspended in the air. The bright blue sky of Rome, and the effect of the vigorous awakening spring in that divinest climate, and the new life with which it drenches the spirit even to intoxication, were the inspiration of this drama."

In the late autumn, in Florence, Shelley wrote a fourth act, which was not part of the original design but which, structurally right, was needed. Between the third act and concluding the fourth he produced, among other poems, *The Cenci, The Mask of Anarchy, Peter Bell the Third,* and *Ode to the West Wind*—each a very different kind of poem as we shall see, although each has its unmistakable origin in Shelley's mind. No wonder that scholars speak of 1819 as an *annus mirabilis*, even as the summit of his career. But there are other summits piercing the sky in the three years more of his life, as the beauty of *The Sensitive Plant*, the wit of *Swellfoot the Tyrant*, the perfection of art of *Adonais*, the power of *The Triumph of Life* —again each is very different, each very great.

Before finishing *Prometheus Unbound* Shelley began his prose *A Philosophical View of Reform*, intended as a "standard book" for reformers. Not published for a hundred years, the tract never served its purpose, but it is important to us as a revelation of the realistic faculty of Shelley's mind. The first chapter presents historical perspective, a survey informed by Shelley's passion for freedom and justice, which are necessary for goodness, greatness, and public happiness; and prophesies liberty in nations the world over. In the second chapter he turns to England and defines the political and economic injustices in the state. At the time of the Long Parliament in 1641, which "questionless, was the organ of the will of all classes of people in England since it effected the complete revolution in a tyranny consecrated by time," one out of eight Englishmen could vote. But in the nearly two centuries since, the proportion has changed to one in hundreds; this proportional diminishing of political rights is a just measure of the loss of freedom. Moreover the national debt, first made an instrument of government in the time of William III, brought to power a new class, those who made wealth out of fraud, manipulating credit and money. The consequence of their manipulations has been economic calamity to the populace. Inflation has made it necessary to labor twice as long for a decent competency; and since there is a limit to what the human frame can endure, men cannot earn enough to care for the sick, the old, nor even for young children, who must work or starve. Although the old, the sick, and the children labor, the populace "eat less bread, wear worse clothes, are more ignorant, immoral, miserable, and desperate." (Whether or not the national debt was the cause, as Shelley believed, economic calamity was walking up and down England.) To reform the political and economic state of England, as was "most just and necessary," Shelley made concrete proposals—that England has adopted most of them attests to their moderation and practicality. It was his philosophic view that made him moderate. His proposals stopped far short of a republic because a "republic, however just in its principle or glorious in its object, would through violence and sudden change which must attend it incur a great risk of being as rapid in its decline as in its growth." That he learned from the course of the French Revolution. I give excerpts of his philosophic view from the third chapter, in which he sets forth the probable means of reform.

The broad principle of political reform is the natural equality of men, not with relation to their property but to their natural rights. That equality in possessions which Jesus Christ so passionately taught is a moral rather than political truth and is such as social institutions cannot without mischief inflexibly secure. Morals and politics can only be considered as portions of the same science with relation to a system of such absolute perfection as Christ and Plato and Rousseau and other reasoners have asserted. . . . Equality of possessions must be the last result of the utmost refinements of civilization; it is one of the conditions of that system of society towards which with whatever hope of ultimate success, it is our duty to tend. . . .

But our present business is with the difficult and unbending realities of actual life, and when we have drawn inspiration from the great object of our hopes it becomes us with patience and resolution to apply ourselves to accommodating our theories to immediate practice. . . .

Any sudden attempt at universal suffrage would produce an immature attempt at a republic. . . . It is no prejudice to the ultimate establishment of the boldest political innovations that we temporize so as, when they shall be accomplished, they may be rendered permanent. . . .

No friend of mankind and of his country can desire that such a crisis [insurrection compelled by the government refusing to begin reform that would gradually create a representative assembly] should suddenly arrive; but still less, once having arrived, can he hesitate under what banner to array his person and his power. . . .

If reform shall be begun by the existing government, let us be contented with a limited *beginning*, with any whatsoever opening . . . it is no matter how slow, gradual, and cautious be the change; we shall demand more and more with firmness and moderation, never anticipating, but never deferring the moment of successful opposition, so that the people may become habituated [to] exercising the functions of sovereignty as they acquire the possession of it. . . . [In] moderate reform . . . for the sake of obtaining without bloodshed or confusion improvement of a more important character, all reformers ought to acquiesce. Not that such are first principles, or that they would produce a system of perfect social institutions or one approaching to [such]. But nothing is more idle than to reject a limited benefit because we cannot without great sacrifices obtain an unlimited one. We might thus reject a representative republic, if it were obtainable, on the plea that the imagination of man can conceive of something more absolutely perfect.

Shelley's knowledge of the "difficult and unbending realities of actual life" and the strength and balance of the rational, realistic faculty of his mind give authority to the "beautiful idealisms of moral excellence" in *Prometheus Unbound*, created as the Preface asserts with the awareness "that until the mind can love, and admire, and trust, and hope, and endure, reasoned principles of moral conduct are seeds cast upon the highway of life which the unconscious passenger tramples into dust, although they would bear the harvest of his happiness." The victory of Prometheus over the idealisms of evil brings into being a perfect world. The vision of a perfect world can shape human history if people follow this principle in *A Philosophical View of Reform*: "Towards whatsoever we regard as perfect, undoubtedly it is no less our duty than it is our nature to press forward; this is the generous enthusiasm which accomplishes not indeed the consummation after which it aspires, but one which approaches it in a degree far nearer than if the whole powers had not been developed by such a delusion." [Delusion here, like illusion, means the ascription of reality to that existing in the imagination. It has no pejorative sense. Similarly Wordsworth speaks of "illusions . . . eminently useful to the mind."] In its vision of a perfect world *Prometheus* works to make society more perfect. In its aspect shaping the mind to "love, and admire, and trust, and hope, and endure," it works to make men more perfect. Those are the ultimate purposes of poetry in Shelley's view, and we should perhaps understand his view more fully before we enter the

91

world of *Prometheus Unbound* so that we may better understand how that world interpenetrates ours. I briefly give what seems most pertinent from *A Defence of Poetry*.

Those people are poets who approximate the beautiful (which is triune: its other aspects are the true and the good) not only in language, music, dancing, architecture, sculpture, painting, but in laws, civil society, the arts of life, and religion. The poet "not only beholds intensely the present as it is, and discovers those laws according to which present things ought to be ordered, but he beholds the future in the present, and his thoughts are the germs of the flower and the fruit of latest time. Not that I assert poets to be prophets in the gross sense of the word, or that they can foretell the form as surely as they foreknow the spirit of events." That is to say, by knowing what is possible in the future, poets can and do direct the course of things from what they are to what they should be. For example, there were "poets among the authors of the Christian and chivalric systems of manners and religions, who created forms of opinion and action never before conceived; which, copied into the imagination of men, became as generals to the bewildered armies of their thought." In that sense poets are the "legislators of the world." Realistically regarding the "present as it is," Shelley wrote, "We have more moral, political and historical wisdom than we know how to reduce into practice; we have more scientific and economical knowledge than can be accommodated to the just distribution of the produce which it multiplies. The poetry [i.e., the beautiful, the true, and the good] in these systems of thought, is concealed by the accumulation of facts and calculating processes." By *calculating* Shelley means selfish as well as reckoning. Never is it more desirable to cultivate poetry than at such times. Poetry in the form of language acts in a diviner manner than setting forth admirable doctrines. "It awakens and enlarges the mind. . . . The great secret of morals is love; or a going out of our own nature, and an identification of ourselves with the beautiful which exists in thought, action, or person not our own. A man, to be greatly good, must imagine intensively and comprehensively; he must put himself in the place of another and of many others; the pains and pleasures of his species must become his own. The great instrument of moral good is the imagination; and poetry administers to the effect by acting on the cause."

When Shelley composed *Prometheus Unbound* his purpose was "simply to familiarise the highly refined imagination of the more select classes of poetical readers with beautiful idealisms of moral excellence." This fit audience would be few among his contemporaries, in Shelley's expectation. But just as every poem is a portion of "that great poem, which all poets, like the co-operating thoughts of one great mind, have built up since the beginning of the world," so the perception of readers is a vast collaboration. "All high poetry is infinite," we may grant, as Shelley wrote of Dante. "Veil after veil may be undrawn, and the inmost naked beauty of the meaning never exposed." Nonetheless, enough meaning has been revealed to reward our minds richly. The few contemporaries of Shelley who coped with *Prometheus Unbound* have since been joined by uncounted thousands. Admirable modern critics, among them C. S. Lewis, think the poem the greatest of the nineteenth century. But nobody makes us choose among the great works of the century which, I believe, gave the world more major poets than any other in history. Temperament may incline us to *The Prelude,* or *Don Juan,* or *Empedocles on Etna,* or *The Ring and the Book,* or another, for a personal favorite. Many are likely to think the great poem they are in at the moment the best of them all.

Of the great long poems of the nineteenth century the *Prometheus Unbound* is perhaps the least read because it is the most difficult. The sources of the difficulty are in the complex, subtle, and compressed thought; in the imagery, particularly in the use of symbols; in the vast range of allusions; in the multiple meanings existing simultaneously; and in the techniques of arranging both language and happenings. The difficulty is justifiable—at the basis of it is originality, and without the originality Shelley could not have said what he wanted to say.

The originality was consciously designed. A contemporary recorded Shelley's saying, "It is original; and cost me severe mental labour." To another Shelley wrote, "It is a drama with characters and mechanism of a kind yet unattempted"; and to yet another asserted that " 'Prometheus Unbound,' is

. . . not, as the name would indicate, a mere imitation of the Greek drama, or indeed if I have been successful, is it an imitation of anything." Shelley accepted the price for his originality, knowing, as he wrote to his publisher, that the *Prometheus* could not "sell beyond twenty copies" (in those days originality had not the popular virtue that any such pretension has today); and he could accept that price because he also knew that it was "durable poetry, tried by the severest test." Two years later he let himself say that "Prometheus was never intended for more than 5 or 6 persons," reflecting his human enough disappointment after the accuracy of his forecast. There were seven reviews in the months after the publication of the 1820 volume, *Prometheus Unbound/ A Lyrical Drama/ In Four Acts/ With Other Poems,* more critical response than to anything he had published earlier, except for *The Cenci,* but even those who praised failed to understand the work; perhaps none of his contemporaries, neither Mary Shelley nor Leigh Hunt, could grasp the work entire.

Difficult as the poem is, meaning is accessible throughout thanks to the labors of many scholars and critics. Meaning reached, the drama rewards us manifold. We may respond with astonishment and pleasure to what Shelley has to say and to his formal excellence. I do not imply a separation between content (that is, the elaboration of subject and theme) and form in literary experience; subject and theme are elements in the formal construct, along with imagery, tone, structure, and so on. What Shelley has to say, as in the case of every poet, emerges from the whole construct. But I do insist that like the other elements of poetry content can be talked about separately and can be judged. Nobody with literary intelligence mistakes the part for the whole.

When the content is especially difficult, as in *Prometheus Unbound,* content perhaps most needs talking about. In my commentary I shall try to come to terms with every difficulty in the drama; and I propose to make clear the continuous thought and action and their formal, dramatic shaping into a genuinely philosophic *poesis.* I shall not explore every image, every allusion, every multiple meaning, every structural technique. Were I to try, I should properly earn nobody's thanks. I hope, in making meaning apparent, to light up more than in-

terpret so that eyes other than mine will see but not necessarily
what I see.

Shelley had no inclination "to restore the lost drama of
Aeschylus"—whose *Prometheus Unbound* "supposed the reconciliation of Jupiter with his victim as the price of the disclo-
sure of the danger threatened to his empire by the consummation of his marriage with Thetis"—such were an "ambition,
which, if my preference to this mode of treating the subject
had incited me to cherish, the recollection of the high comparison such an attempt would challenge might well abate.
But, in truth, I was averse from a catastrophe so feeble as that
of reconciling the Champion with the Oppressor of mankind."
In his own mode Shelley did challenge Aeschylus. His title
page bears as legend a line originally the early poet's, *Audisne
haec Amphiarae sub terram abdite?* Do you hear this, Amphi-
araus, hidden under the earth? Neville Rogers discovered in a
manuscript notebook of Shelley's that this line appears just
preceding the speech of the Spirit of the Hour that closes Act
III, the close of the drama at that time, and that it is addressed
"To the ghost of Aeschylus"—the challenge, which thus demands whether the ghost hears this, the newer poet's version of
Prometheus Unbound, is signed boldly PERCY SHELLEY.

They are two plays not on the same theme, hardly even on
the same subject, but only starting with the same situation, the
opposition of a Titan for the sake of mankind against a powerful God. The only important connection between the two
plays is between their moral conceptions, although these are
divergent. I speak of a connection in the moral divergence of
the two works because Shelley so interpreted it, as do many
scholars. But in truth, to talk of Aeschylus' trilogy is a speculation not worth our trouble for nobody knows what the Greek
poet's moral conception was. If we had the trilogy—there are
only the *Prometheus Bound* and fragments of *Prometheus Unbound,* nothing at all of the first play—we could measure meaning in either play by the other, like measuring the motion of a
star in connection to another going in a different direction.
That were invaluable intellectually and morally, but unhappily we have certain knowledge only that the older star has
perished. There are fragmentary matters that we could fix on.

For example, in both dramatists the gifts conferred by Prometheus are given to mankind out of love. But the nature of mankind before endowment by the Titan is different in the two dramas. Such matters are worth reflection, perhaps, but to use parts in place of Aeschylus' whole is neither candid nor wise. Shelley's verbal echoes are scant. Let us, then, talk only of the modern play.

I have spoken of *Prometheus Unbound* as a play, but we are wrong to think of it so, for if we do we clog our apprehension: any person steadily regarding the work knows that if he looks for what he responds to in a play—for meaning emerging fundamentally from an arrangement of incidents presented through action, no matter what meanings emerge harmonically through arrangements of emotions or ideas—he will find *Prometheus* unsatisfying. But he must then judge that he, not the work, is at fault. I do not mean to say that there are no flaws in the work, only that it must be responded to for what it is, a work with "characters and a mechanism of a kind . . . unattempted" before and after Shelley's *Prometheus*. It is hard to respond to anything for what it is; we rarely respond purely to present experience, almost always we are responding in too large measure to past experience.

Others have spoken of the poem—of the thing made—not as a play but as a rhapsodic drama in the mode of the Old Testament poets; as a symbolic drama; as a myth; as an epic; as a sustained lyric; as odes linked by dramatic poetry and thereby much like opera; as a symphony; even as a frescoed panorama.

We may if we like accept the poet's "a lyrical drama": a drama in that an entire action is imitated and presented rather than narrated (the drama is a comedy in the sense that the change is from bad to good); lyrical because lyrical elements are early brought into the complex tonality of the drama and are sustained throughout the first three acts, and because the emotional logic of those acts must culminate in the lyrical domination of the fourth act, that great "hymn of rejoicing." Compounded with the narrative and lyrical elements in the structural integrity of the poem is the reflective element: there is, as we shall see, extraordinary intellectual power. Shelley perhaps never thought to bring the reflective element into the phrase he used for his form because he took it for granted that

96

a poet wrote poems because he had something vitally important to say and that few would fail to recognize *Prometheus* as a genuine philosophic poem even if only few could cope with the poem. So much for the mechanism which is triune in its structure. Of the characters only this much needs saying now: they are all of the invisible world; that they speak and act, which are their only means of reaching us, lends them the immediacy belonging to drama, the sense of seeing it all happen before our eyes.

While we are on the subject of form, we may as well chase away the misconception that the drama is an allegory. Neither Shelley nor Mary ever spoke of it as such. Shelley wrote in the Preface, "Prometheus is, as it were, the type of the highest perfection of moral and intellectual nature." But he is Prometheus —the Titan, indeed, a God—not a personification or symbol. Even Asia, who in one aspect is Intellectual Beauty and in another is Love, is not primarily a personification; we are meant to take her literally as a spiritual power with personal existence. Allegorical figures are not realities but personified abstractions or symbols. Nor are the actions of the narrative symbolic, which is the fundamental principle of allegory; they are literal, all literal. The poem is mythopoeic rather than allegoric. As is the nature of myth, the vessel contains religious meaning; that religious meaning has the validity of the meaning in the myths, say, of Hinduism or Christianity. [Myth is a way of making meaning of aspects of the "deep truth," which "is imageless," accessible to the mind.] Who chooses not to believe, will not believe, and may or may not suspend his disbelief under the persuasion of imaginative power. Whoever is one's God, whether Jupiter or Jehovah, if belief thinks that God is a symbol and not a literal reality, that belief may be admirably rational but it is not religious; and religious experience, however defunct or negligible to many, has its integrity to some, and neither the will of a dictatorship nor the vote of a democracy can have anything to say about the truth. Those scientists whose faith is that the physical is the only reality may be right, and if they are, *Prometheus Unbound*, like all other expression of religious experience, is wrong.

Let us begin. May I suggest that you hold the poem open before you? What will strike us at once is the philosophic modernity.

Prometheus, bound to the precipice of a ravine of icy rocks in the Caucasus, speaks to Jupiter:

> Monarch of Gods and Daemons, and all Spirits
> But One, who throng these bright and rolling worlds
> Which Thou and I alone of living things
> Behold with sleepless eyes! regard this Earth. (1-4)

[1: *Daemons*, "every thing daemonical hold[s] an intermediate place between what is divine and what is mortal"—Shelley's translation of the *Symposium*.]

Jupiter is not the monarch of Prometheus, the one free spirit in the universe; as such, Prometheus bears the same relationship to Jupiter that Orestes bears in Sartre's *The Flies*. Orestes declares to Zeus: "Your whole universe is not enough to prove me wrong. You are the king of gods, king of stones and stars, king of the waves of the sea. But you are not the king of man."

The earth is multitudinous with enslaved humanity, whom Jupiter requites for "knee-worship, prayer, and praise" with "fear and self-contempt and barren hope" (5-8)—the condition is the nadir of mankind. Blinded by hate, Jupiter has made Prometheus triumph over his misery, a triumph more glorious than the reign of Jupiter, who were omnipotent had Prometheus shared the shame of the God's ill tyranny,

> and not hung here
> Nailed to this wall of eagle-baffling mountain,
> Black, wintry, dead, unmeasured; without herb,
> Insect, or beast, or shape or sound of life. (19-22)

Yet the Titan endures. He asks the Earth if the mountains have not felt, the Heaven if the Sun has not seen, the Sea if the waves have not heard his agony (24-29). Prometheus sustains his suffering in a faith more absolute than Job's, unceasingly tortured:

> The crawling glaciers pierce me with the spears
> Of their moon-freezing crystals. (31-32)

The construction of this phrase seems to say that the crystals are freezing the moon; that is an extension of the primary image, that the crystals are freezing in the light of the moon. The ambiguity works to intensify the cold. Even more interesting than this arrangement of language is the making visible of the slow piercing of the glaciers, which have had three thousand years to give pain. No physical eye could watch the motion of the glaciers, which on Mount Blanc, Shelley wrote, perpetually are "performing a work of desolation . . . at the rate of a foot each day." But our minds can watch the crawling glaciers wound Prometheus: by transposing mentally perceived scientific knowledge to sense perception the poet creates a vital intimacy with those aspects of the universe that are ordinarily grasped, if at all, only abstractly. Shelley's success with such imagery, it seems to me, is unique in English poetry.

After the torture of cold (31-33), which is both physical and symbolic, Prometheus speaks with no self-pity of torments (33-43) that are spiritual (the vulture's poison comes from Jupiter's polluting lips), psychological (the ghastly dream-people), and physical (the wrenching earthquakes, the whirl-winds, the hail). Although the slow hours are laden with afflic-tion, the Titan welcomes day and night, for the hour will come that,

> —As some dark Priest hales the reluctant victim
> Shall drag thee, cruel King, to kiss the blood
> From these pale feet, which then might trample thee
> If they disdained not such a prostrate slave.
> Disdain! Ah no! I pity thee. What ruin
> Will hunt thee undefended through wide Heaven!
> How will thy soul, cloven to its depth with terror,
> Gape like a hell within! I speak in grief,
> Not exultation, for I hate no more,
> As then ere misery made me wise. (49-58)

The images in the first four lines are vindictive; but the thought of disdain brings to a seeming-sudden realization the wisdom that misery has made, and hate changes to pity for the hell of terror that will gape within the dictatorial God. For many minds the change from hate to pity for an afflicting enemy is a psychologically valid experience, as is attested by ancient and modern experience. Prometheus would recall the thunderous curse that terrified the world, and, to the Moun-tains, the Springs, the Air, and the Whirlwinds, says "What was that curse?" They all heard (58-73). [64-65: *Thou serenest Air, Through which the sun walks burning without beams!*—another image made out of scientific knowledge. The "serenest Air" is outside the earth's atmosphere: serene because it is so thin that it has no apparent motion; and because the air is so thin, it does not diffuse the sun's light as beams (the sun would therefore be seen as an enormous star in night).] Prometheus no longer knows what his words were—after he hears the curse he says to the Earth, "Were these my words, O Parent?" (302)—for just as the motives of his defiance heretofore, hatred and desire for revenge, are dead and without memory (70-72), so is the expression of those emotions. In our contemporary parlance, he has suppressed the curse, which he uttered because "Grief for a while is blind, and so was mine" (304).

The four voices reply. There's much more art in the arrangement of the songs than if each voice had its whole say at once; that is, if the first and fifth stanzas, the second and sixth, and so on, had been put together—these pairs of stanzas are a unit in sense. As they stand there are two long, sustained lines, the four stanzaic parts of the first line suspended until their completion in the corresponding parts of the second line. The second line contrasts the fearful effect of the curse on the world with what the world's experience (bad enough) had been before the curse (74-106). [The Voices speak in an imagery out of science, which, as many of the scientific allusions that I shall give, were traced by Carl Grabo. The Second Voice: from the scientist Beccaria, lightning can "explode water into vapor." The Third Voice: so Newton, "Color resides not in the object but in its ability to absorb and to reflect certain of the air-refracted rays of light." The Fourth Voice: underground whirlwinds were thought to cause earthquakes. That the curse could make silent such destructive violence measures its fearfulness.]

The hills, the sky, the ocean cried "Misery" at hearing the terrible curse. The "dread words from Earth to Heaven" made both nature and man ("the pale nations") afraid of Jupiter's rage (99, 107-111). Prometheus, impatient with the Voices' memories, accuses the four voices of Earth's sons of scorning him in not echoing his voice, his curse, scorning him although it has been his will and suffering that have stood between Jove and their destruction (112-119). Why does the spirit that informs (gives form to, and so animates) the lawns and streams

100

not answer the Titan who checked the falsehood and force of Jove, the tyrant who fills their woods with groaning and enslaved humanity (120-129)? For fear of Jupiter they do not dare (130).

"Who dares?" Prometheus cries at large, and hears an inorganic voice, scarcely like sound, from which he can make out only that the Spirit is moving nearby with love. Earth asks how Prometheus who does not know the language of the dead, being immortal, can expect to hear the inorganic voice, that is, with understanding. Prometheus replies that she, a living spirit, interpret in the language of the living. She dare not speak the curse in the voice of the living lest Jupiter hear and tie her to a wheel of pain more torturing than the one she rolls on (the image is a striking conjunction of the myth of Ixion's wheel and the motion of the earth known to science). But, she reflects, Prometheus is more than God, and although the Gods cannot hear the voice of the dead, let him try (131-145). As the Earth speaks in that voice, Prometheus experiences "awful thoughts" (the curse) in his brain but they are too obscure for understanding; they move like dim shadows, rapid and thick; and he also experiences a strange emotion. It is a remarkable creation of images (146-149) that bring into our minds as real this twofold experience, mental and emotional, which no man has ever had. The Earth, still speaking inorganically, believes that she cannot reach him in "this tongue" (150). But Prometheus understands her now, even as she reflects inorganically that he cannot; her voice sounds so different, however, that he does not recognize it as hers, and so questions,

> And what art thou,
> O melancholy Voice? (149-152)

His question would make no sense if she had spoken in the language of the living. Realizing now that he can hear and understand, she replies inorganically and continues speaking so; and in her sense of freedom, Jupiter unable to hear, she lets loose unguarded speech. Through her veins made stony by the cold of Jupiter's sway (we have already seen cold associated with evil; later we shall see warmth associated with good), and stony also because of the nature of the physical earth's interior (veins being a common geologic metaphor)—through her veins

101

joy ran when Prometheus arose in rebellion. [There is ambiguity in "a spirit of keen joy" (158); it may simply be in apposition to "Joy ran" (156), or it may be in apposition to "thou" 157), Prometheus, who is like a cloud that will fertilize the earth with glory.] At his voice Earth's pining sons (Mountains, Springs, Air, Whirlwinds, as in line 113) lifted their faces in hope, and Jupiter grew pale with dread until his thunder chained the Titan. Then the inhabitants of the other worlds—the astronomer Sir William Herschel (1738-1822) believed that other worlds were inhabited, and there are modern astronomers who believe that there are a *million* such worlds—look at the destruction, horror and desolation that visit Earth after Prometheus is bound. In the desert wastes there are no clouds ("my wan breast was dry"), which are the brightest reflectors of light on the earth's sphere, and so the other worlds see her "light wane" (165). This scientific consistency (pointed out by Desmond King-Hele) gives structural strength to the image of the earth as a living organism. The desolation is aggravated by hate, a contagion infecting the "thin air," her breath, that is needed clear by living things. [Adam Walker, a popular lecturer on science whom Shelley heard at Syon House Academy and at Eton, in his *Familiar Philosophy* described air as "thin" and as "exhaled from the earth."] But here Shelley is guilty of a flaw in his characterization of Earth: it is out of character for her to understand that hate is a contagion, for still in "secret joy" she treasures the curse (152-186). [The "inarticulate people of the dead" (183) are inarticulate only to the living; they too, because they suffer or have suffered under Jupiter's evil is the implication, preserve the treasured curse.] Prometheus implores that his mother, Earth, who gives some comfort to all living, suffering beings, deny him not his own words (186-190).

Now, when Earth says that they—she and the seas and mountains and others—"hope these dreadful words, But dare not speak them" (185-186), she must mean that they hope for the fulfillment of the curse in the living world but dare not speak it in that world. It is a natural enough tangent in her thought while she speaks inorganically. In response to Prometheus who has a deep need to know his words, Earth says "They shall be told" (191), because there is no impediment now that he has succeeded in understanding the language of the dead.

102

That the Magus Zoroaster saw his own image is human testimony to the reality of the underworld. [198: *shadows,* phantasms or spirits; 200-203: in the eternity of the underworld there exist also what the minds of men bring into being.] The magi were the "wise men" of the Medes and the Persians; the Persian Zoroaster lived about 1000 B.C. Zoroastrians believed that the power of good would ultimately destroy the power of evil, and foresaw a great deliverer who would bring the world to universal peace. Although only Zoroaster among men ever reached knowledge of the underworld—the most difficult, the most impenetrable knowledge for the human mind—his intellectual power measures what the human mind can become; and Zoroaster's knowledge of reality and eternity gives authority to his prophecy of a great deliverer.

Now Prometheus, the "type of the highest perfection of moral and intellectual nature," is the only living spirit other than Earth (whose nature is dual, organic and inorganic) who can converse with the underworld's inhabitants. To divert Jupiter's wrath to vacant shadow, Earth has Prometheus summon a phantasm (191-218). [212: *mightier Gods* refers only to Hades, the god of the underworld, and to Typhon, the hundred-headed giant who withstood all the gods until Jupiter blasted his strength with lightning and imprisoned him beneath Aetna.] Since the Gods cannot hear the language of the dead, what revenge can Earth fear from Jupiter if a phantasm from the world of death speaks? It is not that her own fears of Jupiter are so great that they confuse her mind; rather, her fears interpret for her. Jupiter has a powerful mind, the gift of Prometheus (II. iv. 44), and will know well enough from the appearance of his phantasm (which Ione and Panthea see) and from the words of those speaking the language of the living what has happened. As it will turn out, Jupiter will react not with wrath but with a sense of triumph; like Earth, he will think that Prometheus has weakened, and he will release the Furies to tear from the Titan the knowledge that will make Jupiter eternally the supreme power in the universe.

The Earth can command the phantasms in the world of the dead, and says that any ghost Prometheus calls shall utter the curse, that any ghost "must reply" (215). The Phantasm called confirms her power:

> Why have the secret powers of this strange world
> Driven me, a frail and empty phantom, hither
> On direst storms? (240-242)

The "hither" and "this strange world" (strange to the Phantasm) make the "secret powers" those of the living world.

Prometheus calls to the Phantasm of Jupiter to appear so that nothing evil may pass his own lips or those of anything resembling him, that is, of his "own ghost" (211); he does so because words have power, they are an act. (218-221)

The imaginative connection between the worlds of the living and the dead exists in folklore and in such different great minds as Homer and Lucretius; the connection possesses a meaning in human experience, a response of intuition to the universe. And the myth makes its suggestions to the modern mind: our conscious and unconscious lives are the two worlds, with living experience which has been suppressed as shadows in our brain becoming vivid although unsubstantial through secret causes; or the archetypes fixed in the memory of the race starting into speech and motion in an individual mind.

Ione and Panthea, daughters of Ocean like Asia, who watch near Prometheus for their sister's sake, as a chorus speak of the Phantasm's approach. Ione, her wings folded over her ears and crossed over her eyes, is the softer of the two, and speaks in a more delicate music; Panthea, steadily listening and regarding, interprets to Ione's fears: the natural forces (underground whirlwinds were thought to cause earthquakes, and earthquakes can cause fire and cleave mountains; scientists now say that rocks slipping underground set up enormous sound waves that make the earth quake) are the "direst storms" (242) that drive the Phantasm. There are terror and power in his figure, and Panthea's last two lines in their psychological insight measure her understanding (222-239).

The Phantasm wonders what "unaccustomed sounds" are on his lips, "unlike the voice" with which his "pallid race hold talk In darkness" (242-245). *Voice* here means "language," synonymous with *sounds,* which are "words"—the Phantasm speaks in the world of the living about matters the dead hold no converse on, therefore in other language.

Prometheus commands the Phantasm to utter the curse, and Earth calls on her children to "Rejoice to hear" although they cannot echo the curse for fear of revenge (246-253). As the Phantasm speaks the curse, his gestures and looks are those of Prometheus (258-260), which tell Jupiter what is being said. The first two stanzas express the defiance of Prometheus; the second two are the curse. The defiance begins with full knowledge of what Jupiter will do to Prometheus and to the humanity he loves "while" (for the limited although long time that) the God "must reign" (262-281).

> Ay, do thy worst. Thou art omnipotent. (272)

—"Omnipotent" only in the sense of physically irresistible during his reign.

> O'er all things but thyself I gave thee power,
> And my own will. (273-274)

Jupiter, having no power over himself, faces an unbridled interior enemy, like the untamed energies of Freud's id, whose nature is destructive of self as of others. Prometheus is free in the moral world for Jupiter cannot subdue his will. The power that Jupiter has, Prometheus gave in the revolution against Saturn, his forethought not equal to Jupiter's bad faith. The curse would transform the God's omnipotence to pain, his agony to be infinite, clinging to him like that poisoned garment that destroyed Hercules; the torture that the curse would clasp the God in is worse than the Titan's, which is finite. The power of the curse is to make Jupiter heap evil deeds on his soul and then, like Milton's Satan, be "damned, beholding good." His "Ill deeds," like good, are as "infinite as is the universe" (293-294)—evil cannot be expunged from existence, but can be cast out to "self-torturing solitude" (295). The image of "burning gold" clinging to Jupiter's brain (291) is a symbol of self; "Self, of which money is the visible incarnation . . . [is the] Mammon of the world," wrote Shelley in *A Defence of Poetry*. Jupiter's fall, although it lag in coming, will come in the hour that will expose what he is (272-301). That the casting out of evil from nature and humanity will come slowly Shelley well understood. In his prose *On the Punishment of Death* he wrote of "that intertexture of good and evil with which nature seems to have clothed every form of individual existence" and in *Essay on Christianity* wrote that "Good and evil subsist in so intimate a union that few situations of human affairs can be affirmed to contain either of the principles in an unconnected state." Mary was wrong in writing in her Note to *Prometheus Unbound,* fifteen years after Shelley died, that he believed "evil is not inherent in the system of creation, but an accident that might be expelled"; in nothing extant that Shelley wrote does he express such a belief.

Prometheus' passion for revenge was terrible, as it is in a man. For a moment he is unwilling to believe that he spoke this curse; his mother confirms that the words were his (302). A changed moral being (although he implies no change in saying that the curse was owing to the grief that blinded him then—Shelley's psychology is subtle), the Titan repents (303-305). *This act changes the history of the universe.*

The Earth cries out her misery, thinking that Prometheus has weakened and surrendered; the voices of her two Echoes are like reverberations of despair. Nor does Ione understand the change; she thinks Prometheus is suffering "but some passing spasm" (314), and even as she speaks sees a Shape approach. Again Panthea interprets: it is Mercury; and when Ione questions her sister about the nine-headed, iron-winged monsters, Panthea announces that they are the Furies (306-334).—Jupiter thinks that this is the hour to tear the fateful knowledge from the Titan.—Ione is consistently thus the quicker to see; Panthea, the maturer in knowledge. These aspects of their character fit them for their choral role.

With dark power Shelley evokes horror:

> *First Fury.* Ha! I scent life!
> *Second Fury.*   Let me but look into his eyes!
> *Third Fury.* The hope of torturing him smells like a heap
>   Of corpses to a death-bird after battle. (338-340)

The First Fury baits Mercury, the Son of Maia [daughter of Atlas, who was a brother to Prometheus, Maia was a virgin companion of Artemis; she was taken by Jove in mountainous Arcadia, where Mercury was born], with the cruel whim of Jupiter. Mercury, no weakling, orders them back hungry to their underworld places, and he summons other monsters [346: *Geryon,* a Spanish king with three bodies whose magnificent oxen, guarded by a two-headed watchdog, ate human flesh; *Gorgon,* a female—with serpents for hair, wings, brazen claws, and enormous teeth—so ugly that whoever looked at her turned to stone; 347: *Chimaera,* a creature with a lion's head, a goat's body, and a dragon's hindpart, that belched fire; *Sphinx,* half woman, half winged lion, who plagued Thebes until Oedipus solved its riddle. The Sphinx consequently destroyed itself, and the Thebans made Oedipus their king by marrying him to their queen—but it was an incestuous marriage whose *unnatural love* polluted the city. After Oedipus' expulsion from the city, his two sons with *unnatural hate* (349) warred for rule of Thebes]. The hell-hounds come to heel (341-352).

To unwilling Prometheus, Mercury is unwillingly driven by Jupiter's will; and Mercury, a "realist" as we would say, advises the Titan against standing alone against the power of Jupiter, as is taught by the clear lamps, the sun and stars, which measure the "weary years From which there is no refuge." Let Prometheus escape "unimagined pains" by revealing the secret of Jupiter's overthrow (353-380). [In Greek myth the secret was that Jupiter would marry Thetis and their child would overthrow him.]

Prometheus knows that nothing good can be done for Jupiter, for "Evil minds Change good to their own nature," and again, "He who is evil can receive no good" (380-381, 389). Jupiter could preserve himself only by changing his evilness to good, but to give him that knowledge would give him nothing that he could profit from. With subtle and accurate psychology Prometheus reflects that Jupiter, incapable of gratitude (Prometheus gave him all he has), "but requites me for his own misdeed" (392). Jupiter would accept no submission but the "death-seal of mankind's captivity" (397). Those who submit to the brief omnipotence of Crime (time is brief measured against eternity) are secure because they will not be punished; vengeance will be no part of the new order (401-405).—By so much more must we admire the resistance of the good and their faith.—But the good do not have to wait for recompense in eternity. In the balance against their pains, better than the "voluptuous joy" of those who live with evil, is a mind within which "sits peace serene, As light in the sun, throned" (430-431), while those who give "benefits and meek submission" (378) to evil, to Jupiter, are "self-despising" (429). So we should like to think; but those who are successful in business, politics, war, or in any other arena where they may practice the infinite variety of evil, no matter what their practice, will not despise themselves. Only the failures despise themselves—only the failures and the good. [398: *the Sicilian's hair-suspended sword*, Dionysius the Sicilian Tyrant hung a sword by a horsehair over the head of Damocles as an emblem of how he, Dionysius, lived, which dispelled Damocles' visions of the Tyrant's happiness.]

Ione, although some scholars ascribe to her only the gift of keen sight and not the gift of understanding, here understands well that the lightning and thunder are Jupiter's work and that the terrible blackening wings, "hollow underneath, like death," are the Furies (432-442)—they are hollow because they are phantasms having no substance (447), and are like death because they are all-consuming. Prometheus' reaction to their foulness measures their spiritually corruptive power, the fascination of ugliness and evil:

> Methinks I grow like what I contemplate,
> And laugh and stare in loathsome sympathy. (450-451)

When they rejoice in being more hideous than they knew, and Prometheus wonders that anything can "exult in its deformity" (Shelley understood that even things human, like Count Cenci, can so exult), the reply to Prometheus is startling:

> The beauty of delight makes lovers glad,
> Gazing on one another: so are we.
> As from the rose which the pale priestess kneels
> To gather for her festal crown of flowers
> The aereal crimson falls, flushing her cheek,
> So from our victim's destined agony
> The shade which is our form invests us round,
> Else we are shapeless as our mother Night. (465-472)

In the structure of the similes the comparison is with contrasts; and the expressive force thereby, a powerful understatement, gives a revelation of the perversion of good. It is the agony of the tortured which gives Furies their shape, which is hollow.

In their threats the Furies imply that they will do worse than tear bone from bone and nerve from nerve, be worse than

> dread thought beneath thy brain,
> And foul desire round thy astonished heart (488-489)

—an index of the evil in all of us. The *astonished* heart is, ambiguously, surprised and stony.

These Furies in an incantation summon others that they need: those who take their mirth and joy from ruin on land and sea, from the bloody bed of multitudinous corpses; those who take their shapes from hatred, from un-love (in sexual unions answering only the senses), from untruth (in minds that can imagine a hell worse than its reality), from the cruelty of the fearful mind that makes others suffer the hell it imagines (495-520).

The summoned Furies come from war, from famine, from "conclaves stern and cold, Where blood with gold is bought and sold" [the contemporary allusion of *conclaves* is to the Congress of Vienna (see page 84)]; a Fury breaks off those who speak, for by revealing their nature and their work they would strengthen Prometheus in his purpose, and another Fury commands the tearing of the veil hiding the Titan's worst agonies (525-539).

The Furies expose a dire misery that the pale stars shine on; and they laugh at the clear knowledge that Prometheus gave to man, for these perishing waters of knowledge cannot allay the feverish thirst they created, the hope, love, doubt, and desire which are forever consuming mankind. To allay this thirst Jesus—not Christ—came, smiling on the bloody earth. But after his death his words were put to poisonous rather than to healing work by Christianity, "the faith he kindled," and looking on that faith's destructiveness his ghost cries out in despair. The past ages crowding on Prometheus do not cancel each other's voice, but each reminds [561: *remembers* is used in its active sense] the Titan distinctly of its feverish misery, mankind having knowledge but living without "truth, peace and pity."

> And the future is dark, and the present is spread
> Like a pillow of thorns for thy slumberless head. (540-563)

The image of the thorns likens Prometheus to Jesus in their suffering, and that image is sustained:

109

Drops of bloody agony flow
From his white and quivering brow. (564-565)

Then the Furies close the tercet with a line shaking with horrible, satisfied ironic laughter:

Grant a little respite now. (566)

The respite is a vision of the French Revolution [567: *disenchanted,* no longer under the spell of slavery], its high hopes and the despair in its failure; more, it is a universal vision of what men could do (567-572) and what they are doing (572-577).

The softer Ione has dared not look at the torture, but hears the Titan's "dreadful groan." Panthea "looked forth twice, but will no more" at scenes of torture and death; she cannot bear to see more grief (578-593).

The Fury has used Jesus as an emblem of the worse than uselessness of resistance, and the Titan can hardly bear the suffering of Jesus. "The wise, the mild, the lofty, and the just," Prometheus sees, are hated by priests and are "hunted by foul lies [609: *hooded ounces,* blindfolded leopardlike beasts trained to hunt in the mountains of Central Asia] from their heart's home," which is love; or are chained to each other in prison, the dead left in their chains; or are burned while the public laughs. But the unheard, unseen evils are the worse. The Fury speaks out of its hellish knowledge:

In each human heart terror survives
The ravin it has gorged. (594-619)

This dread may be ambiguously interpreted. Either terror survives the child's innocence, the prey it has gorged on, in the grown man or woman; or terror, gorging itself on its prey, the human heart, survives from generation to generation, so that the loftiest people irrationally fear what they know is false—in modern terms this terror is in certain respects the superego. Freud observed that in the upbringing of children parents "are severe and exacting. They have forgotten the difficulties of their own childhood, and are glad to be able to identify themselves fully at last with their own parents, who in their day subjected them to such restraints. The result is that the superego of the child is not really built up on the model of

110

the parents, but on that of the parents' superego; it takes over the same content, it becomes the vehicle of tradition and of all the agelong values which have been handed down in this way from generation to generation."

But whereas for Freud the superego is the "origin of conscience," for Shelley the custom and consequent hypocrisy forced on the mind make it a temple where outworn ("agelong" in Freud) values are worshiped. The sources of the terror controlling the mind are in many evils, the external ones being chiefly operative in politics and religion, as in the visions tormenting Prometheus. The divisions among us are tragic, and give the rule to evil:

> The good want power, but to weep barren tears.
> The powerful goodness want: worse need for them.
> The wise want love; and those who love want wisdom;
> And all best things are thus confused to ill.

The clause that the Fury concludes with, "they know not what they do," in echoing Luke 23: 24 exposes a condition of man's pain (620-631).

When goodness, wisdom, power, and love are no longer divided, man's estate will be at its best. At this moment in the drama Prometheus, who is wise and good, Asia, who is love, and Demogorgon, who is powerful, are not conjoined; but when Prometheus expresses pity to the Fury who has spoken these lines for those its words do not torture, pity for those who can live at ease with the evil of the world, he triumphs. Neither hate, fear, nor indifference makes his mind, his soul, vulnerable; in his moral nature pity, love, and justice are triune, perfect. The Fury, knowing the Titan thereby invincible, vanishes (632-634). The spiritual triumph will bring the world's great and radical change.

Prometheus is wracked with pain, seeing the works of Jupiter [642: *This,* This which you do; 645: *they* has "sights" in 643 as its antecedent; 647: *Nature's sacred watchwords* are "Truth, liberty, and love" in 651;654: *Tyrants,* the contemporary allusion is to the Quadruple Alliance, which became the Quintuple Alliance with the admission of France in September 1818, the very month that Shelley was composing this act]. The Earth summons fair spirits from human thought, their home, to cheer her son (656-659). [661: *Its,* the antecedent is "thought";

111

662: *twilight realm*, the "dim caves" of line 559]. The fair spirits come just as the angels came after the temptation of Jesus (Matthew 4:11 and Mark 1:13) and as the angel of the Lord came after the trial of Job (40: 6).

Panthea's and Ione's couplets, beginning with a half rhyme, are a bridge to the Chorus of Spirits. In their natural images heralding the fair spirits are joy and beauty; Panthea's spring image (665) for the spirits is an emblem of regeneration (663-671). The Spirits—"guides and guardians" of evil-oppressed humanity—are from "unremembered ages," from Eternity, in which thought participates; they live in human thought, whether dim or bright, which permeates all but unknowable death, and from human thought they bear their prophecy (672-691), which they make explicit in their last two choruses (780-800). The first spirit sings of the war against false creeds and dictatorship; the second, of a hero of love; the third, of a philosopher kindled to "Pity, eloquence, and woe"; the fourth, of a poet who creates "Forms more real than living man"— three men who are builders of the new world (708-751).

Then Ione and Panthea speak, preparing us for two other spirits; it is Ione who is given voice by their beauty, while Panthea's words are drowned in tears. The shapes come like doves from the ends of the earth; they are "nurslings"—an echo of "Nurslings of immortality" in line 749—of the "all-sustaining air," the atmosphere of human thought inhabited by the fair spirits that sing to Prometheus. These fifth and sixth spirits are Pity and Hope [II. iv. 160: "dove-like eyes of hope"; III. iii. 46: "dove-eyed pity"]. Their "despair Mingled with love and dissolved in sound" is the despair of pity mingled with the love of hope and then dissolved in the sound which is "the soul of Love" (705) [760: *grain*, a synonym for "color," to which the next line is in apposition] (752-762).

The Chorus of Spirits ask whether Pity and Hope have seen the form of Love, for they seem to reflect his beauty and light. And, indeed, Hope saw that "planet-crested Shape" [Love crested with the morning star, which is Goodness ("the Morning Star . . . the great Spirit of Good," *The Revolt of Islam*, I. 356, 373)]. But even as Love scattered the "joy of life" and "paved the world with light," Ruin worked its desolation— just as the Crucifixion and the Church destroyed Jesus and withered his love and truth, just as the failure of the French

112

Revolution smothered the world. Hope wandered over the world dispirited until the assuring smile of Prometheus transformed her sadness brought by the world's wrong to the gladness of remembering the great age to come, when ruin will not follow love (763-771).

But Pity thinks that desolation with subtle fraud cruelly makes the best and gentlest of humanity nurture hopes and dream of joy only to wake to the reality of pain [the "shadow," or manifestation, of the monster they mistake for love], as Prometheus does (772-779). The Chorus of Spirits do not think the discouraged utterance of Pity true. The visions *are* of Love, and although in the world now (as the Furies showed) love brings on ruin that swiftly and wildly and indiscriminately destroys all living things, Prometheus shall overpower this deathless horseman (deathless because evil is an eternal principle of the universe). The Spirits are certain in their knowledge: moral law and natural law are alike: just as natural signs are the sure prophecy of spring, so when "Wisdom, Justice, Love, and Peace . . . struggle to increase" in human thought (the "atmosphere" in 790, as in 676), they will invincibly transform the moral world. The two similes, the natural signs for the herdsmen and the shepherds, are set within the expression of the moral law as though the natural springtime would blossom into intellectual beauty (780-800), the symbol becoming reality.

Ione and Panthea tell us that the Spirits are gone, only a sense of them remaining like the responses to music which echo through the soul after the music has stopped; their rhyming couplets are a bridge from the choruses to the blank verse expressive of heaviness of Prometheus' spirit. Despite the beauty of these spirits from human thought, says Prometheus, their hope is vain; it is otherwise only with the hope that is love. And Asia who is Love, the chalice for his being's overflow that else had spilled to waste (the image is duple: of their union, and of a sacramental wine for mankind), is far away; without her he cannot be what it is his "destiny to be, The saviour and strength of suffering man," nor can he, being what he is, "sink into the original gulf of things." In his spiritual exhaustion—such exhaustion is a characteristic experience, according to psychological studies, on the road of transformation to a better state of mind— Prometheus can only think,

113

There is no agony, and no solace left;
Earth can console, Heaven can torment, no more. (801-820)

Panthea turns his mind to her love, and Prometheus begins to emerge from his spiritual exhaustion. Her love, her hope, is now a knowledge of the reality within their grasp. No longer must she watch Prometheus. His triumph has made possible union again with Asia, and Panthea goes with those tidings to her sister. Asia, waiting, has transformed the desolate and frozen place of her exile to a lovely valley, just as Love can transform the desolate and frozen heart; but her transforming presence must at last fade if her being is not united to Prometheus (821-833). We may incorporate the meaning of that in human experience: love, a spiritual power, needs the mind, or soul, of man as much as man needs love.

PROMETHEUS UNBOUND: ACT II

Scene i

The winter intervened between the writing of the first act and Shelley's shaking off his suffering; the Roman spring drenching his spirits with new life gave him the power to compose again—in an incredible burst, two acts in less than a month.

Twice in the first act the spring was anticipated in images that were symbols of regeneration (by Panthea, 664-666; by the Chorus, 790-800)—as Newman White writes, "not the literal, physical spring, but the mysterious invincible power of which spring was the only adequate symbol." Now Asia speaks, impassioned, to the springtime of the year descending,

> Like genius, or like joy which riseth up
> As from the earth, clothing with golden clouds
> The desert of our life. (10-12)

[3: *horny*, hardened because long without tears] The image shifts from the springtime to the day's sunrise, a reality which Shelley has seen steadily and caught to the life, and which is an objective correlative for the soul's sunrise (1-27). The stunning passage ends with the coming of Panthea [26: *Aeolian*, her wings make music like the harp in the trees blown on by

Aeolus, the god of the winds; *sea-green*, as a daughter of Ocean]. She is late because the ecstasy of her dream-union made her faint (35-36, 79-81). For Asia, Panthea is a manifestation ("shadow") of the soul of Prometheus—"the soul," says Asia, "by which I live" (31); for Prometheus, Panthea is the shadow of Asia (70). Through Panthea they have conversed, Panthea suspended in sleep, or trance, to be able to sustain their "wordless converse," for she failed beneath the music of their communing. When Panthea was "dissolved Into the sense with which love talks," her rest was troubled and yet sweet— better so than to be awake, "full of care and pain." Before the Titan's fall her sleep had been untroubled, when she had known only love and not woe. The intense image of young Ione and her in each other's arms (they still sleep so) reflects sensuous not sensual experience (38-55), as the ecstasy of Panthea's dream-union with Prometheus shows.

Panthea dreamed twice, each dream a meaning passing through her to Asia. The only moments for these dreams were during the Furies' worst torture and Prometheus' spiritual triumph (I. 594-634); it is as though even then the new life was beginning in depths of the Titan's mind beneath consciousness. In her dream his wound-worn body fell from Prometheus, and his form—his essence, his godhead—made the night radiant. The immortal shape of his godhead, although an overpowering light, was a shadow in comparison to the love which came from him like an atmosphere of fire—the scientific similes that follow come in a most unpredictable place and are wonderfully successful—absorbing her as the sun the dew. Her union sounds mystical, an experience with ultimate reality:

> I saw not, heard not, moved not, only felt
> His presence flow and mingle through my blood
> Till it became his life, and his grew mine,
> And I was thus absorbed. (79-82)

After the ecstasy, individual being returned ("was condensed") and as her thought focussed ("gathered") she could hear the sounds of his voice but could only make out Asia's name.

Then comes an inset: Ione has been awakened to a desire that she does not understand, a consequence of sympathy with Panthea just as a tuning fork will vibrate with another:

                    when just now
We kissed, I felt within thy parted lips
The sweet air that sustained me, and the warmth
Of the life-blood, for loss of which I faint,
Quivered between our intertwining arms. (102-106)

The "sweet air" within Panthea's "parted lips" suggests the atmosphere of love that came from the "passion-parted lips" of Prometheus, and "the warmth Of the life-blood" makes us remember that Prometheus' presence flowed and mingled through Panthea's blood (57-106).

Asia, impatient for the "wordless converse" of Prometheus, which is absent from Panthea's words, must look into Panthea's eyes, and there sees her heaven:

> *Asia.* Thine eyes are like the deep, blue, boundless heaven
> Contracted to two circles underneath
> Their long, fine lashes; dark, far, measureless,
> Orb within orb, and line through line inwoven. (114-117)

Eyes become "deep and intricate from the workings of the mind," Shelley believed. The mind of Prometheus is at work in Panthea, like an action of occult science. As Panthea is a daughter of Ocean, a symbol of eternity, it is fitting that the infinite be in her eyes.

[This image of the union of the finite and the infinite expresses a concept that the Romantic imagination seized as truth, a truth at the center of this drama, that the finite human condition can become one with the infinite, that the real and the ideal are not inseparable. Hoxie Fairchild has defined romanticism as "the endeavor . . . to achieve . . . that illusioned view of the universe and of human life which is produced by an imaginative fusion of the familiar and the strange, the known and the unknown, the real and the ideal, the finite and the infinite, the material and the spiritual, the natural and the supernatural"—an excellent definition if "illusioned" is taken not in the pejorative sense that Fairchild intended but as Wordsworth and Shelley used the word. There are like fusions of "the finite and the infinite, the material and the spiritual" in Buddhism and Christianity. The experience is the coalescence, the becoming one, of sensory-intellectual consciousness and mystical consciousness. In Buddhism the two

116

states of consciousness are samsara and Nirvana. In Christianity the state of fusion is sometimes known as "the unitive state."]

Looking at the smiling Prometheus in Panthea's eyes, Asia understands her sister's dream:

> Say not those smiles that we shall meet again
> Within that bright pavilion which their beams
> Shall build o'er the waste world? (124-126)

That reunion of Prometheus and Asia is the dream's promise, and we must understand that the "bright pavilion" is her destination; Demogorgon's cave to which Panthea's other dream (also the "converse" of Prometheus) now will lead, is a way station in the universe. In Demogorgon's cave Love shall do what only now can be done—Prometheus having perfected himself through suffering—and then take the chariot of the hour of the new order, the hour of her reunion with Prometheus. [135: *burst*, burst open; *lightning-blasted*, Jove's destructive power; 136: *When*, when the buds burst open; *Scythian wilderness*, the scene of *Prometheus Bound*—Jove's evil cannot forever control the universe; the blossoms, even while being killed by the frost, tell the way to his overthrow. Sound, image and idea are a marvellous unity.] Asia also has her own dream that will lead to Demogorgon, as though Prometheus and Asia now act from a single impulse. For Asia the dream-summons is on the face and in the voice of natural beauty—on the shadows of the white morning clouds, athwart the mountain; on each herb; in the music of the pines—as well as in Panthea's eyes (108-162). In Asia's mind are the echoes of what she has seen and heard in the prophetic spring imagery (as the "new-bladed grass, Just piercing the dark earth").

The natural echoes are also intelligences, or spirits as Asia says (171)—they are a fusion of the material and the spiritual, drawing Asia and Panthea on their way by "Demogorgon's mighty law" (II. ii. 43); their fusion supports Newman White's interpretation that the mighty law is Spring as a symbol of invincible power, an image used by the spirits from human thought in expressing the prophecy that begins and ends in Prometheus and used also by Asia in her first, great lines. The Echoes summon Asia, Child of Ocean (170) through "caverns hollow, Where the forest spreadeth" (175-176)— i.e., "the Forest, intermingled with Rocks and Caverns" that "Asia and Pan-

117

thea pass into" (stage directions, Scene ii). They will pass through deep noontide darkness in the caverns (181) to the unknown world where Demogorgon sleeps, whom only Asia, Love, can awaken (190-194). In the songs of the Echoes are caverns of calm and beauty (180-184, 199-201) and, at the end, a place where violence created disorder, the effect on the earth of the separation of Prometheus and Asia (the Earth speaks of what happened after the chaining of Prometheus in I. 165-178), who are to "commingle now," the Echoes promise (202-206). In the imagery of their songs the mountains and caverns gave a sense in Shelley's time of a sublimity or majesty not given to us. As Coleridge wrote in a letter, "rocks or waterfalls, mountains or caverns, give me the sense of sublimity or majesty"; and in the ephemeral literature of the day we come upon that theme again and again (e.g., *Annual Register*, 25: 55, 35: 294-295, and 36: 313-316; *Universal Magazine*, 94: 337-339, 95: 78).

Scene ii

The choruses interpret the journey they watch; Asia and Panthea are silent in this scene while they follow the Echoes. A semichorus of spirits first sing of the dark, calm, natural beauty of the forest, piercable only by a "cloud of dew." The cloud of dew is the spiritual power of thought (the "dews of thought" are in the Prologue of *Hellas*), giving a treasure, a pearl, to each flower of poetry, the laurel. (Poetry is the beautiful, the true, the good, in whatever form these are made known—in language, music, architecture, in laws, civil society, religion.) But there is transience in this forest of earthly existence: as the cloud drifts along, the frail wind-flower bends and fades. That transience is echoed by the brief visitation of Intellectual Beauty, the star scattering "drops of golden light," which make the surrounding gloom divine even while we are on the earth, the "mossy ground" (1-23). The divine gloom is an anticipation of Demogorgon's like gloom.

Another semichorus then sings of love—the passionate experience of the nightingales—and of the overflowing music creating joy (24-40) [28: *dying*, the image is sexual but the ecstasy has its source in musical not in physical experience; 36: *when*, at the time that another nightingale "lifts on high The wings of

118

the weak melody"; 37: *rush of wings,* the wings of melody have become strong again].

Other music plays there, the music of the Echoes—of our dreams, or visions which are intelligences; this music is motive power and compass for Asia and Panthea and, indeed, for all spirits (including those of the human mind) on their way to eternity. The music does its work just as streams made strong with the spring thaw bear "inland boats" (a symbol for souls) to the Ocean (41-47), which is the "Ocean Of universal life" (*The Revolt of Islam,* VI. xxix). The act closes with similar imagery. Here and at the act's close the Ocean is also interpretable as the One, the Eternal, of *Adonais,* the Spirit that "Sweeps through the dull dense world" compelling all things to "its own likeness, as each mass may bear" (xliii). [The Ocean is not the One of the great mystic Plotinus, as it is sometimes interpreted. For him the One is the source from which the world flows and to which the soul desires to return, but his One, although Plotinus sometimes called it God, has no personality and no consciousness. In the Upanishads, that part of Hindu sacred literature which speculates on the nature of man and the universe, rivers are individual selves and the ocean the Universal Self, which is pure consciousness and not a person; the Universal Self is the One which is common to all mystical experience. In Hindu mysticism and in Plotinus, the One and the world (both animate and inanimate) are a single substance; the multiplicity of the world has been differentiated from the One. In Christianity, God and the world have separate existence; indeed, in the philosophy of Western religious mystical experience, the physical world is generally regarded as a reality.]

The music begins as a gentle sound come unaware upon spirits (or persons), awakening love, the destined "soft emotion" [in the *Symposium* Agathon says that Love is the "author of all soft affection"]. Then, according to "those who saw"—which sounds very much like Milton's "Some say": the poet is pretending an authority to stand in place of his own—a wind steams up from the earth and lifts their wings, while they think that they are being moved by their own desires. Most commentators interpret this passage as an expression of Necessity, wrongly I think. The "wind" (53) rising betokens the spring, as it often does in Romantic imagery. The wind, like the music, is a visible manifestation of the "law" (43); the wind is to the spirits, once the impulse (which comes as music, "a gentle sound," and which becomes a strong wind, "storm of sound") awakens the destined emotion, what the mountain-thaw is to the streams ("destined" does not mean what *must* happen, as necessity does; destiny is what does happen, or what is envisioned as belonging to a person although not neces-sarily to be his). The "sweet desires" of love do not give power; rather, love brings invincible power for the soul into motion. The power is Demogorgon's, expressed in his law. The power gathers—the music, the storm of sound, acts like a strong wind, "sucked up and hurrying," and becomes visible like clouds—and bears (heads) to the mountain of Demogorgon, the spirits following swiftly (48-63).

The listening Fauns begin to speak. Not in the original ver-sion of the scene, they were a profoundly right afterthought. The Fauns, in their awareness that Prometheus will "make the earth One brotherhood" (94-95) of which they will be part, give a dimension to the play that would not otherwise exist; men would be wrong as characters in this play, and so the Fauns take their place. Their rightness is intensified by their symbolic value: in religious experience they represent the fusion of divinity and worshipper.

The first Faun, who sounds the younger, wonders where the spirits live, whose music they have heard—often heard but never seen by them, although they know the forest intimately. The spirits, Grabo suggests, are perhaps the elements of mat-ter. The second Faun, the more learned, speaking on the authority of "those more skilled in spirits" [the scientist Eras-mus Darwin in his *Botanic Garden*, and the scientific lecturer Adam Walker in *A System of Familiar Philosophy*] gives a scientific account but translates the scientific to a faery world justly praised for its pellucid beauty and natural magic. The imaginative translation retains a vivid physical immediacy, al-though the scientific account is outdated [the bubbles are hy-drogen released by the heat of the sun from the plants at the bottom of the lakes; the inflammable hydrogen bursts into meteors in the air (all aerial phenomena were "meteors" in Shelley's day, and shooting stars were not generally thought to come to the earth's atmosphere from outside) or ignites as will-o-the-wisps]. Also the more philosophical, the second Faun does not want to "stay to speak" lest Silenus [the Satyr who taught Dionysus; he had the gift of prophecy] be cross-tempered at their failure to milk his goats by noon and not sing to them philosophic and prophetic songs, which give more delight than the secrets of nature, songs that charm even the nightingales to silence (63-97).

Scene iii

Asia and Panthea are on the mountain of Demogorgon; a chasm is the gateway,

> Whence the oracular vapour is hurled up
> Which lonely men drink wandering in their youth,
> And call truth, virtue, love, genius, or joy,
> That maddening wine of life. (4-7)

The values are eternal values, coming as they do from the realm of eternity. The men are lonely because all men whose lives are so intensely inspirited are lonely (the word is proleptic, a rhetorical device that Shelley uses again and again), so rare are they. Their madness, their intoxication, metaphorically expresses the intensity of their endowment; the image is religious, like the madness and intoxication of the Maenads worshipping Dionysus [9: *Evoe! Evoe!* is their joyous shout], a god who dies and whose rebirth brings the springtime of the world. The voice of these men will contagiously change the world, transmitting truth, virtue, love, genius, and joy (1-10). Scientific as well as religious imagery gives expression to that revolutionary change, as G. M. Matthews discovered. The entrance to Demogorgon's cave is like a volcano's chasm (3): when seawater made its way into the caves of volcanoes, contemporary science believed, there were eruptions together with earthquakes, mephitic vapors, volcanic storm and lightning—and destruction. The sea goddesses in the cave (a symbol for the human mind) will awaken power, and Demogorgon, the awakened power, in a terrifying struggle will destroy Jupiter's dictatorship.

When Asia speaks, it is in a human aspect rather than as Love or Intellectual Beauty. Responding with lyric intensity to the earth's beauty, Asia spontaneously says that if the earth is a manifestation of Intellectual Beauty, she could worship that spiritual power and its creation, earth, although even if like earth it could not expunge evil (that it cannot is not asserted, nor is it asserted that natural beauty is cause enough for worship). Involuntarily her heart adores (11-17)—that act of worship, her exclamation "Wonderful!" suggests, was summoned up by Intellectual Beauty. Then comes a splendid vision culminating in the avalanche which is an emblem of the triumph of a great truth: the vision of the earth's beauty will become everywhere a reality when the great truth is loosened by Prometheus—all this is in her mind as she approaches Demogorgon (18-42) [18: *vapour*, not the oracular vapor hurled up from the chasm, but the mist rolling toward them which makes Asia's brain dizzy as they watch; 39: *heaven-defying minds*, the contemporary allusion is to the French philosophers]. Nearly all the natural elements in this imaginative experience Shelley had witnessed in his tours and visits.

The sea of mist breaks at their feet, like ocean around men shipwrecked on an island; the mist sweeps over Asia's eyes and makes her brain dizzy (43-50)—these images are an anticipation of the "cloudy strife Of Death and Life" in the first stanza of the song of Spirits, who come out of the mist (50-53), a stanza that summons Asia and Panthea on a passage to reality [59-60: the *veil* gives us perception only of semblances, of "things which seem"; the *bar* divides us from reality, "things which . . . are"]. This song conceives Demogorgon on his "remotest throne" as greater than Asia, rightly so as Asia is in her human aspect. The sound that has brought them to the entrance in the mountain now like a whirlpool takes them down, drawn to the throne with a force curiously expressed in images that culminate in destruction or ill except for the last, magnetic image [66-67: the order in these similes is reversed: the vapor draws the lightning (explicable by meteorology of the day), and the taper the moth]. Such destruction or ill happens in the temporal world; the force in the images is of contrast; no destruction or ill but a treasured spell awaits Asia (88) at the reality of Demogorgon's throne in the eternal world. In the gray abysses that Asia and Panthea descend, Demogorgon is the "One pervading" existence; there no air acts as a prism, that is, life refracts no colors, nor is there the white radiance of heaven nor the gloom of earth.

122

Although light and darkness are images that mystics use, the One, they insist, is nonsensuous and nonintellectual; the experience has in it nothing of the colors, of the multiplicity, of the world, has neither light nor darkness. Mystics use the images of light and darkness to express a paradox: the darkness expresses the emptying of the mind, making it void of multiplicity so that there is only unity, pure consciousness, the light. The darkness *is* the light. Dionysius the Areopagite, a Christian mystic of the fifth century A.D. or later, spoke of God as "the dazzling obscurity." The abyss, too, is a mystical image, which Jan van Ruysbroeck for one, the great Flemish mystic of the fourteenth century, used to express the Infinite. In religious mysticism the Eternal and the Infinite are names for God.

During their descent Asia and Panthea are bound by the spirits (90-92); the binding implicitly symbolizes a mystic trance, in which Asia confronts Eternity. In that confrontation is the spell treasured for Asia (88):

> This is the day, which down the void abysm
> At the Earth-born's spell yawns for Heaven's despotism,
>   And Conquest is dragged captive through the deep:
> Love, from its awful throne of patient power
> In the wise heart, from the last giddy hour
>   Of dread endurance, from the slippery, steep,
> And narrow verge of crag-like agony, springs
> And folds over the world its healing wings. (IV. 554-561)

In lines 83-87 the light in the similes for the spell is in each a symbol of love and intellectual beauty:

> Like veiled lightning asleep,
> Like the spark nursed in embers,
> The last look Love remembers,
> Like a diamond, which shines
> On the dark wealth of mines,
> A spell is treasured but for thee alone.
>   Down, down! (83-89)

The lightning will leap into life from its cloud-veil; the spark (to which the "last look" is in apposition) will flame into life; the diamond will irradiate the wealth of life. The binding

123

explicitly symbolizes a willing submission to a moral condition, the meekness of love:

> Resist not the weakness,
> Such strength is in meekness
> That the Eternal, the Immortal,
> Must unloose through life's portal
> The snake-like Doom coiled underneath his throne
> By that alone. (93-98)

"By that alone" (*that* is meekness) in its brevity and place makes sharply defined the only way to change the world: in his meekness Prometheus recalled the curse, wanting "no living thing to suffer pain"; in meekness is the strength of compassion and Love (43-98).

[There are sometimes contradictions, or rather shifts, in imagery. The snake in the "snake-like Doom" is here a symbol of Demogorgon's eternal sway of goodness (in *The Revolt of Islam*, Canto I, the snake symbolizes the principle of good in the universe), but at the end of *Prometheus Unbound* the "serpent" is "Destruction's strength" (IV. 567, 564), or Jupiter. And there "Eternity," says Demogorgon, is the "Mother of many acts and hours" (565-566), while here "the Eternal, the Immortal" is the masculine Demogorgon (it is "his throne" in line 97), and Demogorgon later calls himself Eternity (III. i. 52). At the drama's end Eternity has an "infirm hand," which is in no wise the "weakness" here, that may not bar forever the serpent in its pit.

In Plato's *Timaeus* the power Demiourgos, who is beneficent, made the world from matter, imitating what existed in idea, and then gave rule to the gods he also made. In later tradition Demiourgos became a terrifying power, and nearly a thousand years after Plato he was the supreme god Demogorgon. In Boccaccio, Demogorgon has Eternity as wife, perhaps the source of that Shape's androgyny—in *Prometheus Unbound* masculine in the aspect of Power, feminine in the aspect of Eternity.]

Scene iv

The veil hiding whatever sits on the black throne falls (1-2); Asia and Panthea are at the culmination of their mystical

trance, time and matter falling away and Eternity confronted;
Eternity has conscious being and the sway of power as a living
Spirit,

> a mighty darkness
> Filling the seat of power, and rays of gloom
> Dart round, as light from the meridian sun.
> —Ungazed upon and shapeless; neither limb,
> Nor form, nor outline . . . (3-7)

Earlier in the act gloom was spoken of as divine (II. ii 22); "Un-
gazed upon" because the spirit imaged as shapeless darkness
cannot be perceived by the eye although it is felt (7). Darkness, as I have said, is a characteristic metaphor in mystical
writings. Dionysius the Areopagite writes of being led "to the
Ray of that divine Darkness which exceedeth all existence" in
the first chapter of his *Mystical Theology*, which he calls
"What Is the Divine Gloom?" I do not know that Shelley read
Dionysius, but mystics in diverse times and in diverse cultures,
with no knowledge of each other, have used similar images
and expressed similar concepts in trying to communicate their
experience.

Demogorgon speaks:

> Ask what thou wouldst know.

And Asia:

> What canst thou tell?

Although Asia has come to Demogorgon in her human aspect,
in the tone of her question she speaks to him as an equal
["When mystical activity is at its height, we find consciousness
by the sense of being at once . . . great enough to be God;
interior enough to be *me*" (quoted and translated by William
James from E. Recejac's *Essay on the Bases of the Mystic
Knowledge*).]; and, indeed, as Asia says after her questioning:

> So much I asked before, and my heart gave
> The response thou hast given; and of such truths
> Each to itself must be the oracle. (121-123)

She is Love. That her heart gave his response, when she earlier
asked herself what the truths of the meaning of the world are,
is a superb allegoric device. But before I suggest the meaning of

125

these lines in the action of the drama, let us return to her questioning.

> *Asia.* Who made the living world?
> *Demogorgon.*   God.
> *Asia.*   Who made all
> That it contains? thought, passion, reason, will,
> Imagination?
> *Demogorgon.* God: Almighty God. (9-11)

The "living world," containing what it does, is the mind. *Hellas* gives a variation of the theme: "Thought/ Alone, and its quick [living] elements, Will, Passion,/ Reason, Imagination cannot die" (795-797). "Almighty" is an intensification of mighty; its meaning is "possessing very great power" rather than "possessing all power" or "having unlimited power." Shelley uses "Almighty" here as he does "omnipotent" in the curse of Prometheus:

> Thou are omnipotent.
> O'er all things but thyself I gave thee power,
> And my own will. (I. 272-274)

The "malignant spirit" of Jove will work without check on Prometheus and on those the Titan loves for the time that Jove "must reign" (I. 276-281). Were God—whoever or whatever God is—possessor of all power, once man reached the "highest perfection of moral and intellectual nature" Jupiter could be quelled for certain eternally, but the drama ends with the possibility of evil seizing sway again.

Shelley wrote elsewhere: "according to the indisputable facts of the case, some evil Spirit has dominion in this imperfect world" (*Essay on Christianity*) but the Power which is God mercifully gives moments of joy in a world of little hope and of loneliness, gives the receptive sense for those moments (God can do only so much until man freely changes). Those moments come during the rare visitation of the winds of Spring (we are now familiar with the symbolic value of this image) or during the rare visitation of a beloved voice when one is alone in youth (the meaning is not "only in youth") filling eyes with tears that make them faint ("faint" is proleptic in "faint eyes"). The tears are the tears of joy and tenderness: "There is an eloquence in the tongueless wind . . . [which

by an] inconceivable relation to something within the soul
. . . [brings] tears of mysterious tenderness to the eyes, . . .
like the voice of one beloved singing to you alone (*Essay on
Love*). The tears fall on flowers that are unbewailing because
they do not live suffering lives, but out of sympathy with human tears their own eyes (one meaning of the ambiguous
"radiant looks") dim even while tears stain their beautiful appearances (the other meaning of "radiant looks"). When that
receptive sense leaves, we are in a "deserted state" although
"surrounded by human beings" (*Essay on Love*). The construction of these lines (12-18) gives the effect of planes of phrase
and meaning transparently overlapping others, like a technique
of Cubism in modern painting. (Elsewhere, it has been much
remarked, Shelley is Turneresque in his anticipation of Impressionism. These illustrative lines from *Julian and Maddalo*,
first offered by King-Hele, were written just before Turner
came to Venice and learned to see the world as none but Shelley had seen it: ". . . as if the Earth and Sea had been/ dissolved into one lake of fire.")

"Did he who made the Lamb make thee?" questions the
speaker in *The Tyger*. And Asia likewise puts this crucial question of the universe (19-28), to which no answer is yet possible
to us. Shelley wrote in plain prose, "That there is a true solution of the riddle [of the origin of evil], and that in our present
state that solution is unattainable by us, are propositions which
may be regarded as equally certain" (Note to *Hellas*, 197-238).
Asia passionately understands the torments of human existence,
which are built into the world ("the great chain of things").
When she demands, Who made these torments? (19-28), and
Demogorgon replies cryptically, "He reigns," anger breaks out
of Asia:

> Utter his name: a world pining in pain
> Asks but his name: curses shall drag him down. (29-30)

There is no meekness here. But it is not psychologically wrong
in her human aspect; even Jesus was angry once.

Twice more Demogorgon says, "He reigns," and Asia, un-
answered, reasons with herself. First there was the timeless
world of Heaven (Ouranos) and Earth (Gaia) and Light (the
essence of Prometheus) and Love (the essence of Asia); then
Saturn (Kronos), a titan born of Heaven and Earth, seized the

127

rule of the world, where now lived inhabitants, earth's first spirits, who were not yet fully men. From Saturn's power ("throne") came its manifestation ("shadow") and vice-regent, Time, who was envious of Light and Love. Earth's first spirits, although they lived in a kind of Eden with the calm joy of unwithered flowers, were as half-living worms, so low in the scale of being because Time refused their birthright, the light of thought and the majesty of love, which would make them fully men. Because of Saturn's bad rule, Prometheus gave "wisdom, which is strength, to Jupiter, And with this law alone, 'Let man be free' " (32-45)—only in liberty can man satisfy his thirst for the light of thought and for love.

> To know nor faith, nor love, nor law; to be
> Omnipotent but friendless is to reign. (47-48)

God—the Power which made the living world and which gives us our moments of joy—does not "reign"; through love he makes, will make, the world harmonious. With Jove's reign came the expulsion from the (unrealized) Eden that the race had lived in (49-58). To make life bearable Prometheus gave his gifts: hope (in Nepenthe, which ends sorrow; in Moly, which escapes brutishness; in the Amaranth, which promises immortality), love, fire, crafts, "speech, and speech created thought," music, sculpture, medicine, astronomy, ocean-going ships, cities [80: *mimicked*, imitated with inferior representations; *mocked*, imitated with superior representations, which are "Forms more real than living man" (I. 748); 84: *Reflected in their race*, in the children of the mothers who gazed on the divine marble; *perish*, men, beholding the love and beauty in their race, are rapt, are lost—Swinburne gave "deperire" for the meaning of perish, comparing Virgil's "Ut vidi, ut perii," When I saw her, how was I lost!].

> Such, the alleviations of his state,
> Prometheus gave to man, for which he hangs
> Withering in destined pain: but who rains down
> Evil, the immedicable plague, which, while
> Man looks on his creation like a God
> And sees that it is glorious, drives him on,
> The wreck of his own will, the scorn of earth,
> The outcast, the abandoned, the alone?

Although these alleviations are glorious, they do not change man's state; evil remains incurable, making him the "wreck of his own will." Who creates that evil? Not Jove, who trembled slavishly at Prometheus' curse (98-109).

> *Demogorgon.* All spirits are enslaved which serve things evil:
> Thou knowest if Jupiter be such or no.
> *Asia.* Whom calledst thou God?
> *Demogorgon.*   I spoke but as ye speak,
> For Jove is the supreme of living things. (110-113)

Demogorgon, replying to Asia's demand, gives no name for Jupiter's master. Whoever or whatever Power created the evil that Jupiter serves, or whether that evil is increate in the universe as a principle that may be overcome but not utterly destroyed, "He reigns" now. Nor does Demogorgon give any clearer image of the nature of God. Demogorgon used that word, which Asia and mankind use for Jove who is now the supreme ruler of living (mortal) things, to signify the greatness of the other, benignant Power in the universe.

Again Asia makes her demand to know the identity of the master of Jove (114).

> *Demogorgon.*   If the abysm
> Could vomit forth its secrets. . . . But a voice
> Is wanting, the deep truth is imageless. (114-116)

Here Demogorgon seems to contradict his earlier saying that he could answer all things that Asia dared demand—unless he thought that her human mind could not ask so much. It is not that Demogorgon does not know the secrets of the abysm (which is ambiguously the depths of the universe and the depths of the human mind, both reflecting the Infinite), but that there is no voice, no language, to give that knowledge expression in human thought ("speech created thought," Asia said a moment ago): "the deep truth is imageless." In like manner Jan van Ruysbroeck wrote of his mystical experience as a "bare and imageless vision" and again as "an imageless and bare understanding."

> For what would it avail to bid thee gaze
> On the revolving world? What to bid speak

Fate, Time, Occasion, Chance, and Change? To these
All things are subject but eternal Love. (117-120)

It would avail nothing to explain what governs the physical world, to have its principles—or rather powers, as they are personified—speak of their nature and function. Knowledge of the physical world explains nothing of good and evil. These powers—Fate, Time, Occasion, Chance, and Change [Fate is synonymous with Destiny, not with Necessity; Chance has no meaning if Necessity exists]—govern the physical but not the moral world.

The modernity of Shelley's theology is manifest in the thought of the mathematician and philosopher Alfred North Whitehead, who saw in "the main structure" of Shelley's mind a scientific outlook "permeating his poetry through and through." Whitehead concludes his chapter on religion and science in *Science and the Modern World*:

We have to know what we mean by religion. The churches, in their presentation of their answers to this query, have put forward aspects of religion which are expressed in terms either suited to the emotional reactions of bygone times or directed to excite modern emotional interests of nonreligious character. What I mean under the first heading is that religious appeal is directed partly to excite that instinctive fear of the wrath of a tyrant which was inbred in the unhappy populations of the arbitrary empires of the ancient world, and in particular to excite that fear of an all-powerful arbitrary tyrant behind the unknown forces of nature. This appeal to the ready instinct of brute fear is losing its force. It lacks any directness of response, because modern science and modern conditions of life have taught us to meet occasions of apprehension by a critical analysis of their causes and conditions. Religion is the reaction of human nature to its search for God. The presentation of God under the aspect of power awakens every modern instinct of critical reaction. This is fatal; for religion collapses unless its main positions command immediacy of assent. In this respect the old phraseology is at variance with the psychology of modern civilizations. This change in psychology is largely due to science, and is one of the chief ways in which the advance of science has weakened the hold of the old religious forms of expression. The nonreligious motive which has entered into modern religious thought is the desire for a comfortable organization of modern society. . . . Above and beyond all things, the religious life is not a research after comfort. I must now state, in all diffidence, what I conceive to be the essential character of the religious spirit.

Religion is the vision of something which stands beyond, behind, and within, the passing flux of immediate things; something which is real, and yet waiting to be realized; something which is a remote possibility, and yet the greatest of present facts; something that gives meaning to all that passes, and yet eludes apprehension; something whose possession is the final good, and yet is beyond all reach; something which is the ultimate ideal, and the hopeless quest.

The immediate reaction of human nature to the religious vision is worship. Religion has emerged into human experience mixed with the crudest fancies of barbaric imagination. Gradually, slowly, steadily the vision recurs in history under nobler forms and clearer expression. . . .

The vision claims nothing but worship; and worship is a surrender to the claim of assimilation, urged with the motive force of mutual love. The vision never overrules. It is is always there, and it has the power of love presenting the one purpose whose fulfilment is eternal harmony. Such order as we find in nature is never force— it presents itself as the one harmonious adjustment of complex detail. Evil is the brute motive force of fragmentary purpose, disregarding the eternal vision. Evil is overruling, retarding, hurting.

"He reigns"; God "never overrules." The minds of the poet and the scientist are in conjunction. But with their planetary minds we are outside the drama.

Demogorgon stopped speaking with the words "eternal Love" (120), and Asia's human aspect, as though in response, begins the change to her aspect as spiritual Power.

> *Asia.* So much I asked before, and my heart gave
> The response thou hast given; and of such truths
> Each to itself must be the oracle.
> One more demand; and do thou answer me
> As my own soul would answer, did it know
> That which I ask. Prometheus shall arise
> Henceforth the sun of this rejoicing world:
> When shall the destined hour arrive?
>   *Demogorgon.*   Behold! (121-128)

Eternity has confirmed her opinion as knowledge (just as her heart was its own intuitive oracle, so must each person's be). She is Love, and *now she is wise,* for absolute knowledge of the faceted truths of the meaning of the universe is wisdom (although ultimate unified truth cannot be given expression in human thought, she knows that it exists). Because she has "wisdom, which is strength" (and Prometheus, who has always had wisdom, now has love), the "destined hour" arrives.

Asia beholds the racing Hours in their chariots:

> Some look behind, as fiends pursued them there,
> And yet I see no shapes but the keen stars: (133-134)

(They look to the past, which is fiendlike but unreal; time is told by the stars.)

> Others, with burning eyes, lean forth, and drink
> With eager lips the wind of their own speed,
> As if the thing they loved fled on before,

(i.e., into the future)

> And now, even now, they clasped it. (135-138)

At once friezelike and incredibly swift, the imagery has an exciting beauty.

A charioteer stops and Asia thinks him meant for her (145). [Here and in IV. 63 the Hours are masculine; in II. iv. 161 the young Hour is neuter; in III. iii. 65 and 70, Hours are feminine. Eternity likewise is three-gendered.] Nor does she at first understand his saying that he is a shadow of a dreadful destiny (this immortal Hour will manifest the action of Demogorgon, of Eternity) and that before the planet Jupiter has set, the God Jupiter will be overcome (although it is just before dawn, v. 1, and Asia's Hour will not rest until noon, iv. 173, the day will stay dark until noon, v. 10). When Panthea turns Asia's mind to Demogorgon ascending the dark chariot and to "watch its path among the stars Blackening the night," Asia understands what the charioteer meant (140-155).

Panthea points to another chariot (156-158), an ivory shell like the veined shell that Love uprose from the sea on (v. 21-23). The young spirit driving this chariot (this spirit is hope, the soul's guide, lines 159-161) will bring Asia to union with the free Prometheus—their union in the next scene precedes the dethronement as cause, or rather *is* the dethronement—and will then blow the mystic shell over the world, heralding the new order.

Scene v

The Earth, whom we know fearful of Jupiter, whispers the warning that "their flight must be swifter than fire" (3-4), that is, swifter than lightning, which moves at the ultimate speed in the universe. Demogorgon, whose Hour is on its way, must not reach Jupiter's throne before Love reaches Prometheus, whom we last saw spiritually exhausted: Demogorgon's manifestation of power cannot precede the union. While the "Car pauses within a Cloud," Asia becomes transfigured (the cloud shall water the earth with love and beauty), and the sun stands still, "held in heaven by wonder" at a light more glorious than his own (1-5, 8-14). Panthea can scarcely endure the radiance of her beauty, which is the effluence of Love. That the glory of her form, her essence, can be manifest in the physical universe means that a good change is at work in its nature. Asia is now as she was on the day when she rose from the sea; love, like intellectual light filling the mind, then burst from her and illumined the world until her grief for Prometheus eclipsed her soul. The whole world, the articulate and the inanimate, now seeks her sympathy, loving her (16-37). By the sympathy of love Shelley meant that "communion not merely of the senses, but of our whole nature, intellectual, imaginative and sensitive" (*A Discourse on the Manners of the Ancient Greeks Relative to the Subject of Love*). Asia listens to music expressive of love for her, and then speaks. It is a high place in Shelley's artistry that her speech is in familiar language:

> all love is sweet,
> Given or returned. Common as light is love,
> And its familiar voice wearies not ever.
> Like the wide heaven, the all-sustaining air,
> It makes the reptile equal to the God:
> They who inspire it most are fortunate,
> As I am now; but those who feel it most

133

Are happier still, after long sufferings,
As I shall soon become. (39-47)

Then a Voice in the Air—the voice of Prometheus, as is explicit in an early draft of the passage—sings to the Life of Life,
Asia's essence, or Love which is Intellectual Beauty giving the
world its best being. The love expressed in her lips kindles the
breath of life, and their smiles turn to fire the cold air of the
world. But such intense love (the kindling "fire") is insupportable: let her screen in her looks the love and smiles of her
lips. Her looking compels a gaze in exchange, and whoever
gazes into her eyes becomes entangled and faints—thus the fire
is screened and does not destroy (48-53). [In a woman's eyes
that are "deep and intricate from the workings of the mind"
the heart of a man can be "entangled . . . in soul-enwoven
labyrinths" (*A Discourse on the Manners of the Ancient
Greeks*)].

Since Prometheus is singing to Asia's essence, "limbs" (synecdoche for body) stand for soul and "vest" (synecdoche for
clothes) for body. The trope shifts: her soul burns through her
body as the morning sun through the clouds; but although
the sun's "radiant lines" will part the clouds and the sun itself
be seen, the divinest atmosphere of her body (the implication
of "divinest" is that the earthly atmosphere of clouds also has
divinity, because it participates in beauty) will always conceal
her (54-59).

"Fair are others," but not so beautiful that they cannot be
seen; none beholds Asia, who is Intellectual Beauty (but her
low and tender voice, matching her beauty, can be heard),
because "liquid splendour" conceals her [*Fair are others*—
"the idea of beauty has a not wholly inadequate embodiment
in the world of sense," *Phaedrus,* 250B]. The "liquid splendour," in apposition to "it," is ambiguous. The splendour is
her body, liquid in beauty like the clouds; it is also the life of
which she is the life (48), the multiplicity of which she is the
unity, and it is the earth of which she is the lamp (66), the
lamp being a metaphor for the "One Spirit." And "all feel,"
now that the world is changing and her voice is heard in and by
all things, as Prometheus now feels, "lost for ever"—in the
sense that we lose ourselves in love to find ourselves (60-65).

The Power which is Love and Intellectual Beauty gives

intellectual, that is, spiritual light to Earth's shapes, which else were dark, wherever that Power moves; and the souls of those the Power loves walk upon the winds, ecstatically,

> Till they fail, as I am failing,
> Dizzy, lost, yet unbewailing!—

they "fail" as in a mystical experience (66-71). That Prometheus has not "failed" in the usual sense is evident in Asia's song: he is pilot and power for her boat.

Asia's soul responds enchanted to his song, sailing on the river of his singing. Just as Prometheus gave pre-eminence to Asia in his song, so Asia gives pre-eminence to Prometheus in hers: his soul like an angel is the pilot at the helm of hers. The winds (betokeners of spring) ring with his melody. Music is not only the river for the boat which is her soul, music fills her sails. The "many-winding river" seems to float her in eternity through a paradise until, as though in deep slumber, Asia floats to an "ocean . . . of ever-spreading sound," which suggests the "wide ocean of intellectual beauty" in Shelley's translation of the *Symposium* (72-84). Or on another level, as life began in the ocean, it is a journey to the source of life, which, to go full circle, is the One. The paradox of Intellectual Beauty going to itself reflects the nature of mysticism, which is always paradoxical and self-contradictory in its expression in language; logic has no relevance to the mystical experience, for logic can exist only where there are distinctions, and only in logic, as Whitehead says, is contradiction the "signal of a defeat: but in the evolution of real knowledge it marks the first step in progress toward a victory."

Meanwhile Prometheus' spirit lifts its wings to catch the winds of the heaven of music, and he and Asia sail on without rational navigation ("Without a course, without a star"), driven by the instinct of music. Prometheus guides her soul's desire among Elysian islands, where mortal souls never were; here the air they breathe is love, and love moving in the winds and on the waves (of Prometheus' music) harmonizes this earth with heaven, that is, with perfection, whose existence is "felt," known intuitively rather than rationally (85-97).

The conception in her third stanza of a paradise on the far side of human birth has a long and imposing history in the human mind: linked to Shelley's are conceptions in Wordsworth's *Ode: Intimations of Immortality,* in Vaughan's *The Retreat,* in Spencer's *The Faerie Queene,* in the *Gospel* of Matthew, in Vergil's *Fourth Eclogue,* in Plato's *Statesman* and *Phaedrus,* in Hesiod's *Works and Days.* I give only brief suggestive passages from *Phaedrus,* translated by H. N. Fowler. Prometheus, Asia says, is the "most beautiful of pilots" (92). In *Phaedrus*: "the lover's perception of the beauty of the beloved reawakens the memory of the lost heavenly vision and kindles that yearning of love for the ideal" (250B); "that which is rightly called the most blessed of mysteries, which we celebrated in a state of perfection, when we were without the experience of the evils which awaited us in time to come, being permitted as initiates to the sight of perfect and simple and calm and happy apparitions, which we saw in the pure light, being ourselves pure and not entombed in this which we carry about with us and call the body" (250C). The modern mind may find it difficult to accept literally any of these conceptions in the history of the human mind, but it would be arrogant to reject all meaning in these conceptions, so great is the imaginative testimony of the authors, so great and so persistent.

Prometheus and Asia have journeyed back through an allegoric lifetime, each stage of which (Infancy perhaps excepted) is hardly worth the living. Now, not everything in *Prometheus Unbound,* of course, needs a symbolic equation; indeed criticism leans to over-interpretation and often loses its balance. When Shelley uses the image of a cave, of an ocean or river and a boat, of music and winds, they may have only a literal sense or, as perhaps here, a metaphoric sense. There is enough metaphoric meaning in the icy caves of Age and the dark and tossing waves of Manhood for them to stand as they are, suggestive of the nature of succeeding undesirable states. [But the temptation to incline to symbolic meaning invites. "Youth's smooth ocean, smiling to betray" stands for the end of innocence, the falseness experienced in the world (the ocean here, a "false ocean" in Shelley's second draft of the line, is not the ocean in lines 84-85 and 110); the "dark and tossing waves" are the emotional storms of manhood; and age has left only the cold mental life to which it retreats. The "glassy gulfs . . . Of shadow-peopled Infancy" is indeterminately ambiguous. In the first version "sunny" was an alternative possibility for "glassy" and nothing modified Infancy; in the second version the line was "Beyond the sunny isles we flee." These images suggest that Infancy is a good state; "shadow-peopled" would then mean that the infant still retains the "heavenly vision" although the apparitions in that vision are dimmed to shadows, and "glassy" would mean clear or transparent. But Shelley may have changed his mind in deciding on "glassy gulfs"—after "smooth ocean," which is unequivocal in meaning, the parallel glassy gulfs suggest a bad state, undesirable because the infant in the mirror of its life ("glassy gulfs"), without the speech needed for thought, sees only reflections, only shadows, and cannot at all understand reality.] After the betrayals of youth, after an infancy without the light of thought, Prometheus and Asia pass through Death (the birth into this world is a death) and Birth (the death into paradise, the "diviner day" that they once lived, is a birth). They are now on the "many-winding river" among the "wildernesses" in the first stanza of her song,

> Peopled by shapes too bright to see,
> And rest, having beheld; somewhat like thee;
> Which walk upon the sea, and chant melodiously!

The beings in that paradise of wildernesses are seen only as shapes; they are too bright—as Prometheus now is—to be seen as they are. They are, like the "happy apparitions" in the "heavenly vision" of *Phaedrus,* essences or forms on the sea of intellectual beauty, walking as Gods whose language is musical; and having beheld them, being among them, Prometheus and Asia come to rest.

Although Prometheus is unbound (or this journey could not have been taken), we are in Act III yet to see the unbinding, just as we are about to witness the overthrow of Jupiter who has already been dethroned. With the union of Prometheus and Asia, time dissolved into eternity. But even in eternity exists a succession of hours, not to speak of the succession necessary in a drama. The third act presents the overthrow, the gladness of Titanian and Olympian Gods who reflect heaven and intellectual light, the unbinding of Prometheus, and the changes in mankind and in the earth. This sequence is a matter of tone rather than of logic. We may think of each of these scenes in the cosmic drama as transpar-

137

ent planes in layers underlying what Prometheus and Asia narrate in their songs. The shapes of earth, wherever Love moves, "are clad with brightness" (67); Prometheus and Asia are in a paradise peopled by bright shapes (108). These shapes are perhaps literally people, or rather their essences—the change in humanity, the last change we are to see in the third act (as our vision penetrates the layers of scenes), having already taken place.

PROMETHEUS UNBOUND: ACT III

Scene i

In a hundred lines of narrative (the techniques are not strictly dramatic) the arrogance, the overweeningness, of Jupiter and his fall are given extraordinary expression.

> *Jupiter.* Ye congregated powers of heaven, who share
> The glory and the strength of him ye serve,
> Rejoice! henceforth I am omnipotent.
> All else had been subdued to me; alone
> The soul of man, like unextinguished fire,
> Yet burns toward heaven with fierce reproach, and doubt,
> And lamentation, and reluctant prayer,
> Hurling up insurrection, which might make
> Our antique empire insecure, though built
> On eldest faith, and hell's coeval, fear;
> And though my curses through the pendulous air,
> Like snow on herbless peaks, fall flake by flake,
> And cling to it; though under my wrath's night
> It climbs the crags of life, step after step,
> Which wound it, as ice wounds unsandalled feet,
> It yet remains supreme o'er misery,
> Aspiring, unrepressed, yet soon to fall:
> Even now I have begotten a strange wonder,
> That fatal child, the terror of the earth,
> Who waits but till the destined hour arrive,
> Bearing from Demogorgon's vacant throne
> The dreadful might of ever-living limbs
> Which clothed that awful spirit unbeheld,
> To redescend, and trample out the spark.
> Pour forth heaven's wine, Idaean Ganymede,

138

And let it fill the Daedal cups like fire,
And from the flower-inwoven soil divine
Ye all-triumphant harmonies arise,
As dew from earth under the twilight stars:
Drink! be the nectar circling through your veins
The soul of joy, ye ever-living Gods,
Till exultation burst in one wide voice
Like music from Elysian winds.
       And thou
Ascend beside me, veilèd in the light
Of the desire which makes thee one with me,
Thetis, bright image of eternity!
When thou didst cry, 'Insufferable might!
God! Spare me! I sustain not the quick flames,
The penetrating presence; all my being,
Like him whom the Numidian seps did thaw
Into a dew with poison, is dissolved,
Sinking through its foundations:' even then
Two mighty spirits, mingling, made a third
Mightier than either, which, unbodied now,
Between us floats, felt, although unbeheld,
Waiting the incarnation, which ascends,
(Hear ye the thunder of the fiery wheels
Griding the winds?) from Demogorgon's throne.
Victory! victory! Feel'st thou not, O world,
The earthquake of his chariot thundering up
Olympus?

[10: *faith,* superstition] In this desire of absolute tyranny, in this egoism and delusion are will and power and passion; and the poetry, a triumph of art, is congruent with the conception of Jupiter.

There are, nonetheless, matters for criticism to resolve.

 All else had been subdued to me; alone
 The soul of man, like unextinguished fire,
 Yet burns toward heaven . . . (4-6)

These lines sound like lines in the curse of Prometheus:

    Thou art omnipotent.
  O'er all things but thyself I gave thee power,
 And my own will. (I. 272-274)

(It is psychologically appropriate that Jupiter speak only of the soul of man not having been subdued to him and not of his personal limitation.) And Jupiter saying "It [the soul of man] yet remains supreme o'er misery" (16) echoes Prometheus:

> Whilst me, who am thy foe . . .
> Hast thou made reign and triumph, to thy scorn,
> O'er mine own misery and thy vain revenge. (I. 9-11)

But the soul of man "burns toward heaven with doubt, And . . . reluctant prayer" (6-7)—not at all like Prometheus. What, then, is the connection between Prometheus and the soul of man? (In Shelley's thought soul and mind are synonymous or, as some prefer, the soul is in the mind.) Let me defer an answer until later in the act, where more matter bears on the question.

Jupiter boasts that his fatal child will trample out the fire of man's soul, but without knowledge enough what God can wield power enough for an overwhelming purpose? Jupiter wrongly thinks of Demogorgon in his own image, theomorphically as it were, as having a body (22-23), and that error makes us doubt that his spiritual offspring will succeed the spirit of Demogorgon, clothing itself in the irresistible power "of ever-living limbs." Jupiter conjoins to that error another, mistaking the sea-goddess, Thetis, "the image of eternity" as Byron wrote of the sea, for eternity itself. Jupiter's egoism exults in his account of their passionate union. That the spirit issuing from that union awaits the destined hour of its incarnation is Jupiter's delusion. His lines (43-48) are not to be interpreted as evil begetting its own destruction; Prometheus, not Jupiter, ends the reign of evil.

The car of the destined Hour, the manifestation of Eternity, arrives. Demogorgon descends and moves toward Jupiter, whose mind is awestruck, shaken, his delusion facing reality. To Jupiter's demand, "what are thou?", Demogorgon first says, "Eternity," and then, with ironic import,

> I am thy child, as thou wert Saturn's child,
> Mightier than thee. (54-55)

He is not the child that Jupiter expected, who serving his father would destroy mankind; rather, he will be to Jupiter

140

what Jupiter was to his father, Saturn. The meaning in the line depends on *as*, the sense being "only as" (51-55).

Jupiter lifts his lightnings against such a "Detested prodigy" (the word, which must be taken in its meaning "out of the ordinary course of nature," is brilliantly chosen—Jupiter rules nature) and threatens Demogorgon with a deeper prison than those of Saturn and the other Titans whom Jupiter chained in Tartarus below Hades. But it is Jupiter who will sink to the abyss, to the dark void. The terrible strife dims the sun and shakes the solid stars. But we know nothing of that struggle, which takes place during the interruption in line 63 (56-63), until the next scene. Shelley could have avoided the awkwardness by extensive stage directions to present the struggle, like those used by naturalistic dramatists after Zola, writing which seems more fit for a novel than for a play; but even if his inventiveness could have anticipated such a technique, prose would never have done and poetry in stage directions would have been ludicrous. Or he could have had a messenger—Apollo speaking to Ocean—narrate the whole first scene of the act. But such a classical narration would also have been awkward, not having been prepared for in the action of the drama; and Shelley apparently wanted to present Jupiter to our eyes, who appears nowhere else in the drama, and was right to do so at this juncture.

Jupiter cries for mercy to the inexorable Power—inexorable because "Evil minds change good to their own nature" (I. 380-381) and because justice is necessary to the world—and entreats Demogorgon to make Prometheus his judge, who, even hanging on Caucasus, would not doom the God.

> Gentle, and just, and dreadless, is he not
> The monarch of the world? What then art thou?

Jupiter's mind reels from the argument that Prometheus as the world's monarch ought be his judge to the unknown nature of Demogorgon, that is, unknown to Jupiter (63-69). In his aspect that overthrows Jupiter, Demogorgon is, in Mary Shelley's Note, the "Primal Power of the world"; we may understand him to be an aspect of the Almighty God who made the living world (II. iv. 11).

In his last extremity Jupiter threatens to drag Demogorgon down to ruin with him [72: *a vulture and a snake*, Jupiter and

Demogorgon; the snake is a symbol of eternity and, as in *The Revolt of Islam*, I. vi-xiv, of good]. His passionate threat is vain: Demogorgon (like a Holy Spirit) speaks to the universe in Act IV. Jupiter cries,

> Let hell unlock
> Its mounded oceans of tempestuous fire,
> And whelm on them into the bottomless void
> This desolated world, and thee, and me,
> The conqueror and the conquered, and the wreck
> Of that for which they combated.

So may a modern dictator with nuclear power act in his last extremity.

But the elements no longer obey Jupiter, and the God sinks, crying "Ai! Ai!",

> Dizzily down, ever, for ever, down. (79-81)
> /——/ /——/— /

The rapid initial dactyl, the especial force on *down* because of the alliteration and the slide over the z sounds and the assonance; that meter repeated in the next four syllables together with alliterative repetition that insists on the *ever*; and in the second breath-group the extra unstressed syllable before the rhetorical pause, which gives renewed force to the final *down*—all go into wonderfully creating the vortex of Jupiter's fall.

Scene ii

Apollo and Ocean are on the shore of Atlantis, west of the straits of Gibraltar, in the river of Ocean girdling the earth; out of and into that river the sun rises and sets, and they talk until the morning star gives the cue for Apollo's rising (37-40). They are the lords of great aspects of the world: the sun is the "eye with which the Universe Beholds itself and knows itself divine" (*Hymn of Apollo*, 31); the sea is "heaven-reflecting" (III. ii. 18). Olympian and Titanian, they are of the two greatest orders of gods, and both are glad of Jupiter's overthrow: Ocean's sea will reflect a purer heaven, his streams flowing around continents and islands of well-being [26: the star is the crest of the moon's unseen pilot; 29-34: the new order will

142

supplant the brutal old shipboard state]; evil will no longer darken the mind of Apollo. As sun and ocean, they are also interpretable as natural forces, or by metonymy as laws of nature. We may speculate that Jupiter's evil is inherent in natural forces or laws, which the mind of man can control only by having no evil in itself subject to those laws; not only having no evil, but having a mind living freely with love, the law that may at last govern matter as well as the moral world. The thematic significance of this scene emerges from the forces of nature being aware of having been freed from evil.

The tonal significance of the scene is in its taking us from Jupiter's arrogant mind and violence to beauty and calm and joy. Apollo has given an account of the cosmic struggle and Demogorgon's victory. Ocean, his voice low-pitched, by his question seems doubtful. Apollo now speaks of Jupiter's fall in two powerful similes. After the first trope Ocean seems still uncertain, wondering; but as Apollo again speaks [11: the line is preceded in sense by "He sunk as"; Jupiter is "caught" in the cloud of victory at the close of III. i], the image of the quelled Jupiter discharges its reality (1-17) and Ocean, now believing in the overthrow of "the supreme of living things" (II. iv. 113), looks to good changes that will follow in the world (18-34). Powerful as Apollo's similes are, because they *narrate* the fall, because they are at a remove from the action, they do not have the direct violence presented to our eyes of Jupiter's wanting to desolate the world with oceans of hellfire, and so the similes serve as a tonal bridge (2-9, 11-17). Ocean's anticipation of changes is a winding ramp off the bridge, as it were: the sea "unstained with blood," as the ramp turns, looks back to the old order; other turns alternately look to the beckoning banks, the banks left behind, and at last upon paradisal images (19-34). And Apollo turns from the eclipses of sorrow to the morning star of love (35-39). When Apollo begins his journey through the new day, Ocean goes to the loud "unpastured sea hungering for calm," which the animal-sea can now have. The "azure calm" that will feed the once wild animal is not arbitrary in its beauty but is seen with the clear eye of a naturalist [43: *which stand*, i.e., which now stand forever full, because Jupiter has fallen]. Then the sea instinct with life and beauty is transformed mythopoeically from its naturalistic azure calm: the waves into wavering limbs, the

143

whitecaps into white arms, the streaming waters into hair, the sea-flowers into garlands and crowns for the sea-goddesses hurrying to grace Asia's joy in the hour of her union with Prometheus.

Scene iii

Hercules begins the scene as though he were a figure in a morality play, conceived as strength ministering to wisdom, courage and love; because Prometheus is most perfect in these properties of mind, or soul, he is the most glorious of living beings (1-4). That Hercules unbinds Prometheus after the overthrow of Jupiter and after Apollo's and Ocean's reflections of the overthrow is a matter of tonal succession, artistically right, not of a traditionally dramatic succession, that is, not of a meaning emerging from cause and consequence in action. Prometheus does not become the "type of the highest perfection of moral and intellectual nature" as a consequence of Jupiter's overthrow. The other way around is the only possible meaning. Once Prometheus evolved to that highest perfection, in Act I, Asia could fulfill herself, in Act II. Their union at the close of the second act (to repeat myself) causes or rather *is* the dethronement. But outside opera there can be no successfully presented polyphony of actions. Shelley solved the artistic problem by using a structural technique like that of Cubism, a technique that he had already used for language (in II. iv. 12-18).

In the two songs closing the second act are the germs of the third act. Again to repeat myself: the scenes in the third act may be experienced, once the whole act is grasped, as transparent overlapping planes so that we see all the scenes happening at the same time. The sequence in the drama is a matter of tonal rhythm rather than of logical cause and consequence. There was Jupiter's power in the first act, spiritually defeated by Prometheus; his power was absent from the second act; it returns with the God in the third act, only to be quelled; and will be absent from the final visions. That simple alternation comprises a large, unifying rhythm. The contrast of Jupiter on his throne in the first scene of the third act, expressing his will and power and passion—the contrast to the change in Asia in the last scene of the second act, to her tribute to love, and to

144

the songs of Prometheus and Asia, is artistically cunning, for the contrast expands our minds with new energy.

In point of time the third act begins before Asia reaches Prometheus. While Jupiter boasts to the congregated powers of heaven, the "Car of the Hour" bearing Demogorgon thunders up Olympus. Then, during their terrible strife the overpowered Jupiter pleads that Demogorgon make Prometheus his judge, "Even where he hangs, seared by my long revenge, On Caucasus" (66-67). Prometheus hangs there until Asia comes (others joining, as named in the stage directions) "borne in the Car with the Spirit of the Hour." Hercules, like a shadow of Demogorgon, unbinds Prometheus. The unbinding, ushering in the union, and the quelling of Jupiter are a single act refracted in the drama. In the third act the unbinding seems to follow the quelling and the scene with Apollo and Ocean—I say *seems* for the quelling of Jupiter also seems to follow the union of Prometheus and Asia, which ends the second act. In a succession formed by logical cause and consequence, the scene with Apollo and Ocean should follow the unbinding, the union and the quelling, but Shelley gave thematic and especially tonal considerations precedence over traditional dramatic structure. One word more: it is also tonally right that the changes in earth and in man, the visions which complete the meaning of the act, should follow the union, as they do in the succession that Shelley chose for the third act. These changes in man and the earth (reaching throughout the universe in Act IV) are the "harvest of his happiness," the purpose to which the poem shapes.

After his courtesy to Hercules, Prometheus turns to Asia who is here the shadow of intellectual beauty ("beauty unbeheld"), not the unseen Power itself—nonetheless, as a manifestation of that Power she is the "light of life"—and turns to her sisters whose love and care "made long years of pain Sweet to remember" (4-9). They will live together in a cave full of natural beauty (even as early as paleolithic man caves were sacred places, where gods were),

> A simple dwelling, which shall be our own;
> Where we will sit and talk of time and change,
> As the world ebbs and flows, ourselves unchanged.
> What can hide man from mutability? (22-25)

145

Clearly the cave is their home, their temple (in the Greek sense of a house for a God, not a place for a congregation), not their world; and Prometheus and Asia, themselves immutable, are here distinct from man and woman, who are subject to time and change (10-25). Prometheus gives an account of how they will spend their hours, an account in ascending order: affectionate, idle moods intermingled with loveliness (26-29); playful, simple creativeness, like a reflection of moral innocence (30-33); spiritual questing and the making of poetry, that is, whatever is true, beautiful, and good (34-39); communion with man through "that best worship love, by him and us Given and returned" (40-60). "The [religious] vision," wrote Whitehead a century later, "claims nothing but worship; and worship is a surrender to the claim of assimilation, urged with the motive force of mutual love."

Prometheus and Asia are here not in the soul, or mind, of man. They are other and greater than man; and a communion of worship, of love, will exist between man and them. Earlier in the act, in Jupiter's speech, Prometheus seemed and did not seem the soul of man. Asia has been a spiritual power having a personality, has been a woman, and in this scene is the shadow of intellectual beauty (in which form she visits the world and inspires worship, as Shelley recorded in *Hymn to Intellectual Beauty*). We can resolve the paradoxes. Or rather William James can. I have already given, in connection with *Hymn to Intellectual Beauty*, elements in his empirical study of religious experience. Here are others, which I abridge.

James first considers whether a common intellectual nucleus exists for all creeds:

The warring gods and formulas of the various religions do indeed cancel each other, but there is a certain uniform deliverance in which religions all appear to meet. It consists of two parts:—

1. An uneasiness; and
2. Its solution.

1. The uneasiness, reduced to its simplest terms, is a sense that there is *something wrong about us* as we naturally stand.

2. The solution is a sense that *we are saved from the wrongness* by making proper connection with the higher powers.

In those more developed minds which alone we are studying, the wrongness takes a moral character, and the salvation takes a mystical tinge. I think we shall keep well within the limits of what is common to all such minds if we formulate the essence of their religious experience in terms like these:—

The individual, so far as he suffers from his wrongness and criticises it, is to that extent consciously beyond it, and in at least possible touch with something higher, if anything higher exist. Along with the wrong part there is thus a better part of him, even though it may be but a most helpless germ. With which part he should identify his real being is by no means obvious at this stage; but when stage 2 (the stage of solution or salvation) arrives, the man identifies his real being with the germinal part of himself; and does so in the following way. *He becomes conscious that this higher part is coterminous and continuous with a* MORE *of the same quality, which is operative in the universe outside of him, and which he can keep in working touch with.*

So far the experiences are only psychological phenomena. They possess, it is true, enormous biological worth. Spiritual strength really increases in the subject when he has them, a new life opens for him, and they seem to him a place of conflux where the forces of two universes meet; and yet this may be nothing but his subjective way of feeling things, a mood of his own fancy, in spite of the effects produced. I now turn to my second question: What is the "objective" truth of their content? [The word "truth" is here taken to mean something additional to bare value for life, although the natural propensity of man is to believe that whatever has great value for life is thereby certified as true.—James]

The part of the content concerning which the question of truth most pertinently arises is that "MORE *of the same quality*" with which our own higher self appears in the experience to come into harmonious working relation. Is such a "more" merely our own notion, or does it really exist? Does it act, as well as exist? And in what form should we conceive of that "union" with it of which religious geniuses are so convinced?

It is in answering these questions that the various theologies perform their theoretic work, and that their divergencies most come to light. They will agree that the "more" really exists; though some of them hold it to exist in the shape of a personal god or gods, while others are satisfied to conceive it as a stream of ideal tendency embedded in the eternal structure of the world. They all agree, moreover, that it acts as well as exists, and that something really is effected for the better when you throw your life into its hands.

147

The "more," as we called it, and the meaning of our "union" with it, form the nucleus of our inquiry. Into what definite description can these words be translated, and for what definite facts do they stand? [As a duty] of the science of religions is to keep religion in connection with the rest of science, we shall do well to seek first of all a way of describing the "more," which psychologists may also recognize as real. The *subconscious self* is nowadays a well-accredited psychological entity; and I believe that in it we have exactly the mediating term required. Apart from all religious considerations, there is actually and literally more life in our total soul than we are at any time aware of.

Let me then propose, as an hypothesis, that whatever it may be on its *farther* side, the "more" with which in religious experience we feel ourselves connected is on its *hither* side the subconscious continuation of our conscious life. Starting thus with a recognized psychological fact as our basis, we seem to preserve a contact with "science" which the ordinary theologian lacks. At the same time the theologian's contention that the religious man is moved by an external power is vindicated, for it is one of the peculiarities of invasions from the subconscious region to take on objective appearances, and to suggest to the Subject an external control. In the religious life the control is felt as "higher"; but since on our hypothesis it is primarily the higher faculties of our own hidden mind which are controlling, the sense of union with the power beyond us is a sense of something, not merely apparently, but literally true.

* * *

Those of us who are not personally favored with . . . specific revelations must stand outside of them altogether and, for the present at least, decide that, since they corroborate incompatible theological doctrines, they neutralize one another and leave no fixed results. If we follow any one of them [their theological doctrines are "over-beliefs"], or if we follow philosophical theory and embrace monistic pantheism on non-mystical grounds, we do so in the exercise of our individual freedom, and build out our religion in the way most congruous with our personal susceptibilities.

Disregarding the over-beliefs, and confining ourselves to what is common and generic, we have in *the fact that the conscious person is continuous with a wider self through which saving experiences come*, a positive content of religious experience which, it seems to me, *is literally and objectively true as far as it goes*.

The further limits of our being plunge, it seems to me, into an al-

148

together other dimension of existence from the sensible and merely "understandable" world. Name it the mystical region, or the supernatural region, whichever you choose. So far as our ideal impulses originate in this region (and most of them do originate in it, for we find them possessing us in a way for which we cannot articulately account), we belong to it in a more intimate sense than that in which we belong to the visible world, for we belong in the most intimate sense wherever our ideals belong. Yet the unseen region in question is not merely ideal, for it produces effects in this world. When we commune with it, work is actually done upon our finite personality, for we are turned into new men, and consequences in the way of conduct follow in the natural world upon our regenerative change. But that which produces effects within another reality must be termed a reality itself, so I feel as if we had no philosophic excuse for calling the unseen or mystical world unreal.

God is the natural appellation, for us Christians at least, for the supreme reality, so I will call this higher part of the universe by the name of God. We and God have business with each other; and in opening ourselves to his influence our deepest destiny is fulfilled. The universe, at those parts of it which our personal being constitutes, takes a turn genuinely for the worse or for the better in proportion as each one of us fulfills or evades God's demands. As far as this goes I probably have you with me, for I only translate into schematic language what I may call the instinctive belief of mankind: God is real since he produces real effects.

That the God with whom, starting from the hither side of our own extra-marginal self, we come at its remoter margin into commerce should be the absolute world-ruler, is of course a very considerable over-belief. Over-belief as it is, though, it is an article of almost every one's religion. Most of us pretend in some way to prop it upon our philosophy, but the philosophy itself is really propped upon this faith. What is this but to say that Religion, in her fullest exercise of function, is not a mere illumination of facts already elsewhere given, not a mere passion, like love, which views things in a rosier light. It is indeed that, as we have seen abundantly. But it is something more, namely, a postulator of new *facts* as well. The world interpreted religiously is not the materialistic world over again, with an altered expression; it must have, over and above the altered expression, *a natural constitution* different at some point from that which a materialistic world would have. It must be such that different events can be expected in it, different conduct must be required.

The whole drift of my education goes to persuade me that the world of our present consciousness is only one out of many worlds of consciousness that exist, and that those other worlds must contain experiences which have a meaning for our life also; and that although in the main their experiences and those of this world keep discrete, yet the two become continuous at certain points, and higher energies filter in.

Both instinctively and for logical reasons, I find it hard to believe that principles can exist which make no difference in facts. But all facts are particular facts, and the whole interest of the question of God's existence seems to me to lie in the consequences for particulars which that existence may be expected to entail. That no concrete particular of experience should alter its complexion in consequence of a God being there seems to me an incredible proposition.

If asked just where the differences in fact which are due to God's existence come in, I should have to say that in general I have no hypothesis to offer beyond what the phenomenon of "prayerful communion," especially when certain kinds of incursion from the subconscious region take part in it, immediately suggests. The appearance is that in this phenomenon something ideal, which in one sense is part of ourselves and in another sense is not ourselves, actually exerts an influence and produces regenerative effects unattainable in other ways. If, then, there be a wider world of being than that of our every-day consciousness, if in it there be forces whose effects on us are intermittent, if one facilitating condition of the effects be the openness of the "subliminal" door, we have the elements of a theory to which the phenomena of religious life lend plausibility. I am so impressed by the importance of these phenomena that I adopt the hypothesis which they so naturally suggest. At these places at least, I say, it would seem as though transmundane energies, God, if you will, produced immediate effects within the natural world to which the rest of our experience belongs.

The ideal power with which we feel ourselves in connection is, both by ordinary men and by philosophers, assumed as a matter of course to be "one and only" and to be "infinite"; and the notion of many finite gods is one which hardly any one thinks it worth while to consider, and still less to uphold. Nevertheless, in the interests of intellectual clearness, I feel bound to say that religious experience, as we have studied it, cannot be cited as unequivocally supporting, the infinist belief. The only thing that it unequivocally testifies to is that we can experience union with *something* larger than ourselves and in that union find our greatest peace. Philosophy, with its passion for unity, and mysticism with its monoideistic bent, both "pass to the limit" and identify the something with a unique God who is the all-inclusive soul of the world. Popular opinion, respectful of their authority, follows the example which they set.

Meanwhile the practical needs and experiences of religion seem to me sufficiently met by the belief that beyond each man and in a fashion continuous with him there exists a larger power which is friendly to him and to his ideals. All that the facts require is that the power should be both other and larger than our conscious selves. Anything larger will do, if only it be large enough to trust for the next step. It need not be infinite, it need not be solitary. It might conceivably be only a larger and more godlike self, of which the present self would then be but the mutilated expression, and the universe might conceivably be a collection of such selves.

I do not imply by this abridgment of James' conclusions that Shelley meant to provide a theology for religious experience. However, we can conceive of Prometheus and Asia as aspects of a "larger and more godlike self" for each human being, man or woman (rather than as such selves respectively for each man and each woman), whose present self is a mutilated expression of what it can become when each is an harmonious element in the whole,

> Man, oh, not men! a chain of linkèd thought,
> Of love and might to be divided not, (IV. 393-394)

> Man, one harmonious soul of many a soul,
> Whose nature is its own divine control. (IV. 400-401)

Such a conception of Prometheus and Asia explains their existing in the drama as they do: Prometheus as man's soul, or mind, and also as the coterminous and other "More," as a God; Asia also as a spiritual power with a personal existence, that is, a God, as a human being, and as a manifestation of Love. [Mary Shelley in her Note on *Prometheus Unbound* interpreted Asia as Nature, but nothing in the drama supports such an interpretation.] The deep truth is imageless, but it is hard to say anything intelligible without images. The existences in the drama give meaning in human measure to the deep truth. The conception, not being one of a universe realiz-

151

ing absolute unity, contains evil as an independent existence, which can be quelled. Were the universe unitary rather than pluralistic, evil must originate in God and forever exist, incapable of being quelled, and is unchangeable even by God. Which is to say, any theism making a systematic philosophy of the universe wants God to be All-in-All and so tends to monotheism and pantheism—at least it has been that way historically; in such a philosophic theism the problem of evil is insoluble unless its God is not absolutely good or not immutable, conditions too hard for such a philosophic theism to admit.

In Shelley's theism there are dual powers: the Almighty and Merciful God who made the living world and all that it contains, and the Evil given no name (II. iv. 9-28). We need not insist that by God Shelley meant an actual Creator, only that the human mind, which is the living world, is of the nature of divinity and is evolving to a larger and more godlike self. Shelley had this to say in his *Essay on Christianity:* "The perfection of the human and divine character is thus asserted to be the same: man by resembling God fulfils most accurately the tendencies of his nature, and God comprehends within itself all that constitutes human perfection. Thus God is a model through which the excellence of man is to be estimated, while the *abstract* perfection of the human character is the type of the *actual* perfection of the divine." If Shelley repudiated the concept of a Creator, that makes his thought no less religious. Buddha, too, apparently repudiated a Creator, but only an uncommonly limited mind, or soul, could think Buddhism not a profound religion. A word of caution: in the dualism of spirit and matter that exists in Shelley's philosophy, good is not synonymous with spirit nor evil with matter (Jupiter is a spirit). If Shelley meant a Creator when Demogorgon spoke of Almighty God, the existence of that higher power need alter nothing that I have said about Prometheus, Asia and humanity.

To Prometheus and Asia in their cave come the "echoes of the human world." The echoes are of love, pity, and music,

> Itself the echo of the heart, and all
> That tempers or improves man's life, now free. (40-48)

There come also mediators of love between man and God,

man's creations in the arts, his spiritual progeny. These "lovely apparitions" (49), here interchangeable with "phantoms" just as when Earth used the words (I. 192-206), are shadows; are manifestations of the forms, or essences, that exist in the world of intellectual beauty. The apparitions are "dim at first" because they are imperfect manifestations of the forms. When the mind embraces beauty, its knowledge won ("gathered") from that union allows it to cast the focussed ("gathered" contains ambiguity) intellectual light (the "rays which are reality") on its creations and make them more perfect; the forms becoming perfect are thereby "radiant," as Prometheus and Asia became radiant when their essences were revealed. The mind's embrace of beauty is the human manifestation of the union of Prometheus and Asia; it is a spiritual act. As "man grows wise and kind," as he becomes his larger and more godlike self, his spiritual progeny (his "shadows," 56) "grow More fair and soft," that is, they more and more have the attributes of beauty and love [the modern critical temper admiring toughmindedness may feel unsympathetic with softness as an image meant to evoke the admirable—nevertheless, love is soft]. This spiritual evolution—"evil and error fall" as "man grows wise and kind"—is possible now that man's life is free (48). The change is not immediate, only begun and sure. "Such virtue," says Prometheus, "has the cave and place around"—this line defines the importance of Prometheus and Asia living there, which is not a retreat from but an action for the world (49-63).

Prometheus gives the Spirit of the Hour one work more to accomplish: to blow over the cities of the world the shell that the prophetic sea-god Proteus gave as a gift to Asia for her first union with Prometheus (the prophecy he breathed into the shell was the only prophecy the god ever willingly made). In the mystic shell the "glowing light" looks "like lulled music," a music that shall be loosened from the "many folded" conch as "thunder mingled with clear echoes" when the Spirit trumpets the prophecy fulfilled in its Hour. The fused images of glowing light and music ("the echo of the human heart") which is oceanic music ("the wide ocean of intellectual beauty") beyond making the gift fitting for Asia suggest that the prophecy is of Love as the law to govern the universe (64-75); and indeed; the Spirit of the Hour returning will say,

153

Soon as the sound had ceased whose thunder filled
The abysses of the sky and the wide earth,
There was a change: the impalpable thin air
And the all-circling sunlight were transformed,
As if the sense of love dissolved in them
Had folded itself round the sphered world. (III. iv. 98-103)

Prometheus through love first changes the Earth—love giving new life and joy—making her natural world fit for "the
coming day." She speaks out of a transforming passion:

all plants
And creeping forms, and insects rainbow-winged,
And birds, and beasts, and fish, and human shapes,
Which drew disease and pain from my wan bosom,
Draining the poison of despair, shall take
And interchange sweet nutriment. (91-96)

Even death shall be as a mother's loving embrace of a child
(84-107), concluding a perfect existence.

For ideality to exist in human life there must be ideality in
nature. So it was in Milton's Paradise before the Fall. So the
Keats of the letters thought, writing, "The point at which
Man may arrive is as far as the parallel state in inanimate
nature and no further"; but unlike the Shelley of *Prometheus
Unbound*, Keats did not at all believe (as he made clear in the
same letter) that the nature of the world would ever change.
The intellectual arguments for mankind's being able to realize
perfection in existence to come are two, the philosophical and
the scientific. If the physical world is a manifestation of an intellectual and moral world, the physical will become more perfect as the intellectual and moral evolve toward perfection. If
the physical world has its own independent existence and
reality, it nonetheless is mutable and may be changed by the
enormous power of science. Act IV gives imaginative expression to that power of science, and thus the scientific imagery
of *Prometheus Unbound* is integral to the imaginative whole.

The love of Prometheus, the touch of his lips to Mother
Earth, shoots a warmth through her that changes her nature.
The cause of the change is both moral and scientific: moral in
the power of love to transform the dense world of matter to
its, love's, own likeness; scientific in the power of energy (heat

154

being metonymous for energy in all its forms) to change matter.

Earth ended her speech with thought of death,

> the last embrace of her [Earth]
> Who takes the life she gave. (105-106)

Asia would know the meaning of death, but the language for this knowledge ("this tongue," 111), and so the understanding which cannot exist until the language does, belongs only to the dead. The music in their exchange softens the hard reality of death:

> *Asia.*   Cease they to love, and move, and breathe, and speak,
>   Who die?
> *Earth.*   It would avail not to reply. (109-110)

Earth can only say in the language of the living,

> Death is the veil which those who live call life:
> They sleep, and it is lifted. (113-114)

Our physical existence makes imperfect our perception of ultimate reality, which is intellectual, spiritual. After our physical lives, our natures, purely intellectual, are unimpeded in our knowledge of ultimate reality, our natures are at one with that reality. The "sleep" ending our physical lives suggests nothing of the dreamlike, only the painlessness of the transition. And meanwhile, Prometheus unbound, our physical lives shall be spent on an earth become an Eden (114-123). Turning from Asia to Prometheus, Earth speaks of a cavern where during Jupiter's reign she panted forth her spirit in anguish, when her son's pain maddened her heart, and those breathing in her anguished spirit became mad too—such were the effects of the Titan's pain on earth and men—so that they built a temple of superstition that lured peoples to bad faith with each other and to war. But now that Prometheus is restored, the breath (her spirit) rising from the cavern like a violet's exhalation fills with a "serener light and crimson air" the lovely natural world around and inspires "calm and happy thoughts," like Earth's. The image of crimson air has a scientific origin, identified by Carl Grabo in the work of Priestley, Davy, and other scientists as nitrous oxide. The influence of the crimson air on our mind has an empirical validity: nitrous oxide, diluted with air, stimulates a consciousness (other than our daily rational consciousness) which William James in his published observations believed was mystical, a state in which the better mind absorbs the worser. It is by right of what Prometheus now is that Earth says, "This cave is thine" (147); it is his "destined cave" (175), other than the cave that Prometheus spoke of. So much is clear from Earth's summoning a spirit to guide Prometheus and the Oceanides from the Caucasus to Greece and from her describing to Prometheus the unfamiliar temple, beside which is the cave. This cave is in closer conjunction than the other with the human world. Prometheus living in Earth's cave will sustain her exhalation of "serener light and crimson air"; and in his aspect as the mind of man will live in nature, he will not be withdrawn to his own cave apart from the human world (40-44). The wisest of living beings, Prometheus accepts Earth's better course. The spirit in the likeness of a winged child that Earth summons is her torch-bearer, her guide. The lamp he let go out in the past while gazing on Asia's eyes, he kindled again on the love in her eyes, "which is as fire" (148-152)—there is a suggestion, perhaps, that the light of natural knowledge gives place to spiritual knowledge. [This spirit's identity is apparent at the beginning of the next scene: its lamp is the light burning on the head of the Spirit of the Earth (2-3); the Spirit of the Earth knows the regions of sea, sky, and earth, having wandered through those regions (10-15); the Spirit of the Earth in the past drank the light of Asia's eyes (16-18); and the Spirit of the Earth is a child (33).] In guiding Prometheus and the Oceanides the spirit will take them from the Caucasus—over the Nysa, where Dionysus was reared and which is a haunt of the frenzied women-worshippers of that mystery god, and through the wilderness watered by the Indus and its tributaries—to Greece where freedom, mind, and intellectual beauty first flowered. The deserted temple, which Earth remembers but which Prometheus in his suffering forgot, was once dedicate to Prometheus. After he was hung in chains in the Caucasian mountains, his pain made Earth exhale an anguish that distorted men's minds; they deserted his temple, whose "living imagery, Praxitelean shapes" filled the air with love, and built another nearby from which superstition ruled (161-168, 124-130). In the temple of Prometheus young men emulating the Titan

bore to his honor through the divine gloom the lamp which
was his emblem, the fire he gave,

> even as those
> Who bear the untransmitted torch of hope
> Into the grave, across the night of life,
> As thou hast borne it most triumphantly
> To this far goal of Time. (168-174)

In Shelley's figurative language we must sometimes single out
the analogous elements: the torch of hope is not wholly correspondent to the lamp which is the Titan's emblem, nor is
the night of life wholly correspondent to the divine gloom;
only the elements of light and darkness are analogous in these
images, and the disagreements in the figures sustain a tension
that the powerful, realistic *untransmitted* forces on us. The
tension dissolves in the triumphant image of Prometheus: here
the far goal corresponds wholly to the grave (the alliteration
underscoring the likeness) and Time corresponds wholly to the
night of life (the assonance underscoring the likeness). To the
night of life and to Time belongs suffering; in the grave a
man awakens to eternity, at the far goal mankind wins to
eternity.

The images were made of actualities in Shelley's experience
and in historical experience. Some months earlier Shelley had
come "to a calm and lovely basin of water [Lake Avernus],
surrounded by dark woody hills, and profoundly solitary,"
where "vast ruins" of a temple were "reflected in its windless
mirror"; and he had seen the "Praxitelean shapes that throng
the Vatican, the Capitol, and the palaces of Rome." (Praxitelean means like the shapes of Praxiteles, not by Praxiteles.)
Pausanias recorded the existence of an altar of Prometheus
(later misinterpreted as a temple) in the grove of Plato's Academy; in worship of Prometheus young men carrying torches
raced from the altar to a goal in Athens. At Colonus near the
Academy, where Oedipus died his mystic and triumphant
death, there was a chasm which was thought an entrance to the
underworld. The temple and cave which actually existed, the
worship of Prometheus and the rich evocation of Colonus—
these are strong towers and cables for Shelley's bridge suspended to symbolic reality.

157

Prometheus and the Oceanides, guided by the Spirit of the Earth, are in a forest near Earth's cave, a "green waste wilderness" (9) echoing an *"Eden* rais'd in the wast Wilderness" in *Paradise Regained.* The light burning "like a green star" (3) corresponds to the image for atmospheric electricity in scientific writings of the day; the light on the sea-spray or cloud, in fields or cities, and in the wilderness (10-14) corresponds to electrical manifestations in the meteorology of the time; and in "long noons . . . work is none in the bright silent air" (28-29) because "at noon . . . the atmospheric electricity . . . is quiescent provided the day is serene and windless"—Carl Grabo extended these findings of his to interpret the Spirit of Earth as electricity, and also equated electricity with love as in the "love, which is as fire" that once kindled the Spirit's lamp (III. iii. 148-151). Although I accept the scientific writings on electricity as sources of the imagery for the Spirit's light and work, I think it imaginatively constricting to equate the Spirit with electricity, thereby rendering it lifeless as a mythical being; on the other hand, the abstract unifying of love ("which is as fire") and electricity is imaginatively fruitful, giving a common reality to the moral and physical worlds. The Spirit of Earth was separated from Asia for the long ages of Jupiter's rule. When Saturn ruled, the Spirit could spend its leisure with Asia, drinking her light [19: *dipsas,* a serpent whose bite caused a consuming thirst], but like "earth's primal spirits" (II. iv. 35) had no intellectual power then; it "idly reasoned what it saw" (III. iv. 22). Its leisure is in "the long noons" (28) when it has no work; this noon hour brought the reunion of Prometheus and Asia (II. v. 10). Asia can now cherish the child "unenvied" (III. iv. 31) because Time who envied Light and Love no longer exists (II. iv. 33; IV. 14). In an imperfect world its "simple talk once solaced"; now, Asia says, it will delight (1-32).

But the Spirit of the Earth is conscious of having changed from a simple being; it has "grown wise . . . within this day; And happier too; happier and wiser both" (33-35). The evil in worms, and beasts, and plants, and humankind used to hinder his walks over the green world and make him sick at heart (36-50). Then using the very human word "well" to make his transition, the Spirit speaks of the change that it witnessed in the world: just before being summoned by Earth to guide Prometheus and the Oceanides, the Spirit was making its way through a great city to the surrounding hills when it heard a long, sweet sound (the conch blown by the Spirit of the Hour) that brought the population into the streets, looking up to Heaven. The Spirit watched a change in people, and in animals, plants, birds. The people, their ugliness fading into the scattering winds,

> seemed mild and lovely forms
> After some foul disguise had fallen, and all
> Were somewhat changed, and after brief surprise
> And greetings of delighted wonder, all
> Went to their sleep again.

The restraint and quietness of tone, the surprise and delighted wonder of the people, and the human return to sleep, make a fine scene. Even toads and lizards—with little physical change—now manifested beauty, for "All things had put their evil nature off." The nightshade, twining a "bright bunch of amber berries" being thinned by two kingfishers, is no longer poisonous; no longer do living things drain the "poison of despair" from Earth, nor do they take any but earth's vegetable nutriment. These water birds were "imaged as in a sky"; as elsewhere Shelley uses the reflection to give an image "more beautiful than the objects it reflects"; the colors and composition, as he wrote of a reflection in a canal in his *Three Fragments on Beauty*, "surpass and misrepresent truth." The reflection, like art, selects and so intensifies beauty, and this image is "as in a sky" because, manifesting moral goodness as well as beauty, it is an image of heaven (51-83).

> *Spirit of the Earth.* So, with my thoughts full of these
> happy changes,
> We meet again, the happiest change of all.
> *Asia.* And never will we part, till thy chaste sister
> Who guides the frozen and inconstant moon
> Will look on thy more warm and equal light
> Till her heart thaw like flakes of April snow
> And love thee.
> *Spirit of the Earth.* What; as Asia loves Prometheus?

159

Asia. Peace, wanton, thou art yet not old enough.
Think ye by gazing on each other's eyes
To multiply your lovely selves, and fill
With spherèd fires the interlunar air?
 Spirit of the Earth. Nay, mother, while my sister trims
 her lamp
'Tis hard I should go darkling. (84-96)

There are several elements to remark in this passage. The personal love of the Spirit for Asia creates more happiness for him than his abstract love for goodness and beauty in humanity and in animals, plants, and birds. Love can change the physical world: its warm light will thaw the moon. The Moon will then claim union with her brother, the Earth, who will leave Asia. The leaving of Asia is like human experience: a man, said Adam, shall "leave his father and his mother, and shall cleave unto his wife." Then comes a human note of comedy in the Spirit's question and Asia's smiling response. Although the amusing passage comes as a discordant surprise in the profoundly serious tonal harmony otherwise sustained from beginning to end, its presence is explicable, even justifiable. The visions between which this passage is set are of the harvest of human happiness; and happiness would seem too theoretical, would be incomplete, were laughter absent—intellectual and moral perfection is not enough. The Spirit of the Earth began to speak of what it had seen (like a messenger) with the human syllable "Well"; and the spirit of the Hour, the other messenger, although beginning sublimely, settles on the ordinary human phrase "As I have said" in coming to the changes in humanity. Shelley used the word and the phrase for the tonality, in the sense that tone is defined in painting; just as a painter using blue in one place on his canvas will use at least traces of blue elsewhere in the picture, so Shelley having the color of human comedy has also the two other human accents. In the moment of comedy the Spirit's teasing, which shows him no longer a child, has no vulgarity in it, and Asia's reply is charming. (Like Schoolmen, we may speculate on the nature of the progeny of Prometheus and Asia.) The Spirit amusingly denies that he is not yet old enough; Asia, like most mothers, thinks her child still a child. While his sister during the interlunar nights (the nights between the waned old moon

160

and the new moon) trims her lamps (the household image for putting the light of the moon, which has gone out, into proper order for illumination is another trace of blue for the tonality), it would be hard for the Spirit of the Earth to go in the dark ("go darkling"): he means, still speaking amused and amusingly, that he will join his sister in her interlunar cave.

Asia stops their conversation with her command "Listen; look!" as the Spirit of the Hour enters, the hour of the new order. Although Prometheus and Asia are attuned to the changes in the world and humankind, it is as feeling not as thought that they know what the Spirit of the Hour has heard and seen; and so the Titan has the Spirit speak, for speech creates thought "Which is the measure of the universe" (96-97; II. iv. 72-73). These two lines are the last words of Prometheus and Asia; they focus our minds on the vision to come, the culmination of the three acts. In the fourth act the union of Prometheus and Asia dissolves into the joy of the universe.

The first vision of the drama, in the songs of Prometheus and Asia closing Act II, was intensely spiritualized. In Act III came the vision of Sun and Ocean; the eye of the universe and the reflection of eternity, they are also the physical laws of the world: a new relation exists between matter and the mind, or soul, of man. The third vision, in the speech of Prometheus to the Oceanides, reveals the connection between divinity and humanity. Earth's vision next concerns itself not with the physical laws of the world but more simply and concretely with the joyous nature of the place for life in the coming day. The fifth and sixth visions, of the Spirit of the Earth and of the Spirit of the Hour, as I have said, are of the harvest of human happiness in the new day. The two visions are needful for us to feel the wide joy and exultation; they create intensity as lyrical expression does by succeeding waves of emotion. The Spirit of the Hour does not repeat the vision of the Spirit of the Earth. The meaning in the narration of the Spirit of the Earth essentially is esthetic and emotional; the meaning in the narration of the Spirit of the Hour essentially is moral and intellectual.

After the heralding music sounded through heaven and earth, the world changed visibly and the Spirit of the Hour could see into the mysteries of the universe (98-105). The sun's horses, which took the Hour's car to this far goal of time, will

161

no longer be harnessed, for the hours of solar time no longer measure existence; the Hour's moonlike car will stand in a temple in the sun in memory of its tidings. That memory and the Phidian forms within the temple will always be in the (intellectual) light of the world (106-115). These Phidian forms, God-made, and the Praxitelean shapes in the temple of Prometheus, man-made, are mediators of "that best worship love" by man and God given and returned (III. iii. 55, 59-61). (It is pleasant to think that Shelley likened the God-made sculpture to the works of the greater and more powerful Greek artist.) The car will be yoked to horses in sculptured flight by an amphisbaenic snake. Shelley probably saw such an antique yoke, as he saw Greek temples open to the sky in southern Italy—his experience constantly entered his poetry. The amphisbaena has a head at each end and moves either way, perhaps suggesting the ever-spreading of the present hour into time past and time future, as though eternity were in an hour (111-121). [120: *mock*, as elsewhere, imitate]. The Spirit of the Hour chides itself for its digression (121-123), which nonetheless has relevance, and speaks again as messenger; the meaning in the digression, by the way, connects the change in sky and earth (98-103) and the change in humanity (125-204). For the Hour it was, and is, "the pain of bliss" to live containing the "mighty change" in humanity, although the Hour was at first disappointed not to see that change "Expressed in outward things" (125-130). The Spirit of the Earth also reported only little outward change (70-71, 74-76)—the theme, which reflects a profound acceptance of the world of living things and a rejoicing in their realities undistorted by evil, reflects no desire to change the physical nature of life.

The Hour witnessed the profoundest political and moral changes: no man ruled others, the race lived as harmoniously as spirits do; those bad emotions that had made the human mind a hell, and that had been inscribed on our foreheads, were gone [135-136: the quotation was inscribed over the *gate of hell* in Dante's *Inferno*, III. 9]. No longer did the subject of another's will become the abject of his own (here the wit of the wordplay, of course, is not used for comic purposes; in *Swellfoot the Tyrant* we shall see Shelley using wordplay for comedy) and thereby self-destructive [140: *abject*, "a man without hope; a man whose miseries are irretrievable"—Johnson's *Dic-*

162

tionary]. None smiled assent to lies that he would not bring himself to speak. None stamped out the sparks of love and hope in his heart until there were only "bitter ashes, a soul self-consumed" and then with "his own hideous ill" infected others [147: *the wretch crept a vampire*, the apparent physiology is that, his heart being ashes, he needs the lifeblood of others; and in taking their blood he infects them with his disease of living loveless and hopeless, as the vampire bat transmits rabies]. None talked away his integrity in polite conversation, realizing after his assent that he did not believe what he had assented to; and although he realized what he had done, he learned to mistrust himself profoundly, for that detected unmeant hypocrisy suggested that he might be living with other hypocrisies undetected (130-152). The Spirit of the Hour has been speaking of men; now he speaks of women. They were "frank, beautiful, and kind As the free heaven"; exempt from custom's evil, they were new creatures intellectually and emotionally, making "earth like heaven"; nor did any once-treasured bitter emotions, the worst of them shame, spoil love, which like the plant nepenthe removes sorrow (153-163).

State and church together with their laws, doctrines, and punishments were "unregarded now," like that ancient sculpture and architecture which celebrated evil power but which now are only an astonishing curiosity (164-179). "And those foul shapes" of evil which were Jupiter ["those foul shapes . . . under many a name and many a form" (180-181) are not "those monstrous and barbaric shapes" (168) carved on the obelisk; the "monstrous and barbaric shapes" are representations of the conquered to glorify the conquerors but which, ironically, have outlasted and so finally triumphed over the palaces and tombs which imaged the dark (truth is in light) but powerful faith that wasted the world, the faith of dictators and priests that served Jupiter; whereas the "foul shapes" are of "the Spirit of evil, One Power of many shapes," as Shelley earlier expressed the idea in *The Revolt of Islam*, I. xxvii. 1-2] —the shapes of Jupiter, not long ago served by the terrified and unhappy peoples of the world, now frown as they moulder like the palaces and tombs emblematic of earlier evils (180-189) [187: *unreclaiming tears*, because of fear their tears—for the love they ruined and killed to flatter Jupiter—neither cried out in opposition nor called them back from moral transgression]. The kind of life men once lived, a painted veil or mask which falsely represented [as in II. ii. 80-82, Shelley generally uses "mimicked" for an inferior representation and "mocked" for a praiseworthy representation] what "men believed or hoped, is torn aside," revealing the true face of man, his best nature:

> the man remains
> Scepterless, free, uncircumscribed, but man
> Equal, unclassed, tribeless, and nationless,
> Exempt from awe, worship, degree, the king
> Over himself. (193-197)

Again the difficulty is the structure of the language, which is Cubistic, the representation (here the direct road of meaning) fragmented into overlapping planes: the man remains absolutely free but each governing himself so that there are no encroachments on others—that direct road is broken up and connected meaning is made part of the design so that what we ordinarily perceive as a sequence of ideas we can perceive at once, this new perception making a conception visible that otherwise would not be. The meaning must come through the formal elements in Shelley's construction. What follows has to do with textural elements rather than with the construction; it is not the meaning but helps make the meaning accessible. The three words "Scepterless [he does not rule others], free, uncircumscribed [he is not ruled by others]," facets cut alike on a diamond, are meant to create lyric intensity as a faceted stone gives brilliance to light; although man has this absolute freedom—and further has absolute equality and individuality, there being no social or political structure (195) and his inner self being exempt from fear or dread or any sense of littleness in some greater presence or power ("awe") and from psychological deference or submission ("worship"—in the secular not in the religious sense as man does give "that best worship love" to Prometheus, who returns it) and from the existence of more or less of any given quality or acquirement ("degree")—he governs himself, equal to living freely and harmoniously. The verbal meanings must be consciously and deliberately restricted; such restriction of meaning is an intellectual experience radically different from the reception or perception of ambiguities.

164

Man is "just, gentle, wise" but not without suffering (the two pertinent meanings of passion are connected: the one, a suffering of imposed or inflicted pain; the other, intense feeling or emotion, which implies the capacity for both pain and joy) although free from that suffering which is the guilt or pain consequent upon any evil that the will effected or permitted (now passion has the Aristotelean meaning of any condition of being following from the action of some cause, a meaning similarly defined by Locke); he experiences such suffering as may be attendant on "chance, and death, and mutability." [A final word on Necessity: since chance exists, necessity can not; and line 199 makes it clear that man's will was always free, although not well used.] Never free of these clogs of his soul, happenings that he must cope with, he nonetheless rules them like slaves, that is, he bends them to his purposes. Were it otherwise, were human life not commensurate with matter, the human soul, the Spirit of the Hour concludes,

> might oversoar
> The loftiest star of unascended heaven,
> Pinnacled dim in the intense inane.

[204: *inane*, literally the void of infinite space]

The vision of the new order although ideal is concrete and solid; the new order, which has what Shelley saw as the best possibilities in human life, requires little outward change. For some the vision is uninteresting; that is perhaps their limitation, not the drama's. For some the heaven of *Paradise Lost* is also uninteresting (after the revolt and battle) presumably because only goodness is there, and they would likewise find Milton's inhabitable and desirable paradise dull were it not for the shadow of Satan falling athwart. For Shelley it was quite otherwise. Prometheus was a character superior to Satan for poetry "because, in addition to courage and majesty, and firm and patient opposition to omnipotent force, he is susceptible of being described as exempt from the taints of ambition, envy, revenge, and a desire for personal aggrandisement, which, in the Hero of *Paradise Lost*, interfere with the interest." That last notion, perhaps, could only have been thought by Shelley. Not that he thought that evil would "interfere with the in-

165

terest" of the many; he wrote *Prometheus Unbound* for the few. In the Preface to his play *The Cenci* he wrote, "Revenge, retaliation, atonement are pernicious mistakes. If Beatrice [the heroine] had thought in this manner she would have been wiser and better; but she would never have been a tragic character: the few whom such an exhibition would have interested, could never have been sufficiently interested for a dramatic purpose, from the want of finding sympathy in their interest among the mass who surround them." That is, who surround them in the theater. The exhibition of Prometheus as the "highest perfection of moral and intellectual nature" could interest the few because the drama was meant only to be read, it was a private experience; *The Cenci* was meant for the stage and so was a public experience in which the response of any person is affected by the response of the surrounding audience. Shelley's image of ideality in *Prometheus Unbound*, in which his consciousness of good is strengthened by his consciousness of evil, found a fit audience, though few, in its own and succeeding ages; and in our time the few are becoming many. The vision that is the whole of Act IV is a triumph of the human spirit.

After Prometheus' moral change, his wisdom purchased by suffering, and its consequence in Asia's action, her descent to Demogorgon, which issues in the enormous struggle between Demogorgon and Jupiter, no conflict can engage the audience, no drama remains. Henceforth the consequences are historic rather than dramatic, and the joy of the world, in Act IV, rightly takes lyric expression.

PROMETHEUS UNBOUND: ACT IV

Shelley completed the third act by April 1819. There was no readiness for a fourth act in his mind; otherwise, the storm of composition still upon him, he would have swept on. Instead, in his excitement he turned to other works (*The Cenci, The Mask of Anarchy, Peter Bell the Third, Ode to the West Wind*). There were months of delay in making arrangements for publication of the drama, which was thought finished in April. It was a fortunate delay (likely owing to uncertainties about Ollier, his publisher) for in the meantime the fourth act gestated. In mid-November he seems not yet to have begun that act, for he wrote to Leigh Hunt, "The Prometheus I wish to be printed and to come out immediately." Shelley had informed Ollier on October 15 that he was on the "point of sending" his *Prometheus* of three acts. There is a draft of a large part of Act IV in a notebook of Shelley's containing an early stage of *Ode to the West Wind*, written in late October; but Shelley's notebook habits were irregular, and I gauge that he simply returned in November to some empty pages in the notebook, other pages of which he had used several weeks earlier. In a letter on December 23 he made the announcement, "I have just finished an additional act to 'Prometheus'." Perhaps *Ode to the West Wind* that autumn scattered from his mind's hearth, as though in psychological answer to his prayer to the spiritual power emblemed by the west wind, the ashes and sparks that blazed into the intellectual light emotionally and formally necessary to culminate the lyrical drama. Although the fourth act came late, it is, as C. S. Lewis judged, "that for which the poem exists. I do not mean by this that the three preceding acts are mere means; but that their significance and beauty are determined by what follows, and that what came last . . . does not add to, and therefore corrupt, a completed structure; it gives structure to that which, without it, would be imperfect. The resulting whole is the greatest long poem in the nineteenth century."

It is also the most modern in its intellectual content: I speak narrowly now of the scientific knowledge. Newman White's counterview is that Shelley's scientific knowledge "is limited to the imagery and does not extend to the general philosophy of the poem," that "Shelley did very little scientific reading after 1815," and that most of the scientific knowledge occurs "in the fourth act, which was written some months after Shelley considered the poem finished." But even if Shelley composed the act after considering the poem finished—possibly the uncertainties about Ollier given as reasons for delaying publication were rationalizations of his feelings that the drama was unfinished—nonetheless the addition of the act (in accordance with the structural principle of harmony) changed the meaning of the whole; and, to my mind, Shelley succeeded in making the scientific knowledge integral to the meaning of the whole. That Shelley read little in science after 1815 is not im-

167

portant: not much happened to change scientific thought between 1815 and 1819, and Shelley's prodigious memory put even the phraseology of things he had read years earlier at his disposal. Nor is the "general philosophy"—I should rather say the thought—of the poem separable from the imagery any more than it is from the structure of the work, or from the tones, or from the myths.

Because the many voices of the visible and invisible worlds are heard in this act, giving a sense of boundlessness and even of immateriality, the reader may not see where the action takes place: in the forest near the cave to which the Spirit of Earth had guided Prometheus and Asia and the two other Oceanides, a place in the human world. We are still in a drama, the poet is artistically conscious of its setting, and in this setting the action comes to us in a structure somewhat like that of Greek drama. There are four divisions: 1) with the actors of the Spirits of air and earth and of the Hours of Time, and the chorus of the two Oceanides, the division ending with line 56; 2) with the actors of the Hours of the new order and of the Spirits of the human mind, and the chorus, the division ending with line 318; 3) with the actors of Earth and Moon, and the chorus, the division ending with line 518; and 4) with the actors of Eternity and the universe concluding the drama, no voice to follow Demogorgon's. The actors in the fourth act, refracting the glory of Prometheus, "Good, great and joyous, beautiful and free," sing in stanzaic forms, while the choral spectators, the Oceanides, speak in blank verse (except for their first lines when it would have been too early to interrupt the movement of song). The presence of the choral spectators makes for our presence in the drama: we may identify with the chorus, and our eyes look through theirs. Their spoken language acts as ballast for our sake, giving the act a steady keel (in a sense, the whole act is an "enchanted boat" floating on a "many-winding river" of song, much like Asia's soul floating to a "sea profound, of ever-spreading sound," piloted by Prometheus).

The act begins with the Voice of unseen Spirits—the Spirits of air and earth (57)—summoning the Hours of eternity; for the new day has already begun, the sun having shepherded the pale stars to their folds in the depths of the dawn (1-8). Not those Hours come in answer to the Voice, but the "past

168

Hours" (31), or rather the spectres of these dead Hours (12-13), who are bearing "Time to his tomb in eternity" (14). Yet death will remain, for, in Shelley's view, acts and hours exist in eternity (IV. 565-566); the difference between time (which is relative) and eternity (which is absolute) is moral and intellectual, not physical. Shelley wrote in a note for *Queen Mab*: "If a mind be conscious of an hundred ideas during one minute, by the clock, and of two hundred during another, the latter of these spaces would actually occupy so much greater extent in the mind as two exceed one in quantity. If, therefore, the human mind, by any future improvement of its sensibility, should become conscious of an infinite number of ideas in a minute, that minute would be eternity. I do not hence infer that the actual space between the birth and death of a man will ever be prolonged." Mythically speaking, Time as vice-regent of Saturn and then of Zeus, envious of Light and Love, is a principle of evil; Eternity, an aspect of the One, is the principle of good. The eternity that man enjoys is not only his succession of absolute hours each having an infinity of intellectual and moral value, but his continued being in ways that the happy Dead reveal later in the act.

The spectral Hours, evil though they were, would mourn deeply, humanly; but they can offer only yew, not hair; dew, not tears—the natural rather than the human; and can spread only faded flowers, nothing beautiful, on Time's corpse (15-20). They melt away; "the children of a diviner day" (of "Eternity, Mother of many acts and hours," 565-566) are to come (24-26). The spectral Hours and their spoil (apparently not worth reclaiming), their conquest rendered vain by Prometheus ("One"), go swiftly "To the dark, to the past, to the dead" (21-39); their gray passage makes more luminous the Light that gives joy to the celebrants.

The Voice of the unseen Spirits of air and earth again sings to the Hours of eternity. Clouds, dew, and waves, anything but passionless, are in a "storm of delight," a "panic of glee," shaking with emotion and dancing in mirth. But where are the Hours?

> The pine boughs are singing
> Old songs with new gladness

—the expulsion of evil, we are reminded, has not changed

things outwardly. There are music and gladness everywhere on land and sea. Where are the Hours? (40-55) The choral spectators announce them:

> *Ione.* What charioteers are these?
> *Panthea.*   Where are their chariots?

Both questions show wonderment at charioteers without chariots. They have none because they are of eternity, not of time. These Hours are not measured by motion, neither by the swift passage of the sun nor of the stars.

> *Semichorus of Hours*
> The voice of the Spirits of Air and of Earth
>   Have drawn back the figured curtain of sleep
> Which covered our being and darkened our birth
>   In the deep.
>
> *A Voice*
> In the deep?
>
> *Semichorus II*
>   Oh, below the deep.
>
> *Semichorus I*
> An hundred ages we had been kept
>   Cradled in visions of hate and care,
> And each one who waked as his brother slept,
>   Found the truth—
>
> *Semichorus II*
>   Worse than his visions were! (56-64)

The voice of the Spirits of Air and Earth could draw back the figured curtain, the dream visions, because these spirits were filled with love:

>   the impalpable thin air
> And the all-circling sunlight were transformed,
> As if the sense of love dissolved in them
> Had folded itself round the spherèd world. (III. iv. 100-103)

The Hours had been born in the realm of the Eternal and had there been cradled a hundred ages—the time it took for the change in mankind envisioned in Act III (if each age is a generation of thirty years, the time is the three thousand years of the suffering of Prometheus)—waking from time to time to truths more horrible than their dream visions of hate. But their dreams were not only visions of hate.

Semichorus I
We have heard the lute of Hope in sleep;
We have known the voice of Love in dreams;
We have known the wand of Power; and leap—

George Woodberry has finely suggested that these three lines correspond to the first three acts; and, we may add, the next line corresponds to the fourth act:

Semichorus II
As the billows leap in the morning beams! (65-68)

The full Chorus of Hours sings, using the second person for their actions, "Weave the dance . . . Pierce with song . . . Enchant the day." There are days and nights in Eternity (69-72). They use the third person for themselves: "Once the hungry Hours were hounds Which chased the day . . ." (73-74). The Hours of Eternity seem only morally other than the Hours of Time. They sing on:

But now, oh weave the mystic measure
Of music, and dance, and shapes of light,
Let the Hours, and the spirits of might and pleasure,
Like the clouds and sunbeams, unite. (77-80)

The mystic measure unifies sound, motion, form, and light. Here the imagery expresses a mystical concept; later the imagery will express a correspondent scientific concept (scientists now suggest an affinity, even a oneness, in the behavior of waves of sound, electric impulses, and light)—in Shelley religion and science are not at odds. The "shapes of light," like those "shapes too bright to see" peopling the calm and green paradise in the diviner day that Prometheus reached in the last stanza of Act II, are humanity's; they are the "spirits of might and pleasure" that the Hours desire union with. The Hours, like the clouds in union with sunlight, will become "heavy with love's sweet rain" (IV. 179). The spirits of might and pleasure are, as Panthea the choral interpreter makes clear, the Spirits of the human mind who are approaching "Wrapped in sweet sounds," their language, "as in bright veils" (81-82). Like flying fish mixing with sea-birds, the

171

Spirits join the dance of the Hours; the Hours wonder where these Spirits came from, who surpass their expectations (83-92).

These Spirits come from the mind of humanity—of Man, not men, as Earth declares,

> A chain of linkèd thought,
> Of love and might to be divided not; (394-395)

and as they say of themselves, they are an ocean, a heaven—words that are emblems of the Eternal (93-98). They come from "that deep abyss [the one mind of Man] Of wonder and bliss [the imaginative and reflective faculties of the mind], Whose caverns are crystal palaces" [the many minds of men, now of transparent clarity and beauty]. They come from the "skiey towers" of "thought's crowned powers"— the aspect of mind that will compel "the elements with adamantine stress" (396). In these caverns and towers of the mind (99-104) are love, wisdom, art, science (105-116) [107: *ye,* the antecedent is "ye happy hours;" the physical image of love suggests that the mind is in the body's passion. 115: *springs,* knowledge; 116: *Daedal wings,* to soar through the universe with]. For years after years—a hundred ages—these Spirits struggled through a "hell of hatreds, and hopes, and fears," finding little happiness to sustain them, but now the love that Man has won to (the Spirits are singing to the Hours who can look "beyond our eyes," that is, through their eyes to the human love in the Mind) transforms the universe to Paradise; love is the sole law governing the moral and physical worlds alike (117-128).

The Spirits singing with the Hours in the next chorus are those of air and earth. To the Spirits of the human mind they say, "Then weave the web of the mystic measure"— the weaving image, right for a dance, gives substance to the abstract design. Let them fill the dance and joyous music,

> As the waves of a thousand streams rush by
> To an ocean of splendor and harmony! (129-134)

—again the image is of multiplicity and unity, of men and man.

172

The Spirits of the human mind have been in "the depths of the sky" and at "the ends of the earth" (130):

> Beyond and around
> Or within the bound
> Which clips the world with darkness round. (138-140)

The "world" is the earth; the bounding "darkness" is the "pyramid of night" in line 444, which reaches some 900,000 miles into space. Now they will go beyond the regions of the stars to the nebulous farthest reaches of matter, where Death, Chaos, and Night have been, which are the absence of Life, Form, and Light (141-146). Wherever the Spirits of the human mind soar, there shall assemble the physical elements and spiritual principles for a creation. Typifying the physical—matter and energy—in this dualism of reality are earth, air, light, and gravitation. Of the three spiritual principles—love, thought, breath—breath is an animating power that shall forever sustain life, although no particular form of life. The spiritual trinity will quell death (see I. 787) not in the sense of utterly destroy, for men will die, but in the sense that life will be spiritually triumphant. The Spirits of the human mind, abstracting a paradigm from the new world of man, will create an ideal world, a heaven (165), whose principles of being will be those of absolute wisdom [154: *void's loose field,* like the hoar deep, the nebulous farthest reaches of matter]. Their "work shall be called the Promethean" (147-158): Man has become divinity, Prometheus, his greater self.

The Hours sing, "Break the dance, and scatter the song," and a semichorus is centrifugally driven beyond the stars along with the Spirits building a new earth and sea, a heaven where until now none could be, while another semichorus is centripetally retained by earth to act "With the powers of a world of perfect light" (159-170). Eternity and the Mind of Man, like Love and Light, are joined. [166: *slow,* that is, only compared to the Hours of Semichorus I]

Semichorus I of the Hours of Eternity whirls around the world being formed out of chaos, singing, and Semichorus II with music of sweet mirth encircles the earth, watching the great change as its forms happily die out of time and are born in eternity (169-174). If we accept the oneness of Man and the

Eternal, the song and the music are the instruments of creation and change; otherwise the song and music of the eternal Hours are an accompaniment, not a cause, the Spirits alone having creative power.

The Hours and the Spirits of the human mind sing together in their last chorus,

> Break the dance, and scatter the song,
> Let some depart, and some remain.

These lines make it clear that they have been dancing together. Those that go to the work of creation beyond the stars and those that stay with the earth will water the new heaven and the new earth with love (175-179).

The Hours and Spirits gone from the forest, Panthea and Ione yet retain their delight,

> As the bare green hill
> When some soft cloud vanishes into rain,
> Laughs with a thousand drops of sunny water
> To the unpavilioned sky! [*unpavilioned*, without clouds]

Shelley is not only using natural images easily to express the spiritual state of delight; in the ease of his art the simile implies an equality between the natural and the spiritual (180-184).

Ione hears new notes, sounds that are full of awe. Panthea says that it is the earth making music as it rolls on the waves of air just as wind makes music in the branches of trees (the Aeolian harp in the image). The air waves that carry sound are, of course, not visible; there seems a correspondence between the invisible world of scientific knowledge and the invisible world of spirit, and indeed, in Shelley's thought, they share an intellectual nature. Ione then hears in the pauses of the earth's music the undernotes of the moon, "awakening tones,"

> Which pierce the sense, and live within the soul,
> As the sharp stars pierce winter's crystal air
> And gaze upon themselves within the sea.

It is a magnificent tribute to the spiritual power of music as a manifestation of beauty (185-193).

Panthea points to the two openings in the forest, expressing in a complex conceit what she sees, hears, and imagines.

174

Through those openings a stream has divided into two runnels; each runnel is a melody; like sisters parting, the two runnels make an isle of lovely grief, lovely because of the sweet sad thoughts that grow there as a wood; but the grief will give way to their meeting in happiness—the image anticipates the love-union of earth and moon. On each runnel of strong sound—which is under an ocean-like enchantment (the melodies, like streams, are being drawn to the ocean "of ever-spreading sound," like the streams in Asia's song at the end of Act II)— floats a vision (194-205).

The first vision is the chariot of the new moon ("that thinnest boat," 206), which bears the moon, or moon-goddess ("Mother of the Months," 207), and which sets with the sun ("By ebbing light," 208)—Shelley's astronomy is accurate [210-213: the image is of "the new moon with the old moon in her arms," the new moon bright with the sunlight it reflects, the old moon seen by virtue of weak light reflected from the earth; 213: *Regard like,* Look like]. The setting sun is also in the image of the storm clouds piled on the "illumined sea When the sun rushes under it" (214-217) [217: *they,* the cloudwheels of the chariot]. The marvelous imagery of the whiteness of the infant deity (the beauty and whiteness intensified by equally marvelous musical attributes of language) takes its source from scientific knowledge as well as from simple observation (the extreme whiteness is owing to there being no atmosphere on the moon to refract light); and the creation of poetry from scientific materials [King-Hele offers as examples the lunar mountain ranges for the sculptural folds, dark craters and their radiating lines for eyes and lashes, Herschel's "dark heat rays" (infra-red rays) for the "fire that is not brightness"] gives modern authority to the mind setting forth a nature divinity, or, rather than a divinity, an intelligence. As the cloud-wheels of the chariot "roll Over the grass, and flowers, and waves," they "wake sounds" (233-234)—music is the effluence of beauty (206-235).

In the complex imagery of the vision which is the sphere —musical, geometric, tactile, intellectual, colored, supernatural, odorous, natural, synaesthetic, human—is the design of an ordering structural power, one which designed simply in the imagery of the moon. The vision which is the sphere— whatever else the richness of its ambiguity may mean: myth-

175

ically, philosophically, mystically—images physical meanings, the center of these meanings being the intricate beauty of the earth as a structure of matter. Now, scholars know that there exists a continuity in the imagery and meaning of the sphere with the vision in the first chapter of *Ezekiel* of the living creatures in a medium of fire, ushered in by natural forces, to which is mystically joined inanimate matter, a mechanism of wheels within wheels, the whole moving with one will and one impulse, and also with the prophet's vision transmitted in the sixth book of *Paradise Lost* of the chariot of God, instinct with spirit. Such distinguished tradition gives lustre and authority to any vision worthy of the tradition; and, in particular, gives imaginative roots in rich soil to the existence of life or spirit in Shelley's vision of matter and motion. But it is the originality, his *continuing* the tradition not changelessly, not lifelessly, but with new imagery, even as science changes the imagery of religion, that can evoke imaginative meaning without our suspending the working of intellect. His originality is in his imaginative power to cultivate a new plant with scientific knowledge. Shelley had the deepest regard for the nature of matter. Quite early he wrote, "Matter . . . is not inert. It is infinitely active and subtle. Light, electricity, and magnetism are . . . not surpassed by thought itself in tenuity and activity" and "seem to possess equal claims with thought to the unmeaning distinction of immateriality. The laws of motion and the properties of matter suffice to account for every phenomenon, or combination of phenomena exhibited in the Universe" (*A Refutation of Deism*). In *Prometheus Unbound* the "deep truth is imageless"—inexplicable by the laws of motion and the properties of matter; and spiritual Power exists governing, or rather harmonizing, the universe through love. The mind of Man, perfected in its greater Self, becomes one with that Power. The earlier belief and the later are not wholly inconsistent. For Shelley matter contains or evolves the consciousness of life, of spirit—the "unimaginable shapes" (244) and the "Intelligible words" (252) suggest as much. Again, in mystical thought (although not in Christian mysticism) the multiplicity of matter and of life are not differentiated from the unity, the oneness, of the Absolute; they, the multiplicity and the Unity, are one substance. The One is the source of being; and the "lampless deep," where ghosts dream

176

that unimaginable shapes dwell (245), is an image consonant with the imagery of mystics in diverse times and cultures for the One.

John Dalton published his atomic theory in 1808; even earlier Sir Humphrey Davy had anticipated the molecular structure of matter. Shelley's imaginative conceptions, based on their work, are close to modern scientific accounts. The one sphere that is the earth is a multiplicity of spheres, the atoms. The structure of matter seems solid; yet the distances of *empty space* between the nuclei of atoms are enormous compared to the size of the electrons revolving around the nucleus of an atom. (Electrons are particles of electricity, which is as love— again, an image symbolizes unity and multiplicity.) Erasmus Darwin spoke of particles of matter as "radiant points" of energy, and modern theory speaks of a flow of radiation from electrons—Shelley's flow of light. The flow of music Shelley perhaps imagined as supersensuous sound waves set up by the motions of electrons and atoms, just as the rushing earth has its *loud and whirlwind harmony*. Atoms, although they are joined together, *involved*, are constantly in motion, *involving*. Every atom has its characteristic color, *Purple and azure, white, and green, and golden;* technically speaking, has its characteristic absorption and emission frequencies although these frequencies, colors, are not necessarily visible to the eye. The intervolving atoms *whirl over each other* even while the concentric shells of electrons are *spinning* upon invisible *axles*. Their own swiftness countering one the other, their *self-destroying swiftness,* the vibration slows the whole. The friction of the powerful rolling earth coming through the forest on the *bright brook* (of sound) *grinds* the brook to an *azure mist* like light—the synaesthesia of sound and light perhaps has its origin in Newton, who noted that the seven colors of the spectrum have a mathematical correspondence to the frequencies of the seven notes in the diatonic major scale. As the multitudinous earth whirls through the forest, the intellectual imagery of science changes to the sensuous imagery of nature; and around the *intense yet self-conflicting* motion (which is the *self-destroying swiftness*) of the vision, the odor, sound and light of nature *Seem kneaded into one.* The synaesthetic imagery (253-259) anticipates the earth's unifying the multiplicity of beauty, the oneness then overcoming sense experience (260-261). Within the

177

earth lies its Spirit, the mythical consciousness of earth, the child that entered the drama to guide Prometheus and Asia to this part of the forest. Its lips are lovingly mocking, that is, imitating, the earth's music (236-269).

From the star upon the Spirit's forehead—the forehead is a metonym for the intellect—shoot "sun-like lightenings" illuminating the secrets of the earth [271-273: *Like swords . . . with tyrant-quelling myrtle . . . Embleming heaven and earth united,* Harmodius and Aristogeiton killed the Athenian tyrant Hipparchus in 514 B.C. (Shelley perhaps saw in Naples a Roman marble copy of the Tyrannicides); in celebration of the liberating act a Greek poet sang of myrtle wreathing the sword of Harmodius—the Greeks crowned their great soldiers with myrtle wreaths. In this passage the light of the mind is the tyrant-quelling sword which, quelling evil and giving the freedom that goodness needs in order to flourish, unites heaven and earth, that is, brings in the new order].

Having portrayed the structure of the earth as matter and having portrayed meaning other than physical, Panthea now gives the history of the earth: the physical evolution manifest in its geological history is continuous with the spiritual evolution in the universal history of *Prometheus Unbound*.

The vast beams flashing from the forehead of the Spirit fill the abyss below the earth, which is the sky, "perpendicular now, and now transverse" (like the northern lights), and pierce the earth. They light up the treasures of mines [281: *valueless,* of incalculable value], caverns of great beauty, deep wells of fire, and underground water that makes oceans and becomes the kingly ermine of mountains. They flash on, deeper, to the buried ruins and navies and armies—"cancelled" (289), destroyed by cataclysm, as were vast cities with their "mortal, but not human" populations (298). The great Linnaeus (1707-1778) and Cuvier (1769-1832) believed that earlier ages had been destroyed by cataclysms; to Erasmus Darwin (1731-1802), the grandfather of Charles, Shelley owed the evolutionary concept implicit in "mortal, but not human." The skeletons and works in these cities are shattered, jammed by the internal pressure of the earth into a "gray annihilation" (301), nothing any longer recognizable for what it was. Over these, as the vast beams pierce upward toward the earth's core, are the fossils of winged things (perhaps pterodactyls or the like), fishes, and serpents that are now only bony chains twisted around iron rocks or buried in the dust of those rocks which they had crushed in their death agonies during the cataclysm; and deeper still the alligator and mastodon which had kinged it on "slimy shores And weed-overgrown continents" like "worms On an abandoned corpse" (311-314), until the ocean deluged the land to cover the foulness or until a comet, passing close, burned it away. Such were the cataclysms that could have ended each epoch. (The change in geological knowledge since Cuvier does not affect the evolutionary meaning implicit in this passage.) Whether the earlier forms of life died by water or by fire, the image is an image of purification, rightly the prelude for the antiphonal singing of the Earth and the Moon —rather, of the Spirit of the Earth and the Spirit of the Moon, for Panthea speaks of the "bright visions" (the chariot and the sphere) "Wherein the singing spirits rose and shone" (514-515).

The two hundred lines of their singing are more than a third of the act. The Earth and the Moon take on such importance because they typify the love "given and returned" (III. iii. 6) everywhere in the universe. They are no longer the child in the sphere and the infant in the chariot, but are come to maturity, as though the geological history of the world were now continuous with eternity wherein the two spirits, brother and sister, now fulfill Asia's prophecy (III. iv. 86-90).

The Earth sings with passionate joy, the gladness bursting from its being expressed in the language of physical science: the "vaporous exultation" is the expansive force of gases. The image conjoins the spiritual and the physical, as does the "animation of delight" (translatable as life-giving joy) which becomes the spiritual atmosphere and motive power of the Earth (319-324).

Although the Earth sounds tumultuous to us, he seems to the Moon a "calm wanderer" (325). "Wanderer" is the literal translation in English for the Greek *planetes*; and the next line, too, is an image of the planet, a "Happy globe of land and air." From the Earth, which is both her brother and the physical structure, a Spirit, "darted like a beam," penetrates her frozen frame (325-331), as foretold by Asia; the Spirit is the Earth's life-giving joy, the "vaporous exultation" (which in an earlier version is the "fire of bursting joy").

Panthea hears the Earth's music as deep and as a loud and

179

whirlwind harmony; Ione and the Earth hear the Moon's music as clear and piercing. The stanzaic forms of the antiphon, until the last two stanzas when the Moon reaches her utmost intensity and the Earth turns to her, are regular. Their stanzaic forms are closely alike, giving a sense of sympathy between Earth and Moon; the subtle differences are for the difference in the music emanating from each being: the Moon's lines are an accent the less and her stanza softly lingers, like an exhalation of joy, in the brief seventh line which rhymes with lovely effect with the long preceding line of the stanza. They do not at first sing the alternate parts of their antiphon in response to each other. The triumphant Earth has as a center of consciousness the change in the universe, love now the law of man's mind; the loving Moon, blossoming with new life, has the Earth in the center of her consciousness.

The Earth's caverns, volcanoes ("cloven fire-crags"), and fountains fill the world with their "vast and inextinguishable laughter." The "Sceptred curse," Jupiter, and his "strong hate" which threatened with black volcanic destruction all that the earth brought forth, are "drunk up By thirsty nothing." Filling the "void annihilation, love Burst in like light on caves cloven by the thunder-ball." In the simile the thunder-ball, or lightning, is love, and the caves are the minds of men separated in darkness (332-355). [335-336: *the abysses, And the deep air's* in Shelley's final extant version is "the abysses Of the deep air's," a better reading.]

Although the Moon speaks to the Earth as "Brother mine," the Earth has just spoken of bringing forth children. James Thomson reconciled the duality so: "the chanting Earth is, in truth, neither the mythological Mother nor the simple Child-Spirit of the preceding acts, but, as was imperative for the full development of the poet's thought, our natural Earth, the living, enduring root of these and all other conceptions, mythologic, imaginative, rational; the animate World-sphere instinct with Spirit, personified as masculine in relation to the feminine Moon, as it would be no less rightly personified as feminine in relation to the masculine Sun."

The Moon sings of the warmth penetrating her, which thaws her frozen oceans and animates her lifeless body (contemporary science thought that there were frozen oceans on the moon and that heat coming from the earth could create an atmosphere for life). The Earth's spirit, "darted like a beam" (327), on her spirit creates an "unexpected birth" (356-362). That the beam is the Earth's light, life and power reflected from the suns and constellations is seen in these lines of the Moon:

> All suns and constellations shower
> On thee a light, a life, a power
> Which doth array thy sphere; thou pourest thine
> On mine, on mine! (440-443)

And the love between the spirit darted from the Earth and the spirit in the Moon's heart is given the imagery of physical love by means of an astronomical image intervolved with the human act:

> As in the soft and sweet eclipse,
> When soul meets soul on lovers' lips,
> High hearts are calm, and brightest eyes are dull;
> So when thy shadow falls on me,
> Then am I mute and still, by thee
> Covered; of thy love, Orb most beautiful,
> Full, oh, too full! (450-456)

[453: *thy shadow*, the moon in eclipse]

Gazing on the Earth, the Moon experiences conscious feeling and conscious knowledge, as both rooted and moving life bursts forth. "Music is in the sea and air," now paradisal, and clouds are soaring dark with the rain of love (363-369).

So far in each part of the antiphon there is imagery of the physical earth or the physical moon: their reality and meaning as structures of matter, portrayed and interpreted by the Oceanides as chorus, are insisted on. Now the Earth sings of the triumph of love, which interpenetrates the inanimate and the animate, and which wakes a life in the dead; love with "thunder, and with whirlwind, has arisen Out of the lampless caves of unimagined being"—like the "lampless deep," an image of the mystical Unity (370-378). Love with the power of earthquake coming from the depths changes Thought, the "living world," heretofore immovable—and "hate, and fear, and pain, light-vanquished shadows,"

181

> Leave Man, who was a many-sided mirror,
> Which could distort to many a shape of error,
> This true fair world of things, a sea reflecting love.

It is the transformation of the world. The imagery fuses the ideal and the real: the world made perfect is a "true fair world of *things*"—matter is now true and beautiful, which are properties of love; matter and love are indistinguishable. Man, made of matter—as a "many-sided mirror," as men, distorted truth and beauty; but now as a sea, as Man—perfectly reflects, that is, absorbs and transmits, love (379-384). Love moves over mankind like the sun's heaven, and mankind reflects not only that light but the radiance and life darting from the other stars; again Cubistic, the syntax seems constructed like transparent overlapping planes, as though making us conscious that the stars are there beyond the sun (385-387).

Hate, fear, and pain leave Man, "even as a leprous child is left"—in the warm human image of the cleansed child wandering home to its mother who "fears awhile It is a spirit, then, weeps on her child restored," the broken syntax seems to reflect the mother's emotional state and through her the Earth's for its child,

> Man, oh, not men! a chain of linkèd thought,
> Of love and might to be divided not,
> Compelling the elements with adamantine stress;

even as the sun's gravitational power rules the fierce opposing centrifugal force of the planets. Man, not men! is a political as well as a mystical conception of humanity as a single whole, an horizontal chain of being; their unity of thought, love, and power makes men Man, who controls matter (388-399) just as the "one Spirit's plastic stress," in *Adonais,*

> Sweeps through the dull dense world, compelling there,
> All new successions to the forms they wear;
> Torturing th' unwilling dross that checks its flight
> To its own likeness, as each mass may bear. (xliii)

"Man, one harmonious soul of many a soul, Whose nature is its own divine control" is man become God; thought, love, and power correspond to Prometheus, Asia, and Demogorgon. But Man become as a God is not to say that Man is the One, the Eternal; for even in the Promethean world there are pain and grief, which are like chance, death, and mutability,

> The clogs of that which else might oversoar
> The loftiest star of unascended heaven. (III. iv. 201-202)

Pain and grief are gentle now (this pain has an external source such as accident; the pain in III. iv. 398 and in IV. 381 has an internal source such as hate) because we control our attitude toward them (400-405). Man's will, bad when it guides, is now powerful in the service of Love, controlling even the most savage impulses of life (406-411).

All things confess Man's strength. His dreams, his imaginings, go into the creation of sculpture and painting, and these make more beautiful the human race [414: *robes,* bodies and faces]; his art of language, forever having the musical power of Orpheus who could charm Gods and stones, with greatest craftsmanship makes a harmony of meaning and form out of what were chaos without such art (412-417), for "speech created thought" (II. iv. 72). No less than the arts, the sciences serve Man. He controls lightning, or electricity, which by analogy with Jupiter's bolts is the most powerful physical energy in the world; his astronomy measures every star; he tames storms as though they were horses and "strides the air" [almost ten years earlier there had appeared an essay on "Aerial Navigation," in *Nicolson's Journal,* formulating the principles for aircraft]; and he lays bare the ocean, who withholds nothing from Man's knowledge.

The ocean, using a sexual image, shouts her abandonment to possession by Man's mind. In the bowers of the Moon, who no longer moves in a white death, a shroud of frost, "Wander happy paramours" who enjoy ideal love, less powerful beings but as mild as the paramours on earth (424-430).

The Earth then gives the vehicle of a simile, and the Moon the tenor. The dawn's warmth dissolves dew to mist, which becomes a cloud and in the setting sun hangs over the sea, a "fleece of fire and amethyst." Like the sea lying beneath that cloud, which comes from the sea and which is lighted marvellously by the sun, the Earth lies in a light which comes from its own joy (the "animation of delight" in Earth's first stanza) and from the divine smile of heaven (emblem of the Eternal). Like rain clouds arraying the earth in green, all suns and constellations shower "a light, a life a power" which array Earth, and Earth rains his light and life on the Moon (431-443).

The Earth "dreaming delight" and "Murmuring victorious joy" in his "enchanted sleep," spins beneath his long cone of shadow that the sun throws into space, as a youth, dreaming love and sighing in his sleep, lies beneath the shadow thrown by his beauty (in analogy to the sun) which keeps a watch of light and warmth around his rest as sunlight surrounds the night (in the geometrical diagram that Whitehead insists Shelley needed to have in mind to picture this stanza, the cone would be a triangle like the side of a pyramid; Shelley knew perfectly well that it was a cone, not a pyramid—he used "cone of night" in *The Triumph of Life*). Comparing his own state to a lover's opens the Earth's consciousness and pride to the Moon's voice: when next he speaks, it will be directly to her (444-449).

When the earth's shadow, the "pyramid of night," falls on the moon, the moon is in eclipse; that moment for the Moon, like the eclipse when soul meets soul in a kiss, fills her with the love of Earth. Her rapture in thought of that moment changes the music of her singing (450-456). The Moon looks at the green and azure earth, shining divinest (its joy like an atmosphere of spiritual light, as in the Earth's first stanza) among all the shining structures of matter ("the lamps") in the universe to "whom life and light is given" (the singular *is* makes a unity of life and light); the "lamps of Heaven" are manifestations of the Eternal, the One, even as the Islamic poet and mystic Jalal al-Din Rumi wrote in the thirteenth century, "The lamps are different, but the Light is the same." Herself a crystal celestial lover (a legitimate meaning for *paramour*), the Moon is carried beside the earth by the power of gravitation which is magnet-like, like the "polar Paradise . . . of lovers' eyes" (I accept the emendation of many scholars who place a comma after "Magnet-like," which may then be read in apposition to "power"). Their eyes like magnetic poles exert always the mutual attraction of love; looking into each other's eyes is paradisal because of their love; and the poles of the earth as its axis shifts are becoming equably warm, like the climate in Paradise, an astronomical change known in Shelley's day. The double "like" and the displacing of "Magnet-like" in the syntax were necessary for the con-

184

struction of image involved within image, that construction being a function of the unity that Shelley conceived. Here Shelley brings into a unifying equation gravitation, magnetism,
and love (457-466).

Elsewhere he has equations for love and electricity, love and
heat, love and light. James Clerk Maxwell (1831-1879) evolved
the mathematical equations for the electromagnetic theory of
light, which united electricity, magnetism, heat, and light; and
Albert Einstein (1879-1955) tried to bring gravitation into a
unified theory. The scientists, of course, unlike the poet, never
brought love into the unifying equation. But it is hard for a
mind without the scientist's self-imposed limitation to resist
Dante's last line of *Paradise*, "The love which moves the sun
and other stars."

The Moon, her brain made weak by the pleasure of love
(*weak* is proleptic), overladen, revolves around the sun maniac-
like; that is, her face seems to wobble because of the pressure
on her brain—her wobbling is the moon's libration, a piece of
technical astronomy that Shelley absorbed from Adam Walker's *Familiar Philosophy*. The Moon revolves, her face wobbling, and she gazes, "an insatiate bride," on the Earth's "form
from every side Like a Maenad, round the cup Which Agave
lifted up"—the Moon gazes insatiately (scientifically, the same
side of the moon always faces the earth) like the Maenad's
thirst for the wine of Dionysus [474: *Agave*, the daughter of
Cadmus, priestess of Dionysus]. Wherever the Earth soars in
its ellipse around the sun, while the sun itself plunges through
the heavens, the Moon must "whirl and follow Sheltered by
the warm embrace" of the Earth's soul "from hungry space"—
gravitation, here equated to the warm embrace of love, holds
the Moon from careening off into the maw of chaos. From
sense and sight of Earth [481: *thy*, of you; in the form of "of
you" it would, of course, come at the end of the line], the
Moon drinks "Beauty, majesty, and might": the multiplicity
of image for her growing like the earth is expressive of the
richness of her experience (467-492).

>And the weak day weeps
>That it should be so. (493-494)

These two lines of the Earth exquisitely echo the Moon's
music (editors are divided on whether the lines belong to the

185

Moon or to the Earth; I believe that they are the Earth's); the likeness in the music mirrors his at last turning to her with the sympathy of love. The meaning is ambiguous. *Weak* is proleptic, as it is in the Moon's song: the day is made weak, is moved to tears by the meaning and beauty in the Moon's three parallel similes (481-492); and the day weeps also because its life is ending with the sunset, and as the day sinks the natural beauty in the vehicles of the similes will die. The transiency of the natural beauty creates a poignant tension with the meaning in the tenor, the Moon's drinking the wine of "Beauty, majesty, and might" from the Earth (as the Maenad drinks from the Dionysian cup), a meaning that exists in the new day which is eternal.

> Oh, gentle Moon, the voice of thy delight
> Falls on me like thy clear and tender light
> Soothing the seaman, borne the summer night,
>   Through isles for ever calm;
> Oh, gentle Moon, thy crystal accents pierce
> The caverns of my pride's deep universe,
> Charming the tiger joy, whose tramplings fierce
>   Made wounds which need thy balm. (495-502)

There is egoism (or pride) in his delight but not in hers, reflecting a difference between male and female in love; the voice of her delight, clear and tender, gives balm to the wounds made by the fierceness of his joy, again reflecting human experience of what a woman can do for a man, owing to their difference. Because the focus of this stanza is different from that of the Earth's other stanzas, the form is different.

Panthea responds to the antiphon, rising, she says,

> as from a bath of sparkling water,
> A bath of azure light, among dark rocks,
> Out of the stream of sound; (503-505)

the image echoes the "enchantment of strong sound" that Panthea saw the visions of moon and earth floating upon (194-203). But Ione more realistically (if such may be said) observes that that "stream of sound has ebbed away" and pays tribute to her sister's language, saying that Panthea claims to rise out of the sparkling water of sound that bathed her because she mistakes that singing for her own voice falling "like the clear, soft dew

Shaken from a bathing wood-nymph's limbs and hair" (505-509). Then, in her choral role until the last, Panthea announces the coming of Demogorgon:

> Peace! peace! A mighty Power, which is as darkness,
> Is rising out of Earth, and from the sky
> Is showered like night, and from within the air
> Bursts, like eclipse which had been gathered up
> Into the pores of sunlight. (510-514)

Shelley in the simile uses science for emotional value with natural and imaginative ease, and the modernity of the mind using science gives a sense of reality and strength to the religious meaning incorporated in the simile, that of godhead bursting out of matter.

In Demogorgon's darkness "the bright visions" of Earth and Moon, streaming away, "Gleam like pale meteors through a watery night" (514-516). Just as Prometheus' and Asia's last words in the drama focussed our minds on the vision of the Spirit of the Hour, so the last words of the choral Panthea and Ione (517-518) focus our minds on the universal antiphony that consummates the drama.

In the triune godhead represented in Shelley's myth, Demogorgon is somewhat analogous to the Holy Ghost. He speaks as divinity. The response of each voice in the antiphony is formally bound to Demogorgon's voice, completing the stanza. The statement is thereby made, purely by formal means, that all things are one with godhead.

Demogorgon first speaks to the Earth, empire of Man, "one harmonious soul of many a soul" (400): "Thou, Earth . . . gathering as thou dost roll The love which paves thy path along the skies"—the laws of planetary motion are a manifestation of love. The Earth responds in an image suggesting the mystical experience of a soul in the presence of the Ineffable (519-523).

Demogorgon speaks to the Moon gazing on the Earth as the Earth gazes upon the Moon (each reflects light to the other); their "beauty, love, calm, harmony" are the birthright of men, beasts, and birds. The image in the Moon's response portrays her not so far along as Earth in the mystical experience (524-528).

Demogorgon summons the Daemons and Gods ruling suns

and stars and the Dominations ruling the ether beyond Man's regions in infinite space, who are orders of being that live in perfect calm, at absolute rest ("Elysian" and "windless"), unlike the stars and solar systems that are forever in swift and scattered motion in the "constellated wilderness" seen from earth. A "Voice from above" answers sublimely, "Our great Republic hears, we are blest, and bless" (529-533).

Then Demogorgon addresses the lower world. The "happy Dead" are supernally radiant, whether they are "made one with Nature" (*Adonais*, 370)—in which case they are of the same stuff as the living, although different spiritually and no longer suffering, and have not passed out of the world—or whether, completes a "Voice from beneath," they have left the world, have changed and passed into "the abode where the Eternal are" (*Adonais*, 495). The implication is that both kinds of futurity exist (534-538).

The beings in the "fortunate abodes" are balanced by the happy Dead, and together their upper and lower worlds balance the Earth and the Moon.

Sustaining a conception of balance in the universe, which reflects his symmetry of mind, Demogorgon awakens the elements of matter from their oblivion (their "confused Voice" suggests the life inherent in matter)—they are in the structures from "man's high mind" to the sullen lead at the earth's center, from the stars to the dull weed at the sea's bottom (539-543) [*dull weed*, the element iodine, discovered only a few years earlier]; and then Demogorgon, as "wind among still weeds," stirs the Spirits in beasts, birds, worms, and fish (they are earth's inhabitants other than man in the *Timaeus*, Plato's cosmology which is connected to Shelley's with several links), in plants, and in the natural phenomena of the air (544-548).

After coupling Earth and Moon, the Beings beyond our wilderness of stars and the Dead, the elemental Genii (from *genere, gignere*, to beget: the elements produce all things) and Spirits, Demogorgon addresses Man singly, who as discordant men lived miserably in the night of time preceding "this immortal day," which is eternity. And remarkably not Man alone but All answer—Man is at one with all—

> Speak: thy strong words may never pass away.

The meaning, of course, is not that Demogorgon's words will

perhaps never pass away but that their nature will never permit them to pass away; his words are eternal (549-553).

Taking up "this immortal day," Demogorgon closes the drama with an utterance beyond praise. This is the day which, at the Titan's spell, opens in the void depths for Jupiter to sink into, and Jupiter is being dragged through those depths. Love, from its throne of patient power in the heart of Prometheus, from his last dizzying hour of dreadful endurance, from an agony incredibly difficult not to plummet from to destruction, "springs And folds over the world its healing wings."

The seals which assuredly bar the pit over Jupiter—Gentleness, Virtue, Wisdom, and Endurance—these seals are given meaning by the existence of evil. And if Eternity's hand should weaken and "free The serpent that would clasp her with its length" (Jupiter in clasping Thetis thought that he was clasping Eternity), these are the powers with which to overthrow the escaped Jupiter, the serpent of evil disentangled from its destiny and ruin:

> To suffer woes which Hope thinks infinite;
> To forgive wrongs darker than death or night;
> To defy Power, which seems omnipotent;
> To love, and bear; to hope till Hope creates
> From its own wreck the thing it contemplates;
> Neither to change, nor falter, nor repent;
> This, like thy glory, Titan, is to be
> Good, great and joyous, beautiful and free;
> This is alone Life, Joy, Empire, and Victory.

We are in the real world here. If such capacity for suffering, for forgiveness, for resistance, for love, for endurance, has belonged to one greater man, it can belong to us all; if saints of any time or place have shown such capacity, they are our measure. Hope is as real as wrong and stronger than destruction; a spiritual power, it "creates From its own wreck the thing it contemplates." The unchanging, unfaltering, unrepenting exertion of the capacity here portrayed is a training in opposition to evil that perfects us physically, intellectually, and morally. The final triplet and Alexandrine fix that glory in our minds. In a working draft the last line had Peace in brackets twice, where Life and Joy now stand; Shelley cancelled one bracketed Peace in ink and the other in pencil (apparently at

189

different times) and substituted above these bracketed words Life and Joy. Life and Joy, in his deliberate judgment, are our primary values, and peace takes no place in glory. It is as though the man were speaking to our time, which has known no peace but need not deny itself the glory of Life and Joy.

I follow the rationalist Gilbert Murray and the mystic W. B. Yeats in my tribute to the religious power of *Prometheus Unbound*. That power will never begin any general movement because the imagery is too personal to Shelley, too personal to enlist general belief. The imagery is personal, but the ideas are not eccentric. They are in conjunction, as astronomers speak of celestial bodies in the same longitude which thereby create a brighter light in the heavens, with the ideas of scientists, philosophers, and mystics; and their power will endure. Just as the ideas of scientists, at first understood by only a small circle of other scientists, at last spread out to the common understanding of our society, changing the physical world we live in, our politics, our economy, our social and private lives, so do religious and philosophic ideas. These ideas may alter as they spread out (even as scientific ideas do), interpreted by other minds who give the ideas guises that are recognizable enough to have immediate meaning. If that meaning serves a deep and common need, the world changes.

1819

THE CENCI

The Shelleys and Claire had reached Rome early in March. Day after day they walked through the ancient and modern purlieus of the city, impressed by the ruins, admiring the fountains and palaces, and taking pleasure in the Borghese Gardens; evenings they enjoyed the *conversazioni* of a Roman bluestocking. In the midst of it all Shelley wrote Acts II and III of *Prometheus Unbound,* in less than a month. They lived easily and pleasantly during April.

Nearly a year earlier, in Leghorn, Mary had made a copy of a manuscript history that told a violent and compelling story, a clash between the Count Cenci and his daughter Beatrice. Shelley had often exhorted Mary to write a tragedy but Mary would not undertake to, thinking herself too young; for tragedy, she said, "requires a greater scope of experience in, and sympathy with, human passion than would have fallen to my lot,—or than any perhaps, except Shelley, ever possessed, even at the age of twenty-six, at which he wrote *The Cenci.*" The matter lapsed until their spring in Rome, where Shelley found the Cenci story everywhere alive in people's minds after two hundred years; and so conceived that the story, because of "its capacity of awakening and sustaining the sympathy of men," had the makings of a great drama. In late April they visited a Roman palace to study a portrait of Beatrice Cenci by Guido Reni. Some sixty years later an Italian scholar showed that the portrait was not Guido's and perhaps not of Beatrice. No matter. Into that face Shelley imagined *his* Beatrice, as revealed in the preface to the play. Excited, he urged the story to Mary "as one fitted for a tragedy. More than ever," Mary confessed in her Note on the play, "I felt my incompetence; but I entreated him to write it instead." Some weeks later they visited the Cenci house in Rome, where early scenes of the play are set, and within days Shelley was at work.

That was the middle of May. About ten days later their son, William, a healthy and spirited boy, became sick, and after a fortnight died. Shelley watched by William's bed for the last "sixty miserable, death-lyke hours." They left Rome, the desolated Mary bearing the loss worse than the nearly wrecked Shelley. They settled for the summer in a house near Leghorn, the Villa Valsovano, out in the country. When Shelley began writing again, he constantly talked with Mary about the play, the only time he ever opened himself to anybody's taking part in his work, to give some ease to her days. Years later, writing her Note on *The Cenci* for her 1839 edition of *The Poetical Works of Percy Bysshe Shelley*, Mary could say with no tone of the "wretchedness and despair" that possessed her after losing "two only and lovely children in one year:"

The peasants sang as they worked beneath our windows, during the heats of a very hot season, and in the evening the water-wheel creaked as the process of irrigation went on, and the fireflies flashed from among the myrtle hedges: Nature was bright, sunshiny, and cheerful, or diversified by storms of a majestic terror, such as we had never before witnessed.

At the top of the house there was a sort of terrace. There is often such in Italy, generally roofed; this one was very small, yet not only roofed but glazed. This Shelley made his study; it looked out on a wide prospect of fertile country, and commanded a view of the near sea. The storms that sometimes varied our day showed themselves most picturesquely as they were driven across the ocean; sometimes the dark lurid clouds dipped towards the wave, and became waterspouts that churned up the waters beneath, as they were chased onward and scattered by the tempest. At other times the dazzling sunlight and heat made it intolerable to every other; but Shelley basked in both, and his health and spirits revived under their influence. In this airy cell he wrote the principal part of *The Cenci*.

It is a measure of Shelley's artistic restraint that none of those sights and sounds, however tempting they were as the stuff of imagery, is in *The Cenci*; they were irrelevant. But the loss of William, which haunted him, made its way into the drama in an expressive and relevant moment. Beatrice speaks to a man of "that fair blue-eyed child who was the lodestar of your life":

> All see, since his most swift and piteous death,
> That day and night, and heaven and earth, and time,
> And all things hoped for or done therein
> Are changed to you, through your exceeding grief. (V. ii. 51-54)

Such transmutation of subjective experience utterly into the stuff of drama, the author nowhere visible in the scene, is another measure of Shelley's artistry. Such, however, was exceptional in this play. In the main his "object was to see how I could succeed in describing passions I have never felt," wrote a friend. Shelley himself wrote that he wanted "to represent the characters as they probably were, and . . . to avoid the error of making them actuated by my own conceptions of right and wrong"; and "in order to move men to true sympathy" he used "the familiar language of men. . . . But it must be the real language of men in general and not that of any particular class to whose society the writer happens to belong." (Wordsworth in his 1800 Preface to *Lyrical Ballads* made his historic argument for the use of "a selection of the real language of men," but the language he argued for was that of farmers and shepherds in his Lake country; Coleridge in *Biographia Literaria*, 1817, showed that Wordsworth in his best practice had used the real language of men in general in opposing the artificial poetic diction of the eighteenth century.)

Shelley wrote the play for production, intending a particular actress at Covent Garden, whose acting he had admired, for Beatrice. But the theater manager, while appreciating the play's power, would not show the play to the actress because of the incestuous rape. After the play was turned down for production, Shelley directed Ollier to publish the 250 copies that had been printed in Leghorn, and the play appeared in the middle of March 1820. In four months there were ten reviews, a considerable notice. The critics were hostile to his "moral perversity" but gave praise to his genius. The small edition sold out (the usual edition of a volume of poems, established poets excepted, numbered 500), and the play went into a second edition.

The pompous morality of the theater managers and critics may irritate or amuse us. In their reviews the critics were often self-important and scoundrelly. The managers dealt in wares for huge dissolute and vulgar audiences (3000 in Covent Garden, fully illuminated during performance) whom Walter Scott described as largely "prostitutes and their admirers." Victorian critics in 1886, reviewing the Shelley Society's production of *The Cenci*, also attacked the play, judging the play undramatic as support for their primary moral attack; but the distinguished audience, in the play's grip for nearly four hours, rose and cheered. The subsequent "long and varied stage history" (traced by Kenneth Cameron and Horst Frenz) confirms the reality and power of the play's hold on the emotions of an audience, and thereby the triumph of Shelley's skill as a dramatist, all the more remarkable because he had practically no experience in the theater. There have been performances in cities of England, France, Germany, Russia, Czechoslovakia, and the United States; a Theatre Guild in the state of Washington had an audience of "enthralled and ever-increasing attention" watching *The Cenci*, and had a better box office than with *Abie's Irish Rose* and *Ah, Wilderness*. The play accomplished that much not only against the odds of Shelley's theatrical inexperience but also against the theatrical conditions of his day.

For our purposes I need only say of theatrical conditions that in serious drama the poetic plays universally imitated

Shakespeare and his contemporaries and the most popular serious plays were those of terror and melodrama. Writing for production, Shelley accepted these conditions, dispensing only (and wisely) with the elaborate spectacle and music typical of the "melo-drama" and with its typical character-izations that make us laugh today. The terror he made distress-ingly human, and the melodrama he put to high artistic purposes, using it in the way of Aeschylus and as Conrad and Pirandello were later to use it, as a necessary balance for the intellectual content. For the intellectual content of *The Cenci* these lines from *Prometheus Unbound* may serve as motto:

> The good want power, but to weep barren tears.
> The powerful goodness want: worse need for them.
> The wise want love; and those who love want wisdom;
> And all best things are thus confused to ill.

Although critics claim that each line of the play has immediate clarity, there are difficulties here and there. What is true is that although the words are not always transparent, the emotional meaning is always understood, and in drama that is what counts most. The difficulties with intellectual or literal meaning are few enough so that explication of the play would be gratuitous.

A playwright hoping to have a tragedy produced had no choice but to model his work after the Elizabethans. We may regret that, as meaning cannot express itself except through form, the expression of the modern, Romantic vision in the nineteenth century was hampered by the older dramaturgy; but it is critically irresponsible to accuse Shelley of imitative-ness in an age when formal originality would have made production a vain hope. Moreover, within the confines of the Elizabethan form, Shelley is original: in his contemporary language (his is the best dramatic verse of his time), in his characterizations, in his themes. Critics speak disparagingly of the debts to Shakespeare in *The Cenci,* but it should be said that these passages have a life of their own, are organic in the play; and while Shelley hardly improved on his source, he nonetheless acquitted himself well. If the like passages are read with a mind not clouded by the prejudice of "imitation," the continuity of human experience that those passages reflect can strengthen the scenes, just as the echoes of the Bible do in *Paradise Lost*. The chief likenesses are the murder scene *(The Cenci* IV. iii. 5-22 and *Macbeth* II. 10-20), Cenci's curse *(The Cenci* IV. i. 114-157 and *Lear* I. iv. 297-311), and the lamp and candle images *(The Cenci* III. ii. 11-18, 51-53 and *Othello* V. ii. 7-13).

Not an historian, Shelley like every good artist made changes in his source to fit his conceptions (that his source gave a prejudiced account favorable to Beatrice has little bearing on literary criticism; we need not turn to a genuine historical account). For example, in his source Beatrice was an orthodox Roman Catholic, and Cenci's worst viciousness was his atheism. In the play there is no orthodoxy in her, and Cenci is devoutly religious although wholly evil. Shelley suggests nothing of Cenci's three convictions for sodomy, having him mulcted for murder instead, and even diminishes the inhumanity of the Pope. The story in his source, as his Preface states, is too "fearful and monstrous" for the stage and would be "insupportable"; so he had to "increase the ideal, and diminish the actual horror of the events." The villainy of Orsino and the subserviency of Camillo are largely Shelley's portraiture; the one serving, the other not opposing, the evil in the world. There are changes in the action, too. For example, in the play the murderers strangle Cenci and throw his body into the garden; in the source Beatrice and Lucretia pull the murdering nails out of Cenci's head and throw the corpse from the balcony. Shelley invented the Pope's envoys coming right after the murder to execute Cenci, not so much for the irony as to accentuate the moral issue in the trial (the castle horn announcing the coming of the Legate for Cenci, which "sounds Like the last trump," echoes the knocking at the gate in *Macbeth*); and Shelley compressed the course of a year into a few days. These changes were all governed by the shaping power of his dramatic imagination.

His shaping power was pre-eminent in making a unity of the play's action. By "unity of action" I mean that logical unity within the plot which binds its beginning, middle, and end, and its climax. These four elements of the plot-structure are *actions* which must be performed by one and the same character, who is thus the character central to the plot.

The beginning, the middle, and the end describe the course of a change in the condition of the central character. The change in condition is the essence of narrative; it is that which happens. It may take any or all of three forms: character may change, as from good to bad, or the reverse; personal circumstances may change, as from prosperity to adversity, or the reverse; relationships to other people may change, as from love to hate, or the reverse. The actions that shape a plot-structure need not, of course, be physical. A discovery or realization is no less a dramatic action for being mental rather than physical. In like manner an emotional change such as falling in love is an action. What defines an action is that it have a consequence.

The beginning action of the plot, which corresponds to the beginning of change in the condition of the central character, contains the roots of the middle. The middle action of the plot gives rise to a question which the play must settle; in terms of plot, this question is what the play is about. The end, or final action of the plot, completing what was begun in the beginning, answers the question posed by the middle.

No plot-structure is complete without a climax. Like the beginning, the middle, and the end of the plot, the climax is an act of the central character; and like the beginning and the middle, the climax moves the action of the play forward. The climax is that act of the central character which determines the course of the rest of the action. (In tragedy the logical cause-and-effect between climax and catastrophe is inevitable. In plays other than tragedies, particularly in those which depend for an effect upon a sudden release of tension, there can occur in the last few minutes of the play a reversal of the course of action indicated by the climax.)

The four actions of the plot-structure must take place on stage if the play is not to lose power. It is the visual presentation of the story that distinguishes a dramatic narrative from other forms of narrative, and it is the visual immediacy that is a play's chief source of power.

For my understanding of these theoretical principles of plot-structure I am indebted to Bernard Grebanier. His method of structural analysis, although evolved for the practicing playwright, is, I believe, a major new instrument for dramatic criticism. Let us now examine the plot-structure of *The Cenci*. Beatrice, of course, is the protagonist, the tragic heroine; Cenci, her antagonist.

1. The beginning of change: Unable to escape, Beatrice is

196

driven by Cenci to chaos of mind by incestuous rape and the threat of its continuance.

2. The middle: Believing that only vengeance will calm her (III. i. 92) and let her live freely (III. i. 216-217), she has him murdered.

3. The end: Will she be able to live calm and free?

Climax: She gives the gold robe to Marzio (the gold robe causes Marzio's capture, IV. iv. 83-86, and his evidence justifies torture of the defendants, V. ii. 75-77).

Although Shelley made a strong armature in the logic of the play's dominating actions, there are structural weaknesses elsewhere—not, however, in Act I, although Newman White and others believe that "All three scenes of Act I barely fall short of being pure character scenes." It is true that Shelley uses his first act for characterization, as Ibsen habitually does; but neither dramatist does merely that. The first scene, swiftly portraying the evil of Cenci, engages us by the fascination of evil, set off by the well-intentioned but inadequate Cardinal Camillo, and engages us, too, by Cenci's threat of violence to the Cardinal (59-65). Cenci's self-portrait issues naturally out of their conflict (66-67) and his contempt for the Cardinal (75-76). He did not discover his best pleasure until he killed a man, and has refined his pleasure to torturing mind and spirit. Such desire is the motive of his rape, the act glanced at in his saying "there yet remains a deed to act Whose horror might make sharp an appetite duller than mine" (100-102)—the audience can now only wonder at the nature of his intent, but at the end of the scene can connect it to Beatrice. Thus the play has begun to move directly to the beginning of change, Beatrice's being driven to chaos of mind.

The second scene begins with a brilliant opening line, Beatrice's "Pervert not truth," its shortness making it emphatic. The line at once reveals the strength and clarity of her mind and her regard for truth, which intensify the paradoxes of her judgments and actions later. We see her selflessness, her loyalty, her love (16-19); her generosity of spirit unhappily darkening her clear sight (27-35, 43-46); her sure knowledge of her father's dark spirit working in the feast Cenci has prepared for the greatest of Rome. In Orsino's soliloquy closing the scene, we see evil closing around her; fear and shame make Orsino different from Cenci but cause no goodness in him, who is "her

197

only hope" (88) and who will betray her. Again, the scene engages the audience emotionally and also moves the play forward. The speeches in these two scenes are worth pausing for; they are perhaps longer, as they are throughout the play, than any other dramatist's except Racine's. Yet they are efficacious, as the stage history of the play reveals. Like Racine's, Shelley's speeches flow with a swift enough movement of internal drama to carry the audience along.

The much admired banquet scene that follows, Shelley built almost entirely out of his imagination to strengthen the drama; his source only briefly recorded that one of Cenci's sons was killed by a surgeon and the other by one Paolo Corso while at a mass, and that the news made Cenci joyful. That Cenci's first address, delivered with "blithe and open cheer" (17), is mockingly ironic is revealed to the audience watching or the person reading by his last line: the nobility of Rome will think him "tender-hearted, meek and pitiful" (13)—qualities we know he despises. The speeches mount skilfully to the dreadful announcement of the cause of his joy. Three guests rise in anger, but Cenci cows the company—too easily, the reflective reader will think, although the passion in the theater may hide that flaw. As the banquet begins to break up, Beatrice pleads to the departing guests for rescue. They waver. Two "would second any one" (144); but Cenci, before "any one" acts and is seconded, laments that "this insane girl Has spoilt the mirth of our festivity" and disperses his guests, saying, "I will not make you longer Spectators of our dull domestic quarrels" (160-164). Beatrice is left alone with Cenci, who threatens to make her "meek and tame" (167); and Beatrice, deserted by the strong and the rich, must face this man alone.

When Beatrice enters the second act, it is with an overwrought mind (12-21). Cenci was in her room for a minute after the feast: he spoke "one word," struck and cursed her (60-64, 75). She routed him then, but now in the aftermath the advantage is his (104-120). The next scene shifts to the Vatican. Camillo, quoting the Pope to Giacomo, reveals the Pope's guilt; the portraiture in the Pope's lines is excellent:

> In the great war between the old and young,
> I, who have white hairs and a tottering body,
> Will keep at least blameless neutrality. (38-40)

Even as we hear these words Cenci is raping his daughter. The Orsino-Giacomo underplot, begun in this scene, is a structural weakness, for it is not integral to the story and impedes the play's movement. In this scene the psychology of Orsino's characterization, subtle and deep, holds our attention; we listen closely to his long soliloquy. As for Giacomo, he is a study of weakness: his doubts, his remorses, his breaking under torture set off Beatrice's fixed and unshakable mind. He has to be involved in the crime, he is needed to betray her. But Orsino and Giacomo reckon too much in the play, and in this scene they delay too long the beginning of change.

The third act opens with Beatrice staggering in and speaking wildly:

> Reach me that handkerchief!—My brain is hurt;
> My eyes are full of blood. (1-2)

But there is no blood in her eyes; the act of rape has made it seem so. In her momentary madness, the pavement sinking under her feet and the walls spinning round, she cries,

> My God!
> The beautiful blue heaven is flecked with blood!
> The sunshine on the floor is black! (12-14)

Her mind gropes toward what "must be done" (86), and that effort steadies her. She determines that it is right that Cenci die (221). Beatrice and Orsino fix on the place for the assassination, a bridge on the road to Petrella. It is Beatrice speaking:

> Two miles on this side of the fort, the road
> Crosses a deep ravine; 'tis rough and narrow,
> And winds with short turns down the precipice;
> And in its depth there is a mighty rock,
> Which has, from unimaginable years,
> Sustained itself with terror and with toil
> Over a gulf, and with the agony
> With which it clings seems slowly coming down;
> Even as a wretched soul hour after hour,
> Clings to the mass of life; yet clinging, leans;
> And leaning, makes more dark the dread abyss
> In which it fears to fall: beneath this crag

199

Huge as despair, as if in weariness,
The melancholy mountain yawns . . . below,
You hear but see not an impetuous torrent
Raging among the caverns, and a bridge
Crosses the chasm; and high above there grow,
With intersecting trunks, from crag to crag,
Cedars, and yews, and pines; whose tangled hair
Is matted in one solid roof of shade
By the dark ivy's twine. At noonday here
'Tis twilight, and at sunset blackest night. (III. i. 244-265)

This is the "single isolated description," if "judged of that nature," as Shelley wrote in the Preface, that exists in the play.
The Theatre Guild in Washington left these lines out of their
production—perhaps mistakenly. The passage intensifies the
psychological atmosphere through which Beatrice moves to
her doom. Whether or not good for the stage, the passage is
superb as literature. (What follows between Orsino and Giacomo is not necessary to the play, although it shows Giacomo
given the strongest motive by his father's domestic oppression
and evil to participate in the murder. The next scene gives us
the doubt-plagued Giacomo again and the news that Cenci
has escaped.)

The fourth act opens with Cenci's passion to destroy his
daughter's will and moral life (10-12). He feeds his rage on
this:

She shall become (for what she most abhors
Shall have a fascination to entrap
Her loathing will) to her own conscious self
All she appears to others. (84-88)

It is a subtle psychology, learned from his own self-anatomy,
which tempted his powers,

Knowing what must be thought, and may be done,
Into the depth of darkest powers:
So Cenci fell into the pit. (II. ii. 110-114)

That temptation into the depth and the consequent perversion
of good to evil in his mind did not eradicate all memory of
beauty and good purposes in the world. Here his hate and
envy answer Beatrice's beauty; if Beatrice, to Cenci a devil,

200

Which sprung from me as from a hell, was meant
To aught good use; if her bright loveliness
Was kindled to illumine this dark world;
If nursed by Thy selectest dew of love
Such virtues blossom in her as should make
The peace of life, I pray Thee for my sake,
As Thou the common God and Father art
Of her, and me, and all; reverse that doom!

He curses Beatrice fearfully, and then exults:

I do not feel as if I were a man,
But like a fiend appointed to chastise
The offences of some unremembered world. (160-162)

The "unremembered" discovers that world in its strange dimension. This is Cenci's rewarding culmination:

My heart is beating with an expectation
Of horrid joy. (166-167)

Then the man, drugged by Lucretia, sinks with a heavy sleep. The murder—the "high and holy deed," as Beatrice conceives it (IV. ii. 35)—is done, while the iron gate, through which arrest will come, is "left open, swinging to the wind" (41). To the murderers Beatrice says,

Thou wert a weapon in the hand of God
To a just use. (54-55)

Even as she speaks they hear the castle horn sounding like the last trumpet (57-58). Beatrice thinks it announces a "tedious guest" and retires with the illusion that "all ill is surely past" (65).

The fifth act opens with the escape of the villainous Orsino: the play takes place in the actual world. That realistic theme of the villainy in the world is made explicit in the next scene when the First Judge, listening to Marzio's confession, reflects, "This sounds as bad as truth" (V. ii. 19).

The hardest thing for us to take in the great trial scene is Beatrice's speech to Marzio (115-117), in which she goes to the extreme, her will and eloquence persuading Marzio to die as the sole guilty person. We wonder at her. It is to her necessary that she be judged guiltless; otherwise the purity of her act will be contaminated. The scene ends with the Judge's righteous cruelty aimed at his prisoners:

> If the Pope's resolution be as grave,
> Pious, and just as once, I'll wring the truth
> Out of those nerves and sinews, groan by groan. (192-194)

Beatrice awakens in her prison cell and tells her young brother that she dreamed they were all in paradise, and adds,

> This cell seems like a kind of Paradise
> After our father's presence. (11-12)

Our sympathy begins to return to her with those lines, and becomes stronger as she says,

> How friendless thou wouldst be, dear child,
> If I were dead. (18-19)

Aristocracy at her heart's core, she judges Lucretia and Giacomo ignoble for having confessed (28-33); and to the Judge who threatens her with torture says, "What a world we make, The oppressor and the oppressed" (73-74), that is, the cruel and the unenduring (like Lucretia and Giacomo). Her brother and stepmother rack themselves for their confessions. Beatrice speaks to them with a Shakespearean calm, and consoles both:

> *Beatrice.*   What 'twas weak to do,
> 'Tis weaker to lament, once being done;
> Take cheer! The God who knew my wrong, and made
> Our speedy act the angel of His wrath,
> Seems, and but seems, to have abandoned us.
> Let us not think that we shall die for this.
> Brother, sit near me; give me your firm hand,
> You had a manly heart. Bear up! Bear up!
> O dearest Lady, put your gentle head
> Upon my lap, and try to sleep awhile:
> Your eyes look pale, hollow and overworn,
> With heaviness of watching and slow grief. (V. iii. 111-112)

The Cardinal brings the sentence from the Pope, who to the pleading Cardinal "said these three words, coldly: 'They must die'." Fearful of dying, of being nothing, Beatrice reels imagin-

202

ing worse, a terrifying vision of her father dominating the
world to come as Cenci dominated this world, in a shape like
himself ravishing her.

> Whoever yet returned
> To teach the laws of death's untrodden realm?
> Unjust perhaps as those which drive us now,
> O, whither, whither? (72-75)

But still strong, she will not let Lucretia and Giacomo hope
further:

> Worse than despair,
> Worse than the bitterness of death, is hope:
> It is the only ill which can find place
> Upon the giddy, sharp and narrow hour
> Tottering beneath us. (97-101)

Beatrice thus rejects Demogorgon's words that would have us,
oppressed,

> hope till Hope creates
> From its own wreck the thing it contemplates.

Nevertheless, Beatrice has her own spiritual triumph, able to
say to Bernardo:

> For thine own sake be constant to the love
> Thou bearest us; and to the faith that I,
> Though wrapped in a strange cloud of crime and shame,
> Lived ever holy and unstained. And though
> Ill tongues shall wound me, and our common name
> Be as a mark stamped on thine innocent brow
> For men to point at as they pass, do thou
> Forbear, and never think a thought unkind
> Of those, who perhaps love thee in their graves.
> So mayest thou die as I do; fear and pain
> Being subdued. Farewell! Farewell! Farewell! (V. iv. 146-156)

Camillo, much moved, cries out, "O, Lady Beatrice!" The violent and passionate story ends with simplicity and calm, Shelley taking the material for her last speech from his source.

> *Beatrice.* Give yourself no unnecessary pain,
> My dear Lord Cardinal. Here, Mother, tie

My girdle for me, and bind up this hair
In any simple knot; ay, that does well.
And yours I see is coming down. How often
Have we done this for one another; now
We shall not do it any more. My Lord,
We are quite ready. Well, 'tis very well. (V. iv. 158-165)

That Shelley, although he wrote the play to be acted, had it published to be read, was nothing unusual. Even a century earlier there were any number of printed plays that were never acted; by the close of the eighteenth century the sales of such works were considerable. The literary play, almost always in verse, and the theatrical play, whether in verse or prose, were popularly recognized as different modes. But nobody felt obliged to say, as Allardyce Nicoll has said, "Drama, if it is to be great, must be theatrical." Tennessee Williams has echoed that judgment. The facts speak against these eminent gentlemen. Only the literary plays have lasted; the "theatrical" plays are neither read nor played. Indeed, it is truer to say, "Drama, if it is to be great, must be literature." No play lasts unless it has literary quality. It is quite true that watching and reading a play are different experiences, the one communal and the other private, each with its own pleasures. To watch is a more powerful, immediate experience when the production is good; it can be more transforming, more exciting. The theatrical production is also more temporal: the people who watch revivals of *King Lear* or *Oedipus Rex* are a minute fraction of those who read the plays. To read is, of course, a more reflective experience, an experience with subtler response to the textural qualities of the play, and for these reasons is perhaps a deeper experience. The person with a predilection for the acted play thinks that the reader should direct the play in the stage of his mind, necessarily a poorer experience than watching the play acted. But it is a misconception to think it well to direct the play mentally. Anybody reading a play reads it as he does a novel, watching the narrative take place in the world and not on a stage, and is right to read it so. That is the nature of the private, literary experience. It is needful only to recognize the differences between the two kinds of experiences, not to judge between them. Nor need we say, Each to his own taste. One taste does not exclude the other.

The death of young William in June, desolating Shelley, made his exile from England especially painful. "O that I could return to England!" he wrote. "How heavy a weight when misfortune is added to exile, and solitude, as if the measure were not full, heaped high on both." His love of England never lapsed; and as the moral and intellectual nature of men could flourish only in liberty, Shelley watched English political events ceaselessly. News of a legal, military massacre on August 16 at a political rally of working men and their families in Manchester reached Shelley early in September; indignation boiled in his veins, and he waited anxiously to "hear how the Country will express its sense of this bloody murderous oppression." Before the month was over he finished *The Mask of Anarchy*, a controlled expression of fierce anger. A passage in his *Philosophical View of Reform*, later that year, will comment on his motive for writing *The Mask*: "The true patriot will endeavour to enlighten and unite the nation and animate it with enthusiasm and confidence. For this purpose he will be indefatigable in promulgating political truth."

Long ago A. Stanley Walker researched the history of the massacre on St. Peter's Fields in Manchester—the bloody oppression became known as Peterloo, after the bloody battle at Waterloo. (In what follows I make some revisions of Walker's account.) The workers had been living in poverty. Twenty years earlier, in 1799, soup kitchens were begun. War taxation made things worse. In the course of a wage dispute in 1808 soldiers killed a weaver, and the next year the courts jailed a man because he agitated for the depressed. In 1812 there were food riots: eight executions followed for mill-burning, housebreaking, and stealing a sack of potatoes. When the Napoleonic War ended, thousands of discharged men returned jobless to England and the first great industrial crisis. There were assemblies on St. Peter's Fields (open ground next to St. Peter's Church) in 1816 and 1817 to agitate for redress of political grievances, but they came to nothing; soldiers broke up an 1817 meeting and arrested two hundred people. In 1819 a bad harvest and industrial depression brought on agitation again for Parliamentary reform. There were two meetings that year before the Manchester Massacre—one on St. Peter's Fields and the other in the Theatre Royal where Henry Hunt (no connection to Leigh Hunt), who was the hero of Peterloo, had clashed with the authorities. "Orator" Hunt had three years earlier spoken at a meeting that unanimously passed motions to relieve economic distress and to call for a "free, full and frequent Representation of the People in the Commons House of Parliament." The northern industrial cities had no Parliamentary representation, while "rotten boroughs" with no population had an M.P. In the summer of 1819 the reformers planned their greatest meeting for Manchester. When they issued a public call for the meeting in August, the municipal authorities published a notice of its illegality, cautioning "all persons to abstain at their peril from attending such Illegal Meeting." Nonetheless over 60,000 people in their Sunday clothes, women holding children in their arms, gathered on St. Peter's Fields. Hunt entered with bands playing; they had progressed through the town with decorum and no disturbance. Banners declared "Equal representation or death." No soldiery were yet in sight. Hunt began by asking for orderliness and silence. Suddenly six troops of soldiers, horse artillery and infantry, were quietly massing. [Lord Sidmouth, the Home Secretary, used war tactics in combating the reform movement. The Home Secretary had a well-organized spy system operating against Englishmen, and stationed soldiers in barracks near the manufacturing centers, like troops of occupation. Lord Eldon, the Lord Chancellor, fortified Sidmouth with the courts. Shelley had good grounds for believing, "The tremendous question is now agitating, whether a military & judicial despotism is to be established by our present rulers, or some form of government less unfavourable to the real and permanent interests of all men is to arise from the conflict of passions now gathering to overturn them."] Hunt, now aware of the massing soldiers, called for a cheer for the military. But three hundred mounted Yeomanry (militia representing the manufacturers), forty of them "young, hot-blooded volunteers from the more affluent Manchester families, and most of them, it would seem, more or less under the influence of drink," charged with drawn sabers, cutting their way to the speakers' platform. The Yeomanry made the arrests, now reinforced by the regular cavalry, shouted "Have at their flags," and again slashed their way, cutting women and even a child coming to them for protection. There were nine people killed and 418 wounded. Rumor swelled the dead. The Government exulted over the victorious violence, alleging that rebellion had been put down. Now, indeed, public journals feared rebellion would break out as meetings multiplied and inflammatory speeches blazed. Nor was the press without fire. Its attacks against the Government, and verse lampoons using Peterloo in their attacks, make Shelley's *Mask of Anarchy* seem moderate. But Leigh Hunt to whom Shelley entrusted his *Mask* and other political poems in the autumn left them unpublished, perhaps solicitous for Shelley's reputation. Leigh Hunt issued *The Mask of Anarchy* as a pamphlet in 1832, and political orators on the side of the Reform Bill used the poem in their speeches. In our own depressed times, in 1932, hunger-marchers in Toronto chanted its verses.

In our own time, too, the poem compels the admiration even of the unsympathetic modern critic of Shelley, no doubt for its toughmindedness, its irony, the vivid reality of its images, and the energy and directness of its language. In *Julian and Maddalo* a year earlier Shelley had used cultivated conversational language with ease and elegance; and in *The Cenci* had just mastered the familiar language of men in over two thousand lines of clear dramatic verse. That mastery prepared him for the use of plain language with powerful, stirring energy as an instrument of revolution.

Shelley could write so, in our best modern manner. If we judge against him because he chose not to do so often, we betray our own limitations. We can be modern and yet as readily recognize the validity of the romantic vision as we do that of the metaphysical, neoclassical, or realistic vision—perhaps more readily, for our culture has its deepest wells in the romantic, which sustain us when the others run dry although we drink mainly from the others these days because they are closer to the intellectual dwelling places of the modern population. Shelley chose his own manner, a manner linked to his own age, as every great artist must, for his greatest work. *Prometheus Unbound* justifies that choice.

Shelley wrote with direct simplicity in *The Mask of Anarchy* even while using literary traditions of artifice. During the Renaissance a masque was a dramatic entertainment, privately and elaborately produced, first only with pantomime and dancing, later with dialogue and song. Abstractions or figures of the spirit world mixed with characters of the real world. Masques such as Ben Jonson's fine productions, for which the great architect Inigo Jones served as stage designer, were presented in the English Court. Later Milton's *Comus*, the first masque with serious moral import informing the whole was presented in Ludlow Castle. The triumph was also a dramatic entertainment, about an act long. John Fletcher, who after Shakespeare's retirement became the leading playwright for the Globe Theatre, wrote four Triumphs, or Moral Representations, as an evening's entertainment. They were perhaps suggested to him by Petrarch's Triumphs, which were narrative poems rather than playlets. Petrarch's six poems are *The Triumph of Love, The Triumph of Chastity, The Triumph of Death, The Triumph of Fame, The Triumph of Time, The Triumph of Eternity*. Fletcher's *Four Plays, or Moral Representations, in one* are The Triumphs of Honour (that is, of Chastity), Love, Death, and Time (but the sources of Fletcher's stories are not in Petrarch). Masque and triumph are sometimes used interchangeably to name these literary forms, which distantly resemble each other.

Shelley's other literary tradition goes back to the middle ages, the first great example being the dream-vision *The Romance of the Rose*. As in Petrarch's masques, or triumphs, which Shelley read that summer, a triumphant pageant—in Shelley's masque, of Anarchy making its swift way through England—comes to the poet in a vision. But the poem has also an English tradition, the greatest accomplishment in that tradition being *The Vision of Piers Plowman*—like that medieval poem Shelley's is a satirical allegory, fierce with indignation and emotional power, compassionate for the suffering, lyrical, tough-minded, immediate in its meaning and appeal. Unlike the vaster *Piers Plowman, The Mask of Anarchy* has a flawless architectural strength.

Stanza 1 announces a vision. Stanzas 2-21 are the triumphal procession of Anarchy to London (the triumph of Anarchy, a tyrant proclaiming himself "God, and King, and Law," is like the ceremonial entrance, or triumph, of a victorious army into ancient Rome). Stanzas 22-23 show the routing of Anarchy by Hope and Love. Stanzas 34-36 are a modulation from the allegory to the revolutionary incitement. The secret of the poem's structural strength is that the ineluctable dream-logic of the allegory in the first part of the poem makes seem inevitable the triumphant outcome of the revolutionary passive resistance that Earth incites the populace to in the second part, stanzas 37-91.

When the dreamer says,

> I met Murder on the way—
> He had a mask like Castlereagh—(stanza 2)

Shelley gave the public he wrote for, which could hardly be expected to know his poem's literary traditions, the immediate meaning of *mask*—a false and cruel face. [The heading of the manuscript that was in Leigh Hunt's possession, written in Shelley's hand, spells the word *Mask*, not *Masque*.] The mask of Anarchy is the face of "God, and King, and Law"; however powerful, that face is also false and therefore can be quelled. Likening Murder's face to Castlereagh is a satirical stroke of brilliant power, making Castlereagh seem the absolute evil measure. Castlereagh, the Foreign Minister and Leader of the House of Commons, during the Great War was responsible for effective reorganization of the army; he selected and supported Wellington, and headed the Powers that overcame Napoleon. The historian John Richard Green praised his "cool judgment, his high courage, his discernment," and G. M. Trevelyan thinks Castlereagh among the great men who led England "through the most terrible ordeal she had ever till then endured" (the others were Pitt, Nelson, and Wellington). These Victorian and modern judgments, reversing the contemporary view of Castlereagh, may or may not be just. In any case Shelley shared the public view expressed by Byron: "As a minister, I, for one of millions, looked upon him as the most despotic in intention, and the weakest in intellect, that ever tyrannized over a country." In England Castlereagh was held accountable for engineering the government's war policy, and in Ireland for bloodily suppressing the 1798 attempt for liberty. After Waterloo, Castlereagh had a leading part in shaping the peace—a euphemism for the suppressing of nationalism and liberty. The most Trevelyan can say for that part of Castlereagh's career is that he "was tending reluctantly to a less close participation in the congressional politics of the con-

209

tinent, when the strain of overwork caused him to commit suicide." (The "congressional politics" allude to the suppressive Congresses of Metternich and Tsar Alexander.) To the end Castlereagh "strongly expressed dislike of the movements of Greek and Italian independence." Not until after Castlereagh's death could a liberal spirit begin to direct the Tory cabinet. Canning succeeded Castlereagh and opposed the reactionaries on the continent; to him Greece largely owed her independence. In the Home Office, Peel ended Sidmouth's spy system and curbed governmental repression of the Radical workingmen.

Eldon, who as Lord Chancellor presided over the courts, was infamous for his crocodile tears, which, turning to mill-stones, knocked out the brains of little children playing about his feet (stanzas 4-5). These two stanzas, when the poem is read aloud, always provoke nervous laughter among the listeners. Sidmouth (stanza 6) made hypocritical speeches in Parliament to justify violent repressiveness. The seventh stanza sustains the image of the mask as a false face: in the "ghastly masquerade" (*masquerade* carries both meanings, as the masked figures are in the triumphal procession), Destructions are "disguised, even to the eyes, Like Bishops, lawyers, peers, or spies." The subtle technique of emphasizing *spies* by the rhyme and making the word parallel to bishops, lawyers, and peers enforces the condemnation of those figures as masks for destructive powers.

The dreamer saw the skeletal figure of Anarchy, like the Apocalyptic vision of Death, proclaiming himself "God, and King, and Law"—that is, a Jupiter, any king, and perverted law—and trampling the "adoring multitude" (stanzas 8-13).

In London, even as Anarchy's hirelings seize the bank and Tower for his bad purposes, and as he goes to a hired Parliament, Hope looking like Despair lays herself down in the way of the procession (stanza 13-25). Her act brings the intervention of Love (the morning planet is Venus, or Love, and the rose light is the dawn's; in *Prometheus Unbound*, I. 765, Love is likewise a "planet-crested shape"). Love, at first small and weak, grows irresistibly strong, perhaps by virtue of Hope's power to create "From its own wreck the thing it contemplates." The thoughts that come into being wherever Love walks are realities that quell the false and cruel powers of Anarchy. In the first five-line stanza of the poem, stanza 33, the

210

Horse of Death, his rider dead, turns and overruns the murderers in Anarchy's triumphal procession (stanzas 26-33).

As if it were the Earth's heart crying aloud to the men born of England and of her to rise like lions from their slavery, Englishmen hear "words of joy and fear":

Ye are many—they are few. (stanzas 34-38)

Stanzas 39-51 are a mirror of English slavery. [44: *The Ghost of Gold,* paper money. Inflationary, given as wages, paper money made the poor poorer; their labor could not sustain their families. So Shelley argued in *A Philosophical View.*] The English endure worse lives than do savages and beasts; but when they are strong, let them not take fierce revenge, let them not "exchange Blood for blood—and wrong for wrong." If the oppressed knew the real meaning of freedom—which is not the unreality and superstition that Rumor makes it out to be—tyrants could no longer stand. Stanzas 54-64 movingly tell what freedom is. Stanzas 65-73 call for a vast assembly of those who suffer to declare that they are free; God made them so. When the tyrants' artillery, bayoneted infantry, and cavalry attack (stanzas 75-78), let the assembly stand, "calm and resolute,"

> 'With folded arms and steady eyes,
> And little fear, and less surprise,
> Look upon them as they slay
> Till their rage has died away." (stanzas 79-85)

The soldiers will quit the field ashamed of the blood they spilled; the boldest and truest will join the multitude passively resisting. The cry of Earth " 'shall then become Like Oppression's thundered doom' ":

'Ye are many—they are few.' (stanzas 86-91)

Shelley knew that passive resistance could not always work. It would not work, say, in a country where those in power and their followers (perhaps the majority of the country) are willing to slaughter millions of people. In *A Philosophical View of Reform,* intended as a "standard book" for reformers, Shelley wrote that passive resistance was desirable for demonstrations in England "not because active resistance is not justifiable when all other means shall have failed, but because in this instance temperance and courage would produce greater advantages than the most decisive victory. In the first place the soldiers are men and Englishmen, and it is not believed that they would massacre an unresisting multitude of their countrymen drawn up in unarmed array before them and bearing in their looks the calm, deliberate resolution to perish rather than abandon the assertion of their rights." Flight or active resistance would incite the soldiers to violence. Passive resistance would reduce them to "impotence and indecision," make them realize the nature of their acts, and might convert them to allies. But if the Government makes insurrection necessary by hiring "armed force to counteract the will of the nation," why, then, the revolution must be waged.

Song to the Men of England

In the autumn of 1819 Shelley wrote other poems to give heart to those facing the oppression of Government. It looked as though revolution must issue. *Song to the Men of England,* meant to inflame, would have caused the prosecution of any publisher and so lay unpublished for twenty years.

The *Song* begins: Why do the men of England submit to the lords, "these stingless drones?" [The drone, stingless, makes no honey; in like manner the lords, having only the weapons the people make, live on the labors of the people. The image, familiar enough to most Englishmen in an age when people lived nearer to the country than most of us do today, has an antecedent in Plato's *Republic,* 552C: "Shall we, then, say of him that as the drone springs up in the cell, a pest of the hive, so such a man grows up in his home, a pest of the state?"] Three stanzas of rhetorical questioning concretely proclaim the wrongness of the many wearing themselves out for the few. There are anger and irony in the fourth stanza. The fifth stanza hammers away, exposing the people's loss; and the sixth, with powerful inverted repetition, calls upon the people to claim the wealth their labor creates and to make good that claim with armed force. If they do not, they deserve the contemptuous tone in the alternative that the seventh stanza without pausing for transition presents, and they deserve the powerful irony in the sadness of the closing stanza.

212

Less well known than *Song to the Men of England,* unde-
servedly, is the acidly satirical *Similes for Two Political Characters of 1819,* also not published until 1839. A manuscript
version bears the heading *To S------th and C--------gh,* Sidmouth
and Castlereagh. The language, rhythms, and images are like
those that make Thomas Hardy now admired. I give the third
stanza:

> As a shark and dog-fish wait
>> Under an Atlantic isle,
> For the negro-ship, whose freight
> Is the theme of their debate,
>> Wrinkling their red gills the while—
>
> Are ye . . .

It would have been foolhardy for a publisher to issue that
satire in face of the libel laws of the time.

PETER BELL THE THIRD

That autumn, too, Shelley wrote a satire of Wordsworth,
Peter Bell the Third; now hilarious, now serious, the poem
mixes genuine praise with its satirical blame. This much the
satire shares with his political poems: a popular language and
the theme of political freedom.

Leigh Hunt's *Examiner* came to Shelley regularly. In a late
April issue John Keats reviewed John Hamilton Reynolds'
Peter Bell: A Lyrical Ballad, a burlesque that Reynolds wrote
before Wordsworth published *Peter Bell: A Tale in Verse* in
1819, the Bard at last satisfied that the pains he had taken with
his poem since 1798 "to fit for filling *permanently* a station,
however humble, in the Literature of our Country" had succeeded; and in an early May issue Leigh Hunt reviewed
Wordsworth's *Peter Bell.* The reviews—quoting stanzas of both
poems—made Shelley laugh aloud. In Wordsworth's poem the
hero, Peter Bell, looking into a smooth river, comes upon a
"startling sight . . . among the inverted trees." Is it the distorted face of the moon, a gallows, a coffin, a grisly idol, shining fairies, a fiend?

> Is it a party in a parlour?
> Cramm'd just as they on earth were cramm'd—
> Some sipping punch, some sipping tea,
> But, as you by their faces see,
> All silent and all damn'd!

This stanza, quoted by Hunt, Shelley used as motto for his *Peter Bell the Third*; the stanza set off his loudest laughter and set loose his satirical imagination. (Wordsworth never printed the stanza in editions after 1819 because the lines offended the pious.)

The *Examiner* reviews reached Shelley early in June, but William's illness and death put amusement out of his mind; when he worked that summer it was on *The Cenci*, and in September it was on *The Mask of Anarchy*. In October perhaps Wordsworth's *Peter Bell* arrived; Mary Shelley's *Journal* records that Shelley "reads 'Peter Bell' " on the 24th, but does not say whether Wordsworth's or Reynolds'. Some scholars mistakenly think that Shelley perhaps never saw Wordsworth's poem, mistakenly because Shelley in his satirical preface used a line from Wordsworth's preface that appeared in none of the reviews, the line anticipating a permanent station in English literature for *Peter Bell*. In any case, in late October his mind could turn to the comic again, and in "six or seven days," taking little pains and letting the "verses & language . . . come as they would," Shelley wrote this "squib," as he put it, although Mary, when she gave the poem its first publication in 1839, protested that it contained "nothing injurious" to Wordsworth himself, who was still alive, only "something of criticism" on his compositions. The critical reception of *Peter Bell* nettled Wordsworth, who in 1820 wrote a sonnet, *On the Detraction Which Followed the Publication of a Certain Poem*, beginning:

> A book came forth of late, called *Peter Bell*;
> Not negligent the style;—the matter?—good
> As aught that song records of Robin Hood;

But a "harpy brood, On Bard and Hero clamorously fell." Poor Wordsworth—his sonnet justified satire.

Keats wrote that Reynolds imitated Peter Bell "as far as that hero can be imagined from his obstinate name," and, indeed, the portrait "is in points the very man: there is such a pernicious likeness in the scenery, such a pestilent humor in the rhymes, and such an inveterate cadence in some of the stanzas." Reynolds was not only laughing at those ballads of Wordsworth that he thought silly; he took Wordsworth's egotism for a ride in his mock-Wordsworthian preface:

It is now a period of one- and twenty years since I first wrote some of the most perfect compositions (except certain pieces I have written in my later days) that ever dropped from poetical pen. My heart hath been right and powerful all its years. I never thought an evil or weak thought all my life. It has been my aim and my achievement to deduce moral thunder from buttercups, daisies*. . . . Out of sparrows' eggs I have hatched great truths . . .

Reynolds dropped this footnote, Wordsworth's footnotes his target:

* A favorite flower of mine. It was a favourite with Chaucer, but he did not understand its moral mystery as I do.

The review gives seven stanzas. Here is one, the most palpable hit in the parody.

> Not a brother owneth he,
> Peter Bell he hath no brother:
> His mother had no other son,
> No other son e'er called her mother;
> Peter Bell hath brother none.

Reynolds anticipated Wordsworth's stanzaic form, except that these rhymes are alternating rather than enclosed; the exaggerated Wordsworthian repetitiousness, no doubt, was meant to expose what Reynolds thought vacuity of mind.

Leigh Hunt began his review with contempt: "This is another didactic little horror of Mr. Wordsworth's, founded on the bewitching principles of fear, bigotry, and diseased impulse"; and went on, contemptuously and ironically, to give a summary of the narrative. The review is not all in that tone. There is praise of a "masterly" passage, "a portrait as true in the colouring as any of Mr. Crabbe's, and deeper thoughted," and six stanzas of the portrait (lines 291-320) are quoted. "But what is to be said of the following Methodistical nightmare?" The quoted "nightmare" contains the stanza Shelley used for his motto. A week later, reviewing Shelley's *Rosalind and Helen*, Hunt contrasted the two poets. He wrote of the older, "The object of Mr. Wordsworth's administration of melancholy is to make men timid, servile, and (considering his religion) selfish. . . . The Poet of the Lakes always carries his egotism and 'saving knowledge' about with him, and unless he has the settlement of the matter, will go in a pet and plant himself by the side of the oldest tyrannies and slaveries."

Very likely not the risibility aroused by the reviews in June and perhaps by the poem itself in October but the political issue which Hunt had brought into focus and which had been preoccupying Shelley in September gave his satire its motive.

Shelley's Dedication (to Tom Moore, who had attacked the Tories) and Prologue need not long delay us. Eyebrows are sometimes raised by people when they come to this: "Your works, indeed, dear Tom, sell better; but mine are far superior. The public is no judge; posterity sets all to rights." The raised eyebrows belong to people unaware that Shelley is satirizing the tone in Wordsworth's Dedication to Robert Southey, which, as Leigh Hunt reflected, "has anything but the look of sincerity." Understanding that his readers would need knowledge of Wordsworth's *Peter Bell*, Shelley observed in his prologue that after the "antenatal Peter," Reynolds',

> "came Peter Bell the Second,
> Who henceforward must be reckoned
> The body of a double soul,
> And that portion of the whole
> Without which the rest would seem
> Ends of a disjointed dream.—

Of his own Peter Bell, Shelley wrote,

> And the Third is he who has
> O'er the grave been forced to pass
> To the other side, which is,—
> Go and try else,—just like this.

While playing a variation on a theme of Wordsworth, the "party in a parlour" stanza, Shelley mixes a serious element with his comic mockery of Wordsworth's tea party. He wrote

216

in his Dedication, "it is not necessary to consider Hell and the Devil as supernatural machinery. The whole scene of my epic is in 'this world which is'—so Peter informed us before his conversion . . . —

> 'The world of all of us, *and where*
> *We find our happiness, or not at all.'* "

The serious element is a variation on this theme:

> *Faustus.* Where are you damned?
> *Mephistopheles.* In hell.
> *Faustus.* How comes it then that thou art out of hell?
> *Mephistopheles.* Why this is hell, nor am I out of it.

Shelley takes up the theme again in his Part the Third, on Hell.

> Hell is a city much like London—
>   A populous and a smoky city;
> There are all sorts of people undone,
> And there is little or no fun done;
>   Small justice shown, and still less pity. (147-151)

(It comes as a surprise to many that Shelley thought life without fun is hellish.) In this city are such as Castlereagh, a law court, manufacturers (these three reflect the oppressors in the Manchester Massacre), the lords in Parliament, an army, "great talk of revolution—And a great chance of despotism," taxes, mincing virtuous women hounding prostitutes, lawyers, judges, bishops, rhymesters, pamphleteers, military heroes, and, also,

> Things whose trade is, over ladies
>   To lean, and flirt, and stare, and simper,
> Till all that is divine in woman
> Grows cruel, courteous, smooth, inhuman,
>   Crucified 'twixt a smile and whimper. (192-196)

The tenor of the crucifixion metaphor, in the powerful last line, is the act of sex; the crucifying nails are the "Things." For Shelley the act of sex without love was a horror.

The populace of hell spend their days at levees, dinners, suppers,

217

teas,
Where small talk dies in agonies;—

that image and rhyme have a satirical power that Pope or Eliot
never bettered. They go to conversazioni, balls, drawing rooms,
law courts, morning visits, clubs, churches, masquerades, and
tombs.

> And this is hell—and in this smother
> All are damnable and damned;
> Each one damning, damns the other;
> They are damned by one another,
> By none other are they damned. (217-221)

This stanza, modelled after the Reynolds stanza I gave as the
most palpable hit among those quoted by Keats, reveals the
difference between a great poet and a clever versifier. Remarkable in Shelley's greatness is the modernity flashing from his
imagination. We have already seen at the beginning of *Prometheus Unbound* his anticipation of the existential theme of
Sartre's *The Flies*. The situation in this stanza is precisely that
of Sartre's *No Exit*.

Well, Peter in Hell's Grosvenor Square serves his master, the
Devil, as a footman. No longer is he the Hero of Wordsworth's
poem, he is the Bard himself. We are in Part the Fourth.

VII

> He had a mind which was somehow
> At once circumference and centre
> Of all he might or feel or know;   295
> Nothing went ever out, although
> Something did ever enter.

VIII

> He had as much imagination
> As a pint-pot;—he never could
> Fancy another situation,   300
> From which to dart his contemplation,
> Than that wherein he stood.

IX

> Yet his was individual mind,
> And new created all he saw

218

In a new manner, and refined   305
Those new creations, and combined
  Them, by a master-spirit's law.

X

Thus—though unimaginative—
  An apprehension clear, intense,
Of his mind's work, had made alive
The things it wrought on; I believe   311
  Wakening a sort of thought in sense.

XI

But from the first 'twas Peter's drift
  To be a kind of moral eunuch,
He touched the hem of Nature's shift,   315
Felt faint—and never dared uplift
  The closest, all-concealing tunic.

XII

She laughed the while, with an arch smile,
  And kissed him with a sister's kiss,
And said—'My best Diogenes,   320
I love you well—but, if you please,
  Tempt not again my deepest bliss.

XIII

"Tis you are cold—for I, not coy,
  Yield love for love, frank, warm, and true;
And Burns, a Scottish peasant boy—
His errors prove it—knew my joy
  More, learnèd friend, than you.

Peter became a poet because of a guest at the Devil's table,
Coleridge:

PART THE FIFTH
GRACE
I

AMONG the guests who often stayed
  Till the Devil's petits-soupers,
A man there came, fair as a maid,   375
And Peter noted what he said,
  Standing behind his master's chair.

II

He was a mighty poet—and
   A subtle-souled psychologist;
All things he seemed to understand,   380
Of old or new—of sea or land—
   But his own mind—which was a mist.

III

This was a man who might have turned
   Hell into Heaven—and so in gladness
A Heaven unto himself have earned;   385
But he in shadows undiscerned
   Trusted,—and damned himself to madness.

IV

He spoke of poetry, and how
   'Divine it was—a light—a love—
A spirit which like wind doth blow
As it listeth, to and fro;   391
   A dew rained down from God above;

V

'A power which comes and goes like dream,
   And which none can ever trace—
Heaven's light on earth—Truth's brightest beam.'   395
And when he ceased there lay the gleam
   Of those words upon his face.

VI

Now Peter, when he heard such talk,
   Would, heedless of a broken pate,
Stand like a man asleep, or balk   400
Some wishing guest of knife or fork,
   Or drop and break his master's plate.

VII

At night he oft would start and wake
   Like a lover, and began
In a wild measure songs to make   405
On moor, and glen, and rocky lake,
   And on the heart of man—

VIII

And on the universal sky—
  And the wide earth's bosom green,—
  And the sweet, strange mystery   410
Of what beyond these things may lie,
  And yet remain unseen.

IX

For in his thought he visited
  The spots in which, ere dead and damned,
He his wayward life had led;   415

—that is, dead to poetry because damned to dullness by his politics.

In Part the Sixth, Damnation, we are told that Peter had a blight rooted in his heart, the belief that " 'Happiness is wrong,' " (578) and this belief undermined his morals.

In the death hues of agony
  Lambently flashing from a fish,
Now Peter felt amused to see
Shades like a rainbow's rise and flee,
  Mixed with a certain hungry wish.[1] (584-588)

[1] See the description of the beautiful colours produced during the agonizing death of a number of trout, in the fourth part of a long poem, published within a few years [*The Excursion*, VIII. 568-571]. That poem contains curious evidence of the gradual hardening of a strong but circumscribed sensibility, of the perversion of a penetrating but panic-stricken understanding. The author might have derived a lesson which he had probably forgotten from these sweet and sublime verses:—

"This lesson, Shepherd, let us two divide,
Taught both by what she* shows and what conceals [*Nature]
Never to blend our pleasure or our pride
With sorrow of the meanest thing that feels."

This is Shelley's only straightforward note, perfectly serious in tone; the others are satirical, several making fun of Wordsworth's factual footnotes.

Things get worse, and Peter "now raved enormous folly" (614).

221

Then Peter wrote odes to the Devil;—
    In one of which he meekly said:
'May Carnage and Slaughter,
Thy niece and thy daughter,
May Rapine and Famine,
Thy gorge ever cramming,
    Glut thee with living and dead!

    'May Death and Damnation,
    And Consternation,
Flit up from Hell with pure intent!
    Slash them at Manchester,
    Glasgow, Leeds, and Chester;
Drench all with blood from Avon to Trent.

'Let thy body-guard yeomen
    Hew down babes and women,
And laugh with bold triumph till
    Heaven be rent!' (634-649)

"Slash them at Manchester"—as the yeomen slashed "babes and women" at Peterloo.

Wordsworth had exposed himself in his Thanksgiving *Ode* on the Battle of Waterloo, which he wrote in 1816. In *Don Juan*, during the battle between Christians and Moslems, Byron reflected satirically, " 'Carnage' (so Wordsworth tells you) 'is God's daughter,' " and quoted these lines that Wordsworth later purged from his *Ode*:

But *Thy*[1] most dreaded instrument
In working out a pure intent,
Is man array'd for mutual slaughter;
Yea, Carnage is thy daughter!

[1] To wit, the Deity's: this is perhaps as pretty a pedigree for murder as ever was found out . . . [Byron's note]

Now the Devil knew his cue, and had a certain lord pay off the poet—" 'fewer Have fluttered tamer to the lure Than he' " (660-662). When Peter was bribed, in the concluding Part the Seventh, Double Damnation,

He hired a house, bought plate, and made
A genteel drive up to his door,

222

> With sifted gravel neatly laid,—
> As if defying all who said,
>   Peter was ever poor. (688-692)

But although Peter walked about with the bloom of health upon his cheek, a disease worked in his soul, dullness. Peter was dull—"Dull—beyond all conception—dull" (707). The account of Peter's dullness swells into a triumph of hyperbole that closes *Peter Bell the Third*. I give specimens.

> His sister, wife, and children yawned,
>   With a long, slow, and drear ennui,
> All human patience far beyond;
> Their hopes of Heaven each would have pawned,
>   Anywhere else to be. (713-717)

> A printer's boy, folding those pages,
>   Fell slumbrously upon one side. (723-724)

> And worse and worse, the drowsy curse
>   Yawned in him, till it grew a pest—
> A wide contagious atmosphere,
> Creeping like cold through all things near;
>   A power to infect and to infest. (733-737)

Woods and lakes grew full of dim stupidity.

> The birds and beasts within the wood,
>   The insects, and each creeping thing,
> Were now a silent multitude;
> Love's work was left unwrought—no brood
>   Near Peter's house took wing. (748-752)

None, except a "half-idiot and half-knave" (759),

> dared within that space,
>   For fear of the dull charm, to enter;
> A man would bear upon his face,
> For fifteen months in any case,
>   The yawn of such a venture. (763-767)

Radiating out of Peter's soul,

> Seven miles above—below—around
>   This pest of dullness holds its sway. (768-769)

223

If only, we may say amid our smiles, there were such poetic justice in the world.

Like most satires, *Peter Bell the Third* reads unevenly in a later age. Nor did Shelley take much care with *Peter*, which he thought of as a joke. To another poem written in the autumn of 1819 Shelley gave profound care, *Ode to the West Wind*.

ODE TO THE WEST WIND

The Shelleys were staying in Florence, for the doctor they wanted to care for Mary, now pregnant, was there; in November the birth of Percy Florence brought them both relief and comfort after the miserable five months following William's death. Working on *The Cenci* and *The Mask of Anarchy* gave a better texture to Shelley's days, but he was still heavy-spirited in October. *The Cenci* and *The Mask of Anarchy* were no personal expression, issued from no interior experience; and the comic *Peter*, written right after the *Ode*, came from no emotional depth. But the subjective, intense *Ode to the West Wind*, happily, worked a change in Shelley, I believe, as prayer may.

Neville Rogers made a revelatory study in six of Shelley's notebooks of the composition of the *Ode*. [His study was anticipated by H. B. Forman, but as Rogers' work is readily available and Forman's is not, I refer only to Rogers'.] In the first two notebooks are fragmentary records of intellectual and emotional experience that were going into the deep well of his mind, and that the *Ode*, once conceived, drew upon. On a day in late October Shelley walked in the woods near Florence while an animating wind was collecting the elements of a storm that began at sunset, a storm of hail and rain, thunder and lightning; and there Shelley conceived the poem. Rogers traces five stages in its composition. The first stage, in Notebook 3, begins with fragments in changing meters and irregular lines, sometimes broken off, that give images of the tangible things the man saw in his walk, and there are lines that with little change (but that little can work wonders) find their place in the *Ode*; but Shelley has not yet reached to "the likeness of something beyond the present and tangible" that will

224

give form and meaning to the poem being made. In stage two, from mood and things in loose verse emerge twenty-two lines of meditative *terza rima*. In this stage Shelley asserts his presumptuousness: he wears a "false laurel," profaning the "wreath to mighty Poets only due," and he may be killed for proudly wearing that crown; but this is his distinction,

> if I fall
> I shall not creep out of the vital day
> To common dust nor wear a common pall
> But as my hopes were fire, so my decay
> Shall be as ashes covering them.

That presumption breaks down in face of the need for prayer. In the third stage are the first three stanzas nearly in their published form; and in Notebook 4 comes a fair copy of these stanzas dated "Oct. 25" at their head, and, as the first fragments give the "20th of October" as the day of his walk in the woods, we know that the first three stanzas took five days. "The source of poetry is native and involuntary but requires severe labour in its development," Shelley once remarked—the Notebooks show that he spoke out of his own experience; the triumph of these laborious days of composition is that the poem, despite its artifice of form, sounds as spontaneous as the wild rush of the wind. Notebook 4 also has an intermediate draft of the fourth stanza. In Notebook 5 are the fourth and fifth stanzas, still in rough draft; and nothing exists beyond this rough draft except Shelley's note on the occasion of the poem's composition in Notebook 6, which contains a draft of *A Philosophical View of Reform*—an underscoring, as it were, of Shelley's weaving private and public experience into a single fabric.

Now to consider the poem made and given to the world: To begin with, critics who should know better wrongly give the verse form as *terza rima*. The form is, rather, a brilliant invention, five fourteen-line stanzas comprising a regular ode. Within each stanza the run-on lines from tercet to tercet (unlike Dante's practice of coming to a stop at the tercet's end) serve the sweep and power of the wind; and the closing couplet, into which the tercets move and to which they are bound by the rhyme scheme, gives the structural pause that is fitted to the invocation, that is needed to make us feel that the man's voice crying out to be heard can be heard. The wind, of course, is an emblem of the spiritual Power being invoked, Autumn's being, which both destroys and preserves for the cyclical regeneration of the world. Thrice the speaker invokes this Power: on the earth, in the sky, over the sea—the Power moves everywhere, commands everywhere, in the world. (That is not to say it is the only power; Shelley's is a pluralistic not a monistic universe.) The patterned recurrence of the invocation, each in its own large setting, creates a large and strong emotional rhythm. In the fourth stanza the first tercet brings together by synecdoche the three regions of the world, each in a line, that were each in a stanza—note the classical arrangement. The man, now speaking in the first person, wishes that he were a leaf, a cloud, or a wave so that he could share the strength of the uncontrollable Power manifest in the wind. No longer with the fresh, high hopes of his unchecked youth; fallen upon the thorns of life, bleeding and weak; chained by the heavy weight of experience, although made of stuff that is tameless, swift, and proud like the west wind, too much so to suffer the chaining, his need is sore. This stanza, then, gives the reason for his prayer. The fifth stanza is his prayer. He wants to be made the instrument of the fierce spiritual Power: let the Power use his dead thoughts, as the wind uses withered leaves, to quicken a new birth of love in the universe; let the Power scatter his words among mankind, words flaring into the fire of liberty like hot ashes and sparks blown from an unextinguished hearth; let the Power speak through his voice a prophecy awakening the earth to the new age.

> O, Wind
> If Winter comes, can Spring be far behind?

The world *will* awaken to freedom and love.

Although I heard that last line overmuch long before I even heard of Shelley, in its context the line never weakens for me. Which brings me to another line, one that several anti-Shelley critics have taken potshots at, "I fall upon the thorns of life! I bleed!" The images, although they do not strike us with intensity, wit, originality, or strength, do give us clarity of substance and of meaning. The metaphor "thorns of life" is low-pitched and conversational but not at all exhausted as metaphor as is "hulk of a man," a phrase in which we see only a vaguely large man and not at all the body of a ship. Because he is in a weak state, the speaker falls upon the thorns of life; the loss of blood weakens him the more. We can easily, once buffeted by experience, stumble into worse, and things become harder and harder. The metaphor is not overdramatic or embarrassing any more than it is exhausted; it is familiar language expressing experience familiar to most grown people. And finally, it is no criterion of greatness in literature that every image in a poem must have intensity, wit, originality or strength. The critics who judge against this line, trying to impugn the poem, do so arbitrarily and so, in this instance, are not worth our regard. Even those who have defended the line have done so on the wrong grounds. They point to the twisted and thwarting circumstances of Shelley's life, especially to the recent shattering and enervating experience of facing little William's death. But the poem is self-contained and wants no biographical illumination; indeed, the voice speaking does not belong to Bysshe, the husband of Mary and father of William, but to the man, or rather a man, in his character as a poet with public work to do. We should have just cause to complain of the man if he weakly exposed the particular experiences of his private unhappiness. He does not do so because he is not weak, he is not a creature of self-pity. His nature is "tameless, and swift, and proud," and he is strong enough to contain the fierceness of the spiritual Power he prays to. That it is a genuine prayer coming from a religious nature, although the Spirit prayed to is in no formulated theology, need not, I trust, be underscored.

Another arbitrary attack was made against the first three tercets of stanza ii—tercets given as Shelley's "characteristic modes of expression" in which there is "a recognized essential trait of Shelley's: his weak grasp upon the actual." We have again and again looked upon the actual in Shelley's strong grasp. Shelley's mode of perception in these tercets is outside that critic's sensory and intellectual ken. "In what respects," he asked, "are the 'loose clouds' like 'decaying leaves'? . . . What again, are those 'tangled boughs of Heaven and Ocean'? They stand for nothing that Shelley could have pointed to in the scene before him." This critic, F. R. Leavis, apparently never saw a waterspout on the Mediterranean, a sometimes tree-shaped cloud extending down from the bottom of a cumulus cloud to a cloud of spray torn up from the sea by strong wind.

In *A Vision of the Sea* Shelley uses the image of "the black trunks of the waterspouts." It is the critic, not Shelley, who must be accused of having seen too little of the actual world. And he goes on, "to scrutinize closely" as he thinks, the images of the stream and the Maenad, neither of which he thinks has real meaning. Well, he was unable to discover logical fitness in the images of these tercets and so thought himself on safe grounds in condemning them. I shall let two other critics answer, each from a single point of view that is separately incomplete although valid; together they reveal a fullness of perception on Shelley's part, at once sensory and intellectual, that is rare and true.

To begin with, as W. K. Wimsatt wrote, "the shift in imagery of the second stanza, the pell-mell raggedness and confusion of loose clouds, decaying leaves, angels and Maenads with hair uplifted, the dirge, the dome, the vapors, and the enjambment from tercet to tercet combine to give an impression beyond statement of the very wildness, the breath and power of the poem's radical metaphor." He added, rather than incline to logic, as metaphysical and neoclassical poetry do, romantic poetry prefers to approach "the directness of sensory impression." Or we may say that such imagery, seeming to give us direct perceptions of multiplicity, opens the way for our immediate apprehension, our intuitive knowledge, of modes of being other than the natural. Whether there be such modes of being or not, when we are not sacrificing our direct perceptions and immediate responses to the authority of our rational minds, we are aware of multitudinous reality. Nor do I say that the intellectual perception of unity abstracted from the complexity of the world is other than reality; it is, at least, what makes the world knowable, what lets us cope with the world. Our modern intellectual perceptions discovering unity are dominantly scientific. Shelley's sensory and intellectual perceptions worked together, neither limiting the other, and there are in the stanza both multiplicity and unity. Let a professional scientist explain the poet's intellectual perception:

In the first 3 2/3 lines of Shelley's stanza, the *loose clouds, shed* like *earth's decaying leaves* into the airstream, are the fractostratus clouds, harbingers of rain. The *tangled boughs* from which these leaf-like clouds are shaken are those regions of air whose slightly adverse pressures, temperatures and humidities make them the destined birth-place for clouds. These parcels of air, turbulent, ever-changing in shape like wind-blown boughs, contain a mixture of water vapour from *Ocean* and air from *Heaven*. The remaining 5 lines describe the mare's-tail cirrus, the *bright hair* spread as if on the *blue surface* of the sky, and streaming like the hair of a girl running into a strong wind. The cirrus stretches from the *horizon,* which is dim because obscured by the scud, to the *zenith.* The simile of the Maenads . . . is apt, for Maenads had the odd habit of rushing around with hair streaming. Since the word "cirrus," coined by Shelley's contemporary Luke Howard, means "a lock of hair," the emphasis on hair is justified. And, as spreading cirrus often heralds a depression, Shelley neatly links his imagery with the weather outlook in the final *locks of the approaching storm,* a phrase which is used as a caption to a photograph of plume cirrus in Grant's *Cloud and Weather Atlas* [1944]. It may be thought that my explanation of these lines has been too detailed. The reason for this detail is that an admired critic, F. R. Leavis, completely misinterpreted the lines because he failed to distinguish between the fractostratus and cirrus clouds.

There are also religious meanings in the stanza. The Maenads in their intoxicated frenzy were destructive, tearing animals to pieces; but in their orgiastic rites they celebrated Dionysus as a fertility god. The fertile God of the vine was also a tree god to whom the Greeks widely sacrificed, as Plutarch records. It is attractive to think that Shelley knew of that aspect of the God, so pertinent is it to the imagery of the *Ode.* In *The Bacchae* of Euripides—Shelley was reading Euripides in 1819, and in the fourth act of *Prometheus* used Agave, a worshipper in *The Bacchae,* for a Dionysian image—the chorus of Lydian priestesses of Dionysus, "the Joy-bestower," sings of the coming of the God as bringing the spring and of the mystery myth of the God's death and resurrection. The eighteenth-century mythologists, whose work Shelley knew, wrote about Adonis, Dionysus, and others as season gods whose death and rebirth were the winter and spring of vegetation. In the tercet that follows the Maenad image, the "dying year" (a subtle echo of the God that dies and is reborn) will be buried in the "vast sepulchre" of the year's last night, its dome "Vaulted with . . . congregated might"—the connotations of a cathedral in these words again are an oblique statement of

229

winter and spring, of death and rebirth. That theme is in the very first tercet of the stanza: the clouds are like decaying leaves: watering the ground they are instrumental in the new birth.

The clouds, again, are "Angels," bringers of good tidings, heralding the fertilizing rain and the intellectually illuminating lightning. "The great writers of our own age are, we have reason to suppose, the companions and forerunners of some unimagined change in our social condition or the opinions which cement it. The cloud of mind is discharging its collected lightning . . ." So Shelley wrote in his Preface to *Prometheus Unbound*. The "I" of the *Ode* is a poet with public work to do, who would be one of those "great writers" heralding social change. No doubt Shelley conceived of himself as such an "I," but it is, nonetheless, a mistake to read the *Ode* as though we were reading autobiography. The *Ode*, as I have said, is a self-contained work of art, and, interesting as the autobiographical elements may be, it is as poetry that the *Ode* claims greatness.

The emotion straining within this poem would break through the form, even as the man making the prayer would be more than himself, a prophetic instrument of a fierce power. The whole is therefore not classical; rather, a tension exists between the romantic and the classical resolved by the calming hope, the calming knowledge, in the last line. The classical elements are in the clarity and balance and perfect ordering of the form and also in the informing metaphor of the ode. The classical formal qualities are apparent. The informing metaphor is classical in that it speaks in harmony with a traditional as well as a contemporary milieu. In the language of the age the rising wind, in the words of M. H. Abrams, was "usually linked with the outer transition from winter to spring"; the wind became "both the stimulus and outer correspondent to a spring-like revival of the spirit after a wintry season"; and the wind paralleled "a purifying revolutionary violence which destroys in order to preserve." In languages of the past—Latin, Greek, Hebrew—the word for wind also signified breath and spirit. In the Old Testament wind and breath renew life and destroy (Ezekiel 37:9, 13:13), and in pagan mythology the wind gods both destroy and animate. The wind, moreover, as the breath of a god was a divine afflatus—literally, an inspiration. And, to continue drawing from Abrams, "In the Biblical commentaries of the Church Fathers it was commonly recognized that the moving air, the breath of the Lord, the Holy Spirit, the life and spiritual rebirth of man, and the inspiration of the Prophets in the Old and New Testaments were connected."

The leaves work in the service of the Wind for the regeneration of the world, a work both natural and symbolic. After many seasons of lying heaped on the forest soil, they fertilize the land (I paraphrase Shelley's exact botany in *Queen Mab*, V. 4ff.). In the first tercet of the *Ode* the dead leaves, like ghosts of themselves, almost weightlessly fly in multitudes through the air. I have only once seen such multitudes of autumn leaves, thick almost as rain in the air, flying swiftly and wildly in the wind. There is fearfulness, I can testify, in such a scene, the emotion I should experience in watching "ghosts from an enchanter fleeing." And the unseen being, working such a profound change in the natural world, is imaginatively well figured as an enchanter. The whole image is an image of wide death—the multitudes are "Pestilence-stricken" (5). Dying, too, are the four races of man—yellow, and black, and pale, and red (I take the suggestion for the symbolic meaning from G. M. Matthews). After the image of death comes the image of regeneration in the natural world and implicitly of resurrection in the human: each seed that the clarion of the Spring will awaken to life is "like a corpse within its grave"; the Spring is their Shepherd (6-12).

We have seen, in the second stanza, that just as the decaying leaves are transformed to fertilize the earth, so are the clouds "from the tangled boughs of Heaven and Ocean" transformed to fertilizing rain; and the lightning discharged illuminates the human mind for the world's change to come; and the images of the Maenad and of the cathedral sustain the religious death-and-rebirth imagery of the first stanza. There has been no abatement of stormy power since the four lines of the Spring's awakening of earth (9-12). Now it is esthetically time for another, longer calm.

The longer calm, in the first half of the third stanza, may lull our minds so that we give the imagery, especially the coiling streams, too little thought. This calm is physical, sensuous, not like the earlier springtime of the world symbolizing spiritual rebirth. Here the Mediterranean god, Neptune—the *his* and *he* make clear the image of the god,—lies "lulled" to a sleep of "summer dreams," an experience idle and unreal. The vividness of dream is his "intenser day"; the analogy is to the water bluer than the day's blue, the sky. In his summer dreams quiver "old palaces and towers" on the pumice, or volcanic, isle beside which he sleeps. In Roman days the town of Baiae, on a small bay west of Naples, was a luxurious resort of nobles and emperors, studded with palaces. Volcanic disturbance submerged shore where palaces stood, and these Shelley had sailed over. These stone ruins, now in the sea (as dreams are in the mind), covered by moss and flowers, are so sweet that "the *sense* faints picturing them"—the pleasure, overwhelming, is sensuous in Neptune's dream as it is in the mind of the poet. The luxurious resort of Baiae was a couch of licentiousness for the powerful (an 1819 *Fragment* speaks of such "a Roman's chamber, Where he kept his darkest revels"). Now we may understand the image in "Lulled by the coil of his crystàlline streams." His streams are nereids, who wound themselves ("the coil") about the god, their loveplay lulling him to sleep. The Wind, who saw him in sleep and saw the old palaces in their sleep, their death (the syntax permits the ambiguity), awakens the god from his summer dreams—by implication to a better life, just as the volcano destroyed Baiae so that a better city could arise. The images are again of regeneration, religious and physical. The Wind then goes out to the Atlantic, and there the storm does its work, despoiling the foliage of the oozy woods, like the wind in the forest. "The phenomenon alluded to at the conclusion of the third stanza," Shelley said in his note to the poem, "is well known to naturalists. The vegetation at the bottom of the sea, of rivers, and of lakes, sympathises with that of the land in change of seasons, and is consequently influenced by the winds which announce it." The images of the leaves in the first three stanzas, which invoke the Destroyer and Preserver, make for textural harmony, just as do the two calms and the religious images and the images of the Wind's dominating power. It is the kind of harmony that Cézanne regretted was going out of modern painting.

The human voice reaches for that Power in the fourth and fifth stanzas, which are bound together by the logic of cause (the sore need) and consequence (the prayer); and which are unified with the first three by the poet's desire to share the strength of the Wind as that strength is manifested in the three regions of the world and by his culminating desire that the Spirit be his spirit, that the poet be the prophetic trumpet of the new order even as the clarion of the Spring promised in the buds the inevitable coming of the new year.

1820

It was a wet, cold January in Florence in 1820, and Shelley and Mary were too much alone. Toward the month's end they left for Pisa. Hills surrounded the quiet town, the Arno flowed through, a forest stood nearby, and these were all steeped in a mild climate. These things meant much to Shelley, and in Pisa and nearby Leghorn the Shelleys had good friends. This region harbored Shelley until his death.

THE SENSITIVE PLANT

For months Shelley wrote little, perhaps constrained by an unhappiness connected to Mary's darkness of mind. Of his major poetry *The Sensitive Plant* shines alone in those dark months. It is an interesting poem to consider critically. To begin with, the poem presents something of a critical paradox. Although less of a personal statement relative to the whole work than is *Ode to the West Wind*, *The Sensitive Plant* profits more than the *Ode* does, and becomes more interesting to criticism, if connected to Shelley's personal experience; and, indeed, the poem forces that connection. The *Ode*, told in the first person (an expression of that *I* connected to public experience, of the poet realizing how far beyond his grasp is a reach to the prophecy that is the cause of the new order unless he becomes the voice of a spiritual Power), translates intensely personal experience to that of a public figure who is the integral element in the poetic whole. The statement of the personal experience, however, is exact. In *The Sensitive Plant* the planes of meaning that are public intersect the plane that is personal; the personal elements as themselves are integral to the whole; and the personal statement is, deliberately I think, inexact.

During the spring and summer a sensitive plant (its botanical name is *mimosa*) grows in a garden which is a paradise,

233

among the loveliest flowers of the world. These flowers are tended by a Lady, who is a careful gardener; the realistic images of her daily work seem to make her an actual woman, who charms.

> She sprinkled bright water from the stream
> On those that were faint with the sunny beam;
> And out of the cups of the heavy flowers
> She emptied the rain of the thunder-showers.
>
> She lifted their heads with her tender hands,
> And sustained them with rods and osier-bands;
> If the flowers had been her own infants, she
> Could never have nursed them more tenderly.
>
> And all killing insects and gnawing worms,
> And things of obscene and unlovely forms,
> She bore, in a basket of Indian woof,
> Into the rough woods far aloof,—
>
> In a basket, of grasses and wild-flowers full,
> The freshest her gentle hands could pull
> For the poor banished insects, whose intent,
> Although they did ill, was innocent. (II. 33-48)

The sanity of her moral values is worth noticing. Unlike the sentimental who will overlook the harm a person may do so long as they think that the person means well, the Lady banishes the insects whose acts are destructive although their motives are innocent. This unsentimental and lovely Lady dies at the summer's end. The flowers of the garden, all perennials except for the mimosa, are utterly destroyed in the autumn, because their principle of life is dead; and before the snow comes, ugly weeds possess the garden. The sensitive plant, which has a principle of being different from that of the other plants, lives into the winter, becomes frozen, and by springtime is a leafless wreck. Only the weeds flourish.

Not enough meaning emerges from the whole if that simple narrative has only literal meaning, and so we are forced to look for an import beyond the theme that a flower garden will not last without a gardener. Who or what is the Lady that wards off the noxiousness of the world? She is a Power, a ruling Grace, a God who acts out of love, as her care of the garden shows. She is, indeed, Love. If that is so, she is immortal and cannot die. When the Lady dies, we consequently are again forced to look elsewhere for meaning, outside the symbolic world (the Conclusion will resolve matters otherwise, but we are here, not there). Here, if we look outside the narrative and symbolic planes, we turn to the plane of Shelley's personal experience and do so justifiably as the planes intersect. But just as there is apparent inconsistency in Love's dying, there is apparent inconsistency in Shelley's being a female: it is as a female that the Sensitive Plant is introduced to us.

At the beginning of Part First the Sensitive Plant opens its leaves, as though they were eyelids, to the light, and closes them beneath Night's kisses, as a woman closes her eyes; and it trembles with love's desire like a doe in the noontide, a female deer. (At the end of Part First, the Sensitive Plant is a child in the embrace of Night, its mother; the image has shifted to express innocence and dependence.) Shelley introduced the Sensitive Plant as a female because he would never "be a party in making my private affairs or those of others to be topics of general discussion," as he said to Leigh Hunt two days after writing the remarks explaining that the first 89 lines of *Euganean Hills* (lines personal to the poet) "were not erased at the request of a dear friend." (Later in Part First the sensitive plant is male; like the traditional male lover, "It desires what is has not, the Beautiful!") In like manner his cry of pain in *Julian and Maddalo* came from the Maniac. Later, his Advertisement to *Epipsychidion* pretended that the "Writer of the following lines died at Florence"—to a friend he privately wrote about the poem, "It is an idealized history of my life and feelings." The personal statement in *Ode to the West Wind* is quite of another kind, for the *I* in that poem is the poet rather than the man; while the man's life is private, the poet's is public. In the plane of personal experience the Sensitive Plant is not Shelley, but reflects intensely, even shares, the man's emotional history; the plant in relation to the Lady and the garden, the man in relation to Mary and his private world. The death of the Lady images Mary's spiritually dying to Shelley after the loss of their children.

Before going on, I wish briefly to speak of another way of regarding *The Sensitive Plant*. Earl Wasserman in his remarkable introductory chapter of *The Subtler Language* illuminates the "conception of the poem [any poem] as somehow a self-constituting and self-sustaining reality," as a symbolic cosmos. In his chapter on *The Sensitive Plant* he writes: "Like the mathematician, the poet, without regard to reality, has declared, 'Let a system be assumed in which . . . ,' then will ultimately ask what penetrating light the imaginative working out of this cosmic assumption has cast on reality. The analogy is Shelley's own: 'The most astonishing combinations of poetry, the subtlest deductions of logic and mathematics are no other than combinations which the intellect makes of sensations *according to its own laws*' (*Treatise on Morals*)." I admire, but I do not accept, his interpretation of *The Sensitive Plant* as "a self-constituting and self-sustaining reality." Nor do I accept the informing metaphysic in his explication, although I do accept many of its details. Wasserman, if I am not mistaken, believes that since "an inclusive and coherent pattern of relations—and, what amounts to the same thing, a coherent meaning—emerges," his interpretation is validated. But just as in mathematics different systems, valid and coherent, can be made by beginning with different axioms, so in criticism interpretations beginning with different premises may give different coherent meanings. Conflicting interpretations may be equally valid; but being an absolutist by temperament, I do not believe that they may both be true.

I am much attracted to the modern critical practice of regarding a work for its own "inclusive and coherent pattern of relations." The *Ode to the West Wind*, I thought, should be so regarded. But we should be mistaken to make the practice a doctrine demanding absolute adherence in criticism, mistaken to make the doctrine a standard of judgment that would say that works not having such a pattern are inferior. Should we bind ourselves to that doctrine, we cut ourselves off from other experience in literature giving pleasure and revelation, elements of whose meaning refer to the world the man writing lived in. Such an experience, as I have said, is Milton's *Sonnet on His Blindness*; such, too, is *The Sensitive Plant*.

A Sensitive Plant in a garden grew . . .

That first line has the innocent air of "Once upon a time a sensitive plant grew in a garden," an innocence both deceptive and real: real because the garden is an Eden, deceptive because the story shall not end happily as "Once upon a time" promises in fairy tales.

> And the Spring arose on the garden fair,
> Like the Spirit of Love felt everywhere;
> And each flower and herb on Earth's dark breast
> Rose from the dreams of its wintry rest. (I. 5-8)

There's an immediacy of beauty in this stanza although no particularity of image, unless I deceive myself. What each flower and herb dreamed in its wintry rest we cannot say, but the stanza's beauty, charging our intellectual atmosphere, suggests the quality of the dreams. The stanza also marks the way of cyclical change.

The stanzas unfolding will say what "each flower and herb on Earth's dark breast" dreamed through the iteration of symbols that, charging the atmosphere of our minds, intensifies and illuminates emotional and imaginative meaning. The flowers awaken again in a morning image:

> And from this undefilèd Paradise
> The flowers (as an infant's awakening eyes
> Smile on its mother, whose singing sweet
> Can first lull, and at last must awaken it),
>
> When Heaven's blithe winds had unfolded them,
> As mine-lamps enkindle a hidden gem,
> Shone smiling to Heaven, and every one
> Shared joy in the light of the gentle sun. (I. 58-65)

Their springtime awakening "on Earth's dark breast" gives "mother" a connotation of Earth; and the lulling and awakening may suggest a death and the consequent birth. Now in their "undefiled Paradise," the flowers unfolded by "Heaven's blithe winds" (the tenor for the vehicle of the mother's sweet singing), share joy in the sun's light, which is Heaven's radiance. The image of the minelamps (another vehicle for the "blithe winds") interrupts the implicit cyclical changing, for lamps can light a gem a long time although not forever. We dare guess, then, that the flowers dreamed of the paradise that they were to be born into. This dream, let us note, is not the bad dream that life can be. Nor are they bad dreams at the

237

end of Part First, "when the day's veil fell from the world of sleep,"

> And the beasts, and the birds, and the insects were drowned
> In an ocean of dreams without a sound;
> Whose waves never mark, though they ever impress
> The light sand which paves it, consciousness. (I. 102-105)

The day's veil hid a reality from living things; its falling away let the beasts, birds, and insects die into an "ocean of dreams," which is perhaps like the "wide ocean of intellectual beauty" in Asia's song ending Act II. These dreams do not mark consciousness, although they do press themselves into consciousness; that is, they are not remembered when living things awaken from that world, are born into this world, although they are in the depths of our consciousness and may therefore influence our lives. The Sensitive Plant in its dream hears snatches of a nightingale's Elysian chant; earlier in Part First "daisies and delicate bells" (perhaps light, i.e., day's eyes, and music) were likened to the beauty of "fabulous asphodels" (I. 53-54), the flowers of Elysium. Thus again the garden is linked with a paradise to come. In Part Second the Lady's dreams are "less slumber than Paradise":

> As if some bright Spirit for her sweet sake
> Had deserted Heaven while the stars were awake,

and this companion in her dream is a presence, although indistinct, in her waking mind, an iteration of the idea in the image of the ocean of dreams impressing the light sand of consciousness (perhaps we may for a moment think of this bright Spirit and the Lady as versions of Prometheus and Asia). Lastly, in her garden are "many an antenatal tomb, Where butterflies dream of the life to come" (II. 53-54), a life that shall be in the garden.

Now to the beginning again. The third stanza reveals the trait of the Sensitive Plant that is the matrix of its being, its desire for love; it is now companionless. Such a trait always and the state of companionlessness then (Mary present in body but not in spirit) belonged also to Shelley; nothing in a first reading of the opening stanzas, of course, can lead us to make that connection. The desire for love and companionship is not limited to either sex, and so the doe-like plant may image

238

elements in a man's emotional history. From the Sensitive Plant the vision widens to others in the garden, the beauty now created with particularity of image:

> The snowdrop, and then the violet,
> Arose from the ground with warm rain wet,
> And their breath was mixed with fresh odour, sent
> From the turf, like the voice and the instrument. (I. 13-16)

The simile of the breath of the flowers mixing with the odor of the turf like the harmony between a voice and an instrument is the first of recurring musical images in the garden. The hyacinth "flung from its bells a sweet peal" (I. 26); the stream in the garden danced with "a motion of sweet sound" (I. 48); the flowers unfold to Heaven as an infant's eyes to its mother "singing sweet" (I. 60); "light winds . . . Shed the music of many murmurings" (I. 78-79); and at night "the sweet nightingale Ever sang more sweet" (I. 106-107). In a later lyric, music reveals "some world far from ours" (*To Jane: "The Keen Stars Were Twinkling,"* 22). And in *Epipsychidion*, also later, on an Ionian island, a "far Eden,"

> every motion, odour, beam, and tone,
> With that deep music is in unison;
> Which is a soul within the soul—they seem
> Like echoes of an antenatal dream.—(453-456)

For an earlier image of music and paradise, I suggest Asia's "sea profound, of ever-spreading sound" at the end of Act II. Clearly, then, the musical images are evocations of paradise, their iteration the technique of symbolism like the iteration of the dream-images. But the music imagery, if understood only intellectually, perhaps does not fulfill itself in our minds; the emotional meaning is more deeply needed, that is, music must induce in our minds a state sympathetic with the state it induces in Shelley's mind.

We may also mark the iteration of the word *sweet* in music images, perhaps meant to reflect in another sense-perception the odorous "flowers of that garden sweet" which "Rejoiced in the sound of her gentle feet" (II. 29-30), the Lady's. It is also a "gentle sun" in whose light the flowers share joy (I. 65). The bells of the lily of the valley are in "pavilions of tender green" (I. 24); and twice there are images of a "tender sky" (I. 36, 97).

These recurring adjectives are meant, of course, to shadow forth qualities of the paradisal world, and they work in the poem much in the way of the dream and music images. If sweetness, gentleness, tenderness are qualities not to our taste in a tough age, we should not like to live in the paradisal world which this garden is.

Also not to the modern taste are the human traits given to the flowers in the garden: the trembling and panting with bliss of the mimosa, the narcissi dying of their own loveliness, the lily of the valley pale with passion, the rose unveiling her glowing breast fold after fold until the "soul of her beauty lay bare," and the wandlike lily lifting its Maenadic cup (I. 9, 20 22, 32, 34). Whether to the modern looker-on's taste or not, Shelley gives these flowers a moral being so that there may be interpenetration with the human looker-on, and the images in the passage go to the gazer through all five senses. Although we may not like what he has done, there is no quarreling with his skill in executing his intention (however much intention may change with the discoveries of composition).

THE QUESTION

When Shelley wants to give flowers a more strictly natural life, as in *The Question*, he can do so with equal skill:

II

There grew pied wind-flowers and violets,
    Daisies, those pearled Arcturi of the earth,
The constellated flower that never sets;
    Faint oxslips; tender bluebells, at whose birth
The sod scarce heaved; and that tall flower that wets—
    Like a child, half in tenderness and mirth—
Its mother's face with Heaven's collected tears,
When the low wind, its playmate's voice, it hears.

III

And in the warm hedge grew lush eglantine,
    Green cowbind and the moonlight-coloured may,
And cherry-blossoms, and white cups, whose wine
    Was the bright dew, yet drained not by the day;

And wild roses, and ivy serpentine,
    With its dark buds and leaves, wandering astray;
And flowers azure, black, and streaked with gold,
Fairer than any wakened eyes behold.

IV

And near to the river's trembling edge
    There grew broad flag-flowers, purple pranked with white,
And starry river buds among the sedge,
    And floating water-lilies, broad and bright,
Which lit the oak that overhung the hedge
    With moonlight beams of their own watery light;
And bulrushes, and reeds of such deep green
As soothed the dazzled eye with sober sheen.

The man who dreamed of the "shelving bank of turf" where these flowers grew made a nosegay and, elated, hastened to "present it!—Oh! to whom?" The poem ends with that despondent question. Newman White suggests that *The Question* could have been written by August 1819 although Mary dated it 1820, and that, like *The Sensitive Plant*, it reflects the crisis that existed in Shelley's and Mary's life. The one image in *The Question* that departs from the strictly natural, likening a flower to a child, movingly reveals Shelley's love of children if we connect the poem to his loss of Clara and William and consequently, as *The Question* seems to say, of Mary. In *The Sensitive Plant* flowers unfold "as an infant's awakening eyes Smile on its mother." Early on, in *Alastor* (1815), "ten thousand blossoms, flow around The grey trunks, and,"

    as gamesome infants' eyes,
    With gentle meanings, and most innocent wiles,
    Fold their beams round the hearts of those that love,
    These twine their tendrils . . . (440-444)

And in *Adonais*, in 1821, again the image comes, in the Roman cemetery where Keats and Shelley's son William lie buried,

    Where, like an infant's smile, over the dead
    A light of laughing flowers along the grass is spread. (440-441)

I make the digression to these flower-child images because, to me at least, they are deeply appealing as a revelation of the man although they were not intended so.

241

Well, to *The Sensitive Plant* once more, and once more let us address ourselves to the technique of symbolism. The wandlike lily lifting up a cup as a Maenad has a fiery star for an eye. On the stream in the garden,

> under boughs of embowering blossom,
> With golden and green light, slanting through
> Their heaven of many a tangled hue,
>
> Broad water-lilies lay tremulously,
> And starry river-buds glimmered by. (I. 42-46)

There are beams darting "from many a star Of the flowers whose hues they bear afar" (I. 80-81); these are "the meteors of that sublunar Heaven, Like the lamps of the air when Night walks forth" (II. 10-11). The flowers are stars or shooting stars; in Shelley's day certain meteors were thought to come from the earth. And flowers are again like stars for three days after the Lady dies (III. 1-2). Fire and stars were for Shelley symbols of the forms, or essences, of love and beauty. Their connection to the Lady is made explicit:

> There was a Power in this sweet place,
> An Eve in this Eden; a ruling Grace
> Which to the flowers, did they waken or dream,
> Was as God is to the starry scheme. (II. 1-4)

She is Love, the Supreme Form.

The garden, then, is no earthly paradise. Shelley recognized only two paradises, the antenatal where only, as in an undefiled Eden, evil is absent (to that existence we may return); or the Promethean world at the far goal of time, from which evil is expunged. The garden in *The Sensitive Plant* is the antenatal paradise whose portals open,

> Through Death and Birth, to a diviner day;
> A paradise of vaulted bowers,
> Lit by downward gazing flowers,
> And watery paths that lie between
> Wildernesses calm and green,
> Peopled by shapes too bright to see,

242

which walk upon the wide ocean of intellectual beauty (*Prometheus Unbound*, II. 103-110). It is here that the Sensitive Plant has its existence in Part First and Part Second.

The flowers—the forms—shared joy in the intellectual radiance (I. 65) of the transcendent world;

> For each one was interpenetrated
> With the light and the odour its neighbour shed,
> Like young lovers whom youth and love make dear
> Wrapped and filled by their mutual atmosphere. (I. 66-69)

The vehicle of the simile again lends the flowers human traits that fit the flowers to our sympathy.

> But the Sensitive Plant which could give small fruit
> Of the love which it felt from the leaf to the root,
> Received more than all, it loved more than ever,
> Where none wanted but it, could belong to the giver,—
>
> For the Sensitive Plant has no bright flower;
> Radiance and odour are not its dower;
> It loves, even like Love, its deep heart is full,
> It desires what it has not, the Beautiful! (I. 70-77)

This is a much interpreted passage. The light and odour that interpenetrate the plants are the fruit of love. The Sensitive Plant, having no bright flower, can give little radiance and odour. Its being is different from that of the forms. But if it can give only small fruit of its love, if only it wanted (lacked) a bright flower, the Sensitive Plant nonetheless received more than all the others could because its "deep heart" had more capacity to receive; and it loved more than belonged to the flowers to give, desiring the Supreme Form, the Beautiful, more than the forms of the flowers. (For a moment let us glance at the plane of personal experience. The Sensitive Plant has no beauty, a reflection of Shelley speaking in the voice of the Maniac in *Julian and Maddalo*:

> Nature nor in form nor hue
> Bestowed on me her choicest workmanship. 465-466)

The light winds shedding music; the beams from the starflowers; the plumed insects bearing light and odor, golden on the green grass; the clouds of dew, fertile power lying like "fire in the flowers till the sun rides high" and then taking fragrance to the stars; the moist, dim noontide like a sea on the warm earth "In which every sound, and odour, and beam, Move, as reeds in a single stream";—these, a multiplicity within unity, were sweet joy, like ministering angels, for the Sensitive Plant to bear (I. 78-95). They gave joy as manifestations of the Beautiful.

The flowers in the garden likewise rejoiced in the Lady, "who moved through the garden ministering" (II. 57) spiritually: the narrator, speaking for the first time in his own person, says,

> I doubt not they felt the spirit that came
> From her glowing fingers through all their frame. (II. 30-13)

It is hard, of course, for the modern mind nurtured in a scientific climate to believe, as Wordsworth and Shelley believed, that all things in nature have a moral life.

At summer's end the Lady died. On the fourth day there were the rites of death. The cold smell of the Lady's corpse, oppressive and dank, penetrated the coffin, and the garden "became cold and foul, Like the corpse of her who had been its soul" (III. 17-18). The plants of the garden,

> The sweetest that ever were fed on dew,
> Leaf by leaf, day after day,
> Were massed into the common clay.
>
> And the leaves, brown, yellow, and gray, and red,
> And white with the whiteness of what is dead,
> Like troops of ghosts on the dry wind passed;
> Their whistling noise made the birds aghast.
>
> And the gusty winds waked the wingèd seeds,
> Out of their birthplace of ugly weeds,
> Till they clung round many a sweet flower's stem,
> Which rotted into the earth with them. (III. 31-41)

Unlike the seeds that the wind blows with the ghostly leaves in the first stanza of *Ode to the West Wind*, these are the seeds of ugliness only that possesses the earth now that the spiritual Power whom Shelley names Intellectual Beauty and Love, its dual aspects, is absent. The Sensitive Plant lives into the winter. When it weeps to see what the world is, its tears are frozen by the world's cold. Winter rules cruelly. Under the roots of the plant,

The moles and the dormice died for want:
The birds dropped stiff from the frozen air
And were caught in the branches naked and bare. (III. 99-101)

In the cycle of change, when "the Spring came back, The Sensitive Plant was a leafless wreck"; only the ugly weeds grew, rising "like the dead from their ruined charnels" (III. 110-113). This world, into which we are born from an antenatal paradise, is a death that we must suffer. That is the theme of the moral allegory, a theme Shelley remembered later on: "this world of life Is as a garden ravaged" (*Epipsychidion*," 186-187). But, as Shelley wrote years earlier, "What opinion should we form of that man, who, when he walked in the freshness of the spring, beheld the fields enamelled with flowers, and the foliage bursting from the buds, should find fault with all this beautiful order, and murmur his contemptible discontents because winter must come, and the landscape be robbed of its beauty for a while again?"

In his Conclusion the narrator reflects on the story.

CONCLUSION

Whether the Sensitive Plant, or that
Which within its boughs like a Spirit sat,
Ere its outward form had known decay,
Now felt this change, I cannot say.

Whether that Lady's gentle mind,
No longer with the form combined
Which scattered love, as stars do light,
Found sadness, where it left delight,

I dare not guess; but in this life
Of error, ignorance, and strife,
Where nothing is, but all things seem,
And we the shadows of the dream,

It is a modest creed, and yet
Pleasant if one considers it,
To own that death itself must be,
Like all the rest, a mockery.

245

That garden sweet, that lady fair,
And all sweet shapes and odours there,
In truth have never passed away:
'Tis we, 'tis ours, are changed; not they.

For love, and beauty, and delight,
There is no death nor change: their might
Exceeds our organs, which endure
No light, being themselves obscure.

First the narrator considers the world realistically, as it were, regarding only the literal actions in the narrative dimension. Whether the dead Sensitive Plant feels the change, or whether its soul, its principle of being, feels the change, that is, whether the soul survives, he cannot say. The lines assert only that the soul or principle of being existed before the plant died. Shelley years earlier defined the soul of a flower as "that which makes an organized being to be what it is, without which it would not be so." The Lady's mind survived her outward form, her body, but whether her mind, like the Sensitive Plant, found sadness after her death, having left delight, the narrator dare not guess.

What we know for certain, in the narrator's view, is that we live in error and ignorance, all things in our lives only a semblance of reality. Life is a bad dream, and we are the shadows (of reality) in it. In such a life it is a modest creed to acknowledge as true that death like everything else is a "mockery," that is, a seeming, a counterfeit. Having made this modest confession of religious faith, the narrator grows stronger in his belief, more forward in his claim. Nothing in that garden, neither the Lady nor the sweet shapes, died; for the forms of love, and beauty, and delight are immutable. It only seemed that they changed when *we* changed as we passed from our antenatal existence to our lives in this world, this wasteland. Our eyes partake of the nature of our death, that is, of our life in this dark world; and being thus obscure in the dark caves of our bodies, our eyes can endure no intellectual light (in which love, beauty, and delight are) at all, just as we could not look at a God in his godhead without suffering destruction.

On some formal matters: Hardly anybody would deny the perfection of verse and diction in the Conclusion. Opinions are divided on the earlier verse. I myself think the four-stress

246

lines and their irregular syllabic patterns masterly. Opinions are also less divided on Part Third than on Part First, perhaps because Part Third satisfies our modern emotional patterns and our sense of reality better. That Part First and Part Third are not a single world where good and evil, beauty and ugliness are inextricable from each other troubles some critics who cannot accept the metaphysic of the poem (however they interpret its metaphysic) or who come to poetry ready to judge, I should say prejudge, by this or that critical rule or prejudice, as, for example, the formula of "dissociation of sensibility." Shelley, however, is not the only man to whose mind in a dark mood the world was "an unweeded garden," possessed absolutely by "things rank and gross in nature." Such a view of the world is a psychological reality, or Hamlet also spoke nonsense (I. ii. 135-137). One further formal matter: in *The Sensitive Plant* Shelley anticipates the intensive use of symbolism in modern literature. I do not speak of the symbols used structurally in the allegory, that is, of the symbolic figures and symbolic actions that form the story, but of the symbols used technically, the technique of iteration functioning to charge the atmosphere.

LETTER TO MARIA GISBORNE

Whatever his personal unhappiness, Shelley these months passionately watched the politics of Europe. Excited by the March revolutionary victories in Spain, the first revolt in Southern Europe, where the insurgents restored the Constitution drawn up during the resistance to Napoleon and abolished the Inquisition, Shelley thought to go to Spain. Nothing came of that impulse. (In 1822 the Quadruple Alliance authorized a French army to intervene in Spain; the army from France was hardly opposed; and Spanish liberalism came to an end.) But the "glorious events" of 1820 stirred Shelley's answerable mind to compose his *Ode to Liberty*, not a Pindaric ode but in the grand style. Later on when pigs in the market square outside his window grunted an accompaniment to the "ode to liberty," Shelley broke into laughter and, thinking of Aristophanic choruses, imagined the germ for *Swellfoot the Tyrant*. Politics were the ground of much of his work in 1819 and 1820. In May

247

of 1820 he twice wrote Leigh Hunt to suggest a publisher for his *Philosophical View of Reform* and for political songs written "to awaken and direct the imagination of reformers," and in April had written chiding Hunt for ignoring *Peter Bell the Third.*

In June Shelley had to go to Leghorn from Pisa to scotch a slander that a rascally, discharged servant thought to injure the Shelleys with, unless Shelley paid blackmail. The man threatened to spread a story in the English colony that Shelley had had a bastard by Claire. In Leghorn Shelley "succeeded in crushing" that "most infernal business," but the slander, like ugly weeds, sprang up again a year later, and has not entirely died yet. The unrelenting money demands of Godwin were a harder trouble those days, and Shelley had to intercept his letters to Mary, "whose agitation of mind produced through her a disorder in the child" in whose life her own seemed wholly bound up, Shelley told Godwin. The Shelleys and Claire stayed in Leghorn, in the house of the Gisbornes who were in England, until August. There Shelley wrote his verse *Letter to Maria Gisborne.* His study was the engineering workshop of the young Henry Reveley, Mrs. Gisborne's son by an earlier marriage. The *Letter*, never meant for publication, openly speaks of Shelley and his ways. The first lines light the poem imaginatively.

> The silk-worm in the dark green mulberry leaves
> His winding sheet and cradle ever weaves;
> So I, a thing whom moralists call worm,
> Sit spinning still round this decaying form,
> From the fine threads of rare and subtle thought—
> No net of words in garish colours wrought
> To catch the idle buzzers of the day—
> But a soft cell, where when that fades away,
> Memory may clothe in wings my living name
> And feed it with the asphodels of fame,
> Which in those hearts which must remember me
> Grow, making love an immortality. (3-14)

What follows has good humor, charm and warmth. He is amused by the incongruous picture he makes among the "shapes of unintelligible brass . . . tin and iron" and "un-

248

imaginable wood," on the brick floor, that would "puzzle Tubal Cain,"

> Great screws, and cones, and wheels, and groovèd blocks,
> The elements of what will stand the shocks
> Of wave and wind and time. (44-54)

(The "elements" were the elements of a Mediterranean steamship that Shelley and Reveley, who later became a noted Victorian engineer, were in partnership to build; Reveley gave up its construction, claiming that Shelley had stipulated for too huge an engine.) Looking out of his study to the beauty of the world Shelley reflects, "Their [critics'] censure, or their wonder, or their praise" are not worth heeding (113-131). Distrustful that Maria Gisborne and he will meet again, Shelley takes respite in memory of their communion:

> —how on the sea-shore
> We watched the ocean and the sky together,
> Under the roof of blue Italian weather;
> How I ran home through last year's thunder-storm,
> And felt the transverse lightning linger warm
> Upon my cheek—and how we often made
> Feasts for each other, where good will outweighed
> The frugal luxury of our country cheer,
> As well it might, were it less firm and clear
> Than ours must ever be;—and how we spun
> A shroud of talk to hide us from the sun
> Of this familiar life, which seems to be
> But is not:—or is but quaint mockery
> Of all we would believe, and sadly blame
> The jarring and inexplicable frame
> Of this wrong world:—and then anatomize
> The purposes and thoughts of men whose eyes
> Were closed in distant years;—or widely guess
> The issue of the earth's great business,
> When we shall be as we no longer are—
> Like babbling gossips safe, who hear the war
> Of winds, and sigh, but tremble not;—or how
> You listened to some interrupted flow
> Of visionary rhyme,—in joy and pain
> Struck from the inmost fountains of my brain,

249

With little skill perhaps;—or how we sought
Those deepest wells of passion or of thought
Wrought by wise poets in the waste of years,
Staining their sacred waters with our tears;
Quenching a thirst ever to be renewed! (145-174)

His mind comes to the present again.

You are now
In London, that great sea, whose ebb and flow
At once is deaf and loud, and on the shore
Vomits its wrecks, and still howls on for more.
Yet in its depth what treasures! You will see
That which was Godwin,—greater none than he
Though fallen—and fallen on evil times—to stand
Among the spirits of our age and land,
Before the dread tribunal of *to come*
The foremost,—while Rebuke cowers pale and dumb.
You will see Coleridge—he who sits obscure
In the exceeding lustre and the pure
Intense irradiation of a mind,
Which, with its own internal lightning blind,
Flags wearily through darkness and despair—
A cloud-encircled meteor of the air,
A hooded eagle among blinking owls.—(192-208)

Coleridge was a friend of the Gisbornes. Shelley speaks of others whom he misses: Hogg, who hides his virtues; Peacock, whose fine wit and learning he admires; and Horace Smith, a banker and man of letters who was a most excellent friend to Shelley, who combined, we may believe,

Wit and sense,
Virtue and human knowledge; all that might
Make this dull world a business of delight. (192-250)

Maria may look at the night, cloudless and lovely in moonlight or starlight, or with rare stars rushing through the windblown clouds, in London.

All this is beautiful in every land.—
But what see you beside?—a shabby stand
Of Hackney coaches—a brick house or wall
Fencing some lonely court, white with the scrawl

250

Of our unhappy politics;—or worse—
A wretched woman reeling by, whose curse
Mixed with the watchman's, partner of her trade,
You must accept in place of serenade—(264-271)

Against these unattractive realistic details of London Shelley
sets pleasant Italy—let her choose!

Next winter you must pass with me; I'll have
My house by that time turned into a grave
Of dead despondence and low-thoughted care,
And all the dreams which our tormentors are; (292-295)

as to nerves—
With cones and parallelograms and curves
I've sworn to strangle them if once they dare
To bother me—when you are with me there. (312-315)

Their "friendly philosophic revel," next winter, will "Outlast
the leafless time."

THE WITCH OF ATLAS

As the summer heat closed in on Leghorn, the Shelleys and
Claire escaped to the Baths of San Giuliano, four miles outside Pisa. Before leaving Leghorn early in August Shelley, having heard of Keats' illness from the Gisbornes, warmly invited
Keats to come to Italy for the winter as his and Mary's guest.
Keats told a friend that he could not accept the invitation for
fear of not remaining a free agent in Shelley's company.

Shelley found a "pleasant and spacious" house overlooking
the village square. Behind the house a canal, connecting the
Serchio and Arno rivers, bounded the garden. The nearby
mountain of San Giuliano bloomed with myrtle. They spent
their time quietly, once making a two-day excursion to Lucca.
While Mary and Claire looked about the town, Shelley climbed
Monte San Pellegrino with delight and came down with *The
Witch of Atlas* in his mind; in three days Shelley composed 78
ottava rima stanzas of imaginative grace, delicacy, playfulness,
and beauty that absorb even the evils of the world. Not many
years ago a critic praised *The Witch* as "Shelley's best long
poem, the most individual and original of his visions, and the

251

supreme example of mythmaking poetry." Well, maybe; I confess I think that praise extravagant. Mary condemned these verses because they discard "human interest and passion" (in her words) and because "they tell no story, false or true" (in Shelley's). But there is a passage whose human interest and feeling are deep. The lady-witch, a playful Intellectual Beauty, wrote "strange dreams upon the brain" (617) that transformed people.

LXXVI

And timid lovers who had been so coy,
   They hardly knew whether they loved or not,
Would rise out of their rest, and take sweet joy,
   To the fulfilment of their inmost thought;
And when next day the maiden and the boy
   Met one another, both, like sinners caught,
Blushed at the thing which each believed was done
Only in fancy—till the tenth moon shone;

LXXVII

And then the Witch would let them take no ill:
   Of many thousand schemes which lovers find,
The Witch found one,—and so they took their fill
   Of happiness in marriage warm and kind.
Friends who, by practice of some envious skill,
   Were torn apart—a wide wound, mind from mind!—
She did unite again with visions clear
Of deep affection and of truth sincere.

As Santayana said in another context: "So purely ideal and so deeply human are the visions of Shelley."

SWELLFOOT THE TYRANT

It was that August in San Giuliano that Shelley read his "ode to liberty" to a visitor and found himself answered by a chorus of pigs; the seed for an Aristophanic play that his laughter planted gave its fruit two months later. Shelley enjoyed the comic; we have already heard several tones of comedy in his work. In July Shelley had translated Homer's *Hymn to Mercury*, the best of his translations (his translations, from five lan-

252

guages, are about a fifth of the volume of his poetry). It is his best translation perhaps because it was done with the most pleasure, and was done with such pleasure because, as he wrote crossways on a letter of Mary's in July, the *Hymn* "is infinitely comical." In that letter he also wrote, "So the Green Bag is opened. I expect, at least, that the accusation [against the Queen] is as terrible as that made against Pasiphae"—material that went into his own comic masterpiece, which is full of vitality, *Oedipus Tyrannus; or, Swellfoot the Tyrant.* Horace Smith had this political satire published; but threatened with prosecution by the Society for the Prevention of Vice, the publisher had to surrender the edition; only seven copies were sold. (No court ever summoned Aristophanes for his audacious laughter at state or priest.) Mary did not print *Swellfoot* in her first 1839 edition of the *Poetical Works,* and when she included it in her second edition belittled the play; she was too serious, unappreciative of the comic and unresponsive to the free play of satire.

To me this play is the only great Aristophanic lashing comedy, fantastic and grotesque, in our language; our literature has preferred to follow the tradition of realistic later Greek comedy. Edith Hamilton, whom I admire beyond bounds, wrote "W. S. Gilbert: A Mid-Victorian Aristophanes" for the *Theatre Arts Monthly.* Miss Hamilton, I think, was never wrong. But for all that Gilbert shared with Aristophanes, he was a *mid-Victorian* Aristophanes without the grotesquerie and bite of the Athenian. The Savoy operas of Gilbert and Sullivan are closer in spirit to the fantastic *extravaganzas,* a popular entertainment of the nineteenth century, than to Old Comedy. *Swellfoot the Tyrant,* which does owe much to Aristophanes' Old Comedy, is nonetheless an original work of art. The structure is much freer, the tone is Shelley's, the language and ideas are modern, the mock-mythology shows a vitality in his awareness of the world about him.

The history of Swellfoot began with the marriage of Princess Caroline to the Prince of Wales in 1795; she left him a year later. Her reputation started to tumble after the Delicate Investigation of 1806, and she faced the charge of adultery by another investigating Commission in 1818. Whether adulterous or not, the woman had been touring Europe scandalously. When the "mad, blind, despised" George III died in 1820, the

Tory ministers denied Caroline a place in the Prince Regent's Coronation. The brash Caroline howled. The Whigs gallantly rallied to her, or, we may say, used the issue to oppose the new King who had disappointed their expectation of power on his becoming Regent ten years earlier; the people made Caroline a heroine because the Government accused her of adultery. As Shelley reflected in July, "Nothing, I think shows the generous gullibility of the English nation more than their having adopted her Sacred Majesty as the heroine of the day." It is an absurdity "that a vulgar woman, with all those low tastes which prejudice considers as vices, and a person whose habits and manners everyone would shun in private life, without any redeeming virtues should be turned into a heroine, because she is a queen." But her husband the king, "no less than his ministers, are so odious that everything, however disgusting, which is opposed to them, is admirable." That letter explains how Shelley could make Caroline, after a fashion, the heroine of his play. The "Queen's Trial" for adultery, lasting from August to November, stuffed maw and crop up and down the country with scandal. In November mobs celebrated the throwing out of the Bill against the Queen, and towns were illuminated. But the show over, the country tired of their heroine. Caroline tried in vain to break into Westminster Hall for the Coronation in July 1821, and died a week later.

The Advertisement to *Oedipus Tyrannus; or, Swellfoot the Tyrant* tells us that Oedipus has been rendered literally as Swellfoot—as fit a name, we may reflect, for a presumably gouty King George as for the Theban king named for the misshaping of his feet bound by thongs when he was a child. Swellfoot, however, is not the central character of the play; he is portrayed to show the kind of thing that Mammon (Church) and Purganax (Government) serve. These two, acting with a single intention, perform the actions of the plot and climax.

1. The beginning of change: Mammon and Purganax recognize the danger of Iona's presence in Thebes.

2. The middle: Mammon gets the poison bag which Purganax will entice Iona to and thereby wreak her downfall.

3. The question that the end must resolve: Will they succeed?

The climax: Purganax accepts Iona's offer.

It is formally right that they are central to the play's action, not Iona, because it is a structural principle in drama that a satire be built on the change in fortune of that character against whom the play's criticism is directed. The minor characters Dakry (Law) and Laoctonos (Army) fit logically into the allegory. The characters as well as representing abstractions in the way of moral allegory were also representations of public figures; Laoctonos, for example, whose name translates to "people-slayer," is Wellington.

Swellfoot, King of Thebes, like Oedipus begins the play; but here the magnificent temple is built of thigh-bones and death's-heads, and clinging around the Altar of Famine are boars, sows, and sucking pigs in place of the suppliants around the altar before the palace of Oedipus. Swellfoot speaking to the statue of the goddess Famine over the altar condemns himself morally:

> Thou supreme Goddess! by whose power divine
> These graceful limbs are clothed in proud array
> [*He contemplates himself with satisfaction.*
> Of gold and purple, (1-3)

and then makes himself a laughing stock:

> and this kingly paunch
> Swells like a sail before a favouring breeze,
> And these most sacred nether promontories
> Lie satisfied with layers of fat; and these
> Boeotian cheeks, like Egypt's pyramid,
> (Nor with less toil were their foundations laid)
> Sustain the cone of my untroubled brain,
> That point, the emblem of a pointless nothing. (3-10)

The economy is superb but for the last line which, despite the well-turned quibble, should have been let go. It is wrong dramatically, and the brilliant image of "the cone of my untroubled brain" with its fool's "cone" and ambiguous "untroubled" says it all. But it is the only superfluous line in the play.

The Swinish king has the pigs under his heel. They lament the loss of their golden age:

> Under your mighty ancestors, we Pigs
> Were bless'd as nightingales on myrtle sprigs,

255

Or grasshoppers that live on noonday dew,
And sung, old annals tell, as sweetly too; (39-42)

the lyricism may stir our pity, but the incongruity makes us
smile. The tone shifts to the realistic; the timing that dissipates
the half-pathetic half-amusing lyric yearning is excellent.

But now our sties are fallen in, we catch
    The murrain and the mange, the scab and itch;
Sometimes your royal dogs tear down our thatch,
    And then we seek the shelter of a ditch. (43-46)

In a fury when the pigs ask for hog-wash and clean straw, he
orders them spayed—the earth is loaded with pigs, nor (in an
un-Malthusian way) has moral restraint, starvation, disease,
war, or prison any effect—and then, his tyranny running amok,
commands them killed:

let me hear
Their everlasting grunts and whines no more. (94-95)

It is a swift, powerful portrait of a dictator's contempt for life,
done dramatically. The gelder, butcher, and trader who will
do the murderous work—Moses, Zephaniah, and Solomon,
names suggested, of course, by the Hebraic aversion to pork—
are recognizable enough people in a world that has seen Nazi
and can guess at Communist horrors. There is no anti-Semit-
ism, it should be needless to say, on Shelley's part; he simply
had no use for churches and their high figures, whether Christian, Jewish, or Moslem.

Then the play turns to Mammon, the Arch-Priest, and Purganax, Chief of the Council. Purganax, who fears that matters
are ominous in the state, speaks swellingly like an orator; Mammon, in a lively familiar style. Most of all the oracle (which
Shelley uses as a motto for the play) makes Purganax afraid:

"Boeotia, choose reform or civil war!
When through the streets, instead of hare with dogs,
A Consort Queen shall hunt a King with Hogs,
Riding on the Ionian Minotaur." (113-116)

Mammon, who is amusing in his scoundrelly way, unlike the
superstitious Purganax does not take these things seriously, but

nonetheless wants to know what the Chief of Council has done to baffle the oracle:

> For prophecies, when once they get abroad,
> Like liars who tell the truth to serve their ends,
> Or hypocrites who, from assuming virtue,
> Do the same actions that the virtuous do,
> Contrive their own fulfilment. (131-135)

There is a fine ironic wit in his simile. In the service of Purganax are a leech (waste; see I. 263-264), a gadfly (calumny; see I. 351), and a rat (disease; see I. 265-266, 354-356).

> The Gadfly was the same which Juno sent
> To agitate Io[1], and which Ezekiel[2] mentions
> That the Lord whistled for out of the mountains
> Of utmost Aethiopia, to torment
> Mesopotamian Babylon. The beast
> Has a loud trumpet like the scarabee,
> His crookèd tail is barbed with many stings,
> Each able to make a thousand wounds, and each
> Immedicable; from his convex eyes
> He sees fair things in many hideous shapes,
> And trumpets all his falsehood to the world.
> Like other beetles he is fed on dung—
> He has eleven feet with which he crawls,
> Trailing a blistering slime, and this foul beast
> Has tracked Iona from the Theban limits,
> From isle to isle, from city unto city,
> Urging her flight from the far Chersonese
> To fabulous Solyma, and the Aetnean Isle,
> Ortygia, Melite, and Calypso's Rock,
> And the swart tribes of Garamant and Fez,
> Aeolia and Elysium, and thy shores,
> Parthenope, which now, alas! are free!
> And through the fortunate Saturnian land,
> Into the darkness of the West. (152-175)

[[1] The *Prometheus Bound* of Aeschylus.—(SHELLEY'S NOTE.)
[2] And the Lord whistled for the gadfly out of Aethiopia, and for the bee of Egypt, etc.—EZEKIEL.—(SHELLEY'S NOTE.)]

The artistry here is worth pausing for. The epic tone of the passage is controlled by the familiar syntax and phrases in the first three lines, then by the grotesquerie of the beast, and, after the tracking of Queen Iona through isles and cities whose names are musical and evocative (for sympathy with Iona), the descent to Mammon's plain consideration, so that the whole is all of one piece with the play. When Mammon plainly says,

> But if
> This Gadfly should drive Iona hither?

Purganax bursts out,

> Gods! what an *if!* but there is my gray RAT:
> So thin with want, he can crawl in and out
> Of any narrow chink and filthy hole,
> And he shall creep into her dressing-room,
> And—   (175-181)

The implication is that the Rat shall defame her, ambiguously by act and/or assertion. The imagery could hardly be more sexually suggestive. It is idle to say that Shelley could not or would not write so, if he did. We must remember not only that Queen Caroline was accused of adultery (alluded to in II. i. 83) but that Aristophanes was Shelley's model. Mammon thinks that Iona is on her guard against such as the Rat; anyway "rats, when lean enough To crawl through *such* chinks—" (183-184) can do nothing, is the comic implication. Sex is Aristophanically used for comedy twice again, as we shall see.

Satisfied that the leech will suffice for Queen Iona, Mammon yet fears the Swinish multitude. "[*A most tremendous humming is heard.*" The Gadfly, the Leech, and the Rat are arrived. There follow lyrics that anticipate those of W. S. Gilbert, and like his invite comic music:

> *Gadfly.*
> Hum! hum! hum!
> From the lakes of the Alps, and the cold gray scalps
>   Of the mountains, I come!
> Hum! hum! hum!
> From Morocco and Fez, and the high palaces
>   Of golden Byzantium;
> From the temples divine of old Palestine,
>   From Athens and Rome,

With a ha! and a hum!
I come! I come!

All inn-doors and windows
    Were open to me:
I saw all that sin does,
    Which lamps hardly see
That burn in the night by the curtained bed,—
The impudent lamps! for they blushed not red,
    Dinging and singing,
    From slumber I rung her,
Loud as the clank of an ironmonger;
        Hum! hum! hum! (220-239)

The Gadfly has driven the Queen to Thebes, and we hear the Swine within chanting,

        Ugh, ugh, ugh!
    Hail! Iona the divine,
    We will be no longer Swine,
    But Bulls with horns and dewlaps. (272-275)

"Well, Lord Mammon," says Purganax, "This is a pretty business" (278-279). Mammon swiftly converts the "pretty business": he will go invent "some scheme to make it ugly then" (280). It is he, the Arch-Priest, who brings the ugly, deadly liquor to destroy Iona. That bane is sealed by law and blessed by religion. Purganax and Mammon must make the Pigs believe that this perilous liquor in the green bag (the prosecution in the Queen's Trial carried its evidence to the House of Lords in a green bag; lawyers commonly used green bags) is the true test of guilt or innocence, that it transforms the guilty to something hideous and the innocent to an angel,

    And they will see her flying through the air,
    So bright that she will dim the noonday sun;
    Showering down blessings in the shape of comfits.
    This, trust a priest, is just the sort of thing
    Swine will believe. I'll wager you will see them
    Climbing upon the thatch of their low sties,
    With pieces of smoked glass, to watch her sail
    Among the clouds, and some will hold the flaps

259

Of one another's ears between their teeth,
To catch the coming hail of comfits in. (394-403)

It is an extraordinary scene that Mammon imagines.

In Act II Purganax goes to the public sty where the boars are in full assembly. They want to know what Iona has been accused of.

> *Purganax.* Why, it is hinted, that a certain Bull—
> Thus much is *known:*—the milk-white Bulls that feed
> Beside Clitumnus and the crystal lakes
> Of the Cisalpine mountains, in fresh dews
> Of lotus-grass and blossoming asphodel
> Sleeking their silken hair, and with sweet breath
> Loading the morning winds until they faint
> With living fragrance, are so beautiful!—
> Well, *I* say nothing;—but Europa rode
> On such a one from Asia into Crete,
> And the enamoured sea grew calm beneath
> His gliding beauty. And Pasiphae,
> Iona's grandmother,——but *she* is innocent!
> And that both you and I, and all assert. (II. i. 59-72)

(Shelley saw "teams of milk-white or dove-coloured oxen" by the river Clitumnus in Umbria.) The beauty in this speech of Purganax subserves the deceit and sharpens the comic climax "*she* is innocent." Let Iona therefore be tested, persuades Purganax, echoing Mammon,

> If innocent, she will turn into an angel,
> And rain down blessings in the shape of comfits
> As she flies up to heaven. (II. i. 86-88)

Enraptured by the image, the Second Boar exclaims,

> How glorious it will be to see her Majesty
> Flying above our heads, her petticoats
> Streaming like—like—like— (II. 1. 95-97)

What he suddenly realizes he will see beneath her petticoats stops his mind short of the simile. (It is not that the Second Boar lacks the inventiveness to make a simile, for when Purganax showed the green bag, the Second Boar interrupted him, saying,

> Oh! no GREEN BAGS! ! Jealousy's eyes are green,
> Scorpions are green, and water-snakes, and efts,
> And verdigris, and—)

The Third Boar, a nincompoop, fills in "Anything." Then
Purganax the orator:

> Oh no!
> But like a standard of an admiral's ship,
> Or like the banner of a conquering host,
> Or like a cloud dyed in the dying day,
> Unravelled on the blast from a white mountain;
> Or like a meteor, or a war-steed's mane,
> Or waterfall from a dizzy precipice
> Scattered upon the wind.   (II. i. 97-104)

The heroics for her Majesty's petticoats are comic enough, but
a finer stroke follows with the First Boar's

> Or a cow's tail. (104)

It is, again, an Aristophanic image, and again done with ambiguity. The cow's raised tail was suggested insensibly to the
First Boar by the image of the "waterfall from a dizzy precipice," preposterously like the physical function for which she
raises her tail. The cow also raises her tail when sexually
aroused: in the First Boar's mind, as well as the waterfall image
are the images of Europa and Pasiphae yielding their love to
the milk-white bulls; and these boars who "boast their descent
From the free Minotaur . . . still call themselves Bulls" (I. i.
139-141). There is further ambiguity for *tail*: the slang meanings of the female pudenda and a harlot. In the next line the
Second Boar, having recovered his wits, satirically puns on
"boar": "Or *anything*, as the learned Boar observed" (105).
   [Shelley liked puns and quibbles. Visiting the Welsh estate
of Thomas Grove, an uncle by virtue of marriage to his
mother's sister, the young Shelley wrote, "Here are rocks, cata-
racts, woods and Groves." Edward Trelawny recorded a quibble
and a pun of Shelley's last year. Trelawney wanted to know
whether the dirty, card-playing Greeks on their squalid cargo
ship in port were a scene realizing Shelley's idea of Hellenism.
"No!" Shelley retorted, "but it does of Hell." And again Trelawny lectured Shelley, this time on his incompetence as a

261

sailor, saying that in a squall "we should have to swim for it."
Shelley, eying the *Don Juan's* ballast, two tons of pig iron,
quipped, "Not I: I should have gone down with the rest of the
pigs in the bottom of the boat."

I am tempted to give another fragment of Shelley's sense of
comedy, humor rather than wit. Byron named her, Shelley's
sailboat, the *Don Juan.* "We must suppose," Shelley reflected,
"the name to have been given her during the equivocation of
sex which her godfather suffered in the harem." (Sold into
slavery by Haidée's father, young Juan is purchased by the
Sultan's latest bride and taken to her disguised as a girl. Haidée
still in his head, our hero spurns Gulbeyaz, but begins to melt
when tears follow her rage. At that moment the Sultan comes,
and Juan is marched off to the seraglio. There he spends the
night with the luxuriant Dudû—who, regretting her sudden
scream, tells the other maids she has awakened from a dream
of an apple and a bee—much to the vexation of the Sultana the
next morning.)]

Iona Taurina offers to stand the test, although the Pigs are
ready to pawn their lives that none dare lay a finger on her.
The expiation will be at the approaching feast of Famine.

The last scene takes place inside the temple of Famine. Swellfoot and his ministers and Iona and the Swine come in. The
priests of Famine invoke their Goddess, a skeleton in parti-
colored rags seated upon a heap of skulls and loaves of bread.
Their theme is this:

> The earth pours forth its plenteous fruits,
>   Corn, wool, linen, flesh, and roots—
> Those who consume these fruits through thee grow fat,
>   Those who produce these fruits through thee grow lean,
> Whatever change takes place, oh, stick to that! (II. ii. 9-13)

The trial proceeds. Unnoticed, the figure of Liberty walks
through the temple and chants to Famine,

> I charge thee! when thou wake the multitude,
> Thou lead them not upon the paths of blood.
> The earth did never mean her foison
> For those who crown life's cup with poison
> Of fanatic rage and meaningless revenge—(II. ii. 90-94)

The character of Liberty and her speech seem out of tone in

the play, but the passage serves the satire by being a criticism of the hunt that rages at the end. During her chant Mammon, Dakry, Laoctonos, and Swellfoot surround Iona Taurina. Purganax is about to pour the bane upon her when her saintlike resignation of innocence gives place to a loud laugh of triumph; she seizes the green bag and empties it over Swellfoot and his Court, who are transformed to filthy and ugly animals and who rush away. Pigs scramble for the loaves; those who eat are turned into bulls. Famine sinks through a chasm, and a Minotaur rises.

> *Minotaur.* I am the Ionian Minotaur, the mightiest
> Of all Europa's taurine progeny—
> I am the old traditional Man-Bull;
> And from my ancestors having been Ionian,
> I am called Ion, which, by interpretation,
> Is JOHN; in plain Theban, that is to say,
> My name's JOHN BULL.   (II. ii. 104-110)

Iona tucks up her hair and leaps on his back. The play ends fiercely, like the excesses of the French Revolution:

> *Iona Taurina.* Hoa! hoa! tallyho! ho! ho!
> Come, let us hunt these ugly badgers down,
> These stinking foxes, these devouring otters,
> These hares, these wolves, these anything but men.
> Hey, for a whipper-in! my loyal Pigs,
> Now let your noses be as keen as beagles',
> Your steps as swift as greyhounds', and your cries
> More dulcet and symphonious than the bells
> Of village-towers, on sunshine holiday;
> Wake all the dewy woods with jangling music.
> Give them no law (are they not beasts of blood?)
> But such as they gave you. Tallyho! ho!
> Through forest, furze, and bog, and den, and desert,
> Pursue the ugly beasts! tallyho! ho!

> *Full Chorus of* IONA *and the* SWINE.
> Tallyho! tallyho!
> Through rain, hail, and snow,
> Through brake, gorse, and briar,
> Through fen, flood, and mire,
> We go! we go!

Tallyho! tallyho!
Through pond, ditch, and slough,
Wind them, and find them,
Like the Devil behind them,
Tallyho! tallyho!

[*Exeunt, in full cry;* IONA *driving on the* SWINE, *with the empty* GREEN
BAG.

THE END.

Shelley used much contemporary material for his play,
worth noting for what it shows of one of his modes of composition. Newman White studied *Swellfoot the Tyrant* in relation
to contemporary political satires antedating the play. In all
the contemporary literature, as in Shelley's play, "the symboli-
cal green bag figures prominently." Cartoons suggested the
play's climax: one, called *Opening the Green Bag*, "represents
the conspirators being routed by the dragon and serpents in
the bag"; another, "called *The Filth and Lies of the Green Bag
visiting their Parents and Friends*, shows the Green Bag full of
reptiles poured over the heads of its owners." Leigh Hunt in a
June issue of the *Examiner* made the change to poison. Again,
in a cartoon Caroline rides a bull, "calling 'Justice,' while the
Archbishop, King and counsellors are fleeing in panic." Shelley and the pamphleteers were agreed on the "obesity, dullness,
heartlessness, gluttony and lechery of the King, the cynical
deceit and corruption of Castlereagh [Purganax], the reaction-
ary character of Liverpool [Mammon], the brutality of Laoctonos [Wellington], the cant and lachrymosity of Eldon
[Dakry]." There were other contemporary allusions: the leech
was Sir John Leach, who organized the 1818 Commission; the
rat and gadfly were other members of that Commission, both
"well known as agents of Castlereagh against Caroline." That
Shelley used these journalistic sources the way he did, shows a
likeness in his mentality to theirs, a common realism in his
mentality not often recognized. The bawdy jokes, too, so far as
I know never recognized by Shelley scholars, must alter nar-
rower conceptions of a rarefied mentality. In his letters such
common realism extended to money matters: he wrote to a
friend negotiating with his publisher for him, "I am, all
citizens of this world ought to be, especially curious respecting

the article of money." But the next work to consider has little of a mentality common to mankind in it.

1821

EPIPSYCHIDION

The Serchio overflowed near the end of October in 1820, and the Shelleys left the little village of San Giuliano, embarking from a second-story window. They settled in Pisa, in a commodious *palazzo*, where Shelley was constantly studious, sometimes lively and witty, and sometimes terribly despondent, the idea of suicide darkening his mind. Distressed by Shelley's dark moods, Tom Medwin (Shelley's cousin, who was visiting) thought to bring good company to Pisa as an antidote, Edward Ellerker Williams and his wife, Jane. They arrived in January of 1821, and the happy friendship that flourished for Shelley and Williams gave Shelley his best months in Italy.

Before the year closed Shelley had made other new acquaintances. Among these was Prince Alexander Mavrocordato of Greece, who visited often and whom Mary liked; he left Italy after the Greek revolution against the Turks began in 1821. The Prince presided over the first Greek national assembly in 1822; led an army into western Hellas, met a defeat, but successfully resisted the first siege of Missolonghi; in 1825 became secretary of state; and after the war served as Greek envoy to Germany, England and Turkey, and was four times the prime minister of Greece. To him Shelley dedicated the lyrical drama *Hellas*. Another was Professor Francisco Pacchiani; confessor to the Governor of Pisa, he was a priest who contemned the priesthood, who held a post in Physical Chemistry at the University of Pisa and enjoyed a reputation for his experimental work, and who lived disreputably. Pacchiani took Mary and Claire to visit Teresa Emilia Viviani, daughter of the Governor of Pisa, at her convent school, a "prisoner" there until a marriage arranged by her father would release her. She was an Italian beauty of nineteen with sensitivity and an answerable mind—the being who inspired Shelley's *Epipsychidion*, which he wrote in February after two months of visits and letters. Or rather it was not Emilia who inspired the poet but two visions: one of her beauty as incarnating the spiritual beauty "Of light, and love" (24) and the other of an intensest and completest sympathy with that incarnation. The visions gave Shelley "certain intoxicating moments" for which, he wrote that spring, "I live," but which at last failed him. Out of the experience a realism matured, recorded in a letter over a year later. "If you are anxious, however, to hear what I am and have been," the *Epipsychidion* "will tell you something thereof. It is an idealized history of my life and feelings. I think one is always in love with something or other; the error, and I confess it is not easy for spirits cased in flesh and blood to avoid it, consists in seeking in a mortal image the likeness of what is perhaps eternal."

In his Advertisement Shelley wrote that his idealized history would be "sufficiently intelligible to a certain class of readers without a matter-of-fact history of the circumstances to which it relates; and to a certain other class it must ever remain incomprehensible." The Advertisement says, too, quoting from Dante's *New Life*, that "it would be a great disgrace to him who should rhyme anything" if he could not reveal "a true meaning" under the figures and rhetoric of the concealing language. But scholars are not agreed on either the ideal or matter-of-fact meaning. The Advertisement lastly makes a "presumptuous application" of lines translated from a Canzone of Dante's:

> My Song, I fear that thou wilt find but few
> Who fitly shall conceive thy reasoning,
> Of such hard matter dost thou entertain;
> Whence, if by misadventure, chance should bring
> Thee to base company (as chance may do),
> Quite unaware of what thou dost contain,
> I prithee, comfort thy sweet self again,
> My last delight! tell them that they are dull,
> And bid them own that thou art beautiful.

The "hard matter" in passages *is* difficult and I have never seen any attempt to explicate certain of those lines. The difficulty they present, however, does not fall within my present purposes. Not long after Shelley composed *Epipsychidion* Edward Williams reflected, "His ordinary conversation is akin to poetry, for he sees things in the most singular and pleasing lights: if he wrote as he talked, he would be popular enough."

266

In this poem, far from the common mentality of mankind, Shelley could nonetheless write as he talked:

> I never was attached to that great sect,
> Whose doctrine is, that each one should select
> Out of the crowd a mistress or a friend,
> And all the rest, though fair and wise, commend
> To cold oblivion, though it is in the code
> Of modern morals.   (149-154)

>   True Love in this differs from gold and clay,
> That to divide is not to take away.
> Love is like understanding, that grows bright,
> Gazing on many truths; 'tis like thy light,
> Imagination! which from earth and sky,
> And from the depths of human fantasy,
> As from a thousand prisms and mirrors, fills
> The Universe with glorious beams, and kills
> Error, the worm, with many a sun-like arrow
> Of its reverberated lightning. Narrow
> The heart that loves, the brain that contemplates,
> The life that wears, the spirit that creates
> One object, and one form, and builds thereby
> A sepulchre for its eternity.   (160-173)

However singular the light in these lines, their morality, which is Shelley's most radical social statement, could never publicly please in the nineteenth century; and if they are popular enough in the twentieth, they are perhaps applauded without an understanding that grows bright. Luckily Shelley revised his earlier draft of "True Love in this differs from gold and clay, That to divide is not to take away." Modern idiom has made the earlier phrase vulgar: "Free love has this, different from gold and clay, That to divide is not to take away." My own judgment of the meaning of these lines is that they speak of love in human relationships, including physical love (as the lines in the preceding verse paragraph make perfectly clear); my evaluation as poetry of the paragraph on love (in *A Defence of Poetry*, composed right after the *Epipsychidion*, Shelley defined poetry as the true, the beautiful, and the good) is high.

To suggest that *Epipsychidion* composes variations on the theme of "spiritual affinity," on the "non-physical quality of 'true' Love," as some scholars do, distorts the meaning. Such Platonics were never Shelley's conception of love. In *A Discourse on the Manners of the Ancient Greeks Relative to the Subject of Love* Shelley wrote that love is "the universal thirst for a communion not merely of the senses, but of our whole nature, intellectual, imaginative, and sensitive [of the senses]. . . . The sexual impulse . . . serves, from its obvious and external nature, as a kind of type or expression of the rest, a common basis, an acknowledged and visible link. Still it is a claim which even derives a strength not its own from the accessory circumstances which surround it, and one which our nature thirsts to satisfy." The sexual act "ought always to be the link and type of the highest emotions of our nature." Shelley wrote this essay after translating *The Symposium* in 1818. He expressed a similar conception in *On Love*, written perhaps about the time of *A Discourse*, perhaps some years earlier. The "invisible and unattainable point to which love tends" is the "meeting with an understanding capable of clearly estimating our own; an imagination which should enter into and seize upon the subtle and delicate peculiarities which we have delighted to unfold in secret; with a frame [a body] whose nerves, like the chords of two exquisite lyres, strung to the accompaniment of one delightful voice, vibrate with the vibrations of our own." In his prose, at least, there is no mistaking that true love includes the human body.

The union of Shelley and Emily, or, if you will, of the speaker of *Epipsychidion* with the incarnation of Intellectual Beauty, comes in the third movement. The union with that incarnation gives this lifetime a value of ultimate reality. The third movement begins with an explicit statement of a spiritual union, the sexual taking no part. But the pressure for completeness of love will overcome this restraint.

> The day is come, and thou wilt fly with me.
> To whatsoe'er of dull mortality
> Is mine, remain a vestal sister still;
> To the intense, the deep, the imperishable,
> Not mine but me, henceforth be thou united
> Even as a bride, delighting and delighted. (388-393)

The island itself, the "far Eden" (417) of the speaker and Emily, seems a physical reality, given its meaning by the por-

268

tion of the Eternal that burns within the island's center and makes itself felt over rock, and water, and forest.

> the isle's beauty, like a naked bride
> Glowing at once with love and loveliness,
> Blushes and trembles at its own excess:
> Yet, like a buried lamp, a Soul no less
> Burns in the heart of this delicious isle,
> An atom of th' Eternal, whose own smile
> Unfolds itself, and may be felt, not seen
> O'er the gray rocks, blue waves, and forests green. (474-481)

The speaker and his "heart's sister" (415), who will become his spouse, will live in a dwelling on that island which a "wise and tender Ocean-King" had built as "a pleasure-house Made sacred to his sister and his spouse" (488-492).

> We two will rise, and sit, and walk together,
> Under the roof of blue Ionian weather,
> And wander in the meadows, or ascend
> The mossy mountains, where the blue heavens bend
> With lightest winds, to touch their paramour;
> Or linger, where the pebble-paven shore,
> Under the quick, faint kisses of the sea
> Trembles and sparkles as with ecstasy,—
> Possessing and possessed by all that is
> Within that calm circumference of bliss,
> And by each other, till to love and live
> Be one:—or, at the noontide hour, arrive
> Where some old cavern hoar seems yet to keep
> The moonlight of the expired night asleep,
> Through which the awakened day can never peep;
> A veil for our seclusion, close as night's,
> Where secure sleep may kill thine innocent lights;
> Sleep, the fresh dew of languid love, the rain
> Whose drops quench kisses till they burn again.
> And we will talk, until thought's melody
> Become too sweet for utterance, and it die
> In words, to live again in looks, which dart
> With thrilling tone into the voiceless heart,
> Harmonizing silence without a sound.

Our breath shall intermix, our bosoms bound,
And our veins beat together; and our lips
With other eloquence than words, eclipse
The soul that burns between them, and the wells
Which boil under our being's inmost cells,
The fountains of our deepest life, shall be
Confused in Passion's golden purity,
As mountain-springs under the morning sun. (541-572)

Even to the blue heavens and the earth, to the pebble-paven shore and the sea, Shelley gives the imagery of physical love, so much is it part of his universe. If the sexual imagery is being used mystically, the imagery is nonetheless not a metaphor for mystical experience; it is the experience itself, the union with ultimate reality in this, physical, lifetime. Shelley and Emily are, on the island,

Possessing and possessed by all that is
Within that calm circumference of bliss,
And by each other, till to love and live
Be one;   (549-552)

for love "is the bond and sanction which connects not only man with man, but with everything which exists" (*On Love*). If the noonday love (552-572) after their morning walk in the mountains or by the sea is not a sexual union, what is? That union, of course, is part of a completer union, "one Spirit within two frames"; indeed, even their bodies become one (573-577),

Touch, mingle, are transfigured; ever still
Burning, yet ever inconsumable:
In one another's substance finding food,
Like flames too pure and light and unimbued
To nourish their bright lives with baser prey,
Which point to Heaven and cannot pass away:
One hope within two wills, one will beneath
Two overshadowing minds, one life, one death,
One Heaven, one Hell, one immortality,
And one annihilation. Woe is me!
The wingèd words on which my soul would pierce
Into the height of Love's rare Universe,
Are chains of lead around its flight of fire—(578-590)

Words are unequal to express that consummate union, and the attempt of the poet's soul to "pierce Into the height of Love's rare universe" ends with an image of physical consummation.

Even if the physical consummation is only a shadow of the consummate union in "Love's rare universe," in this world inalterably, even in an idealized history, "there exist spirits cased in flesh and blood." Although Shelley could say, "As to real flesh & blood, you know that I do not deal in these articles,—you might as well go to a ginshop for a leg of mutton, as expect anything human or earthly from me," the very images deny what the words apparently state. For "deal in these articles" and "ginshop" are commonly human, and "leg of mutton" is earthly enough. In like manner, and with deliberate intent, the sexual imagery in the third movement denies the theme stated in the opening lines of the movement. It is hard not to believe that flesh and blood are integral to Shelley's conception of perfect love.

Mutability

Shelley generally wrote little during the winter months. Act IV of *Prometheus Unbound* is the only companion exception to *Epipsychidion*. But he would write lyrics now and then. Perhaps *Mutability* came out of a wintry mood. In any case, it is interesting to place this lyric after the intensely romantic *Epipsychidion*. Classical in its clarity and unblurred outlines, like the things seen in luminous Attic light, *Mutability* is a poetry of statement, not of suggestion; the images are apt rather than rich or intense, the only image with original force belonging to the marketplace:

> Love, how it sells poor bliss
> For proud despair!

But the value of such poetry is not in originality, it is in the immediacy of our assent. The structural movement of the poem is steady: from a definition of delight, to our surviving whatever joys we call ours, to our awakening and tears. The sadness of the theme is balanced by the artistic control, which reflects spiritual control; nothing is slack, nothing is tense.

271

I

The flower that smiles to-day
　　　To-morrow dies;
All that we wish to stay
　　　Tempts and then flies.
What is this world's delight?
Lightning that mocks the night,
　　　Brief even as bright.

II

Virtue, how frail it is!
　　　Friendship how rare!
Love, how it sells poor bliss
　　　For proud despair!
But we, though soon they fall,
Survive their joy, and all
　　　Which ours we call.

III

Whilst skies are blue and bright,
　　　Whilst flowers are gay,
Whilst eyes that change ere night
　　　Make glad the day;
Whilst yet the calm hours creep,
Dream thou—and from thy sleep
　　　Then wake to weep.

In the middle of January the Williamses came to Pisa. Medwin and Williams had served in the East India Army together.
After retiring from the Army on half pay, as Medwin had, Williams met Medwin again in Geneva. The Cornish adventurer
Edward Trelawny, who drifted into their company there, says
that Medwin "talked of nothing" but Shelley, making Trelawny and Williams want to go to Italy in the spring for the
sake of knowing the man. Medwin's letter from Pisa, as matters turned out, brought Williams to Italy a year earlier than
Trelawny.

Williams and Jane were man and wife by common law, Jane
having been deserted (by a husband who was good riddance)
and desertion being no ground for divorce; loving each other,
they managed well. Williams wrote of himself, as though
scarcely interested, "I was in the Navy at eleven years old. I

272

liked the sea but detested the tyranny practised on board men-of-war. I left the Navy, went into the Dragoons, and was sent to India. My mother was a widow; a man married her for her money. Her money he would have, and he defrauded me of a large portion of my inheritance. I sold my commission, marred my prospects of rising by marrying, and drifted here [Pisa]." Although Jane had beauty and sang well, perhaps because her conversation was tethered to domesticity Shelley could not reconcile himself to her until May; but in time Jane was an island of calm for him. The open, spirited, and manly Williams was a pleasure at once. In April Shelley purchased a small marsh punt made of lath and canvas, fitted it with rudder and sails, and he and Williams often and happily sailed the unsafe boat on the canal between Pisa and Leghorn. Williams had always been a sportsman. In India, hunting passionately, he had killed or been in at the kill of 26 tigers and 18 lions, and recorded his hunts in a journal of talented drawings. With Shelley in Italy Williams changed his pursuits and began to study and write. His water-color portrait of Shelley is the best portrait we have, indeed, the only one worth looking at.

The spring moved along quietly. In May the Shelleys returned to the Baths of San Giuliano, again to spend a pleasant summer and autumn there—the happier for the company of the Williamses almost daily. They lived in a village four miles away, Williams working on a play and Jane tending her kitchen and their two children. The four miles were a green hour's walk or an enchanting sail on the quiet, deep canal linking the Arno and the Serchio. Branches hanging overhead checkered the water with light and shade; myriads of ephemera, slender and delicate, beat their membranous wings near the water for their brief May hours; cicadas prolonged their shrill notes in the day's heat; fireflies glimmered in the twilit shrubbery; and the aziola, that little downy owl, stirred listeners in the evening with its sad cry.

THE BOAT ON THE SERCHIO

Sometimes Williams and Shelley sailed down the Serchio to the sea. Here are lines from the fragmentary *The Boat on the Serchio*. It is early morning, and their boat is asleep.

273

The helm sways idly, hither and thither;
  Dominic, the boatman, has brought the mast,
  And the oars, and the sails; but 'tis sleeping fast,
Like a beast, unconscious of its tether. (3-6)

The stars burned out . . .

Day had awakened all things that be,
The lark and the thrush and the swallow free,
  And the milkmaid's song and the mower's scythe,
And the matin-bell and the mountain bee:
Fireflies were quenched on the dewy corn,
  Glow-worms went out on the river's brim,
  Like lamps which a student forgets to trim:
The beetle forgot to wind his horn,
  The crickets were still in the meadow and hill:
Like a flock of rooks at a farmer's gun
Night's dreams and terrors, every one,
Fled from the brains which are their prey
From the lamp's death to the morning ray. (17-29)

There is deep pleasure in the everyday reality, to which are
linked the sudden images of sleep.

EVENING: PONTE AL MARE, PISA

Quite in another tone, anticipating the symbolist and the im-
pressionist, in Pisa Shelley wrote a city poem, *Evening: Ponte
al Mare, Pisa.*

The sun is set; the swallows are asleep;
  The bats are flitting fast in the gray air;
The slow soft toads out of damp corners creep,
  And evening's breath, wandering here and there
Over the quivering surface of the stream,
Wakes not one ripple from its summer dream.

The dust and straws are driven up and down,
And whirled about the pavement of the town.

Within the surface of the fleeting river
  The wrinkled image of the city lay,
Immovably unquiet . . .   (1-6, 11-12, 13-15)

274

Both these poems were unfinished. But between late April and early June Shelley created his most finished work, the *Adonais* —in his own judgment, only days before completing the poem, "a highly wrought *piece of art*, perhaps better in point of composition than anything I have written." Some months later he wrote to his publisher, "The *Adonais*, in spite of its mysticism, is the least imperfect of my compositions, and, as the image of my regret and honour for poor Keats, I wish it to be so." Only to Byron—who had no high opinion of Keats; who, Shelley gauged, would think him "carried too far by the enthusiasm of the moment;" and to whom he habitually deprecated himself, for Byron was a poet Shelley was in "despair of rivalling" and there was "no other with whom it is worth contending"—did he say, "I fear it is worth little." The importance of the *Adonais* to Shelley is measurable by the more than thirty times he speaks of the poem in his letters.

Shelley himself had no high opinion of Keats' poetry, except for *Hyperion*, which he thought "certainly an astonishing piece of writing." In a letter to Byron about the death of Keats, Shelley said that Keats clothed his writings in "narrow and wretched taste" but that such taste was dispersed in *Hyperion* by "the energy and beauty of his powers." A half year later, his tribute in *Adonais* notwithstanding, Shelley's judgment in a letter to Hogg was the same: "Keats, a young writer of bad taste, but wonderful powers and promise." Those "wonderful powers and promise" are, I take it, what Shelley meant when he wrote of Keats as "the great genius whom envy & ingratitude scourged out of the world." Shelley mistakenly believed, as he wrote to the dubious Byron (the account came to Shelley from Leigh Hunt), "Young Keats, whose 'Hyperion' showed so great a promise, died lately at Rome from the consequences of breaking a blood-vessel, in paroxysms of despair at the contemptuous attack on his book in the *Quarterly Review*," the "consequences" being the tuberculosis that Keats actually died from although the critical attack was not the cause.

If genius is apparently wasted by the world, what meaning, what value, is in its exercise? Questions of meaning and value can be answered only with knowledge of what is real, what is true. The *Adonais* works out the nature of ultimate reality and

275

the connection of the meaning and value of a man's life—centrally, of a man who is a poet—to that reality. Milton had coped with that problem, too, in his elegy for Edward King, a poet whom Milton knew no better than Shelley knew Keats and whose "powers and promise" as a poet Milton could not regard as praiseworthy as Shelley regarded Keats'. For both Milton and Shelley the man they were honoring, however, represented much. In *Lycidas* Milton faced the question of committing his own life to loss should he, like King, be cut off early; in *Adonais* Shelley faced the question of committing his life to loss should he, like Keats, find no sympathy in what he wrote (in the sense of a tuning fork vibrating to another). And, indeed, Shelley brings to his elegy as formal elements the pastoral conventions that Milton accepted for his (other pastoral elements come from Virgil and the elegies attributed to the Greek poets Bion and Moschus), as though conscious of the continuity of human experience. [These are the paralleled conventions:—The poets are mountain shepherds: *Lycidas*, 23-31; *Adonais*, 262-302. There is an invocation to a goddess of poetry: *Lycidas*, 15-17; *Adonais*, 28-29. Mythological figures are in the world of the elegy: *Lycidas*, 15-16, 58, 96-99; *Adonais*, 12, 127-134, 140-141, 239-240, 249-250. Christian figures are in the same world: *Lycidas*, 109, 163, 173; *Adonais*, 306. The elegist questions protective deity: here the echo is least changed: *Lycidas*, "Where were ye nymphs," 50-51; *Adonais*, "Where wert thou, mighty Mother," 10-13. The natural world mourns: *Lycidas*, 39-40, 60; *Adonais*, 120-144. Flowers adorn the hearse or grave: *Lycidas*, 136-151; *Adonais*, 440-441. Mourners come: *Lycidas*, 103-111, 165; *Adonais*, 262-315. There is a questioning of divine justice: *Lycidas*, 64-76, 88-99; *Adonais*, 38-43, 177-180. Corruption in the age is condemned: *Lycidas*, 113-129; *Adonais*, 235-261, 316, 335. A vision overleaps mortality and grief to the immutable, spiritual reality: *Lycidas*, 78-84, 165-185; *Adonais*, 337-495.] The religious value and meaning that Shelley comes to are a revelation radically other than Milton's, but I like to think that Milton would have responded deeply to the radiance in Shelley's celebration of the spiritual power the later poet believed in, the star to his wandering bark:

> That Light whose smile kindles the Universe,
> That Beauty in which all things work and move,

That Benediction which the eclipsing Curse
Of birth can quench not, that sustaining Love
Which through the web of being blindly wove
By man and beast and earth and air and sea,
Burns bright or dim, as each are mirrors of
The fire for which all thirst. (478-485)

The *Adonais* is the most widely read of Shelley's major poems and, "in spite of its mysticism," its explicit and primary meanings are well enough understood. The implicit meanings are rich—"All high poetry is infinite"—in the literary allusions and myth, in the philosophical content, in the imagery and structure. For those who wish to pursue these matters I suggest four essays that I think the most rewarding: "Shelley's *Adonais*" in Edward B. Hungerford's *Shores of Darkness*, 1941; "The Evening Star: *Adonais*" in Carlos Baker's *Shelley's Major Poetry*, 1948; "*Adonais*" in James A. Notopoulos' *The Platonism of Shelley*, 1949; and "Shelley: *Adonais*" in Earl R. Wasserman's *The Subtler Language*, 1959 (first published in the *Journal of English Literary History*, 1954, under the title "*Adonais*: Progressive Revelation as a Poetic Mode").

The *Adonais*, ironically, made Shelley lose "the strong excitement of an assurance of finding sympathy in what you write." In 1820 and 1821 his work attracted some thirty reviews and forty brief notices, much of the attention favorable; there were also poems addressed to him in the journals and even a book published on him. But he seems to have been unaware of this considerable response. In cancelled passages of the Preface to *Adonais* Shelley, conscious of his "publications simply as the instruments of that sympathy between myself and others which the ardent and unbounded love I cherished for my kind excited me to acquire," grieved that "Persecution, contumely, and calumny have been heaped upon me in profuse measure." Like Keats, in whose fate he saw his own (line 300), he suffered from the reviewers, who, "with some rare exceptions, are a most stupid and malignant race." Shelley's burning curse in the *Adonais* set the important reviewers against him, and they dammed the tide of favorable recognition before his reputation could take the flood. Shelley was anxious to know how the *Adonais* fared in England: "I should very much like to hear what is said of my Adonais" and again "I am especially curious

277

to hear the fate of Adonais.—I confess I should be surprised if *that* Poem were born to an immortality of oblivion." He never lost a sense of its value, writing in 1822, "It is absurd in any review to criticize Adonais, & still more to pretend that the verses are bad" and "—I know what to think of Adonais, but what to think of those who confound it with the many bad poems of the day, I know not.—" He was saying, too, "I can write nothing, & if Adonais had no success & excited no interest what incentive can I have to write?" In the spring of 1821 a pirated edition of *Queen Mab* became a trumpet for working-class radicalism, but that notoriety was small comfort for Shelley, who now thought little of its "furious style" and "all the bad poetry in it." This trumpet kept sounding through at least fourteen more pirated editions in the next twenty years, and made Shelley a force for radicalism not only in England but in Germany and Italy.

To—. ("Music, When Soft Voices Die")

Shelley often visited Pisa during the spring and summer months, twice a week going to Emilia, who now had two suitors. Shelley, much to his own amusement, had to "quiet and console" the frantic loser, and wrote to Claire, "I am worthy to take my degree of M.A. in the art of Love, for I have contrived to calm the despairing swain." In September Emilia married. From the deep currents of Shelley's imaginative life, a handful of lyrics and narratives issued, for the matter-of-fact history caused volcanic tremors in his idealization. Among these poems is a lyric that the classicist Walter Landor "would rather have written . . . than all" that the Elizabethans "ever wrote . . . excepting Shakespeare" and that T. S. Eliot, even in his early antipathy to Shelley, granted "a beauty of music and a beauty of content."

> Music, when soft voices die,
> Vibrates in the memory—
> Odours, when sweet violets sicken,
> Live within the sense they quicken.
>
> Rose leaves, when the rose is dead,
> Are heaped for the belovèd bed;

And so thy thoughts, when thou art gone,
Love itself shall slumber on.

[Shelley uses "thy thoughts" in the sense of "thoughts of you,"
a common enough construction in his time.]

Just as Emilia called on Shelley to ease her personal circumstances, so did Byron, who in August requested that Shelley
come to Ravenna and engaged Shelley to persuade his mistress, the Countess Guiccioli, to stay in Italy. The Countess,
now in Florence, wished to go to Switzerland with her brother
and father, revolutionaries expelled from Ravenna. Giving an
account of his days to Mary, Shelley reflected, "L.B. is greatly
improved in every respect—in genius in temper in moral views,
in health in happiness. The connexion with la Guiccioli has
been an inestimable benefit to him. . . . He has made *me*
write a long letter to her to engage her to remain.—An odd
thing enough for an utter stranger to write on subjects of the
utmost delicacy to his friend's mistress.—But it seems destined
that I am always to have some active part in every body's affairs whom I approach." As fee for his success Shelley was re-
warded with Byron's commissioning him to secure the best
palace in Pisa.

His absence from the Baths of San Giuliano stretched out by
Byron's need for his company, Shelley missed Mary to whom
he confessed, "My greatest content would be utterly to desert
all human society. I would retire with you & our child to a
solitary island in the sea, would build a boat, & shut upon my
retreat the floodgates of the world. . . . —If I dared trust my
imagination it would tell me that there were two or three
chosen companions beside yourself whom I should desire.—
But to this I would not listen.—Where two or three are gathered together the devil is among them, and good far more than
evil impulses—love far more than hatred—has been to me, except as you have been it's object, the source of all sort of mischief. . . .—But this it does not appear that we shall do.

"The other side of the alternative (for a medium ought not
to be adopted)—is to form for ourselves a society of our own
class, as much as possible, in intellect or in feelings: & to connect ourselves with the interests of that society. . . .—We must
do one thing or the other: for yourself for our child, for our

existence." In Pisa Shelley formed such a society, the "Pisa Circle," which held together until his death. But it was a male society, Byron and Shelley the chief conversationalists at the gatherings; they and their companions ate together, rode, and practiced with pistols, Shelley pleased that his markmanship rivalled Byron's. He and Byron were "constant companions: no small relief this after the dreary solitude of the understanding & the imagination in which we past the first years of our expatriation, yoked to all sorts of miseries & discomforts."

That society lay ahead of his stay in Ravenna, where both his life and personal reputation met darkening circumstances. Earlier in the year Marianne Hunt had cried out her wish in a letter to Shelley to come to Italy for the sake of her husband. Leigh Hunt, too ill to work, had driven himself into a fearful nervous state; they needed money. Shelley gave what he could, but had too little to float the Hunts. In Ravenna Shelley spoke to Byron, who thought favorably of Hunt, and suggested that they embark on a journal Hunt would edit. Shelley borrowed the passage money for the Hunts. A year later the reunion with Hunt ushered Shelley to his death in a Mediterranean squall. His last act for Hunt was persuading the inconstant Byron to offer his *Vision of Judgment* for the first issue of the *Liberal* and that superb work launched the short-lived journal. Shelley brought out Byron's best in another way. The first evening of Shelley's arrival Byron, who for eleven months had harbored in his mind a scandal that Claire had given birth to a child of Shelley's in Naples, that they had destroyed or abandoned the child, and that they had been brutal to Mary, cut the lie loose from its moorings. In Shelley's presence Byron could apparently not believe what eleven months earlier he had been willing to reply to the writer of the scandalous letter was "just like them." Byron showed the letter to Shelley, who immediately wrote to Mary of this "desperate and wicked malice" in a "hellish society," for only Mary could "effectually rebut" the charge. Such infamy had to be suppressed if "only for the sake of our dear Percy." Mary, of course, passionately repudiated the story. To her husband she wrote: "love me, as you have ever done, and God preserve my child to me, and our enemies shall not be too much for us. . . . Adieu, dearest! Take care of yourself—all yet is well. The shock for me is over, and I now despise the slander; but it must not pass uncontradicted." The ill wind, at least for the moment, blew Shelley and Mary together. The whole story of the scandal (the same that Shelley thought he had crushed in Leghorn) is not worth telling. The proof against it excludes any reasonable doubt. I speak of the malice at all only because there are those who, temperamentally antipathetic to Shelley, still use the story to write Shelley off.

POEMS TO JANE: INTRODUCTION

In October the Shelleys moved back from the Baths to the city of Pisa. They and the Williamses settled in a house on the north side of the Lung' Arno; they looked across open country. Byron moved into a neighboring *palazzo*, his amiable and sentimental mistress already in Pisa. In January Edward Trelawny reached Pisa. The dark Cornishman, who had deserted the Royal Navy in Bombay and taken to piracy on French privateers, whose native intelligence and strong body let him survive, even as a stripling, rough times in Madagascar and Java, and years later in Greece, admiringly took to Shelley; sometimes morally questionable, Trelawny was never so in relationship to Shelley and Mary. Mary, who especially enjoyed his company, described the newcomer as a "kind of half Arab Englishman . . . who recounts the adventures of his youth [Trelawny, like Shelley, was not quite thirty] . . . eloquently and well . . . 6 feet high—raven black hair which curls thickly and shortly like a Moor's—dark grey expressive eyes, overhanging brows, upturned lips and a smile which expresses good nature and kindheartedness [Shelley had his reservations about Trelawny but Trelawny, happily for his own mind, never was aware of them] . . . his voice is monotonous yet emphatic and his language as he relates the events of his life energetic and simple—whether the tale be one of blood and horror or of irresistible comedy." The day after Trelawny's arrival, Shelley and Williams had the Cornishman begin negotiations with an English shipbuilder he knew in Genoa for their "fatal and perfidious bark," built against the better judgment of Trelawny and the shipbuilder on a design that Williams was in love with.

Trelawny spent much time—walking, riding, dining—with the Shelleys and Williamses those days, and although Shelley had earlier that month written *To Jane: The Invitation* and *To Jane: The Recollection*, this steady and acute observer, talkative as his *Recollections* are, says nothing of Shelley and Jane—perhaps because there was nothing to observe other than their friendship (some writers speak of Jane as Shelley's "Platonic mistress," an appellation considerably revealing about the minds of the writers). The poems written to Jane are generally interpreted with biographical referents rather than as self-sustaining pieces of art. [A referent is that outside the poem which a word or group of words in the poem refers to.] We again face the view that the best poetry is entirely self-sustaining and self-contained, is its own cosmos, and that insofar as referents are needed to experience the poem the experience is less valuable esthetically. This critical issue, which bears crucially on a reading of Shelley, is worth our turning to once more, partly because only opinion, no knowledge, exists about the biographical referents, and that state complicates the critical issue.

Early in the winter Shelley and Williams had begun to look eagerly to a summer on the coast for the pleasures of sailing. When in February they explored the coast along the Gulf of Spezia, they were discouraged by the dearth of houses. The Williamses and Claire, who was visiting in Pisa and was to spend the summer with the Shelleys, tried again on April 23, but found only one, unfurnished house, too incommodious for both families. While they were gone Shelley heard of the death by typhus of Claire's daughter, Allegra, in the convent school were Byron had placed her. Shelley decided that they had bettre rush Claire out of Pisa, away from Byron, for Claire would look upon Byron as her child's murderer and would react wildly. The others in the little community—the Williamses and Claire were returned from house-hunting—were not in favor of going but Shelley's obstinacy for Claire's sake was not to be overcome, and the others gave in. On April 26 Mary and Claire, Trelawny escorting them, went to Spezia to see what could be done, Shelley and Williams staying in Pisa another day to take care of shipping the furniture they would need. Mary rented the house, on the shore between villages that neighbored Spezia; and as there was nothing else, Williams, Jane and their two children crowded into one of the three bedrooms (nobody forced them to go along, of course).

In this house Claire learned the shattering news. In her wildness her reason seemed threatened. To her it seemed that the Shelleys were accomplices of the murderer Byron, since they had not rescued Allegra. After the shock and her wildness, Claire somehow won to a stoical calm, and returned to her quarters in Florence.

On the promontories shaping the lovely little bay of San Terenzo in the Gulf of Spezia, chestnut and ilex trees flourished. A primitive fishing village, foothills descending to the beaches, and the sea—these were the world, hardly roomier to Mary's spirit than the house they lived in, the first story unpaved and useless, the second story a common dining room and three bedrooms; the kitchen and servants' quarters were in the outbuildings. Jane liked the place and circumstances little better than Mary did, but both women gave in to their husbands' pleasure and agreed to stay. For Shelley and Williams, living outdoors and sailing their skiff until the *Don Juan* came, each day rang with delight.

Two hundred rocky meters along the shore the village houses of San Terenzo clung like wild and barren bushes on a steep hillside, dominated by an old, grey castle. Along the coast in the other direction about a mile's distance, in its own bay, Lerici lay under a shelter of hills, its houses built along the shore and going steeply up to another old castle, pleasing to romantic eyes for its pentagon of a grey tower circled by myriads of swallows. Petrarch composed a sonnet to Laura there, the idealism of his love tempered by a wry humor and sadness.

1822

LINES: WE MEET NOT AS WE PARTED

In May, Shelley composed the sad *Lines Written in the Bay of Lerici* and possibly *Lines: We Meet Not as We Parted*. [Both were first published by Richard Garnett in 1862 from manuscripts in Boscombe Manor, where Shelley's daughter-in-law, Lady Jane, had made a voluminous collection of Shelley materials.] Newman White thinks the second poem a sequel to the first, and that they record an incident with Jane, "a relatively trivial one, heightened and magnified by an idealizing mood." They are the "only authentic record of the high-water mark of Shelley's attraction to Jane Williams. . . . What happened can never be known, but a kiss or a passionate declaration, followed by a rebuke, could have produced the known results." Ivan Roe thinks the "favourite interpretation" of *We Meet Not as We Parted* as the record of a refusal of a kiss by Jane a mistake, and I think so too. As the lines are a fragment, they cannot be regarded as a self-contained poem. The lines reveal clearly enough the consequences of a momentary experience of the speaker, but obscure the cause, obscure the nature of that experience. The lines are good, but not good enough to trouble with were they not crucial to the present critical issue, that is, the value of the referent in the literary experience. The lines begin,

I

We meet not as we parted,
    We feel more than all may see;
My bosom is heavy-hearted,
    And thine full of doubt for me:—
    One moment has bound the free.

These lines seem to say that something has happened *since* they have parted that has changed the nature of their relationship. His present emotional state is clear, but hers is ambiguous. Is she full of doubt about her feelings for him or about his for her? Which moment no longer lets them—or only him? —live freely, a moment before or after their parting? We know for certain only that their relationship has changed and that they hide their deepest feelings.

II

That moment is gone for ever,
    Like lightning that flashed and died—
Like a snowflake upon the river—
    Like a sunbeam upon the tide,
    Which the dark shadows hide.

The moment apparently had brightness and beauty, at least so the images say. And so now we take it that the brightness and beauty "bound the free," even as love binds, although with the one heavy-hearted and the other full of doubt they might be better free of each other.

III

That moment from time was singled
As the first of a life of pain;
The cup of its joy was mingled
—Delusion too sweet though vain!
Too sweet to be mine again.

But the joy of brightness and beauty was delusive. Its cup was mingled with something that gave lifelong pain. (It seems to me incredible that such a moment could be interpreted as the refusal of a kiss, or that the refusal or the altered relationship consequent upon his indiscretion could cause such pain that the mature Shelley would declare it lifelong. There is nothing of Cavalier hyperbole in the tone of these lines. The tone is realistic, the lines are autobiographical, the pain has actually existed in his life for years—indeed, if I interpret well, Jane is nowhere in the speaker's mind as he writes.) Perhaps the most interesting aspect of these lines as a poem is their "progressive revelation" (to use Earl Wasserman's phrase for the structural principle of *Adonais*) of the nature of the moment.

IV

Sweet lips, could my heart have hidden
That its life was crushed by you,
Ye would not have then forbidden
The death which a heart so true
Sought in your briny dew.

It is this stanza that commentators are sure speaks of a kiss. "Sweet lips," then, would be the lips his own were refused; with that refusal his life was crushed and he wanted to die, but she would not suffer him to make her guilty of his suicide. It is preposterous to think that Shelley wanted to kiss Jane on pulling her out of the sea after a spill from his skiff, and then, refused, wanted to drown in the sea, the "briny dew." But in an age when everybody may be thought to be equally right, we can hardly register surprise at the serious reception of such an interpretation. Her sweet lips, of course, are a metonym, the grammatical subject of "would not have forbidden"—they are sweet in the mixture of his emotions because he loves her still; and her tears, the "briny dew," by metonymy again, the cause of her tears, tempted his death.

285

The cause of her tears may only be guessed at. I take the tears to be Mary's; for Mary, not Jane, fits the emotional context of the poem, and only in connection to Mary could Shelley speak of a life of pain. One editor, C. D. Locock, dates the poem 1814. There is no certain evidence to establish the time and place of composition. If the lines were composed that early, the cause of Mary's tears could be the confession of her love to a man already married. The moment was rapturous and, releasing his love, "bound the free." The rest can be worked out without comment from me. For myself, on stylistic grounds, I do not think that Shelley could have composed this poem in 1814. But even the fragmentary last stanza, for which only the final two lines exist, are consistent with the "moment" suggested by an 1814 date:

> Methinks too little cost
> For a moment so found, so lost.

These lines seem to say that the brightness and beauty of the moment were more than worth the cost of a lifetime of pain that followed his elopement with Mary. Browning, too, believed that a moment could weigh in the balance against a lifetime.

Ivan Roe thinks the lines "a comment on a quarrel (not a flirtation) in which the woman refused one moment's opportunity of reconciliation," and that the woman was Mary, but attempts no reconstruction of that moment. I shall try, taking from Roe a suggestion he makes in another context, that "Mary caused a kind of earthquake in Shelley's spirit" when she "told Shelley, in a moment of intense grief following Clara's death . . . that she had once taken another lover," who was William's father. The affair took place in 1815 with Hogg; the story is told by the Madman in *Julian and Maddalo* and in Mary's 1815 letters to Hogg. She never named her lover to Shelley.

If after little Clara's death Mary made such a confession, that moment could have seemed one of deep love and honesty; but the emotional reaction of a man whom the practice of promiscuity revolted, whatever his theory expressed in *Epipsychidion*, had to set in. (It was Mary, it is true, who was later alien, but that is no psychological contradiction.) The lines are wholly explicable on the assumption of such a moment,

286

and the assumption gives a psychological validity to the lines that makes their expression proportional to the cause. But along with the assumption must go, as it were, a suspension of disbelief, the assumed biographical referent serving to give a sense of wholeness to a construct not self-sustaining, a sense of particularity that strengthens the too general, and a sense of clarity to the ambiguous or rather to the obscure. It is a critical tightrope to walk, but worth the risk.

LINES WRITTEN IN THE BAY OF LERICI

Now we may work backward from *Lines: We Meet Not as We Parted* to *Lines Written in the Bay of Lerici*, still for the sake of the critical issue and the bearing of that issue on a reading of Shelley. Unlike the supposed sequel these lines (although technically fragmentary) are, I think, self-sustaining. However, there are elements of tropal richness that a referent may give even to a self-sustaining, self-contained poem, or, if you will, to our reading of the poem. If such richness is available, why should we enclose our experience in the cosmos of the poem? Let me take the reading of *Lines Written in the Bay of Lerici* as a self-contained cosmos for granted and proceed to a reading with a referent—again, not Jane but Mary.

> She left me at the silent time
> When the moon had ceased to climb
> The azure path of Heaven's steep,
> And like an albatross asleep,
> Balanced on her wings of light,
> Hovered in the purple night,
> Ere she sought her ocean nest
> In the chambers of the West. (1-8).

If we enclose our minds in the cosmos of the poem, the speaker and she are *personae*, they are thoughts mediated by words from the mind of the poet and are connected to nothing ouside the poem. But suppose the opening of the *Lines* had used the Mother of Months in place of the moon. We should then have to bring knowledge of that mythological figure into the cosmos of the poem, and perhaps knowledge of the symbolic value Shelley gave her. I do not think that any

287

critical theorist would deny the validity of our doing so. If literary allusions are at all admitted, that is, a knowledge of matter outside the poem, it seems arbitrary to exclude biographical allusions. If it were the Mother of Months, we might have to bring knowledge of her chastity to "the delusive flame" (48). If it is Mary, we do well to bring knowledge of how she reckons in Shelley's life and other poetry into this poem. (We need not reject truths because they are obvious: there is more than one kind of literature to experience, there is more than one way to experience a particular piece of literature, and we are foolish to lose any of the pleasures or values of literature —I am speaking, of course, of poetry and not of biography— because of a critical frame of reference.) In Shelley's mind, at least, there would be little difference between Artemis and Mary as matter for poetry. For him both are alike in being an "object of thought—that is, any thought upon which any other thought is employed with an apprehension of distinction . . . and such is the material of our knowledge."

Scholars are agreed that Mary is the moon in *Epipsychidion*. The three opening lines here give not only a literal meaning, the time and quality of the night when the woman left after speaking to him, but also a figurative meaning; the moon, the woman, left the speaker when she was in the zenith of his heaven. The vehicle of the moon in turn becomes the tenor of a simile: the moon, like "an albatross asleep, . . . sought her ocean nest In the chambers of the West." Both elements in the simile suggest death: the albatross by echoing the slain albatross (of *The Ancient Mariner*) in the image of sleep, the sinking to the chambers of the West by the traditional force of its symbolic meaning. The woman, in leaving, spiritually died to the man.

> She left me, and I stayed alone
> Thinking over every tone
> Which, though silent to the ear,
> The enchanted heart could hear,
> Like notes which die when born, but still
> Haunt the echoes of the hill. (9-14)

Here commentators interpret "every tone" as Jane's guitar music, but as the vehicle of the simile makes "every tone" like musical notes, it would be an inept figure if every tone were not a word; and it seems to me that only a blind or prejudiced mouth could argue the case for such an ineptitude. As for the touch of a gentle hand on the speaker's brow (15-18), although Shelley speaks of Jane's hand on his brow in another poem (Jane would hypnotize Shelley to ease physical pain), we make ourselves into a caricature of a critic if we think that Mary's hand never stroked his forehead.

> Memory gave me all of her
> That even Fancy dares to claim:—(20-21)

I read these two lines as stating that Shelley remembers actual experience with Mary that was as perfect as Fancy anticipates.

The speaker, "disturbed and weak," sits watching the ships, as if they were sailing to some star "for drink to medicine Such sweet and bitter pain" as his.

> And the fisher with his lamp
> And spear about the low rocks damp
> Crept, and struck the fish which came
> To worship the delusive flame. (45-48)

In Mary, Shelley at first saw Intellectual Beauty incarnated; the lamp is an image for Intellectual Beauty, as the flame is for Love, the other aspect of that spiritual power (therefore do the fish worship). But it was a delusion. . . . I have given metaphorical meaning in the lines, a meaning easily missed without knowledge not in the lines. As for the stylistic excellence of these four lines, I beg off speaking about that although there are effects worth attention. The poem ends in a way very untypical for Shelley, with a moral.

> Too happy they, whose pleasures sought
> Extinguishes all sense and thought
> Of the regret that pleasure leaves,
> Destroying life alone, not peace! (49-52)

But whereas a moral usually expresses a truth commonly accepted, Shelley's moral does not. Although the fisher lines are concrete and particular, the lines for the moral fittingly use general and abstract language in the best Neoclassical manner. The first two lines of the moral have a balance, movement, and ease worthy of Pope (notice, too, the skill in the use of assonance and near-assonance), but the swift run-on into the third line hurries us away from the Neoclassical. The subtle jarring of the failure quite to rhyme in the final couplet, the sound echoing the sense of disharmony, of unfulfillment, in the speaker's life, seems a masterly original technique; it is actually an emendation by Richard Garnett, who first published the *Lines* and the supposed sequel.

[The manuscript of these *Lines* is among the manuscript sheets of *The Triumph of Life* in the Bodleian Library. G. M. Matthews observed that there is no holograph authority for the "plausible verb, 'leaves,' " in the last couplet of the poem, which has no word at all to rhyme with "peace." Matthews believes that the *Lines* really begin with what was published by Garnett as *Fragment to the Moon*:

> Bright wanderer, fair coquette of Heaven,
> To whom alone it has been given
> To change and be adored forever,
> Envy not this dim world, for never
> But once within its shadow grew
> One fair as you, but far more true

Matthews also believes that in the last couplet "*Destroying* is firmly cancelled in MS." and is replaced by "Seeking," which, of course, radically alters the meaning. But Donald Reiman, who has also made a careful study of the manuscript, is "unable to agree that Shelley intended 'Seeking' to replace 'Destroying.' " (Reiman also observes that as a colon is the mark after "peace," the *Lines* "must still be regarded as fragmentary, making it dangerous to explicate it as a self-contained unit.")

These two scholars are also opposed on the biographical problem. Matthews argues that there is objective evidence in the MS of *The Triumph of Life,* that *Lines Written in the Bay of Lerici* is about Jane Williams, that there was "a love-affair, passionate on Shelley's part and at least complaisant on Jane's." Reiman's study makes the objectivity of Matthews' evidence doubtful in the extreme; Reiman does not once read Jane's name in the manuscript where Matthews does five times. (Reiman, however, also believes that the poem is about Jane.) If Matthews should be right, that would argue against (although not conclusively) my application to these *Lines* of the critical principle I have talked about, that is, the value of

290

the referent in the literary experience, but it would not invalidate the principle.]

To Jane: The Invitation, The Recollection

We may continue working backward, now from May in San Terenzo to January in Pisa, the time and place of composition of two fine poems, *To Jane: The Invitation* and *To Jane: The Recollection*. These poems have generally been understood in the light of the later poems mistakenly thought (to my mind) addressed to Jane, and have consequently been misunderstood. The poems form two parts of a whole. Let us remember that in the work of a writer who knows what he is doing the meaning of a part cannot be determined without knowledge of the whole.

In *The Invitation* Jane, "Best and brightest," seems a shadow of Intellectual Beauty, able to redeem the speaker from sorrow, transforming his winter to spring. They will go away, away,

> from men and towns,
> To the wild woods and the downs—
> To the silent wilderness
> Where the soul need not repress
> Its music lest it should not find
> An echo in another's mind, (21-25)

like the sympathy of tuning forks. Then comes a little allegory, in familiar language that uses homely and business images, extraordinary for the life breathed into the abstractions.

> I leave this notice on my door
> For each accustomed visitor:—
> 'I am gone into the fields
> To take what this sweet hour yields;—
> Reflection, you may come tomorrow,
> Sit by the fireside with Sorrow.—
> You with the unpaid bill, Despair,—
> You, tiresome verse-reciter, Care,—
> I will pay you in the grave,—
> Death will listen to your stave.

291

Expectation too, be off!
To-day is for itself enough;
Hope, in pity mock not Woe
With smiles, nor follow where I go;
Long having lived on thy sweet food,
At length I find one moment's good
After long pain—with all your love,
This you never told me of.'   (29-46)

Perhaps the success of these lines (their language and versification aside) is owing to their making our thought and the abstractions together with their actions and qualities interpenetrate each other. In any case the passage shows still another mode that Shelley could master.

In the woods where he and Jane will walk are "pools where winter rains Image all their roof of leaves" (5-51)—an image crucial to *The Recollection*; knowledge of its meaning will make us understand that the restrained ideality with which *The Invitation* ends, as though balancing the ideality of the beginning, is ironic.

To Jane: The Invitation, The Recollection was first published by Mary Shelley in an earlier version as one piece, *The Pine Forest of the Cascine near Pisa* (in *Posthumous Poems*, 1824, and in the first edition of *Poetical Works*, 1839; in the second edition of 1839 she gave the revised version). The first version, for whatever the psychological reason, addresses itself to Jane as a "bright image" that an "unwelcome thought" blots out of Shelley's mind (as the wind destroys the reflected image of forest branches in the pools)—unwelcome because she is "good and dear and kind" as the forest is ever green. There is nothing sexual in the tone; Jane is a friend. The revised version changes "bright image" to "one dear image," thereby changing the referent. The change makes meaning of the forest imagery clearer, deeper, and stronger.

In *The Invitation* Jane was "Fairer far than this fair Day" the morning of the walk. In *The Recollection* Shelley praises these "many days" as having been as "beautiful and bright" as Jane; now the "loveliest and the last, is dead." Memory will write that day's "epitaph of glory,"

For now the Earth has changed its face,
A frown is on the Heaven's brow.   (1-8)

292

We shall see how the natural scene and Shelley's mind are woven together with an ideality and spirit beyond either in one fabric. The loveliness of the day has as its foil the disturbance in his mind. That much is self-contained in the poem. Yet the considerable literary quality of this poem becomes richer if we bring to it knowledge of Shelley's life, a knowledge that the poem's use of his name, willy nilly, invites us to determine. The change in Earth and Heaven, of course, is not only a change in the weather. There is wrong manifesting itself on the earth, and Heaven frowns to see that. Shelley's mind suffers from that wrong. They "wandered to the Pine Forest That skirts the Ocean's foam" (10),

> And on the bosom of the deep
>   The smile of Heaven lay;
> It seemed as if the hour were one
>   Sent from beyond the skies,
> Which scattered from above the sun
>   A light of Paradise. (15-20)

The "seemed" gives the sense of ideality of the hour a restraint so that the hour's actuality does not dissolve but remains itself and palpable. In contrast to the earth's beauty and brightness are the pines they paused among, the "giants of the waste, Tortured by storms." Happily these pines in calm days are "soothed by every azure breath." Now Shelley and Jane are in the depths of the ocean of life and beauty, the "harmonies and hues" around them as tender as Heaven's, the tree-tops lying asleep overhead like "green waves on the sea" (21-32). "How calm it was!" In the "inviolable quietness" they drew the "breath of peace"—a "momentary peace" to which a spirit, interfused in the circle of their world from the remote white mountain waste to the soft flower at their feet, bound their "mortal nature's strife" (33-48).

> And still I felt the centre of
>   The magic circle there
> Was one fair form that filled with love
>   The lifeless atmosphere. (49-52)

The "still" I take to mean that the momentary peace was magically extended by his awareness of the form of beauty filling with love the circle of their world, whose atmosphere otherwise were lifeless—magically because in the ordinary experience of our mortal nature peace is only momentary. The earlier version of these lines suggests an ambiguity:

> And still, it seemed, the centre of
>   The magic circle there,
> Was one whose being filled with love
>   The breathless atmosphere. (73-76)

In this version it is possible to interpret "still" in the sense of "yet" or "nevertheless," the "one" that is radiating love being Jane.

> We paused beside the pools . . .

The pools, each seeming "a little sky . . . Which in the dark earth lay, More boundless than the depth of night, And purer than the day" (53-60), are images of Heaven on the earth; the reflections (like art) select and so intensify the shapes and hues of the forest to the perfection of ideality. Just as the "water's love" imaged that "fair forest green, And all was interfused beneath With an Elysian glow" (72-74),

> Like one beloved the scene had lent
>   To the dark water's breast,
> Its every leaf and lineament
>   With more than truth expressed. (77-80)

The truth of the forest is a truth that is in the world of things; the "more than truth" is ideality. In the way of the world we live in,

> an envious wind crept by,
>   Like an unwelcome thought,
> Which from the mind's too faithful eye
>   Blots one dear image out. (81-84)

Mary was on the walk in the Cascine forest with Shelley and Jane. There is nothing of her physical presence in *The Recollection*, but I take the images in the pools to be images of the time when Mary's love gave an "Elysian glow" to their life; it was a "softer day" (76), that is, as Shelley used "soft," a day that had more love. It lasted until the evil of the world exacted its toll in the form of "an envious wind" (as Time, in *Prometheus Unbound*, was "envious" of Light and Love, of Prometheus and Asia). The wind shatters the beauty in the pools as "an unwelcome thought" disrupts the work of Memory, which has been praising this day of the walk in the pine forest and the "softer day" that the beauty in the pools imaged. The likening of the wind to a thought blotting out "one dear image" superimposes consummately Mary's image on the image of the forest in the pools. The thought, perhaps, was of her unfaithfulness, blotting out the ideality to which "the mind's . . . eye" has been "too faithful." We can hardly tell whether the tone of "too" is sad or bitter, whether or not it denies that the ideal is true. The earlier version had "my mind's" rather than "the mind's too faithful eye"—in writing about his deepest emotional experience, when he changed the referent from Jane to Mary, Shelley put on his concealing mantle of reserve. *The Recollection* closes, as it opened, speaking to Jane:

> Though thou art ever fair and kind,
>   The forests ever green,
> Less oft is peace in Shelley's mind,
>   Than calm in waters, seen.

Neither Jane nor the forest—the "ever green" is both literal and tropal, the natural world in contrast to the human mind—can give peace to Shelley.

WITH A GUITAR, TO JANE

Well, the winter passed and in the green spring Shelley composed *With a Guitar, to Jane* in the Cascine forest, under the lee of a pine fallen into a dark pool. Mary and Trelawny were searching for him that brilliant spring morning, and while the tired Mary waited on the outskirts of the wood, Trelawny found Shelley watching the reflections in the water. Trelawny having spoken of Mary as a forsaken lady, Shelley started up, saying, "Poor Mary! hers is a sad fate. Come along; she can't bear solitude, nor I society—the quick coupled with the dead." The society Shelley could not bear was the society of the tedious, as in *The Aziola*, which Mary well understood:

295

I

'Do you not hear the Aziola cry?
 Methinks she must be nigh,
  Said Mary, as we sate
In dusk, ere stars were lit, or candles brought;
  And I, who thought
 This Aziola was some tedious woman,
  Asked, 'Who is Aziola?' How elate
 I felt to know that it was nothing human,
  No mockery of myself to fear or hate:
  And Mary saw my soul,
And laughed, and said, 'Disquiet yourself not;
 'Tis nothing but a little downy owl.'

Shelley wrote in a *Song* addressed to the Spirit of Delight, like *The Aziola* composed in 1821,

  I love tranquil solitude,
   And such society
  As is quiet, wise, and good. (37-39)

To stop Shelley's self-reproaches Mary bantered cheerfully, and the three walked back to Pisa in high spirits.

At the pool's edge Trelawny had come upon Shelley's scrawl of a manuscript, words smeared out, words written over each other, and all run together—like "a sketch of a marsh overgrown with bulrushes, and the blots for wild ducks." Answering Trelawny, Shelley described a mode of his composing, using homely kitchen imagery, and humorously explained his motive for publication by playing on *a printer's devil.* "When my brain gets heated with thought, it soon boils, and throws off images and words faster than I can skim them off. In the morning, when cooled down, out of the rude sketch as you justly call it, I shall attempt a drawing. If you ask me why I publish what few or none will care to read, it is that the spirits I have raised haunt me until they are sent to the devil of a printer. All authors are anxious to breech their bantlings" [their bastards]. Trelawny could make out only the first two lines,

  Ariel, to Miranda take
  This slave of music.

296

With a Guitar, to Jane needs no praise. I have argued the value and validity of biographical allusions in an esthetic experience. For the esthetic experience of this poem it does not matter whether or not the reader knows that Ariel and Ferdinand are Shelley and Williams, however interesting the poem is in terms of the fine relationship between these men. Indeed, for the esthetic experience we perhaps do better to exclude that knowledge, for the equation of the actual to the fanciful may weigh down the tone. However, the esthetic experience is likely to be the richer for a close knowledge of the literary allusion. I am again saying that it may profit us to bring a knowledge of matter outside the poem to our reading. The literate reader may be expected to know who Ariel, Miranda, Ferdinand and Prospero are as well as he knows the meanings of the other words in the poem; in that sense the poem contains knowledge of these *personae*, that is, these names, like the other words in the poem, contain their meaning. But the literary allusion goes beyond knowledge that the poem contains, demanding a close knowledge of *The Tempest* without which the reader loses a measure of the poem's tropal richness. The opening lines state an analogy:

> Ariel to Miranda:—Take
> This slave of Music, for the sake
> Of him who is the slave of thee . . .

Later lines implicitly elaborate the analogy between Ariel and the guitar, and, failing intuitive perception, we shall lose that implicit meaning without detailed knowledge of *The Tempest*. In Shelley's poem Ariel has been Miranda's guardian spirit from life to life, for he can find his own happiness only in pursuing hers. When Miranda dies, the deserted Ariel (who cannot die) exists in sadness. When she lives again on earth, Ariel guides her over the sea of life. Now, in her "humbler, happier lot," none of this is remembered ("humbler" because in this life she is Jane, as the last line of the poem tells us, not the titled Miranda);

> And now, alas! the poor sprite is
> Imprisoned, for some fault of his,
> In a body like a grave;—
> From you he only dares to crave,

For his service and his sorrow,
A smile to-day, a song to-morrow.
The artist who this idol wrought,
To echo all harmonious thought,
Felled a tree . . .
From which, beneath Heaven's fairest star,
The artist wrought this loved Guitar. (35-45, 57-58)

A sculptor frees the form that he sees imprisoned in stone or wood; just so, the artist wrought the guitar. There is an analogy between this artist freeing the guitar from the wood and Prospero, also an artist, freeing Ariel from a cloven pine, where Sycorax had imprisoned him because he was "a spirit too delicate To act her earthy and abhorr'd commands, Refusing her grand hests." The first we know of Prospero is in the first line after the opening storm-scene. Miranda speaks,

If by your art, my dearest father, you have
Put the wild waters in this roar . . .

And Prospero says to her some lines later,

Lend thy hand,
And pluck my magic garment from me.—So:
Lie there, my art.

The smile that Ariel craves is for his sorrow—as in *The Invitation* Jane's smile brings a springtime of the spirit to those in sorrow—and the song is for his service [40-42: this criss-crossing is an example of the rhetorical device of chiasma]. Just as Ariel's service to Prospero earns his freedom, so Ariel's soul is freed from the prison of his body by Jane's artistry when, in return for his service, she plays the guitar and sings; for music can "hale souls out of men's bodies" as Shakespeare and Shelley knew. For absolute freedom Ariel, imprisoned in "a body like a grave," must die. The artist felled the tree "while on the steep The woods were in their winter sleep," dreaming of the other seasons and of love,

and so this tree,—
O that such our death may be!—
Died in sleep, and felt no pain,
To live in happier form again. (45-56)

298

There is more than an analogy between the guitar and Ariel's soul, there is a congruency, even an identity. In Euclidian geometry analogies, being parallel, cannot intersect; but in the cosmos of this poem, where reincarnation and eternity are realities, perhaps non-Euclidian geometry is the truer, parallel lines do intersect, and identity exists at the point of intersection. The guitar echoes "all harmonious thought" (44), which is also the work of poets; Ariel is a poet, although not in language, making harmony in Miranda's life. The Spirit (of music) inhabiting the guitar—or, as the contemporary philosopher James K. Feibleman would put it, that in the world of possibility which can enter the world of actuality; that which is in the former realm of being does not depend upon becoming actual for its reality—"talks according to the wit Of its companions," as poets do (and as Shelley was conscious that he did).

> But, sweetly as its answers will
> Flatter hands of perfect skill,
> It keeps its highest, holiest tone
> For our belovèd Jane alone.

The fine compliment to *Jane* has a richness of connotation that makes me of two minds about the nature of the esthetic experience in this poem. Jane, of course, is Miranda in a "humbler, happier lot," and her "highest, holiest tone" frees, if only momentarily, the imprisoned Ariel. But we are simply being contrary if we blot out from our mind's eye the actual person who is "our belovèd Jane." The Miranda of the fictive world has become, as it were, actual in the cosmos of the poem; and the transformation, rather than weigh down the fanciful tone, gives it the substance of a reality more familiar to us. *Jane* creates another tangential relation, outside the cosmos of the poem, for those who prefer to include biographical allusion in the experience of the poem. Jane's music, overpowering and revelatory, gave a freedom to Shelley's spirit. As Shelley wrote to Jane,

> Though the sound overpowers,
> Sing again, with your dear voice revealing
> A tone
> Of some world far from ours,

299

Where music and moonlight and feeling
Are one.   (*To Jane*, 19-24)

THE TRIUMPH OF LIFE

There were dark times in San Terenzo, although Williams and sailing made that spring more happy than not for Shelley. Mary suffered a severe miscarriage; Shelley saved her life. By taking "the most decisive resolutions, by dint of making her sit in ice, I succeeded in checking the hemorrhage . . . so that when the physician arrived all danger was over," and the physician applauded him for his boldness. Nightmares possessed Shelley: of the sea flooding their house, of his strangling Mary. Such dark experiences, perhaps, and his conviction "that the mass of mankind as things are arranged at present, are cruel deceitful & selfish, & always on the watch to surprise those few who are not," were the impulse for *The Triumph of Life*. Whatever the impulse, it was powerful. In June Shelley was saying, "I write little now. It is impossible to compose except under the strong excitement of an assurance of finding sympathy in what you write. Imagine Demosthenes reciting a Philippic to the waves of the Atlantic!" For Shelley a poem had to mean, not merely be, and mean enough to the listener to summon up his response. He went on to say, "I feel too little certainty of the future, and too little satisfaction with regard to the past, to undertake any subject seriously and deeply. I stand, as it were, upon a precipice, which I have ascended with great, and cannot descend without *greater*, peril, and I am content if the heaven above me is calm for the passing moment." Yet right after this letter of June 18th Shelley began work, or renewed work (the history of its composition is uncertain), on *The Triumph of Life*. On July 1, Shelley suspended work to sail to Leghorn to take care that matters with the cooling Byron would go well for Leigh Hunt, who was now in the port. A week later, the Hunt family having been settled in Pisa and Byron brought around, Shelley and Williams were driven by storm to their death.

What the fragmentary poem would have become without its final interruption, there is no knowing. A minority says, "It

300

is hardly to be doubted that *The Triumph of Life* was to have marked a new and important path in the wanderings of Shelley's careful thought." The majority think that Shelley "would probably have ended *The Triumph of Life* as he had *Prometheus Unbound, Adonais,* and *Hellas,* on a note of affirmation." I think it a mistake to turn either speculation to the interpreting of the fragment. Shelley was a poet who had considerable structural power, as I have tried to show in such varied works as *Mont Blanc, Lines Written among the Euganean Hills, Prometheus Unbound, The Cenci, The Mask of Anarchy, Ode to the West Wind, The Sensitive Plant, Swellfoot the Tyrant,* and *Mutability.* Moreover the importance of structure was a conscious element in his formal art. Less than half a year before he began work on *The Triumph of Life* he said, "I have done some of Charles I [a play begun in late 1819 and taken up again in January 1822] but although the poetry succeeds very well I cannot seize the conception of the subject as a whole yet, & seldom now touch the *canvas.*" I take it from the way Shelley was working on *The Triumph* that he had a "conception of the subject as a whole." Only *his* execution of the whole, whatever the relation of his execution to his conception, could warrant a critic's confidently making statements about the theme or themes or about meaning of the parts, for such statements can have authority only in relation to the whole. Faced with the impossibility of determining the unity and harmony of the structure, which correspond, as Joyce put it, to "phases of artistic apprehension;" faced with the impossibility of apprehending theme and meaning that can come only with knowledge of the whole and of the relations of the parts to the whole, critics have made interpretations frankly based on a scholarly guess of what the whole would have been. Modesty, at least, should restrain us from such crossing of the province of criticism over to authorship. What we can do, given a fragment, is to examine the texture, what Shelley in speaking about *Charles I* called "the poetry" as distinguished from the "whole."

> Swift as a spirit hastening to his task
>   Of glory & of good, the Sun sprang forth
> Rejoicing in his splendour, & the mask

Of darkness fell from the awakened Earth.
The smokeless altars of the mountain snows
Flamed above crimson clouds, & at the birth

Of light, the Ocean's orison arose
To which the birds tempered their matin lay. (1-8)

Careful art gave these opening lines their assured mastery, meaning coming to us through the musical attributes of the language perhaps even before our minds take in the lucid images wholly. To achieve these lines Shelley worked his way through four earlier versions. He moved steadily toward making the texture more perfect and making completer the spiritual harmony of the natural world (at least for that morning). The birds, living creatures, are not heard until the fourth version, which says,

the Ocean's orison arose
Amid the music of the birds of day. (7-8)

The first version began,

Out of the eastern shadow of the earth
Amid the clouds upon its margin grey—
Scattered by Night to swathe in its bright birth

In fleecy snow & gold the infant day,
The glorious Sun arose . . . (1-5)

The lines now in *The Triumph* proceed with great dignity:

And in succession due, did Continent,

Isle, Ocean, & all things that in them wear
The form & character of mortal mould
Rise as the Sun their father rose, to bear

Their portion of the toil which he of old
Took as his own & then imposed on them. (15-20)

We do not know the nature and purpose of the toil the Sun "of old Took as his own & then imposed" on living things; nor, in the fragment, do we learn. The speaker,

whom thoughts which must remain untold

Had kept as wakeful as the stars that gem
The cone of night, now they were laid asleep, (21-23)

302

stretched himself beneath the hoary branch of "an old chestnut flung athwart . . . a green Apennine." The speaker remembers,

before me fled
The night; behind me rose the day; the Deep

Was at my feet, & Heaven above my head   (26-28)

when he experienced a strange trance. There is a dizziness in
these rhythms that precede the trance, subtly right. There is
rightness, too, in the images for the trance: he is on a green
mountain, suspended between night and day, the ocean at his
feet and the sky over his head ("the Deep" and the shock of its
assonance with "my feet," and "Heaven" alliterating with "my
head," reverberate with other than natural meaning)—it is as
though he is not quite in the dimension of time and as though
he is no whit less or lesser in the world than earth, sky, and
ocean. Once before, the narrator knew,

> That I had felt the freshness of that dawn,
> Bathed in the same cold dew my brow & hair
> And sate as thus upon that slope of lawn
>
> Under the self same bough, & heard as there
> The birds, the fountains & the Ocean hold
> Sweet talk in music through the enamoured air.
> And then a Vision on my brain was rolled . .   (35-40)

But when it was he had experienced that dawn and that same
cold dew, sat there under that self-same bough and listened to
the talk in music, or why it is that he is here again listening,
we cannot learn from the fragment.

[These forty lines are fair copy in the Bodleian manuscript.
I have followed the text as edited by Donald Reiman in *Shelley's "The Triumph of Life": A Critical Study*, 1965, which
with clear authority from MS capitalizes words that other editions do not. The punctuation varies, too. Both sorts of changes
may alter meaning. As Reiman supplies a conservative text in
a variorum edition, his is the text to use for close study of the
fragment. Now and then I shall silently use alternative readings.]

The first tercet not to run on is the thirteenth, which is
stopped by a period. Dante inclined to close his tercets. I do

303

not think that Shelley ran his tercets on out of a desire to make his *terza rima* original or out of need to manage the difficult rhyme scheme (difficult in English because in our language rhyme is internal in the structure of a word, whereas in Romance languages continuing triple rhymes are relatively easy to manage because of the constantly recurring same syllables at the end of inflected words). The running on of the tercets intensifies the sense of motion inherent in the interlocking rhyme scheme of *terza rima*, while the formal pattern of the tercets stays fixed. This stylistic tension accords with meaning in the imagery: first there is the swift motion of the sun and the motions of all things in the natural world, while the speaker stretched beneath a chestnut experiences a trance; then comes the intenser motion of the triumphal pageant in his vision, while the speaker and the weary Rousseau are by the wayside. The motion in Shelley's imagery and verse, carrying the world of the fragment along, accords, too, with the modern intellectual image of the universe in which nothing is at absolute rest.

[The *terza rima*, the directness of speech, techniques in imagery, the allusions to Dante and *The Divine Comedy*, make critics regard the English and Italian poets together. Nonetheless, it is Shelley's own style and soul, not Dante's, that makes *The Triumph* what it is. Indeed, not only elements from Dante but also from Petrarch, Milton, and Rousseau are compounded in the fragment. Shelley pays this tribute to Dante:

> "Behold a wonder worthy of the rhyme
>
> "Of him whom from the lowest depths of Hell
> Through every Paradise & through all glory
> Love led serene, & who returned to tell
>
> "In words of hate & awe the wondrous story
> How all things are transfigured, except Love. (471-476)]

In his trance the speaker thought himself "beside a public way Thick strewn with summer dust" where people hurried to and fro,

> Numerous as gnats upon the evening gleam,

All hastening onward, yet none seemed to know
　　Whither he went, or whence he came, or why
He made one of the multitude . . .

　　And as I gazed methought that in the way
The throng grew wilder, as the woods of June
　　When the South wind shakes the extinguished day.—

And a cold glare, intenser than the noon
　　But icy cold, obscured with　　　　light
The Sun as he the stars.　(46-49, 74-79)

That cold glare shone from a chariot drawn by winged shapes
lost in thick lightnings; the narrator could only hear their
wings. A charioteer with four faces (like the Janus who presided over the seasons, the changes of the earth in time) and
blindfolded eyes badly guided the car.

a Shape
　　So sate within as one whom years deform

Beneath a dusky hood & double cape
　　Crouching within the shadow of a tomb.　(87-90)

The crowd gave way, & I arose aghast,
　　Or seemed to rise, so mighty was the trance,
And saw like clouds upon the thunder blast

　　The million with fierce song and maniac dance
Raging around; such seemed the jubilee
　　As when to greet some conqueror's advance

Imperial Rome poured forth her living sea
　　From senatehouse & prison & theatre
When Freedom left those who upon the free

　　Had bound a yoke which soon they stooped to bear.
Nor wanted here the true similitude
　　Of a triumphal pageant, for where'er

The chariot rolled a captive multitude
　　Was driven; althose who had grown old in power
Or misery,—all who have their age subdued,

　　By action or by suffering, and whose hour
Was drained to its last sand in weal or woe,
　　So that the trunk survived both fruit & flower;

305

All those whose fame or infamy must grow
　　Till the great winter lay the form & name
Of their own earth with them forever low.　(107-127)

[126: *the great winter*, "Buffon's sublime but gloomy theory,
that this earth which we inhabit will at some future period be
changed into a mass of frost"—Shelley reflecting on the glaciers
of Mont Blanc. Our earth will, at last, turn stone cold.]
　　Some were not conquered by the Shape, were not in the savage dance of life, those who died young and uncorrupted, and
those of Athens and Jerusalem (Socrates and Jesus) who put
aside earthly power and wealth and who were invulnerable.
Chained to the car were "the mighty captives"; in the van the
tempestuous young danced, "tortured by their agonizing pleasure," joining in "bright destruction"; in the rear,

　　　　Old men, and women foully disarrayed
　　　　　Shake their grey hair in the insulting wind,

　　　　And limp in the dance.　(165-167)

These are destroyed by frost, as the young by fire.

　　　　Struck to the heart by this sad pageantry,
　　　　Half to myself I said, "And what is this?
　　　　Whose shape is that within the car? & why"—

　　　　I would have added—"is all here amiss?"
　　　　But a voice answered . . "Life". . . I turned & knew
　　　　(O Heaven have mercy on such wretchedness!)

　　　　That what I thought was an old root which grew
　　　　To strange distortion out of the hill side
　　　　　Was indeed one of that deluded crew,

　　　　And that the grass which methought hung so wide
　　　　　And white, was but his thin discoloured hair,
　　　　And that the holes it vainly sought to hide

　　　　Were or had been eyes.—"If thou canst forbear
　　　　To join the dance, which I had well forborne,"
　　　　　Said the grim Feature, of my thought aware,

　　　　"I will now tell that which to this deep scorn
　　　　　Led me & my companions, and relate
　　　　The progress of the pageant since the morn;

"If thirst of knowledge doth not thus abate,
Follow it even to the night, but I
  Am weary" . . . Then like one who with the weight

Of his own words is staggered, wearily
  He paused, and ere he could resume, I cried,
"First who art thou?" . . . "Before thy memory

  "I feared, loved, hated, suffered, did, & died,
And if the spark with which Heaven lit my spirit
  Earth had with purer nutriment supplied

"Corruption would not now thus much inherit
  Of what was once Rousseau—nor this disguise
Stained that within which still disdains to wear it.—
                                        (176-205)

[These are the lines of which T. S. Eliot said, "Well, this is better than I could do. But I quote it as one of the supreme tributes to Dante in English, for it testifies to what Dante has done, both for the style and for the soul of a great English poet."] The holes which were or had been eyes were, of course, thought to be holes in the ground, as the hair was thought to be grass and the body an old root. The image of Rousseau as a piece of vegetation and earth on the hillside is a wonder of imaginative meaning. Nor do the humanity and careful plainness of the two tercets bringing us to Rousseau seem less praiseworthy to me.

As for those chained to the car—"The Wise, The great, the unforgotten," bishops, generals, kings, philosophers—

                        their lore

  "Taught them not this—to know themselves; their might
Could not repress the mutiny within. (211-213)

Among those ignorant of what they were, fallen, was Napoleon,

        Whose grasp had left the giant world so weak

    That every pigmy kicked it as it lay—
      And much I grieved to think how power & will
      In opposition rule our mortal day—

307

And why God made irreconcilable
Good & the means of good. (226-231)

[The pygmies are the rulers of the European monarchies in
Napoleon's wake.] Lines like these make their mark esthetically and contentually in analytic criticism: one scholar, Milton
Wilson, admires the combination of the concrete and the abstract in the language of the passage; others speculate on what
this God is, myself accepting the notion of C. E. Pulos that the
"God is an inconceivable power differing from man and the
mind of man" as is "the unknown God" of *Hellas* worshipped
in Jerusalem (211-212) and in Athens (733-735).

After the spoilers of the modern world, Rousseau points to
those of Greece, Rome, and the Christian world whose phantoms are chained to the car. [261: *The tutor & his pupil*, Aristotle and Alexander. Bacon on Aristotle: "I will think of him
that he learned that humour of his scholar with whom it
seemeth he did emulate, the one to conquer all opinions, as the
other to conquer all nations." Just as only what is mortal of
Plato is there, in expiation of his love for a boy, the "star," so
do the mortal elements of Bacon and the great bards expiate
what exposed them to corruption. The rulers of Rome and
Church are utterly condemned for their destruction of body
and spirit.] The narrator of the vision interrupts Rousseau:

> "Whence camest thou & whither goest thou?
> How did thy course begin," I said, "& why?
>
> "Mine eyes are sick of this perpetual flow
> Of people, & my heart of one sad thought.—(296-299)

Rousseau then speaks of his own history, able to tell partly
whence he came and how he reached this dread pass but not
why this should be nor whither life hurries him. What Rousseau cannot tell he may learn from the questioner if the questioner "from spectator turn Actor or victim in this wretchedness." The detachment of the spectator from the action or suffering in the vision, although not from sympathy with its
unhappy pageantry, is the matrix of the fragment's singular
tone.

Rousseau's history, nearly half the fragment, is difficult, imperfectly explicable, nor do I have the space now to cope with

its matter. I must beg release. It has sufficed, I trust, to show a new tone, a new style, a new set of intellectual and emotional co-ordinates in the geometry of the work Shelley was building.

Mary, ill and fearful and weeping, tried to hold Shelley in San Terenzo on the first of July. In Pisa a letter from Mary urged her husband to come back, her mind darker than ever with foreboding of disaster hanging over their child. On the docks in Leghorn, Leigh Hunt watched an aspect of the aristocratic Shelley new to him, Shelley's gift of connecting easily and naturally with ordinary people, whether rough captains or common sailors. Shelley's business done at week's end, and purchases made for their household, Williams and Shelley and a young sailor boarded the *Don Juan*, their "perfect plaything for the summer" as Williams boyishly recorded in his diary the day the craft sailed into their little bay. The skies were threatening. But Williams, who had sat in Leghorn chafing at his absence from Jane but unwilling to go back to San Terenzo without Shelley, wanted to shove off; and the wind was blowing fair for the Gulf of Spezia, promising a fast run. They set sail. A squall began to come up. A watcher in the Leghorn tower saw the crew taking in sail ten miles away; then the storm broke and thick rain stopped their vision. An Italian captain later testified that the Englishmen would not come aboard his safer vessel; that he had warned them to reef their sails or they were lost; that one man had begun to lower the sails and the other had forcibly stopped him—but that does not jibe with what the Leghorn watcher saw. Salvaged, the *Don Juan* showed her stern violently stove in and her masts broken off. The Italian captain had seen a third boat in the storm, perhaps the Livornese felucca that, in a story going around Leghorn, followed the *Don Juan* out of port. Shelley had money aboard. The stove-in stern suggests to some that the felucca's crew tried to pirate the *Don Juan* but succeeded only in ramming and sinking her; naturally, they saved nobody. Trelawny believed a dubious account told years later of a dying boatman's confession to a priest: "he was one of five who, seeing the English boat in great danger, ran her down, thinking milord Inglese was on board, and they should find gold." Ten days later the bodies of Shelley and Williams, mutilated by fish, were washed ashore, ending the fearful doubts and hopes. Tre-

309

lawny brought the news to Mary and Jane. There were strict Italian laws, against the danger of plague, that washed-up bodies be buried on the shore with quicklime, but through the British minister in Florence Trelawny got permission to cremate and take the ashes to Rome for burial. Shelley's heart would not burn. Trelawny rescued it, singeing his hand. Mary carried her husband's heart to her grave. Trelawny purchased ground near the pyramid in the Protestant cemetery in Rome and built two tombs. In the first Shelley's ashes were placed; in the other, Trelawny's, sixty years later. Before Trelawny left for Greece with Byron (where the Cornishman fought with the insurgent chief Odysseus, whose stronghold was on Mount Parnassus), he gave Mary money to go to England. There she lived for her son, managing on an allowance that Shelley's father provided her and on her writings until Percy Florence inherited the Shelley baronetcy and estates. A generation later George Henry Lewes, a fine mind, in the *Westminster Review* spoke of Shelley as a great Englishman.

Shelley perhaps had the most brilliant intelligence and finest sensibility of his age, and, although indeed a fallible human being, he ranked among its few greatly good men. If he wrote much not worth our reading, and if much of his best work is flawed, there are still enough greatness and range in his work to say that he was the first poet of his age. His was a manifold radical voice: in politics, in economic thought, in religious experience, in social philosophy, and therefore in literary expression. Response to his poetry, as to any poetry, finally depends on our immediate or enlarged sympathy with the meaning—intellectual, emotional, and esthetic—of his works. My own venture is that his voice will speak to new listeners long after his critics who praise or blame are silent.

APPENDIX

The Socrates-Diotima Discourse from Shelley's Translation of the *Symposium*, as edited by James A. Notopoulos in his *The Platonism of Shelley*, 1949

—Then Socrates thus began.

"I applaud, dear Agathon, the beginning of your discourse, where you say, we ought first to define and declare what Love is, and then his works. This rule I particularly approve. But, come, since you have given us a discourse of such beauty and majesty concerning Love, you are able, I doubt not, to explain this question, whether Love is the Love of something or nothing? I do not ask you of what parents Love is; for the enquiry, of whether Love is the love of any father or mother, would be sufficiently ridiculous. But if I were asking you to describe that which a father is, I should ask, not whether a father was the love of any one, but whether a father was the father of any one or not; you would undoubtedly reply, that a father was the father of a son or daughter; would you not?"—"Assuredly."—"You would define a mother in the same manner?"—"Without doubt."—"Yet bear with me, and answer a few more questions, for I would learn from you that which I wish to know. If I should enquire, in addition, is not a brother, through the very nature of his relation, the brother of some one?"—"Certainly."—"Of a brother or sister is he not?"—"Without question."—"Try to explain to me then the nature of Love; Love is the love of something or nothing?"—"Of something, certainly."

"Observe and remember this concession. Tell me yet farther, whether Love desires that of which it is the Love or not?"—"It desires it, assuredly."—"Whether possessing that which it desires and loves, or not possessing it, does it desire and love?"—"Not possessing it, I should imagine."—"Observe now, whether it does not appear, that, of necessity, desire desires that which it wants and does not possess, and no longer desires that which it no longer wants: this appears to me, Agathon, of necessity to be; how does it appear to you?"—"It appears so to me also."—"Would any one who was already illustrious, desire to be illustrious; would any one already strong, desire to be

311

strong? From what has already been conceded, it follows that he would not. If any one already strong, should desire to be strong; or any one already swift, should desire to be swift; or any one already healthy, should desire to be healthy, it must be concluded, that they still desired the advantages of what they already seemed possessed. To destroy the foundation of this error, observe, Agathon, that each of these persons must possess the several advantages in question, at the moment present to our thoughts, whether he will or no. And, now, is it possible that those advantages should be at that time the objects of his desire? For, if any one should say, being in health, 'I desire to be in health'; being rich, 'I desire to be rich, and thus still desire those things which I already possess,' we might say to him, 'You, my friend, possess health, and strength, and riches; you do not desire to possess now, but to continue to possess them in the future; for, whether you will or no, they now belong to you. Consider then, whether, when you say that you desire things present to you, and in your own possession, you say anything else than that you desire the advantages to be for the future also in your possession.' What else could he reply?"—"Nothing, indeed."—"Is not Love, then, the love of that which is not within its reach, and which cannot hold in security, for the future, those things of which it obtains a present and transitory possession?"—"Evidently."—"Love, therefore, and every thing else that desires anything, desires that which is absent and beyond his reach, that which it has not, that which is not itself, that which it wants; such are the things of which there are desire and love."—"Assuredly."

"Come," said Socrates, "let us review your concessions. Is Love anything else than the love first of something; and, secondly, of those things of which it has need?"—"Nothing."—"Now, remember of those things you said in your discourse, that Love was the love—if you wish I will remind you. I think you said something of this kind, that all the affairs of the Gods were admirably disposed through the love of the things which are beautiful; for there was no love of things deformed; did you not say so?"—"I confess that I did."—"You said what was most likely to be true, my friend; and if the matter be so, the love of beauty must be one thing, and the love of deformity another."—"Certainly."—"It is conceded, then, that Love loves that which he wants but possesses not?"—"Yes, certainly."—"But Love wants and does not possess beauty?"—"Indeed it must necessarily follow."—"What, then! call you that beautiful which has need of beauty and possesses not?"—"Assuredly no."—"Do you still assert, then, that Love is beautiful, if all that we have said be true?"—"Indeed, Socrates," said Agathon, "I am in danger of being convicted of ignorance, with respect to all that I then spoke."—"You spoke most eloquently, my

312

dear Agathon; but bear with my questions yet a moment. You admit that things which are good are also beautiful?"—"No doubt."—"If Love, then, be in want of beautiful things, and things which are good are beautiful, he must be in want of things which are good?"—"I cannot refute your arguments, Socrates."—"You cannot refute truth, my dear Agathon; to refute Socrates is nothing difficult.

"But I will dismiss these questionings. At present let me endeavour, to the best of my power, to repeat to you, on the basis of the points which have been agreed upon between me and Agathon, a discourse concerning Love, which I formerly heard from the prophetess Diotima, who was profoundly skilled in this and many other doctrines, and who, ten years before the pestilence, procured to the Athenians, through their sacrifices, a delay of the disease; for it was she who taught me the science of things relating to Love.

"As you well remarked, Agathon, we ought to declare who and what is Love, and then his works. It is easiest to relate them in the same order, as the foreign prophetess observed when, questioning me, she related them. For I said to her much the same things that Agathon has just said to me—that Love was a great deity, and that he was beautiful; and she refuted me with the same reasons as I have employed to refute Agathon, compelling me to infer that he was neither beautiful or good, as I said—'What then,' I objected, 'O Diotima, is Love ugly and evil?'—'Good words, I entreat you,' said Diotima; 'do you think that every thing which is not beautiful, must of necessity be ugly?'—'Certainly.'—'And every thing that is not wise, ignorant? Do you not perceive that there is something between ignorance and wisdom?'—'What is that?'—'To have a right opinion or conjecture. Observe, that this kind of opinion, for which no reason can be rendered, cannot be called knowledge; for how can that be called knowledge, which is without evidence or reason? Nor ignorance, on the other hand; for how can that be called ignorance which arrives at the persuasion of that which it really is? A right opinion is something between understanding and ignorance.'—I confessed that what she alledged was true.—'Do not then say,' she continued, 'that what is not beautiful is of necessity deformed, nor what is not good is of necessity evil; nor, since you have confessed that Love is neither beautiful or good, infer, therefore, that he is deformed or evil, but rather something intermediate.'

" 'But,' I said, 'Love is confessed by all to be a great God.'—'Do you mean, when you say all, all those who know, or those who know not, what they say?'—'All collectively.'—'And how can that be, Socrates?' said she laughing; 'how can he be acknowledged to be a great God, by those who assert that he is not even a God at all?'—'And who are they?' I said.—'You for one, and I for another.'—'How can you say that, Diotima?'—'Easily,' she replied, 'and with truth; for tell me, do you not own that all the Gods are beautiful and happy? or will you presume to maintain that any God is otherwise?'—'By Jupiter, not I!'—'Do you not call those alone happy who possess all things that are beautiful and good?'—'Certainly.'—'You have confessed that Love, through his desire for things beautiful and good, possesses not those materials of happiness.'—'Indeed such was my concession.'— 'But how can we conceive a God to be without the possession of what is beautiful and good?'—'In no manner, I confess.'—'Observe, then, that you do not consider Love to be a God.'—'What then,' I said, 'is Love a mortal?'—'By no means.'—'But what, then?'—'Like those things which I have before instanced, he is neither mortal or immortal, but something intermediate.'—'What is that, O Diotima?'—'A great Daemon, Socrates; and every thing daemoniacal hold[s] an intermediate place between what is divine and what is mortal.'

" 'What is his power and nature?' I inquired.—'He interprets and makes a communication between divine and human things, conveying the prayers and sacrifices of men to the Gods, and communicating the commands and directions concerning the mode of worship most pleasing to them, from Gods to men. He fills up that intermediate space between these two classes of beings, so as to bind together, by his own power, the whole universe of things. Through him subsist all divination, and the science of sacred things as it relates to sacrifices, and expiations, and disenchantments, and prophecy, and magic. The divine nature cannot immediately communicate with what is human, but all that intercourse and converse which is conceded by the Gods to men, both whilst they sleep and when they wake, subsists through the intervention of Love; and he who is wise in the science of this intercourse is supremely happy, and participates in the daemoniacal nature; whilst he who is wise in any other science or art, remains a mere ordinary slave. These daemons are, indeed, many and various, and one of them is Love.

" 'Who are the parents of Love?' I enquired.—'The history of what you ask,' replied Diotima, 'is somewhat long; nevertheless I will explain it to you. On the birth of Venus the Gods celebrated a great feast, and among them [came] Plenty, the son of Metis. After supper, Poverty, observing the profusion, came to beg, and stood beside the door. Plenty being drunk with nectar, for wine was not yet invented, went out into Jupiter's garden, and fell into a deep sleep. Poverty wishing to have a child by Plenty, on account of her low estate, lay down by him, and from his embraces conceived Love. Love is, therefore, the follower and servant of Venus, because he was conceived at her birth, and because by nature he is a lover of all that is beautiful, and Venus was beautiful. And since Love is the child of

Poverty and Plenty, his nature and fortune participate[s] in that of his parents. He is for ever poor, and so far from being delicate and beautiful, as mankind imagine, he is squalid and withered; he flies low along the ground, and is homeless and unsandalled; he sleeps without covering before the doors, and in the unsheltered streets; possessing thus far his mother's nature, that he is ever the companion of Want. But, inasmuch as he participates in that of his father, he is for ever scheming to obtain things which are good and beautiful; he is fearless, vehement, and strong; a dreadful hunter, for ever weaving some new contrivance; exceedingly cautious and prudent, and full of resources; he is also, during his whole existence, a philosopher, a powerful enchanter, a wizard, and a subtle sophist. And, as his nature is neither mortal nor immortal, on the same day when he is fortunate and successful, he will at one time flourish, and then die away, and then, according to his father's nature, again revive. All that he acquires perpetually flows away from him, so that Love is never either rich or poor, and holding for ever an intermediate state between ignorance and wisdom. The case stands thus:—no God philosophizes or desires to become wise, for he is wise; nor, if there exist any other being who is wise, does he philosophize. Nor do the ignorant philosophize, for they desire not to become wise; for this is the evil of ignorance, that he who has neither intelligence, nor virtue, nor delicacy of sentiment, imagines that he possesses all those things sufficiently. He seeks not, therefore, that possession of whose want they are not aware.'—'Who, then, O Diotima,' I enquired, 'are philosophers, if they are neither the ignorant nor the wise?'—'It is evident, even to a child, that they are those intermediate persons, among whom is Love. For Wisdom is one of the most beautiful of all things; Love is that which thirsts for the beautiful, so that Love is of necessity a philosopher, philosophy being an intermediate state between ignorance and wisdom. His parentage accounts for his condition, being the child of a wise and well-provided father, and of a mother both ignorant and poor.

" 'Such is the daemoniacal nature, my dear Socrates; nor do I wonder at your error concerning Love, for you thought, as I conjecture from what you say, that Love was not the lover but the beloved, and thence, well concluded that he must be supremely beautiful; for that which is the object of Love must indeed be fair, and delicate, and perfect, and most happy; but Love inherits, as I have declared, a totally opposite nature.'—'Your words have persuasion in them, O stranger,' I said; 'be it as you say. But this Love, what advantages does he afford to men?'—'I will proceed to explain it to you, Socrates. Love being such and so produced as I have described, is, indeed, as you say, the love of things which are beautiful. But if any one should

315

ask us, saying: O Socrates and Diotima, why is Love the love of beautiful things? Or, in plainer words, what does the lover of that which is beautiful, love in the object of his love, and seek from it?'—'He seeks,' I said, interrupting her, 'the property and possession of it.'— 'But that,' she replied, 'might still be met with another question, What has he, [who] possesses that which is beautiful?'—'Indeed, I cannot immediately reply.'—'But if, changing the beautiful for good, any one should enquire,—I ask, O Socrates, what is that which he who loves that which is good, loves in the object of his love?'—'To be in his possession,' I replied.—'And what has he, who has the possession of good?'—'This question is of easier solution: he is happy.'—'Those who are happy, then, are happy through the possession; and it [is] useless to enquire what he desires, who desires to be happy; the question seems to have a complete reply. But do you think that this wish and this love are common to all men, and that all desire, that [that] which is good should be for ever present to them?'—'Certainly, common to all.'—'Why do we not say then, Socrates, that every one loves? if, indeed, all love perpetually the same thing? But we say that some love, and some do not.'—'Indeed I wonder why it is so.'—'Wonder not,' said Diotima, 'for we select a particular species of love, and apply to it distinctively the appellation of that which is universal.'—

" 'Give me an example of such a select application.'—'Poetry; which is a general name signifying every cause whereby anything proceeds from that which is not, into that which is; so that the exercise of every inventive art is poetry, and all such artists poets. Yet they are not called poets, but distinguished by other names; and one portion or species of poetry, that which has relation to music and rhythm, is divided from all others, and known by the name belonging to all. For this is alone properly called poetry, and those who exercise the art of this species of poetry, poets. So, with respect to Love. Love is indeed universally all that earnest desire for the possession of happiness and that which is good; the greatest and the subtlest love, and which inhabits the heart of every human being; but those who seek this object through the acquirement of wealth, or the exercise of the gymnastic arts, or philosophy, are not said to love, nor are called lovers; one species alone is called Love, and those alone are said to be lovers, and to love, who seek the attainment of the universal desire through one species of Love, which is peculiarly distinguished by the name belonging to the whole. It is asserted by some, that they love, who are seeking the lost half of their divided being. But I assert, that Love is neither the love of [the] half or of the whole, unless, my friend, it meets with that which is good; since men willingly cut off their own hands and feet, if they think that they are the cause of evil to them. Nor do they cherish and embrace that which may be-

316

long to themselves, merely because it is their own; unless, indeed, any one should choose to say, that that which is good is attached to his own nature and is his own, whilst that which is evil is foreign and accidental; but love nothing but that which is good. Does it not appear so to you?'—'Assuredly.'—'Can we then simply affirm that men love that which is good?'—'Without doubt.'—'What, then, must we not add, that, in addition to loving that which is good, they love that it should be present to themselves?'—'Indeed that must be added.'—'And not merely that it should be present, but that it should ever be present?'—'This also must be added.'

" 'Love, then, is collectively the desire in men that good should be for ever present to them.'—'Most true.'—'Since this is the general definition of Love, can you explain in what mode of attaining its object, and in what species of actions, does Love peculiarly consist?'—'If I knew what you ask, O Diotima, I should not have so much wondered at your wisdom, or have sought you out for the purpose of deriving improvement from your instructions.'—'I will tell you,' then she replied: 'Love is the desire of generation in the beautiful, both with relation to the body and the soul.'—'I must be a diviner to comprehend what you say, for, being such as I am, I confess that I do not understand it.'—'But I will explain it more clearly. The bodies and the souls of all human beings are alike pregnant with their future progeny, and when we arrive at a certain age, our nature impells us to bring forth and propagate. This nature is unable to produce in that which is deformed, but it can produce in that which is beautiful. The intercourse of the male and female in generation, a divine work, through pregnancy and production, is, as it were, something immortal in mortality. These things cannot take place in that which is incongruous; for that which is deformed is incongruous, but that which is beautiful is congruous with what is immortal and divine. Beauty is, therefore, the Fate, and the Juno Lucina to generation. Wherefore, whenever that which is pregnant with the generative principle, approaches that which is beautiful, it becomes transported with delight, and is poured forth in overflowing pleasure, and propagates. But when it approaches that which is deformed, it is contracted and sad[ness], it is repelled and checked and does not produce, but retains unwillingly that with which it is pregnant. Wherefore, to one pregnant, and, as it were, already bursting with the load of his desire, the impulse towards that which is beautiful is intense, on account of the great pain of retaining that which he has conceived. Love, then, O Socrates, is not as you imagine the love of the beautiful.'—'What, then?'—'Of generation and production in the beautiful.'—'Why then of generation?'—'Generation is something eternal and immortal in mortality. It necessarily, from what has been

317

confessed, follows, that we must desire immortality together with what is good, since Love is the desire that good be for ever present to us. Of necessity Love must also be the desire of immortality.'

"Diotima taught me all this doctrine in the discourse we had together concerning Love; and in addition, she enquired, 'What do you think, Socrates, is the cause of this love and desire? Do you not perceive how all animals, both those of the earth and of the air, are affected when they desire the propagation of their species, affected even to weakness and disease by the impulse of their love; first, longing to be mixed with each other, and then seeking nourishment for their offspring, so that the feeblest are ready to contend with the strongest in obedience to this law, and to die for the sake of their young, or to waste away with hunger, and do or suffer anything so that they may not want nourishment. It might be said that human beings do these things through reason, but can you explain why other animals are thus affected through love?'—I confessed that I did not know.—'Do you imagine yourself,' said she, 'to be skilful in the science of Love, if you are ignorant of these things?'—'As I said before, O Diotima, I come to you, well knowing how much I am in need of a teacher. But explain to me, I entreat you, the cause of these things, and of the other things relating to Love.'—'If,' said Diotima, 'you believe that Love is of the same nature as we have mutually agreed upon, wonder not that such are its effects. For the mortal nature seeks, so far as it is able, to become deathless and eternal. But it can only accomplish this desire by generation, which for ever leaves another new in place of the old. For, although each human being be severally said to live, and be the same from youth to old age, yet, that which is called the same, never contains within itself the same things, but always is becoming new by the loss and change of that which it possessed before; both the hair, and the flesh, and the bones, and the entire body.

" 'And not only does this change take place in the body, but also with respect to the soul. Manners, morals, opinions, desires, pleasures, sorrows, fears; none of these ever remain unchanged in the same persons; but some die away, and others are produced. And, what is yet more strange [is] that not only does some knowledge spring up, and another decay, and that we are never the same with respect to our knowledge, but that each several object of our thoughts suffers the same revolution. That which is called meditation, or the exercise of memory, is the science of the escape or departure of knowledge; for, forgetfulness is the going out of knowledge; and meditation, calling up a new memory in the place of that which has departed, preserves knowledge; so that, tho' for ever displaced and restored, it seems to be the same. In this manner every thing mortal is preserved:

318

not that [it] is constant and eternal, like that which is divine; but that in the place of what has grown old and is departed, it leaves another new like that which it was itself. By this contrivance, O Socrates, does what is mortal, the body and all other things, partake of immortality; that which is immortal, is immortal in another manner. Wonder not, then, if every thing by nature cherishes that which was produced from itself, for this earnest Love is a tendency towards eternity.'

"Having heard this discourse, I was astonished, and asked, 'Can these things be true, O wisest Diotima?' And she, like an accomplished sophist, said, 'Know well, O Socrates, that if you only regard that love of glory which inspires men, you will wonder at your own unskilfulness in not having discovered all that I now declare. Observe with how vehement a desire they are affected to become illustrious and to prolong their glory into immortal time, to attain which object, far more ardently than for the sake of their children, all men are ready to engage in any dangers, and expend their fortunes, and submit to any labours and incur any death. Do you believe that Alcestis would have died in the place of Admetus, or Achilles for the revenge of Patroclus, or Codrus for the kingdom of his posterity, if they had not believed that the immortal memory of their actions, which we now cherish, would have remained after their death? Far otherwise; all such deeds are done for the sake of ever-living virtue, and this immortal glory which they have obtained; and inasmuch as any one is of an excellent nature, so much the more is he impelled to attain this reward. For they love what is immortal.

" 'Those whose bodies alone are pregnant with this principle of immortality are attracted by women, seeking through the production of children what they imagine to be happiness and immortality and an enduring remembrance; but they whose souls are far more pregnant than their bodies, conceive and produce that which is more suitable to the soul. What is suitable to the soul? Intelligence, and every other power and excellence of the mind, of which all poets, and all other artists who are creative and inventive, are the authors. The greatest and most admirable wisdom is that which regulates the government of families and states, and which is called moderation and justice. Whosoever, therefore, from his youth feels his soul pregnant with the conception of these excellencies, is divine; and when due time arrives, desires to bring forth; and wandering about, he seeks the beautiful in which he may propagate what he has conceived; for there is no generation in that which is deformed; he embraces those bodies which are beautiful rather than those which are deformed, in obedience to the principle within him which is ever seeking to perpetuate itself. And if he meets, in conjunction with loveliness of form, a beautiful, generous and gentle soul, he embraces both at once, and immediately undertakes to educate this object of his love, and is inspired with an overflowing persuasion to declare what is virtue, and what he ought to be who would attain to its possession, and what are the duties which it exacts. For, by the intercourse with, and as it were, the very touch of that which is beautiful, he brings forth and produces what he had formerly conceived; and nourishes and educates that which is thus produced together with the object of his love, whose image, whether absent or present, is never divided from his mind. So that those who are thus united are linked by a nobler community and a firmer love, as being the common parents of a lovelier and more enduring progeny than the parents of other children. And every one who considers what posterity Homer and Hesiod and the other great poets have left behind them, the sources of their own immortal memory and renown, or what children of his soul Lycurgus has appointed to be the guardians, not only of Lace-daemon, but of all Greece; or what an illustrious progeny of laws Solon has produced, and how many admirable achievements, both among the Greeks and Barbarians, men have left as the pledges of that love which subsisted between them and the beautiful, would choose rather to be the parent of such children than those in an hu-man shape. For divine honours have often been rendered to them on account of such children, but on account of those in human shape, never.

" 'Your own meditation, O Socrates, might perhaps have initiated you in all these things which I have already taught you on the sub-ject of Love. But those perfect and sublime ends, to which these are only the means, I know not that you would have been competent to discover. I will declare them, therefore, and will render them as in-telligible as possible: do you meanwhile strain all your attention to trace the obscure depth of the subject. He who aspires to love rightly, ought from his earliest youth to seek an intercourse with beautiful forms, and first to make a single form the object of his love, and therein to generate intellectual excellencies. He ought, then, to consider that beauty in whatever form it resides is the brother of that beauty which subsists in another form; and if he ought to pursue that which is beautiful in form, it would be absurd to imagine that beauty is not one and the same thing in all forms, and would therefore remit much of his ardent preference towards one, through his perception of the multitude of claims upon his love. In addition, he would consider the beauty which is in souls more excellent than that which is in form. So that one endowed with an admirable soul, even though the flower of his form were withered, would suffice him as the object of

320

his love and care, and the companion with whom he might seek and produce such conclusions as tend to the improvement of youth; so that it might be led to observe the beauty and the conformity which there is in the observation of its duties and the laws, and to esteem little the mere beauty of the outward form. The lover would then conduct his pupil to science, so that he might look upon the loveliness of wisdom; and that contemplating thus the universal beauty, no longer like some servant in love with his fellow would he unworthily and meanly enslave himself to the attractions of one form, nor one subject of discipline or science, but would turn towards the wide ocean of intellectual beauty, and from the sight of the lovely and majestic forms which it contains, would abundantly bring forth his conceptions in philosophy; until, strengthened and confirmed, he should at length steadily contemplate one science, which is the science of this universal beauty.

" 'Attempt, I entreat you, to mark what I say with as keen an observation as you can. He who has been disciplined to this point in Love, by contemplating beautiful objects gradually, and in their order, now arriving at the end of all that concerns Love, on a sudden beholds a beauty wonderful in its nature. This it is, O Socrates, for the sake of which all the former labours were endured. It is eternal, unproduced, indestructible, neither subject to encrease nor decay; not, like other things, partly beautiful and partly deformed; not at one time beautiful and at another time not; not beautiful in relation to one thing and deformed in relation to another; not here beautiful and there deformed; not beautiful in the estimation of one person and deformed in that of another; nor can this supreme beauty be figured to the imagination like a beautiful face, or beautiful hands, or any portion of the body, nor like any discourse, or any science. Nor does it subsist in any other thing that lives or is, either in earth, or in heaven, or in any other place; but it is eternally uniform and consistent, and monoeidic with itself. All other things are beautiful through a participation of it, with this condition, that although they are subject to production and decay, it never becomes more or less, or endures any change. When any one, ascending from a correct system of Love, begins to contemplate this supreme beauty, he already touches the consummation of his labour. For such as discipline themselves upon this system, or are conducted by another beginning to ascend through these transitory objects which are beautiful, towards that which is beauty itself, proceeding as on steps from the love of one form to that of two, and from that of two, to that of all forms which are beautiful; and from beautiful forms to beautiful habits and institutions, and from institutions to beautiful doctrines;

until, from the meditation of many doctrines, they arrive at that which is nothing else than the doctrine of the supreme beauty itself, in the knowledge and contemplation of which at length they repose.

" 'Such a life as this, my dear Socrates,' exclaimed the stranger prophetess, 'spent in the contemplation of the beautiful, is the life for men to live; which if you chance ever to experience, you will esteem far beyond gold and rich garments, and even those lovely persons whom you and many others now gaze on with astonishment, and are prepared neither to eat or drink so that you may behold and live for ever with these objects of your love! What, then, shall we imagine to be the aspect of the supreme beauty itself, simple, pure, uncontaminated with the intermixture of human flesh and colours, and all other idle and unreal shapes attendant on mortality; the divine, the original, the supreme, the self consistent, the monoeidic beautiful itself? What must be the life of him who dwells with and gazes on that which it becomes us all to seek? Think you not that to him alone is accorded the prerogative of bringing forth, not images and shadows of virtue, for he is in contact not with a shadow but with reality; with virtue itself, in the production and nourishment of which he becomes dear to the Gods, and if such a priviledge is conceded to any human being, himself immortal.'

"Such, O Phaedrus, and my other friends, was what Diotima said. And being persuaded by her words, I have since occupied myself in attempting to persuade others, that it is not easy to find a better assistant than Love in seeking to communicate immortality to our human natures. Wherefore I exhort every one to honour Love; I hold him in honour, and chiefly exercise myself in amatory matters, and exhort others to do so; and now and ever do I praise the power and excellence of Love, in the best manner that I can. Let this discourse, if it pleases you, Phaedrus, be considered as an encomium of Love; or call it by what other name you will."

The whole assembly praised his discourse, and Aristophanes was on the point of making some remarks on the allusion made by Socrates to him in a part of his discourse, when suddenly they heard a loud knocking at the door of the vestibule, and a clamour as of revellers, attended by a flute-player.—"Go, boys," said Agathon, "and see who is there: if they are any of our friends, call them in; if not, say that we have already done drinking."—A minute afterwards, they heard the voice of Alcibiades in the vestibule excessively drunk and roaring out:—"Where is Agathon? Lead me to Agathon!"—The flute-player, and some of his companions, then led him in, and placed him against the door-post, crowned with a thick crown of ivy and violets, and having a quantity of fillets on his head.—"My friends," he cried out, "hail! I am excessively drunk already, but I'll drink with you, if

322

you will. If not, we will go away after having crowned Agathon, for which purpose I came. I assure you that I could not come yesterday, but I am now here with these fillets round my temples, that from my own head I may crown his head who, with your leave, is the most beautiful and wisest of men. Are you laughing at me because I am drunk? Aye, I know what I say is true, whether you laugh or not. But tell me at once, whether I shall come in, or no. Will you drink with me?"

Agathon and the whole party desired him to come in, and recline among them; so he came in, led by his companions. He then unbound his fillets that he might crown Agathon, and though Socrates was just before his eyes, he did not see him, but sat down by Agathon, between Socrates and him, for Socrates moved out of the way to make room for him. When he sate down, he embraced Agathon and crowned him; and Agathon desired the slaves to untie his sandals, that he might make a third, and recline on the same couch. "By all means," said Alcibiades, "but what third companion have we here?" And at the same time turning round and seeing Socrates, he leaped up and cried out:—"O Hercules! what have we here? You, Socrates, lying in ambush for me wherever I go! and meeting me just as you always do, when I least expected to see you! And, now, what are you come here for? Why have you chosen to recline exactly in this place, and not near Aristophanes, or any one else who is, or wishes to be ridiculous, but have contrived to lie down beside the most beautiful person of the whole party?"—"Agathon," said Socrates, "see if you cannot defend me. I declare my love for this man is a bad business: from the moment that I first began to love him I have never been permitted to converse with, or so much as to look on any one who is beautiful. If I do, he is so jealous and suspicious that he does the most extravagant things, and hardly refrains from beating me. I entreat you to prevent him from doing anything of that kind at present. Procure a reconciliation: or, if he perseveres in attempting any violence, I entreat you to defend me, for I am seriously alarmed at the fury of his amatory impulse."—"Indeed," said Alcibiades, "I will not be reconciled to you; I shall find another opportunity to punish you for this. But now," said he, addressing Agathon, "lend me some of those fillets, that I may crown the wonderful head of this fellow, lest I incur the blame, that having crowned you, I neglected to crown him who conquers all men with his discourses, not yesterday alone as you did, but ever."

BIBLIOGRAPHY

Abrams, M. H. "The Correspondent Breeze: A Romantic Metaphor,"
The Kenyon Review, XIX (Winter 1957), 113-130.
Annual Register, XXV, 55; XXXV, 294-295; XXXVI, 313-316.
Baker, Carlos H. *Shelley's Major Poetry: The Fabric of a Vision*.
Princeton, 1948.
Bates, Ernest Sutherland. *A Study of Shelley's Drama "The Cenci."*
New York, 1908.
Bloom, Harold. *Shelley's Mythmaking*. New Haven, 1959.
Blunden, Edmund. *Shelley: A Life Story*. London, 1946.
Booth, Wayne C. *The Rhetoric of Fiction*. Chicago, 1961.
Butter, Peter. *Shelley's Idols of the Cave*. Edinburgh, 1954.
Cameron, Kenneth Neill. *The Young Shelley: Genesis of a Radical*.
New York, 1950.
—— and Frenz, Horst. "The Stage History of Shelley's *The Cenci*,"
PLMA, LX (December 1945), 1080-1105.
Chambers, E. K. *Samuel Taylor Coleridge: A Biographical Study*.
Oxford, 1938.
Coleridge, Ernest Hartley and R. E. Prothero. *The Works of Lord
Byron*. 13 vols. London, 1905-1930.
Clark, David Lee. *Shelley's Prose; or, the Trumpet of a Prophecy*.
Albuquerque, 1954; corrected edition, 1966.
Cline, C. L. *Byron, Shelley, and Their Pisan Circle*. Cambridge
(Mass.), 1952.
Coleridge, Samuel Taylor. *Biographia Literaria*, ed. J. Shawcross. 2
vols. Oxford, 1907.
Critical Review, LIX, 33.
De Selincourt, Ernest and Helen Darbishire, eds. *The Poetical Works
of William Wordsworth*. Oxford, 1940-1949.
The Dictionary of National Biography, ed. Sir Leslie Stephen and Sir
Sidney Lee. Oxford, 1917–
Eliot, T. S. *Selected Essays*. New York, 1932.
——. "A Talk on Dante," *Kenyon Review*, XIV (Spring 1952), 178-
188.
Elton, Oliver. *A Survey of English Literature: 1780-1830*. 2 vols.
London, 1912.
Fairchild, Hoxie N. *The Romantic Quest*. New York, 1931.
Feibleman, James K. "The Truth-Value of Art," *Journal of Aes-
thetics and Art Criticism*, XXIV (Summer 1966), 501-508.
Frazer, Sir James George. *The New Golden Bough*, ed. Theodor H.
Gaster. New York, 1959.

Freud, Sigmund. *New Introductory Lectures on Psychoanalysis*, tr. W. J. H. Sprott. New York, 1933.

Grabo, Carl H. *A Newton among Poets: Shelley's Use of Science in "Prometheus Unbound."* Chapel Hill, 1930.

Grebanier, Bernard. *Playwriting.* New York, 1961.

Green, John Richard. *History of the English People.* 4 vols. New York, 1878.

Grylls, R. Glynn. *Trelawny.* London, 1950.

Hamilton, Edith. "W. S. Gilbert: A Mid-Victorian Aristophanes," *Theatre Arts Monthly*, XI (October 1927), 781-790.

Havens, Raymond D. "Julian and Maddalo," *Studies in Philology* XXVII (October 1930), 648-653.

————. *The Mind of a Poet: A Study of Wordsworth's Thought.* 2 vols. Baltimore, 1941.

Hibernian Magazine, 1790, ii: 132.

Hogg, Thomas Jefferson. *The Life of Percy Bysshe Shelley.* See Wolfe, Humbert.

Hungerford, Edward B. *Shores of Darkness.* New York, 1941.

Hunt, Leigh. *The Examiner*, February and March 1818.

Hutchinson, Thomas, ed. *The Complete Poetical Works of Percy Bysshe Shelley.* London, 1905, 1934.

James, William. *The Varieties of Religious Experience: A Study in Human Nature.* London, Cambridge (Mass.), 1902.

Jones, Frederick L. *The Letters of Percy Bysshe Shelley.* 2 vols. Oxford, 1964.

Joyce, James. *The Portrait of the Artist as a Young Man.* New York, 1916.

Kapstein, I. J. "The Meaning of Shelley's 'Mont Blanc,'" *PMLA*, LXII (December 1947), 1046-1060.

King-Hele, Desmond. *Shelley: His Thought and Work.* London, 1960.

Kitto, H. D. F. *The Greeks.* Harmondsworth, 1951.

Landor, Walter Savage. *The Complete Works of Walter Savage Landor*, ed. T. Earle Welby and Stephen Wheeler. 16 vols. London, 1927, 1933.

Leavis, F. R. *Revaluation: Tradition and Development in English Poetry.* London, 1949.

Levy, G. Rachel. *The Gate of Horn.* London, 1948.

Lewis, C. S. *Rehabilitations and Other Essays.* Oxford, 1939.

Locock, C. D., ed. *The Poems of Percy Bysshe Shelley.* 2 vols. London, 1911.

McAdam, E. L., Jr., and George Milne, eds. *Johnson's Dictionary: A Modern Selection.* New York, 1963.

Mack, Maynard. "The Muse of Satire," *Yale Review*, XLI (September 1951), 80-92.

Matthews, G. M., ed. *Shelley: Selected Poems and Prose.* Oxford, 1964.

———. "Shelley and Jane Williams," *Review of English Studies,* N. S., XII (February 1961), 40-48.

Medwin, Thomas. *The Life of Percy Bysshe Shelley: A New Edition* . . . , ed. Harry Buxton Forman. London, 1913.

Murray, Gilbert. "Myself When Young," *The Listener,* XLII (August 18, 1949), 272-273.

Nicoll, Allardyce. *A History of Early Nineteenth Century Drama, 1800-1850.* 2 vols. Cambridge, 1930.

———. *A History of Late Eighteenth Century Drama, 1750-1800.* Cambridge, 1927.

Notopoulos, James A. "The Dating of Shelley's Prose," *PMLA* (June 1943), 477-498.

———. *The Platonism of Shelley: A Study of Platonism and the Poetic Mind.* Durham, 1949.

Partridge, Eric. *Dictionary of Slang.* 2 vols. London, 1961.

Peacock, Thomas Love. *Memoirs of Shelley.* See Wolfe, Humbert.

Plato. *The Dialogues of Plato,* tr. Benjamin Jowett. 4 vols. 4th ed. London, 1953.

———. *Phaedrus,* in *Plato,* vol. 1, tr. H. N. Fowler. London, 1914.

Pulos, C. E. *The Deep Truth.* Lincoln, 1954.

Raysor, Thomas M., ed. *The English Romantic Poets: A Review of Research,* rev. ed. New York, 1956.

Reiman, Donald H. *Shelley's "The Triumph of Life": A Critical Study.* Urbana, 1965.

———. "Shelley's 'The Triumph of Life': The Biographical Problem," *PMLA,* LXXVIII (December 1963), 536-550.

———. "Structure, Symbol, and Theme in 'Lines Written among the Euganean Hills'," *PMLA,* LXXVII (September 1962), 404-413.

Roe, Ivan. *Shelley: The Last Phase.* London, 1953.

Rogers, Neville. *Shelley at Work: A Critical Inquiry.* Oxford, 1956.

Santayana, George. *The Winds of Doctrine.* New York, London, 1913.

Sartre, Jean-Paul. *No Exit & The Flies,* tr. Stuart Gilbert. New York, 1949.

Shelley, Mary Wollstonecraft. *Mary Shelley's Journal,* ed. Frederick L. Jones. Norman, 1947.

———, ed. *The Poetical Works of Percy Bysshe Shelley.* 4 vols. London, 1839.

———, ed. *The Poetical Works of Percy Bysshe Shelley.* London, 1839 [1840].

Shelley, Percy Bysshe. See Clark, David Lee; Jones, Frederick L.; Hutchinson, Thomas; Locock, C. D.; Shelley, Mary; Woodberry, George; Zillman, Lawrence John.

Stace, Walter T., ed. *The Teachings of the Mystics: Being Selections from the Great Mystics and Mystical Writings of the World*. New York, 1960.

Thomson, James ("B. V."). "Notes on the Structure of Shelley's 'Prometheus Unbound'," *Atheneum* (July-December 1881), 597-598.

Trelawny, Edward John. *The Recollections of Shelley & Byron*. See Wolfe, Humbert.

Trevelyan, George Macaulay. *A Shortened History of England*. New York, 1942.

Trilling, Lionel, ed. *The Selected Letters of John Keats*, enl. ed. New York, 1955.

Universal Magazine, LXXXVI, 60-61; XCIV, 337-339; XCV, 78.

Walker, Stanley A. "Peterloo, Shelley, and Reform," *PMLA*, XL (March 1925), 128-164.

Wasserman, Earl R. *Shelley's* Prometheus Unbound: *A Critical Reading*. Baltimore, 1965.

————. *The Subtler Language: Critical Readings of Neoclassic and Romantic Poems*. Baltimore, 1959.

Westminster Review, April 1841.

White, Newman Ivey. *Shelley*. 2 vols. New York, 1940. (His *Portrait of Shelley*, 1959, written for the general reader, is admirable.)

————. "Shelley's *Swellfoot the Tyrant* in Relation to Contemporary Political Satires," *PMLA*, XXXVI (September 1921), 332-346.

Whitehead, Alfred North. *Science and the Modern World*. New York, 1925.

Wilson, Milton. *Shelley's Later Poetry: A Study of his Prophetic Imagination*. New York, 1959.

Wimsatt, W. K. *The Verbal Icon*. Lexington, 1954.

Wolfe, Humbert, ed. *The Life of Percy Bysshe Shelley, as Comprised in* The Life of Shelley *by Thomas Jefferson Hogg,* The Recollections of Shelley & Byron *by Edward John Trelawny,* Memoirs of Shelley *by Thomas Love Peacock*. 2 vols. London, 1933.

Woodberry, George, ed. *The Complete Poetical Works of Percy Bysshe Shelley*. Boston, 1901.

Wordsworth, Christopher. *Memoirs of William Wordsworth*. 2 vols. London, 1851.

Wordsworth, William. *The Poetical Works*. See de Selincourt, Ernest.

Yeats, William Butler. *Ideas of Good and Evil*. London, 1903.

Zillman, Lawrence John, ed. *Shelley's Prometheus Unbound: A Variorum Edition*. Seattle, 1959. (The bibliography is complete until 1957.)

INDEX

Abrams, M. H., 230
Adonais, 275-278
Aeschylus, Shelley's attitude towards, 95
Alastor, 12-21
allegory in familiar style, 291-292; see also *Mask of Anarchy*
allegory of the cave, Plato's, 32-33
Allegra, 71-72, 75, 282-283
allusions, literary, and the esthetic experience, 297-299
"Almighty," limited meaning of, 126
Ancient Mariner, The, 288
annus mirabilis, Shelley's, 88-89
Apollo-Ocean scene (III.ii), thematic and tonal functions of *Prometheus Unbound*'s, 137-138, 142-143
Aristophanes, 253
Arnold, Matthew, 86
Asia, 111, 113-118, 121-129, 131-138, 144-146, 151, 152-153, 160-161, 166
Aziola, The, 296

Bacon, Francis, 308
Baker, Carlos, 71, 277
Baths of San Giuliano, 251, 273
biography and criticism, 56-58, 63, 227, 233, 235-236, 282, 284, 287-288, 297, 299

Bloom, Harold, 251
Boat on the Serchio, The, 273-274
Booth, Wayne, 57
Boscombe Manor, 283
Byron, 8, 22, 37, 62, 80-83, 140, 222, 275, 279, 280, 282, 300

Cameron, Kenneth, 52, 193
Carlyle, Thomas, 37
Castlereagh, Robert Stewart, 2nd Viscount, 209-210, 213
cave as the temple, or home, of the united Prometheus and Asia, 145-146
cave of Prometheus, importance of, 153
cavern, Earth's, which replaces Prometheus', 155-157, 158
Cenci, The, 190-204
Cézanne, Paul, 232
Chamouni, 25
Charles I, 301
children, Shelley's love of, 241
Clairmont, Claire, 21, 58, 61-62, 71-72, 248, 280, 282-283
Clark, David Lee, 26
classicism in Shelley, examples of, 85, 226, 230, 271
closet drama, tradition for, 204
Coleridge, Samuel Taylor, 11, 21, 45, 46, 118, 192, 219, 250

comic sense, Shelley's, 3, 62, 160, 213, 252-253, 258, 260, 261, 278, 296
Congress of Vienna, 84, 109
contrapuntal effect, 20-21
Covent Garden, 193
criticism and biography, *see* biography and criticism
Cubism, Shelley's,
  in language, 127, 164, 182
  in structure, 137-138, 144-145
Culture and Anarchy, 86

Dalton, John, 177
Dante, 185, 266, 304
Darwin, Erasmus, 120, 177, 178
Davy, Sir Humphrey, 177
death of Shelley, 309-310
dedicated life, Shelley's, 53-54
"deep truth is imageless, the," 129
Defence of Poetry, A, 27, 92-93
"delusion," Romantic meaning of, 91
Demogorgon, 111, 122-129, 140-142, 187-189
Destiny, 52
difficulty and originality, 93
Dionysus, Shelley's knowledge of as a fertility god, 229
"dissociation of sensibility," 247
Don Juan, Byron's, 222

Eldon, John Scott, 1st Earl of, 206, 210
Eliot, T. S., 278, 307
Elton, Oliver, 78
Epistle to Dr. Arbuthnot, 57
Epipsychidion, 244, 266-271
eternity, difference between time and, 169, 170, 171
Eton, 4
Evening: Ponte al Mare, Pisa, 274

evil,
  nature of, 105-106, 107, 129, 152
  no solution to the riddle of, 127
  Shelley's consciousness of, 4, 62
evil in the human mind, 49-50

Fairchild, Hoxie, 14, 16
familiar style in Shelley, 39, 68, 133, 192, 207, 291-292
Fauns, symbolic value of, 120
Feibleman, James K., 299
finite and the infinite, fusion of, 116-117
Flies, The, 98
form communicating meaning, 187
French Revolution, 110
Frenz, Horst, 193
Freud, Sigmund, 105, 110-111
fun, Shelley's attitude that life is hellish without, 217
fun, Shelley's sense of, *see* comic sense
fusion of finite and the infinite, 116-117
fusion of real and ideal, 182
future state, 188

Garnett, Richard, 283, 290
geology, 178-179
Gilbert, W. S., Shelley's anticipation of, 258
Gisborne, Maria, 248-251
Godlike self of man, 151
Godwin, Mary, 7; *see also* Shelley, Mary
Godwin, William, 4, 7, 21, 55, 83, 248
gold as a symbol of self, 105
good and evil, intertexture of, 105-106

330

Grabo, Carl, 100, 155
Gray's *On the Death of a Favorite Cat*, 3
Greek drama, Act IV of *Prometheus Unbound* similar to the structure of, 168
Green, John Richard, 209
green bag, 259

Hamilton, Edith, 253
Hamlet, 247
Hardy, Thomas, 9, 213
Havens, Raymond D., 71
Hellas, 24-25, 28, 52, 126
Hercules, 144
Herschel, Sir William, 102
Hogg, Thomas Jefferson, 5-6, 286
Hope, 132, 189
humor, Shelley's sense of, *see* comic sense
Hungerford, Edward B., 277
Hunt, Leigh, 36-37, 213, 215-216, 248, 280, 300, 309
human mind, evil and misery in the, 49-50
Hymn to Intellectual Beauty, 21-25, 53

ideal, pressure in Shelley's life to incorporate the, 14; *see also* intellectual beauty, or love
ideality, 48, 154, 294; *see also* new order, paradise, visions
ideal order, strong feelings in, 169
imagery, example of originality and tradition in, 176
images
    made of actualities in Shelley's experience, 16, 88, 157
    made of scientific knowledge, *see* science used for poetry
implied author, 57
Impressionism, Shelley's anticipation of, 127, 274

Intellectual Beauty, 22-24, 45, 54, 134-135, 243, 244, 251, 268, 276-277, 289, 291; *see also* Asia
intellectual beauty, or love, Shelley's need to find embodied in a woman, 54
Invocation to Misery, 86-87

James, William, 24, 63, 146
Jesus, Prometheus' likeness to, 109-110
Joyce, James, 301
Julian and Maddalo, 62-75, 87
Jupiter, 98-101, 103, 105, 107, 128-129, 138-142, 163, 189
Jupiter, child of, 140
Jupiter's phantasm, 103-105

Keats, John, 37, 213, 214-215, 251, 275
King-Hele, Desmond, 102, 127, 228
Kitto, H. D. F., 20, 85
knowledge
    Shelley's passion for, 36
    Shelley's use of, 54

Lake Leman, 22
Landor, Walter Savage, 71, 278
Leavis, F. R., 227
Leghorn, 248, 309
Lerici, 283
Letter to Maria Gisborne, 247-251
Lewes, George Henry, 310
Lewis, C. S., 93, 167
liberty
    necessity of for an ideal world, 48
    necessity of for spiritual values, 24-25
Lines ("The cold earth slept below"), 8-10

originality, conscious design of in *Prometheus Unbound*, 93

Oxford, 5

Pacchiani, Prof. Francesco, 265

paradise
earth and human society transformed to, 158-159, 162-165, 182-183
moon transformed to, 183
universe transformed to, 171-174
see also ideality, new order, visions

paradise, antenatal, 135-137, 242-243

paradise, music as an image for, 239

passive resistance, 50, 211-212

Peacock, Thomas Love, 12-13

persona, or mask, 57, 62, 63, 70-71, 72, 81, 227, 287, 297

Peter Bell the Third, 213-224

Petrarch, 75, 80, 283, 304

Phaedrus, 134, 137

Philosophical View of Reform, A, 89-91

Pisa, 233, 265

"Pisa Circle," 280

pity, Prometheus', 111

Pity and Hope, Spirits of, 112-113

Plato, 32-33, 212

poet, Shelley's definition of, 92

poetry, Shelley's definition of, 92

Pope, Alexander, 57

practical affairs, Shelley's handling of, 35-36

"progressive revelation," 285

Prometheus, 52, 95-96, 97, 98-114, 134-138, 140, 141, 144-146, 151, 152-157, 161, 165-166, 189

Prometheus Bound, 95

Prometheus Unbound, 87-190

Pulos, C. E., 308

puns and quibbles, Shelley's liking for, 261-262

Quadruple Alliance, 84, 111, 247

Queen Mab, 6, 7, 278

Question, The, 240-241

radical influence, Shelley's, 278

realism, Shelley's, 68, 89, 189, 264, 266, 274, 285

"realism" of Mercury, 107

real and ideal, fusion of, 182

Reiman, Donald, 290, 303

religion, Whitehead's definition of, 130-131

religious experience
Prometheus Unbound as an expression of, 97
tributes to *Prometheus Unbound* for the power of its, 190

religious life, governing beliefs of, 24

Republic, The, 212

reserve, Shelley's; *see* restraint

restraint, examples of Shelley's, 10, 71, 78, 192, 235, 295

Reveley, Henry, 248-249

Revolt of Islam, The, 37-56

revolution, grounds for, 50, 212

Reynolds, John Hamilton, 213-215

Roe, Ivan, 284, 286

Rogers, Neville, 224

romanticism, definition of, 14

Rousseau, 304, 306-307

San Terenzo, 283, 300

Santayana, George, 252

This book is set
in 10 point Linotype Baskerville,
leaded 2 points, with display in Letraset
Baskerville, and printed by letterpress
on 60 lb. Warren's 66 Antique.
The endpapers are Multicolor Muscatel,
and the binding cloth is Columbia
Bayside Chambray

DATE DUE

OCT 8 1993 F		
NOV 1 6 '93		
JAN 2 4 '94		
DEC 0 5 2...		

DEMCO